Autobiography without Apology

T0324093

AZTLÁN ANTHOLOGY SERIES

Aztlán Anthology Series, Volume 7

Authobiography without Apology
The Personal Essay in Chicanx and Latinx Studies

Edited by

Chon A. Noriega, Wendy Laura Belcher, and Charlene Villaseñor Black

UCLA Chicano Studies Research Center Press
Los Angeles
2020

CSRC Director: Chon A. Noriega
Senior Editor: Rebecca Frazier
Business Manager: Darling Sianez
Manuscript Editor: Catherine A. Sunshine
Design and Production: William Morosi

Front cover: Ruben Ochoa, *Pachuco a la Vidrio*, 1999. Glass and zoot suit, worn by the artist.
Photography by Patrick Miller.

Library of Congress Cataloging-in-Publication Data

Names: Noriega, Chon A., 1961- editor. | Belcher, Wendy Laura, editor. |
  Black, Charlene Villaseñor, 1962- editor. | University of California,
  Los Angeles. Chicano Studies Research Center. Press
Title: Autobiography without Apology : The Personal Essay in Chicanx and
  Latinx Studies / edited by Chon A. Noriega, Wendy Laura Belcher, and
  Charlene Villaseñor Black.
Description: Los Angeles : UCLA Chicano Studies Research Center Press,
  2020. | Series: Aztlán anthology series ; volume 7 | Includes
  bibliographical references and index. | Summary: "This collection of
  essays, drawn from 'Aztlán: A Journal of Chicano Studies,' focuses on
  the personal experiences of Chicanx and Latinx scholars, writers, and
  artists. Each essay is a reflection on the process of self-naming-the
  role of "I"-in the authors' work and research. 'Autobiography without
  Apology' expands the earlier CSRC Press publication 'I Am Aztlán' with
  the inclusion of ten essays that bring the collection up-to-date. The
  new title acknowledges Aztlán's growing scope as it embraces Latinx,
  LGBT, and Indigenous studies as well as Chicanx studies"-- Provided by
  publisher.
Identifiers: LCCN 2020025719 | ISBN 9780895511737 (paperback)
Subjects: LCSH: Mexican Americans--Biography. | Mexican Americans--Ethnic
  identity. | Mexican Americans--Intellectual life. | Mexican
  Americans--Social conditions.
Classification: LCC E184.M5 A885 2020 | DDC 305.8968/72073--dc23
LC record available at https://lccn.loc.gov/2020025719

♾ This book is printed on acid-free paper.

UCLA Chicano Studies
Research Center
193 Haines Hall
Los Angeles, California 90095-1544
www. chicano.ucla.edu

Distributed by the University of
Washington Press
PO Box 50096
Seattle, Washington 98145-5096
www.washington.edu/uwpress

CONTENTS

Testifying

Field Reports

Autobiography without Apology

Chon A. Noriega, Wendy Laura Belcher, and Charlene Villaseñor Black

In Rudolfo A. Anaya's novel *Heart of Aztlán* (1976), the protagonist leaves the barrio of Barelas in Albuquerque to search in the mountains for Aztlán, the mythical homeland of the Aztecs.

> Time stood still, and in that enduring moment he felt the rhythm of the heart of Aztlán beat to the measure of his own heart. Dreams and visions became reality, and reality was but the thin substance of myth and legends. A joyful power coursed from the dark womb-heart of the earth into his soul and he cried out I AM AZTLÁN! (131)

We take this cry as the starting point for this anthology. Anaya's protagonist had been looking for a myth of origins by returning to the sacred lands he had been forced to leave in order to seek employment in the city. But he finds, instead, himself—a "plural self" (Sommer 1988, 130), a singularity that nevertheless embodies a collective experience and call to action. Anaya's novel, published in the latter years of the Chicano civil rights movement, weaves together the communal and the personal through a narrative about labor relations, social protest, ethnic identity, and pre-Columbian spirituality. Indeed, the protagonist first learns about Aztlán at a meeting of striking union members!

We focus on the process of self-naming—the ubiquitous "I am . . ."—because it is found not just in early Chicana/o literary, performing, and visual arts, but in Chicana/o scholarship as well. Consider, for example, *Aztlán: A Journal of Chicano Studies*, which was founded in 1969 by a group of graduate and undergraduate students associated with the UCLA Chicano Studies Research Center. In the first issue, published in the spring of 1970, the editors announced that the center's publications "were created to provide responsible and reliable sources for materials on Chicanos" (vi). The journal

in particular was seen as "a forum for scholarly writings" and as the first
university-sponsored serial publication on the Chicana/o population. Given
this academic orientation, then, it is of note that preceding the essays in the
first issue is an excerpt from "El Plan Espiritual de Aztlán," which ends by
explicitly linking its political agenda with self-naming. "We are AZTLAN,"
it declares (iv).

With this beginning, the editorial staff of Aztlán—which included
Juan Gómez-Quiñones (history), Roberto Sifuentes (Spanish), Reynaldo
Flores Macías (education), Andres Chavez (political science), and Deluvina
Hernández (sociology)—not only challenged the earlier scholarly literature
on Chicana/os for its biases and prejudices but also opened up a space for
a Chicana/o voice within academic publishing. That is, by using the first
person ("I" and "we") as part of a larger social and academic project, the
editorial staff articulated a worldview and set of collective experiences
that had been excluded from higher education, public policy, and popular
discourse within the United States.

In this era, then, to be autobiographical often represented an applied
dimension within a scholarly article. By using "I," the Chicana/o scholar
made particular claims within a field of study or discipline, often in sharp
contrast to the general and more stereotypical arguments put forth by
some non-Chicana/o scholars. But by drawing upon personal experience
and self-reflection, the Chicana/o scholar also provided an arena within
which these ideas could be tested, put to use, and improved. Thus, in the
second issue of Aztlán, Gilbert Benito Córdova (1970) wrote a brief memoir
on his teaching experiences, which starts with a very atypical academic
essay opening.

> During the summer of 1969 I was in charge of Head Start at my little
> community—Abiquiú, New Mexico. For the first time I was on my own
> professionally! Now I could try out all I had learned at college about
> child education. (103)

Arriving at the school, Córdova was quickly struck by the inappropriateness
of the English and Castilian Spanish storybooks provided to the children,
and he invited local elders to the school to tell the stories to the children.
This worked marvelously well: "The children fell in love with their story-
tellers and stories" (104). The article includes a transcription of a unique
folktale by Steven Suazo, one of the elders, for use by other teachers of
Chicana and Chicano schoolchildren.

Córdova did not offer a close reading or analysis, but neither was he
content to just reproduce the tale. Instead, he expressed concern about

the general approach to Chicana/o children as "underprivileged children, underachievers, underdeveloped children, culturally deprived, and so on" (104). After citing some scientific sources on the topic, Córdova wrote,

> It seems to me that if any of these experts would stop for just a minute and think, it might occur to them that there is no such thing as a culturally deprived child. Either a child has a culture or he does not have a culture; and if the child does not have a culture, then he is not a human being. He is some other form of animal than human. As for the other terms, how about underprivileged children? Would its counterpart be overprivileged children? (105)

Córdova's use of the "I" in this short essay is not only moving but also important. From it, we gain insight into the motivations and efforts of early Chicana/o scholars and their intertwined educational and political struggle. It encapsulates the commitment of so many Chicana/o scholars who have sought to return their own advantages in education to the community, but who have also approached their community as a resource in its own right and not as a "disadvantaged" place.

Since the publication of Córdova's article, many scholars have commented on the necessity of expressing the self and drawing from "our own specific racial and cultural experience" to contribute to public knowledge and overcome the strictures of the dominant culture (Herrera-Sobek 1996, 38). Yvonne Yarbro-Bejarano (1996) points out that in the context of oppression, to focus on the self is not a selfish act: "The Chicana writer finds that the self she seeks to define and love is not merely an individual self, but a collective one" (215). Indeed, "individual subjectivity" emerges "through the articulation of collective experience and identity" (218).

And yet, as the editors of *Autobiographical Writing across the Disciplines: A Reader* observe, "At no point in the evolution of higher education was the autobiographical or personal as a mode of learning or genre of writing considered valid" (Freedman and Frey 2003, 8). As such, there has traditionally been, at times, a defensive tendency among those who champion autobiography as a literary or scholarly form. But in looking at Chicana/o studies, which has always been interdisciplinary, we see something different: autobiography without apology. This phrase alludes to Edén E. Torres's *Chicana without Apology* (2003), itself an excellent example of the critical self in cultural studies and the inspiration for the title of this volume and this introduction. Such an approach is not new. Consider Ernesto Galarza's *Barrio Boy* (1971), written as an anecdotal response to the "psychologists, psychiatrists, social anthropologists and other manner of 'shrinks' [that] have spread the rumor that these Mexican immigrants and their offspring have lost their 'self-image'" (2). In contrast to this scientific "rumor," Galarza wryly notes, "I can't remember a time I didn't know who I was. . . . It seemed to me unlikely that out of six or seven million Mexicans in the United States I was the only one who felt this way" (2). What is of special interest here is that *Barrio Boy* is not just an autobiography. It was written and published as part of the United States–Mexico Border Studies Project at the University of Notre Dame and sponsored by a grant from the Ford Foundation. In other words, not unlike Torres's more recent book, Galarza's memoir was positioned institutionally as a scholarly contribution to the emerging field of Chicana/o studies. Ramón Saldívar (1990), echoing Renato Rosaldo, situates Galarza's text in this broader context: "Replacing the political or philosophical essay, his autobiography is a personal document where historical self-explanation, philosophical self-analysis, and poetic self-expression merge to tell with irony and humor a social story: an individual's participation in one of the grandest migrations of modern times—the influx of Mexicans into the American Southwest" (168).

In the 1990s and 2000s, memoir and autobiography gradually came to greater acceptance in the academy (Smith and Watson 2010, 12), a side effect of a critique of notions of objectivity, including the centering of a supposedly detached, neutral voice in scholarly writing. This critique encouraged authors to break the third wall—to use a theater metaphor—revealing their own subjectivity. Autobiographical and personal essays continue to do the important work of representation, thereby fostering acceptance of diverse viewpoints. Important contributions from women, members of the LGBTQ community, undocumented immigrants, the formerly incarcerated, youth, and others make underrepresented voices audible (Brumble 2018; Delgadillo 2015; Espinoza, Cotera, and Blackwell 2018; Fernández-García 2020; González 2013, 2018). Latinx personal essays, memoir, and autobiography also undertake the important work of documenting the voices of leaders and participants in the civil rights struggles of the 1960s and 1970s, a task of increasing urgency as these *veterana/os* grow older (Blackwell 2011; Guevara 2018). Additionally, scholars are at work recovering important historical voices from centuries past that would be otherwise lost to history (Howe 2015). Correspondingly, the secondary literature has developed at a rapid pace, analyzing and suggesting important new methodologies and theories for using memoir, autobiography, and testimonio, especially in the areas of literature and history (Abrahão 2012; García 2016; López 2011; Walker 2017). Continued interest in the personal essay promises exciting new developments, particularly as theoretical work related to posthumanism destabilizes notions of a fixed, constant self (Bost 2019), moving from understandings of self as individual to interconnected, relational models. New research and theorizing around indigeneity, decoloniality, queer theory, and disability studies promise to reshape our perceptions further.

In this volume, we bring together a number of important personal essays published in *Aztlán* since 1997. The contributors are Chicana and Chicano, but also Indigenous, Puerto Rican, and Cuban American, and they include scholars as well as writers and artists. The common thread involves their contribution to a Chicana/o studies journal and its fifty-year mission of creating "a forum for scholarly writings" related to the Chicana/o and Latinx community. In these essays, the authors ask not so much the traditional autobiographical questions of "Who am I?" or "How did I become who I am?" but "How did we live and think?" They focus on where their lives intersect history writ large and small. In other words, the presence of the self is a given within the text. It is done without apology, which is not to say without being self-critical.

In the first section, "Exile and Going Home," four writers who are also artists and/or art historians reflect on exile and the process of going home as an integral aspect of the creative process. Max Benavidez writes about internal exile and displacement as a Mexican Angeleno. He writes lyrically about constructing his own identity through the process of recollection. He remembers learning English, listening to his great-grandmother's stories, reading *Don Quixote*, seeing the bruises on a beautiful bride, and following a Hopi Indian painter. He tells us that through the human drama of family, we absorb, struggle, and grow up, and that having created an identity through home, we must learn to tell those stories. Harry Gamboa Jr. documents and interprets the contemporary urban Chicano experience through almost a dozen short essays first circulated on Chicle, an electronic discussion list. He deconstructs the freeway, perceptual pollution, stereotypes, fine dining, call–in shows, anti-representatives, solipsistic conversations, and the death of self. Santa C. Barraza, the painter, remembers her journey home, after a twenty-five-year absence, to the Texas town where she was born. Reflecting on what she has learned in the interim, she concludes that her artistic vision has been shaped by the landscape of South Texas and, in particular, the maguey, the symbol of home and identity. Cuban American Alejandro Anreus reflects on his family's arrival from Cuba to the United States on one of President Lyndon Johnson's "freedom flights" in the wake of the

Cuban Revolution. Although initially supportive of Castro, his family grew disillusioned and eventually fled to Florida, only to flee a second time from Miami's right-wing exiles. Anreus's family went to New Jersey, where they settled in an Italian American neighborhood. Anreus recounts a Christmas Eve adventure that involves his grandmother, a live chicken, and a tense ride on a city bus. His story reminds us of immigrants' resilience, survival skills, and coping strategies.

In the second section, "Home/Work," three scholars examine their work and find that some notion of "home" informs their intellectual inquiries. Chon A. Noriega writes about the influence of his father, who inspired the author's "ongoing intellectual quest." After discovering that his sister had saved all their father's Mexican LPs, Noriega uses his skills as a historian and critic to examine the albums and come to a "more compassionate understanding of my father" and his father's career as a journalist, thereby gaining insights into his own career as a scholar. Frances Negrón-Muntaner, a filmmaker, writer, and cultural critic, asks how we can move beyond the supplemental status of the "cinema of the other" in order to produce "another cinema." Originally presented at a panel, the essay went unpublished as too controversial. Negrón-Muntaner addresses the idea of home as an unresolved and politically charged problem to which film gives witness. In her film *Brincando el charco: Portrait of a Puerto Rican* (1994), she addresses the metaphorical sense of "homelessless" felt by the island's excluded populations, including Afrodescendant Puerto Ricans and members of the LGBTQ community, as well as Puerto Ricans residing in the United States. Catherine S. Ramírez writes about growing up as a nerdy Chicana girl who loved science fiction. "Nobody told us that girls, much less Mexican girls, weren't supposed to like science fiction," she recalls. Ramírez's love of science fiction led her to a career dedicated to scholarly study of the literary genre and related expressions such as futuristic Chicana art. Ramírez—who introduced the concept of "Chicanafuturism," a theoretical approach inspired by Afrofuturism—posits a new, hopeful future for Chicanas by challenging traditional constructions of the future as white.

In the third section, "Entre Familia," four scholars critically challenge the code of silence about "internal" matters within the Chicana/o community that is signaled by the phrase *entre familia*. To identify an issue, such as sexism or homosexuality, as *entre familia* was to say that it could not be talked about in public—and, hence, not at all—since doing so would betray or undermine the Chicana/o community in its political struggle. Vincent Pérez engages with both the literary tradition and the critical scholarship on Mexican American autobiography in telling the story of his grandfather. Through family anecdotes, memories, and secrets, he brings personal and national history together as he tells us about Francisco Róbles Pérez and the secret rape that shaped his family history. Any biography has a complicated relationship to the truth, and Pérez examines testimonial memory as a form of repression and resistance. Jerry Garcia, in a provocative opening paragraph, addresses the role of cocks in his father's life. Playing with ideas of masculinity and machismo, Garcia describes the illegal cock fighting in which the men in his family, all Mexican immigrants, participated. He considers how cockfighting shapes familial relationships and its role in the daily life of his family. Renee M. Moreno reflects on family tragedy and the persistence of grief as she recalls the history of her father, Colorado artist and labor activist Raymond Moreno (1932–1972), who died prematurely while driving while intoxicated. She describes her lifelong journey to reconcile her grief over his death, in which documenting his life became a means to resolution. "History is not always found in the places we expect," she observes as she recounts her father's history as a founding member of the Group Workshop, an artists' collective in Denver. In the final essay in this section, Chicana artist Judith F. Baca remembers her journey back in time into her own family's history. Their migration north during the years of the Mexican Revolution became the inspiration for her 2001 digital mural, *La Memoria de Nuestra Tierra: Denver*, which was commissioned for the Denver International Airport. In this personal essay, she considers her family's history and her creative process as an artist. She reveals the complexity of her family's saga and that of all Mexican Americans as well.

In the fourth section, "Testifying," six authors address the creation of works of art and politics, recounting or reflecting on their roles within public history. The first, tatiana de la tierra, offers a fascinating and thoughtful account of two Latina lesbian journals she co-founded and co-edited in the early 1990s. In addition to presenting this important history, her essay offers a model for a self-critical account of Latinx publications and their role within cultural and intellectual production. Alma López creates digital artwork of fantastically surreal images that recontextualize major cultural icons, bringing issues of race, gender, and sexuality into relationship with transnationalist myth and the urban environment. She reports from the field on censorship attempts against the exhibition of her work in New Mexico. Her response is a modern-day *respuesta* to the Catholic Church, among others, and it provides an inspiring model for challenging institutional policies. Next, Ruben Ochoa responds to the glass walls and ceilings that have limited Chicana/o access to social and cultural institutions with . . . a glass zoot suit! In the fine tradition of Chicana/o conceptual art, Ochoa turns his body into a cutting commentary on the exclusionary "white cube" of the American museum. Anita Tijerina Revilla and José Manuel Santillana present their "queerstories" as "counterstories," bringing what they call "Jotería-historia" to visibility. "There is a direct connection between who we are as individuals and how we participate in an activist and academic community of queer Latina/os and Chicana/os," they write. Transborder activist Cynthia Bejarano recounts her experiences as part of Amigos de las Mujeres de Juárez, a group advocating on behalf of the victims of feminicide along the border. Her work demonstrates the power of personal testimonio in the process of truth seeking, a tactic that is particularly important when victims can no longer speak on their own behalf. Writing from the realm of theater, playwright Ricardo Gamboa recounts his experiences growing up in Chicago and how his personal history inspired him to diversify the theater world. In his project *Meet Juan(ito) Doe* (2017), people without prior theater experience used their personal stories to make space for brown and black narratives in the world of theater.

In the fifth section, "Field Reports," five scholars offer personal reflections on their pedagogy and research methodology. While in some ways these essays are less "personal" than the others in this collection, the authors' observations hit closer to home in terms of how we work in the academy. Alvina E. Quintana considers her experiences as a native Californian and a Chicana professor teaching East Coast students about Los Angeles and shows us a slice of academic life in the post-diversity moment. Quintana's thoughts on multicultural pedagogies, particularly the responses of her mostly white students to course readings on ethnicity and social change, are illuminating. Arlene Dávila draws upon her ethnographic research on US Hispanic marketing to raise questions about methodology and to offer a larger critique of the challenges posed to fieldwork and ethnography in the age of globalization. She argues that there is much to be learned from the predicaments of fieldwork and how researcher's ethnic backgrounds intersect with their research. In particular, she describes how her access to marketing agencies and employees was mediated by their perceptions of her. Dávila's concerns and insights echo those found in the first issues of *Aztlán*, for they speak to the necessary presence of the Chicana/o and Latina/o scholar within the very world he or she would study and thereby change. Ana Clarissa Rojas Durazo tells the story of her involvement in painting a community mural along the border between Mexicali and Calexico.

The daughter of the project's organizer, María del Carmen Durazo, Rojas provides special insight into this binational art project. Growing up on both sides of the border, she experienced firsthand its militarization in the twentieth century; yet, as a participant in the mural project she became an eyewitness to the creation of community across borders. Carlos Francisco Jackson writes about the future political potential of Chicanx posters from his perspective as a printmaker and director of the Taller Arte del Nuevo Amanecer. Jackson's vast knowledge of poster production facilitates his thinking about the future of Chicanx poster making in the digital age. He advocates for the continued and future importance of actual printed post-ers, not just digital analogs, as tangible objects that exist in the real world and play relevant roles in creating community. Identifying herself as "Ndé scholar, activist, poet, legal defender, and community member," Margo Tamez researches the violence of settler colonialism and the effects of the militarized border on Indigenous communities along the Texas-Mexico border. She relates her personal history, her experiences working with elders and other community members, and her archival research. Her goal is to unearth the lives of the past nineteen generations of Ndé people in South Texas, work she describes as "Activist Research in the Shadow of the Wall."

We hope that these essays will prove useful not only to scholars of Chicanx, Puerto Rican, Cuban American, Indigenous, and Latinx studies but also to students just embarking on their academic and professional careers. What better way to learn about one's writerly options as a scholar than to see the array of choices these writers have made in telling their personal yet public stories? Rather than modeling some dry formula, these essays are instructive in their innovation, creative technique, and complex modes of addressing identity. As Norma Cantú (2008) notes in her collection of autobiographies by Chicanas in science, mathematics, and engineering, such stories "provide a roadmap" for navigating systems and professions that have "traditionally denied access to and marginalized" Latinas and Latinos in the United States (xiii). Since developing a voice is one of the most difficult challenges facing students, the humor and verve of these essays is particularly illustrative. And, since students often want to represent their families but feel anxious about doing so, the sensitivity and directness of these writers' approaches to their loved ones offer guid-ance. The emotional richness of these essays, which dramatize the human consequences of personal choices and historical movements, will inspire critical thinking about the varieties of connection that shape us.

Works Cited

Abrahão, Maria Helena Menna Barreto. 2012. "Autobiographical Research: Memory, Time and Narratives in the First Person." *European Journal for Research on the Education and Learning of Adults* 3, no. 1: 29–41.

Anaya, Rudolfo A. 1976. *The Heart of Aztlán*. Berkeley: Editorial Justa Publications, Inc.

Blackwell, Maylei. 2011. *¡Chicana Power! Contested Histories of Feminism in the Chicano Movement*. Austin: University of Texas Press.

Bost, Suzanne. 2019. *Shared Selves: Latinx Memoir and Ethical Alternatives to Humanism*. Urbana: University of Illinois Press.

Brumble, H. David. 2018. *Street-Gang and Tribal-Warrior Autobiographies*. London and New York: Anthem Press.

Cantú, Norma E., ed. 2008. *Paths to Discovery: Autobiographies from Chicanas with Careers in Science, Mathematics, and Engineering*. Los Angeles: UCLA Chicano Studies Research Center Press.

Córdova, Gilbert Benito. 1970. "A Hispano Tale from Abiquiú, New Mexico." *Aztlán: A Journal of Chicano Studies* 1, no. 2: 103–10.

Delgadillo, Theresa. 2015. *Latina Lives in Milwaukee*. Urbana, Chicago, and Springfield: University of Illinios Press.

Espinoza, Dionne, María Eugenia Cotera, and Maylei Blackwell, eds. 2018. *Chicana Movidas: New Narratives of Activism and Feminism in the Movement Era*. Austin: University of Texas Press.

Fernández-García, Andrea. 2020. *Geographies of Girlhood in US Latina Writing: Decolonizing Spaces and Identities*. Cham, Switzerland: Palgrave Macmillan.

Freedman, Diane P., and Olivia Frey, eds. 2003. *Autobiographical Writing across the Disciplines: A Reader*. Durham, NC: Duke University Press.

Galarza, Ernesto. 1971. *Barrio Boy*. Notre Dame, IN: Notre Dame University Press.

García, Mario T. 2016. *Literature as History: Autobiography, Testimonio, and the Novel in the Chicano and Latino Experience*. Tucson: University of Arizona Press.

González, Rigoberto. 2013. *Autobiography of My Hungers*. Madison: University of Wisconsin Press.

———. 2018. *What Drowns the Flowers in Your Mouth: A Memoir of Brotherhood*. Madison: University of Wisconsin Press.

Guevara, Rubén Funkahuatl. 2018. *Confessions of a Radical Chicano Doo Wop Singer*. [[no subtitle]] Oakland: University of California Press.

Herrera-Sobek, María. 1996. "Introduction." In *Chicana Creativity and Criticism: New Frontiers in American Literature*, edited by María Herrera-Sobek and Helena María Viramontes, 1–46. 2nd ed. Albuquerque: University of New Mexico Press.

Howe, Elizabeth Teresa. 2015. *Autobiographical Writing by Early Modern Hispanic Women*. Farnham, UK: Ashgate.

López, Marissa K. 2011. *Chicano Nations: The Hemispheric Origins of Mexican American Literature*. New York: New York University Press.

Saldívar, Ramón. 1990. *Chicano Narrative: The Dialectics of Difference*. Madison: University of Wisconsin Press.

Smith, Sidonie, and Julia Watson. 2010. *Reading Autobiography: A Guide for Interpreting Life Narratives*. 2nd ed. Minneapolis: University of Minnesota Press.

Sommer, Doris. 1988. "'Not Just a Personal Story': Women's Testimonios and the Plural Self." In *Life/Lines: Theorizing Women's Autobiography*, edited by Bella Brodzki and Celeste Schenck, 107–30. Ithaca, NY: Cornell University Press.

Torres, Edén E. 2003. *Chicana without Apology: The New Chicana Cultural Studies*. New York: Routledge.

Walker, Anthony. 2017. "Critical Autobiography as Research." *Qualitative Report* 22, no. 7: 1896-1908.

Yarbro-Bejarano, Yvonne. 1996. "Chicana Literature from a Chicana Feminist Perspective." In *Chicana Creativity and Criticism: New Frontiers in American Literature*, edited by María Herrera-Sobek and Helena María Viramontes, 213–19. 2nd ed. Albuquerque: University of New Mexico Press.

Exile and Going Home

Subterranean Homesick Blues

Max Benavidez

> We are the river of Heraclitus, who said that the person of yesterday is
> not the person of today, who will not be the person of tomorrow. We
> change incessantly.

> —Jorge Luis Borges, *Seven Nights*

I was born in Los Angeles, the quintessential temple of dreams. It is a
megalopolis—willed out of a smoky desert—where mythmaking and illusion
arise on a grand scale: a perfect setting for creating a defiant vision. Like
every other place on earth, Los Angeles breeds its own aesthetic sense; it
creates its own aesthetic moments. Here its basis is impersonal freeways,
visual clutter, vast economic disparities, and a restless cultural eccentricity
surrounded by disorder and fragmentation.

For a Mexican born in Los Angeles, it is a also a city of internal exile
and displacement. The Mexican Angeleno is often seen as part of a sub-
working class with little formal education, scant resources, and no viable
future. In a city founded by Mexican settlers, the Mexican floats within
and around a highly stratified urban social structure. Not Native American,
yet of the Indian. Not Spanish, yet of Europe. Not even Mexican in the
strictest sense of the term. And the US-born Mexican is rarely, if ever,
considered "American."

As many have said, "History is hysterical." And US Mexicans have
experienced more than their share of racial and cultural hysteria.

I myself have lived such a life. I have lived through and survived
hysterical cultural imperialism. Yes, I have also devoured the dominant
culture. I learned to speak English without a Spanish accent. I read all the
Western classics. Watched the great Hollywood movies as well as European
and Japanese art films. Consumed Coke and 7-Up. Went to Disneyland.
I even owned a Chevrolet and then an Alfa Romeo once upon a time.

1

Quixote in Durango

Above all, I was influenced by the English language. Ironic, really, since I come from a family where Spanish was in the air, woven into the texture of my aural life, a *sotto voce* soundtrack of the mind. I recall my maternal great-grandmother sitting in a rocking chair rolling her own cigarettes by hand, an ink-stained copy of *Don Quixote* in the original Spanish sitting on a table by her side, while she watched flickering black-and-white images of Mexican movies on the local Spanish-language television station. From time to time, she would talk to herself in Spanish. Years later, I memorialized her in a poem called "Durango." (Here is an excerpt.)

Grandmother
Great grandmother

I see your old trunk
the one you brought
from Mexico in 1913

Wood, painted flowers
cracked
leather straps

the tarot cards
wrapped
in black velvet

whose fortune did you tell?
yours? Mexico's?

Grandmother
great grandmother
you read *Don Quixote*
I touched your book
I read the passages
marked by your hand
in thick India ink

I remember
you liked old movies
They said you loved
"The Hunchback of Notre Dame,"
the 1939 version

In writing the poem, I recollected my memory. And, that process of recollection is one example of how I discovered and constructed my sense of cultural identity. I realized I was of Mexico in a very real sense through the traces of my great-grandmother's DNA that pulsed within me, along with her brave actions and eccentric predilections. When I touched her trunk, the one she had dragged all the way from Durango, Mexico, to Los Angeles, California, I touched a vestige of the dust roads and harsh tribulations of an actual refugee from the crimes and glories of the Mexican Revolution. When I read her copy of *Don Quixote*, I read a book she had handled with her two hands for many, many years. Those pages were infused with her energies and her essence.

In reading that particular book, I experienced a strange sort of empathy. Perhaps just as she entered into the work of art created by Miguel de Cervantes, I entered or "felt into" the book and through it, both in a tactile and intellectual sense, into her life. That feeling can be compared to the theory of *Einfühlung*, where the spectator (or reader in this case) feels an instantaneous emotional identification with the work of art. I felt an intense identification with her, the book, and the author, and a commingling of all three in my mind.

Don Quixote became a building block of my personal literary cultural history. This cinematic Spanish novel that comments about a major historical transformation with great irony, humor, and literary creativity is a touchstone for me that "says" Mexico, culture, grandmother, Spanish, revolution, duality, and art all at once. Whether reading Vladimir Nabokov's lectures on *Don Quixote* or Borges's "Pierre Menard, Author of the Quixote," I was always reminded of the old woman who sat in my living room watching faded prints of old Mexican movies on Spanish-language television. In essence, my cultural sensibility was formed at an early age. As time went on and new cultural experiences entered my consciousness, I had already learned how to process them and even place them on a cultural list of priorities.

As Nabokov said, "The key to the problem of reestablishing the past turns out to be the key of art." In the same way, the key to the problem of establishing a cultural identity turns out to be the key of art. Just as in a novel, for example, there is a narrator who is created by the author, in cultural identity there is the consciousness that makes choices and takes bits and pieces from various life experiences to create a specific sense of self.

Stealing Beauty

I remember a beautiful young woman from my childhood. She was my mother's cousin, Chata. At her wedding, as she walked down the aisle, her beauty seemed to stun everyone into speechless awe. And her groom, who looked like a bronze Elvis Presley, fell back with his hand raised in mild shock. It was as though he were saying, "She's too beautiful for me."

The wedding reception was a happy mélange of Mexican music, food, and dancing. I will never forget the green chile enchiladas or the perfection of the flan. For one moment in time, life seemed golden.

A few weeks after the wedding, my mother began getting mysterious phone calls from the bride. My mother would often take them in her bedroom and whisper in hushed Spanglish. I instinctively wanted to protect Chata.

Then, one night, very late, she showed up at our house with a suitcase. She was distraught. My mother told me to go to bed. I could hear crying in the living room. It was the bride sobbing.

My mother then took Chata into her bedroom. I had to see what was going on. With great stealth I tiptoed down the dark hallway and toward my parents' bedroom door. It was open just a crack. In the low light I could see my mother helping the bride undress. Chata stood still in a black silk slip, large purple bruises and welts on her arms and thighs. She took off her slip and showed my mother dark bruises on her firm brown breasts.

Her husband had been beating her for weeks. Every night he whipped her and then raped her.

I went back to my bed with a strange mixture of arousal and rage. I felt liquid. It was as though I was melting into the bed, into the floor, down into the earth. I realized I was crying.

I learned that night that beauty can be destroyed. I realized that there are destroyers. That a Cortés can come into a place, into a family, and destroy everything. It dawned on me that not just physical beauty can be destroyed but also our insides. The bruises could heal and disappear. The welts would fade away. Although Chata didn't see Francisco, her husband, again, she was never the same.

Years later, we heard that she had died in a car crash. We all went to the wake. Her face looked so tired. They said it had to be reconstructed. Everything was all wrong. I remembered that the actor Montgomery Clift had lived that way for many years, with one side of his face reconstructed. Like a fallen angel. Beauty can be lost or stolen, just like anything else. Like a movie star, Chata was the beautiful celebrity of our family and the object of our dreams and desires. And like a Marilyn Monroe or a Montgomery Clift, she could be broken into pieces; she could fall from grace.

Chata lay on the white pillow inside the coffin. She was dead but I think she really had died long before the car accident. She was already dead inside when she came to our house that night. It seemed to me then that some people were too fragile for life.

Years later, when I was reading *Pedro Paramo* by Juan Rulfo, I was reminded of Chata's husband, Francisco. Paramo and Francisco were the same: brutal bullies who enjoyed destroying beauty. They were the fascists. But I was also reminded of Chata when I came to the section in the book where two people converse inside their common grave.

One asks the other, "And your soul? Where do you think it's gone?" The other says her soul is wandering on earth, that it hated her and wanted her to keep living, but finally she just sat down to die.

"'This is the end,' I told it. 'I can't go any farther.' I opened my mouth so it could leave, and it left. I felt something fall into my hands. It was the little thread of blood that tied it to my heart."

That was Chata to me. She was tired of living her life. The man she adored, beat her. One day she simply could not stand it any longer. Perhaps she told her soul to leave and the next thing we knew she was dead in a car accident.

A Mexican Daedalus

All through my childhood I was absorbing pop culture, continental literature, and foreign films, but also observing the human dramas that were playing themselves out in my family. Since my family was Mexican on my mother's side and New Mexican on my father's side, drama, conflict, and the centrality of death were always close and laced with the Spanish language. *Muerto. Chismes. La familia.* Etcetera. I remembered the ancient Greek artist Daedalus, who created the Labyrinth, a huge underground maze. I lived in a cultural labyrinth, a maze of my own making.

I also struggled with the undercurrent of prejudice that seemed to swirl around me as I was growing up. I remember going into a department store to buy some clothes and asking my mother if I could give the clerk the money. As I handed the money to the clerk she instinctively pulled back at the sight of my little brown hand. Her mouth tightened as she forced herself to take the money from me and then toss the change back into my waiting palm. I would never forget that little exchange because it made me realize that there were people who saw me as something to be avoided and looked down upon, an outcast.

Although English was the main language of my natal home, Spanish was the magical tongue. That dichotomy was the beginning of my consciousness about the power of language and the nature of duality. I remember being aware that I was involved in a life-and-death struggle. My intuition told me to master English. Study it. Dissect it like a scientist in a sociolinguistic laboratory.

Years later I read the self-exiled Irish writer, James Joyce, and realized he was a kindred soul. He, too, lived under cultural domination. He, too, knew what it was like to hear English spoken by its owners. Even more, he wrote down what it was like to bear linguistic and cultural dislocation. He wrote:

> The language we are speaking is his before it is mine. How different are the words *home, Christ, master,* on his lips and on mine! I cannot speak or write these words without unrest of the spirit. His language so familiar and so foreign, will always be for me an acquired speech. I have not made or accepted its words. My voice holds them at bay. My soul frets in the shadow of his language.

There it is. The "acquired speech." Something "foreign," like an invisible microbe, that insinuates its way deep into one's consciousness until every intimate thought is in English. This living, ever-present juxtaposed consciousness of something strange yet "familiar" made Joyce's soul fret "in the shadow." Like Joyce I vowed to be a shadow warrior. Unlike him, I wanted to find an island of tranquility in my troubled psychic landscape.

I searched for maps that could show me the way beyond bitterness and self-loathing. One map or path I found was Dante, the Italian poet and author of the *Divine Comedy*.

He was someone who started out with many difficulties and conflicts in his nature and yet he was able to turn them into something positive. I knew that in one way or the other, I had to create. That in the process of creation, in the process of transformation, there was salvation. Dante shows us in the *Divine Comedy*, in his epic of descent into the abyss, the journey of an individual from a state of confusion to a state of self-actualization. By studying Dante and his work, I was able to see that one can overcome conflict and produce something worthwhile out of that conflict.

Spider Woman's Son Spins Stories

Another path was shown to me by a Hopi Indian painter and poet whom I had met while on a magazine assignment. He helped show me the connection between creativity and spirituality. I spent a lot of time on the

Hopi Reservation with him. In some strange way, he was the indigenous reflection of my roots. He and his father, a famous artist who had painted Hopi-inspired murals on walls of the US embassy in India during the Franklin Roosevelt Administration, were extensions of my paternal roots in the pueblos of New Mexico.

Once he wanted to show me some ruins. A place called Awatovi. It was an old Hopi village that had been destroyed by the Hopi themselves in a conflicted mad rage in the 1600s because the village had converted to Catholicism. He wanted to show me some murals that still remained on the walls of crumbling kivas. He said they were his inspiration.

He borrowed his father's old pickup and we took off—to Awatovi. Out near Antelope Mesa. About halfway there it started to snow.

The snow fell in a white blur. We were on a dirt road filled with gashes, holes, and bumps, bouncing around inside the truck. I remember looking over to my right and seeing a group of wild horses. There must have been fifteen or twenty. I think they saw us at the same time that we saw them, and they started to run alongside us in the same direction.

We were heading south along this road with the snow driving down. The horses galloped right beside us. We could see their breath steaming in the cold air, fuming out of their flared nostrils as they strained to keep abreast.

It was a like a dream.

At that point he told me he was a member of the Snow/Water clan and the snow meant that his dead relatives were watching out for us. And then he said, "In Hopi you are identified as a cloud when you die. Clouds bring rain and snow. They bring life. When I die I hope to return as a cloud."

In the midst of the wild horses, the steady snowfall, and the closeness of ancient, forbidden ruins (you needed a special permit to visit Awatovi)—he began to talk about one of his paintings. It was called, "Coming to Pick Up the Dead, or Entering into the Spirit World." In that painting, *kachinas*, the Hopi's masked gods, carry off a dead body.

He said, "The cloud spirits carry us into the cloud world."

We arrived at the ruins, the site of a massacre. The snow began to let up as we wandered around the old village, destroyed one night over three hundred years ago because it had converted to another religion, my birth religion.

We studied the faded paintings, peered down into abandoned kivas. The horses stood nearby, as if they were guardians sent by watchful gods to protect us from the toxic vapors of hate and destruction that subtly permeated the ruins.

7

That evening we sat in his mother's house. She lived in the old village of Shuongpovi on Second Mesa. It was pitch dark outside. A deathly quiet surrounded us. It was as if we were engulfed by a great, deafening silence.

He told me that the Hopi were still practicing their ancient ceremonies, that they live by a ceremonial calendar.

The next morning I awoke before dawn. I went outside and saw waves of gray clouds rolling above the mesas from the east, rushing toward me at a great speed. I didn't believe it then. I couldn't believe it. But the clouds were people who had died during the night. And above me, in the form of fleeting clouds, the dead were being carried off into the spirit world.

From this Hopi painter I learned that I had to go back to my home and my culture and tell the world about the stories that I found there.

Notes from the Underground

So I came back to Los Angeles and began telling the stories of Chicano artists in Los Angeles. I was especially attracted to Asco (Spanish for nausea or repulsion), the underground art group from East LA. To me they were the Beatles of the Chicano art scene. Before they broke up, they epitomized life in Los Angeles as a Mexican. Their work captured the essence of the times, the harsh yet ironic truth hidden behind the ideological and cultural facade of Chicano fundamentalism.

The Chicano art that has come to occupy my attention is about alienation and estrangement. It is about the duality of presence and invisibility: about the coexistence of pride and self-loathing; about moral corruption and cultural redemption. Taking my cue from the fictional antiheroes of nineteenth-century gothic literature, who were aware of their duality and torment, I attempted to outline Chicano gothic art.

Such art brings us images of tormented and heightened self-consciousness laced with grim cynicism. One aspect of this antithetical or double identity is self-abhorrence.

All my life I have never felt hatred or bitterness toward "white" or Anglo people. Hatred and racism are my enemies and I never wear their masks because I find these twin sins disfiguring.

But there was a period in my life when I simulated whiteness in response to my experiences of prejudice and discrimination. It was not assimilation because I still retained a secret sense of my Mexican self and what that meant in this society. However, it was simulation. I couldn't change the color of my skin but I could act white, speak white, even pretend to think white. Simulation is to assume a false appearance. This simulation of a plastic whiteness was a pretense, a false front that I presented to the world, even to myself. I was very good at it. In a sense, it was my first performance art.

So self-abhorrence can come in many forms. Some Chicanos loathe the created "white" self as well as the Mexican self who allowed the creation of the simulated, masked persona. While it is an act of creation, this manufactured self can be a monster, not a beautiful creation but a horrible one.

Like the tormented creature in Mary Shelley's "ghost story," *Frankenstein*, the self-aware Chicano knows what it's like to be maligned, misunderstood, caught in the tangle of an anxious but romantic terror of hyper self-consciousness and, as Harold Bloom put it, living as "the antithetical halves of a single being." As artists and individuals, we Chicanos survive racism and its malignant growths by taking the real, if somewhat abstract, torment of our metaphysical desires and transforming them into a calculated and often subtle assault on the cultural status quo.

In the twenty-first century, the circumstances we find ourselves in have an eerie resemblance to those encountered by the creators of gothic fiction. The early nineteenth-century was a time of great turbulence: political, social, economic, cultural, and existential. The Chicano has lived with this type of turbulent upheaval throughout history. Ironically, it is this very awareness that gives Chicano art, especially the art made in Los Angeles, a spectacular resonance with our times. It also seems that the rest of American society has caught up with the ironic disillusion born of barrio-influenced life.

If there is one painting that represents our historical moment for me, it is Gronk's signature piece for his *Hotel Senator* exhibition. With that one painting, he reached a gothic height. The blue creature, whose head is on fire, functions as a signifier for the whole series.

I noted in an essay at the time: "This thing has intuited Auschwitz, Chernobyl, Soweto and San Salvador—not by reading the international news but through the banal experience of life's incessant brutality. . . . this being has been emotionally lobotomized by incremental violations of the spirit." It could be about accursed humanity at any point in history, anywhere. It could be the LA riots. The Oklahoma City bombing. That power to "read" the raw depravity of humanity gives *Hotel Senator* a mythic edge. What I saw was the impermanence and horror of life elevated to a supernatural level where the two become that thing that art and high religious ritual can be: witness to our being.

"For one translucent moment," I wrote, "within the confines of our brief existence we are totally transfixed by our reflection. That's when we experience what someone once called the 'ecstasy of catastrophe.' The depravity and ungraspable forces we see in 'Hotel Senator' are frightening not because they exist somewhere downtown but because they exist within us."

What many Chicano artists in Los Angeles have accomplished is to present us with images that come out of a long line of defiant questioning and self-questioning, not only of our own position in this society but our very circumstance as human beings. Because of our acute awareness of our bicultural reality, of our divided selves, many of us have reached excessive levels of self-consciousness. Like the Romantic writers such as Mary Shelley, we have tried to overcome this through the use of our imaginations. Although our cultural and social heritage cannot be divorced from our very existence, there is in our work a potential opening that amplifies our experience and illustrates the parallels between our specific cultural condition and the existential reality we all face.

Keeping the Demons Out

When Frankenstein's creature asks, "Who was I? What was I? Whence did I come? What was my destination?" he is unable to find an answer.

But there is an answer; there is an escape route. Liberation comes with the knowledge of who we are, what we are, where we came from, where we are going.

A. I. Becker, in an essay on the *wayang kulit*, the Bali shadow puppet theater, asked a master puppeteer how the *wayang* controls power gone amuck, demons, disease, or stupidity? Sources of chain-reacting linear power? The closest answer to his question: "'The music and shadow play move round and round and keep the demons out.' Then the puppet master paused, laughed heartily, and added, 'Demons think in straight lines.'"

The answer for those of us still in the ever-constant process of creating a cultural identity is to move round and round. To recognize the wisdom in coincidence. To realize that paradox is a form of logic. As the puppeteer also said, "Demons and people possessed go in straight lines." It is time for us to curve around each other. To not talk straight and to keep the demons out.

Note

"Subterranean Homesick Blues," by Max Benavidez, is reprinted from *I Am Aztlán: The Personal Essay in Chicano Studies* (Los Angeles: UCLA Chicano Studies Research Center Press, 2004) and from *Aztlán: A Journal of Chicano Studies* 22, no. 2 (1997).

Phantoms in Urban Exile

Harry Gamboa Jr.

Man under the Asphalt

I've heard rumors that the freeways in LA are the concrete ribbons of a package that will never be opened before exodus. The asphalt coating of billions of square feet is the icing on the multiple social layers of a dysfunctional environment. I speed along at 70 mph, attempting to tie a perfect knot of the Pasadena Freeway, the Golden State Freeway, and the Ronald Reagan Freeway. Miles accumulate as I repeat the round trips, week after week, until finally a metallic implosion—compounded by leaking oil, burnt rubber, and bent plastic—causes my '88 Ford Festiva to succumb to 192,006 miles of abuse. I walk across an urban desert in search of an oasis. My cup of sand runneth over. I am crawling under the oppressive smog and heat until my bones are bleached white near the anonymous necropolis of stranded motorists. Within a few days, a new coating of asphalt decorates the urbanscape with an opaque black facade. I cannot see or hear the traffic that speeds by as I rest in peace and silence.

Amnesia in the Air

Faces, places, and names are all a blur as I run to the nearest pay phone. I dial numbers at random until my fingers are bloodied. The operator demands to know what this is all about. I can't explain but it is extremely urgent that I get through to someone who can make sense of what I've just witnessed. The victims are sprawled across the hoods of cars, across parking lots, sidewalks, public spaces, private homes, and freeways. The worst of it is that they have no idea of what has happened to them. They are vanishing like aimless ants descending into the catacombs of self-nullification. The buzzing of the phone harmonizes with the sad melody of the victims who whistle while nothing works. The concrete tumbleweeds stampede against the one-way street like anonymous heads that roll in disbelief. I continue to dial until I reach you, hoping that no explanation will suffice, and that the sound of a hissing noise will provide a lost memory of adequate human communication.

No Tears in Dystopia

The brutal marks have disappeared via erase relations. The beautiful smile, awkward glance, flick of the wrist as the knife heads toward its victim, all of the images vanish when exposed to the hypnotic toxic whitewash. The Santa Ana winds have kicked up the dust and for a brief moment the veneer of normalcy is exposed as an artificial portrait of decay. The actual surface of experience is stretched beyond transparency. Awareness bursts as the tip of the blade finds its mark at the societal jugular. Nothing bleeds because it is all a hoax. The collapse of memory is contagious and we are all lost on our own turf. Zombies execute poor judgment but we are nevertheless under the law and order of the walking dead. I have irradiated dust in my eyes and everything appears to be glowing and eternal. The mirage of personal perspective persists even when the lights are out. My iris is in crisis. My cries against perceptual pollution are manifested by the evaporation of tears that are scattered as lost angel dust by the violent winds.

The Sky Has Fallen

The shattered glass takes on the form of a distended chandelier that encompasses my field of vision. The buildings continue to shake as the windows are propelled beyond the horizon. I am dancing on the high wire as the domino effect causes a perpetual wave of social collapse. There are no survivors as the pattern of collective shock eliminates perceptual stability. The wire becomes increasingly taut with each step as the distance between the rumba, cha cha, the twist, and the disaster below is exaggerated by a tremendous height. The harsh winds make coexistence with erratic cyclones a fact of life. Glass particles penetrate the solitude of the dead. I look forward and see that the wire heads skyward into nothingness. Each step requires a certain tap of the shoe, a particular realignment of the toe, and a major pivotal response. In order to counter imbalance, I must present an assertive attitude that rejects the forces of gravity and aerodynamics. The rubble and rotting flesh blends easily with the scintillating facade that was once a valid environment. Altitude and direction become increasingly irrelevant as a dark fog settles in. I continue to dance to the beat of fundamental forces that are beyond awareness. Intuition takes the lead as I follow.

Eating My Own Memory

MENU: When the crash course is the main course, no tip is required. There isn't time to digest the images or to discuss the issue of disgust. A quick byte leads to perceptual deprivation.

WAITER: I recommend the atomic burrito special. Not too spicy and there are plenty of hot neutrons wrapped in a wonderful blanket of lead tortillas.

CUSTOMER: I'll have the number 5. Can you replace my tacos with something less invasive?

WAITER: You can have plutonium in your guacamole as a substitution but you'll have to pay in advance and in cash.

CUSTOMER: Is that the normal policy of this restaurant or have you just been through too many unexpected detonations in your time?

WAITER: I've seen it all and I promised never to be stiffed by someone who doesn't intend to be around for too long anyway.

CUSTOMER: Let me talk to the manager. Your attitude stinks.

WAITER: So does the food. It's the manager's day off. I settle all complaints. What's the problem?

CUSTOMER: You're the problem. All I wanted was a slight change in my order and I wanted to put it on my green charge card.

WAITER: That's impossible. No exceptions. I reserve the right to refuse service to anyone and since you're just "anyone," get the hell out of here.

CUSTOMER: OK. Here's $20.00 and a promise not to complain. I'm very hungry and desperate for the chain reaction of anonymous beans. Keep the change.

WAITER: The customer is always right.

MENU: Not responsible for lost or stolen stereotypes.

Refried Has-Been

RADIO: WE MUST REMEMBER THAT EACH EFFECT HAS A CAUSE BUT THAT NOT EVERY CAUSE IS EFFECTIVE.

LISTENER: Racist brainwasher. Give me a jingle not jingoistic poetry.

RADIO: THE COUNTRY SUPPORTS OUR POSITION. SHOOT EVERYONE ON SITE IF THEY DON'T HAVE WHITE IN THEIR "I."

LISTENER: Is this AM, FM, or Exterminate 'em?

RADIO: OUR BORDERS NEED TO BE BLOCKADED. OUR SCHOOLS NEED TO BE DESIGNED FOR CUL-TURAL DRAINAGE. OUR PRISONS MUST BE POPULATED TO SUPPORT THE NEW MIDDLE CLASS OF SECURITY PERSONNEL.

LISTENER: This isn't a voice, it's a hypnotic mantra. Shut up.

RADIO: THEY EVEN HAVE THE AUDACITY TO PEN-ETRATE SUBURBIA. THEY SHOULD GO BACK TO THEIR URBAN HELLHOLES. I DON'T WANT THEM IN MY NEIGHBORHOOD.

LISTENER: I prefer to listen to music, not dangerous static. Maybe if I push a button . . .

RADIO:GOT A RUSH FROM THE BLOOD THAT GUSH FROM YOUR HEAD
ON MY WAY FOR THAT HAPPY MEAL
NOT MUCH OF A LAST SUPPER

JACKING EVERYTHING IN SIGHT
I KNOW IT AIN'T RIGHT
FEELING GOOD
MUNCHING ON FAKE FOOD

AIN'T GOT THE CHANGE
BUT THE GLOCK IS AS GOOD AS GOLD
GIVE ME SOME FRIES AND A COKE
PUT SOME 9 MM PEPPER ON YOU

LISTENER: I shouldn't believe everything I hear. Sometimes the noise just keeps me company.

Defy the Reign

Dear Anti-Representative,

I am writing to you out of concern for the safety of my culture, my children, my job, my health, my air, my water, my skin, and my existence/coexistence/subsistence. Your veiled hatred has holes in it. Are you gasping for that final breath or are you spewing venom? Your public persona comes in crisp and clear whether the TV is on or off. You have made a mess of things with surgical precision. How did you manage to produce such a plague of self-hatred? Certainly mass hypnosis is a trick.

The rabid rabbit in your hat has been gnawing on everything that generates positive self-esteem. The lucky rabbit's foot you've been passing around spreads the germ of doubt, paranoia, violence, and unnatural disaster. There are many of your nonconstituents who have voted to cure our environment of your infectious waste. With the help of the many concerned citizens and noncitizens who have incurred your wrath, please be advised that an antidote is forthcoming. No thanx for your lack of concern.

Siempre,

Anonymous Anomaly

(This message has been rubber stamped onto the foreheads of unassuming party members, party crashers, and part-time employees who work for the overthrow of exploiters in blue suits or starched skirts.)

No Magic in Realism

There is a card trick in which all of the aces are burned, the hearts are broken, the diamonds are lost, the joker is rabid, the clubs and spades are buried up the sleeves of quick-talking dealers who manage to read your mind as they empty your pockets. A similar game can be played with exploding dice, poisoned dominoes, and 9 mm roulette. The game of NO CHANCE is as popular as ever.

Round and around it goes, where it stops nobody knows. Life and death are on the same coin.

People vanish but they never reappear. Is that a trick?

Mass hypnosis vs. mass hysteria, is that a question or a trick with mirrors?

Tossing knives into the air and running out into the rain, is that a trick?

Never any answers to the important questions. Pick a number, spin the wheel, and let it ride. Bet it all.

Premonition of a Déja Vu

MYSELF: I knew I would have been there before but the opportunity was lost before it had ever begun.

YOURSELF: You're losing it. Get a grip. Make sense.

MYSELF: I didn't feel it would happen so suddenly. Everyone is gone. I can't recognize anyone anymore. There really isn't much difference between inorganic and organic matter.

YOURSELF: In your case that is quite obvious. I could carbon date your brain and wind up with a date somewhere near July of next year.

MYSELF: Everything looks like it will be so familiar tomorrow. But what am I supposed to do about today?

YOURSELF: Masturbation is out of the question. You've got no sense of passion or privacy.

MYSELF: My watch is permanently set to high noon. It is OK to be correct at least twice a day.

YOURSELF: I liked it better when you were in a coma.

MYSELF: Every time I blink I am convinced that I'm dying.

YOURSELF: Do caffeine IV.

MYSELF: My awareness is mainlined to eternity but it's boring.

YOURSELF: Close your eyes and count backwards from one billion.

MYSELF: Zzzzzzzzzzzzzzzzzzzzzzzzzzzzzzzzzzzzzzzzzzzzzzzzzzzz.

Tiptoe through the Aftermath

(A man/woman is walking in his/her neighborhood without the aid of a gun. Toes are exposed through torn socks/stockings. His/her shoes were blown off by an unexpected burst of energy. He/she is looking for meaning in the charred ruins. Fragments of objects jut out from the ground to form a random path of chaotic swirls. The man/woman is amused by an endless landscape of smoke and ash. He/she steps into the first of many paths to come. Each step leads closer to the end. He/she entertains himself/herself by singing a song to the mysterious shadows, which remain eternally motionless. The unintentional melancholy and melody become a subtle memory of disaster.)

He/she: You stick your right foot out,
 You stick your left foot in,
 There's never a partner when you need to
 Overdosey dose.

C'mon baby,
Let's do the twist,
C'mon honey,
It's a nuclear mist,
'Round and around we go,
In a brilliant cloud like this,
Let's do the twist,
Let's do the fission twist.

(He/she suddenly slips into an abyss of redundancy as the swirling path runs into itself causing a frightening array of high voltage sparks and violent chemical reactions. He/she is vaporized into a sour note that no one hears.)

Notes

"Phantoms in Urban Exile," by Harry Gamboa Jr., is reprinted from *I Am Aztlán: The Personal Essay in Chicano Studies* (Los Angeles: UCLA Chicano Studies Research Center Press, 2004) and from *Aztlán: A Journal of Chicano Studies* 22, no. 2 (1997).

Phantoms in Urban Exile (1995–97) was an original series of email communications first distributed via The Chicle electronic discussion list hosted at the University of New Mexico. To learn more about Gamboa's work, please see www.harrygamboajr.com.

The Maguey
Coming Home

Santa C. Barraza

In the hot, humid summer of 1996, after twenty-five years of absence from Kingsville and the South Texas soil where I was born, I am driving home. I am moving back. I am traveling on a surreal, blacktop highway, straight and flat as can be found only in South Texas. I was born in a flat place, a place of marshlands and prairie grass, where you can see for miles and where the intensity of the heat rises as vapor on the horizon. You can see it rising as steam and escaping into the sky. I begin to reflect back on a time when my ancestors occupied that land. I loosely combine those thoughts with what I have learned while I have been away from my birthplace. . . .

My artistic vision comes from this timeless land. It comes from looking at the South Texas horizon line and observing the land melting into the sky—the two merging together in infinity. I am entranced by the combination of these opposing forces—the earth and the sky, the physical and the immaterial ethereal, blending and becoming one. This perspective inspires creativity and moves me to question why—to question the unknown, to ponder the unconscious. The creative forces come forth from this source, from this land. And I am moved to wonder about those who came before us—our *antepadres* and *antemadres*. What did they do? Did they feel the same way about nature, about the sky, about the cosmos? Because it is so powerful, so overwhelming, this harsh, sometimes unforgiving land, whose history Gloria Anzaldúa describes as "una herida abierta" (open wound) (1987, 3), inspires creation. I have learned that this land centers me. It envelops, teaches, and compels me to become one with it—to create, to bring forth those ideas, those forces.

As I drive down the monotonous blacktop, the undulating hum of the tires against the road reminds me that I have embarked upon a journey. Leaving Chicago, upon reaching the outskirts of the windy city, I found abundant cornfields lining the highway on either side. Those beautiful, bountiful fields lined the charcoal road, creating an opening, a gateway. They formed a passageway leading me back to Texas. . . .

As I continue to drive deeper into Texas, I see a large maguey slightly ahead of me, on my right. I stop the car. The maguey—or, more specifically, its image—has become an icon for me. Because it is indigenous to this area, it is a symbol of home and identity. My mother, Frances Contreras, always told us, "Plant a maguey in front of your house, in your front yard; it brings good luck to the house." Thus she planted a maguey in front of our house. When you think about home, you think about your mother. She was creative—she conceived you and gave you life. Like the maguey, woman is life sustaining. As the plant renews and sustains life, woman procreates and maintains. The maguey is the symbol of home, of *hogar*.

I would use the maguey in my own work because I could relate to it—because of the legends, myths, history, folklore, and spirituality affiliated with it, and because it is tied directly to my mother. I remember her stories about the maguey, and then I recall her dissatisfaction with my using it as a symbol in my artwork. Her worries stemmed from a local story about soldiers in the Mexican Revolution who would copulate with the maguey in the battlefields. Its leaves then would produce ghost images of a fetus. She felt that it was bordering on witchcraft to use the plant in my artwork.

To fully appreciate the importance and symbolism associated with the maguey, one needs to consider the plant's origin. According to myth, the young goddess Mayahuel was stolen by Ehecatl-Quetzalcoatl. She was chased by the feared star demons, Tzitzimime, who destroyed her. Ehecatl-Quetzalcoatl buried her body. The first maguey plant sprouted over her grave (Miller and Taube 1993, 112). Consequently, Mayahuel is represented emerging from this particular plant, symbolic of vegetation-fertility.

It is not surprising that, similar to the maguey goddess, the Virgin of Guadalupe appeared above a maguey. In 1531, ten years after the conquest, the Lady appeared at the hill of Tepeyac, the same site where the earth goddess Tonantzin was worshipped. She left her imprint on maguey fiber—on the *tilma* of Juan Diego.

In pre-Columbian times, the actual maguey plant also was the temple of worship for the Aztecs. The victim was sacrificed over the plant; and the human heart—the life force of the body—was offered to Huitzilopochtli, their supreme deity of war, and placed over it. Thus, through the process of sacrificing and offering the victim, life, death, and spirituality were combined and integrated into this plant. Metaphorically, the plant then became a significant point of departure from which the soul of the sacrificed victim carried his or her message from the immediate community to the gods. A mythico-religious concept of the central force of life and death of this entity—of life and death, resurrection, rebirth, and regeneration—was embodied in the image of the maguey. This is how, personally, the cactus has become an important symbol of the incarnation of the forces of nature and humanity.

In the summer of 1996, my journey is coming to an end as I ponder all these things during the fifteen-hundred-mile drive from the Midwest to South Texas. I contemplate my decision, at age forty-five, to return to Kingsville to begin another *etapa* (stage) in my lifelong struggle to reclaim my own Chicana identity. I've done much of my work elsewhere, outside *Tejas*, especially in Pennsylvania and Chicago. But now I am returning home, to the place that it hardest of all to live in—the disputed, often violent space of South Texas, the Borderlands. I am returning to the contradictions, dualities, and daily resistance to the historical obliteration of our female selves—as *nativas, indígenas, mestizas,* Chicanas, Mexica-*Tejanas*. Gloria Anzaldúa, Chicana *patlache* feminist theorist and writer, as well as author Pat Mora, uses the concept of *Nepantla* to describe the in-between spaces that Chicanas always have occupied, the spaces within which we have constructed ourselves and our history. This concept articulates the structure of the artwork I have been doing all my life.

Yet I do not feel that I am "at home" until I notice water standing in the highway. This optical illusion is caused by the intense heat of this area rising from the roadway into the surrounding dry air. The movement distorts the vision and creates wavy images that appear to be situated directly above a roadway with water lying on it. Since the terrain is so flat, I can see for miles ahead of me as I drive. The entire horizon begins to shimmer. This is a South Texas mirage. I am being welcomed by the topography and climatology.

Within a couple of days, I have seen the land slowly transformed from an urban Chicago scene into a South Texas landscape—a unique experience. It is a hot, humid, arid place, but it is home. Finally I am home again.

Notes

"The Maguey: Coming Home," by Sanza C. Barraza, is reprinted from *I Am Aztlán: The Personal Essay in Chicano Studies* (Los Angeles: UCLA Chicano Studies Research Center Press, 2004) and from *Aztlán: A Journal of Chicano Studies* 26, no. 1 (2001).

Excerpted from "Santa C. Barraza: An Autobiography," *Santa Barraza: Artist of the Borderlands*, edited by María Herrera-Sobek. Number 5, Rio Grande/Río Bravo Series. College Station, Texas: Texas A & M University Press, 2001. Used with permission. To order, call toll-free 1-800-826-8911.

Works Cited

Anzaldúa, Gloria. 1987. *Borderlands/La Frontera: The New Mestiza*. San Francisco: Aunt Lute Books.
Miller, Mary Ellen, and Karl Taube. 1993. *The Gods and Symbols of Ancient Mexico and the Maya: An Illustrated Dictionary of MesoAmerican Religion*. New York: Thames and Hudson.

Chickens on the Bus

Alejandro Anreus

For my daughter Isabel

It was our first winter in Elizabeth, New Jersey. We had arrived in September, and the warm fall weather had not prepared us for the brutal winter that appeared two days after Thanksgiving. The year was 1972 and "we" were my mother Margarita; my aunts Dinorah and Nereyda; the family matriarch, my grandmother María Otilia Anreus; and of course me, an underweight and scrawny twelve-year-old named after the infamous anarchist (and lousy shot—remember Frick?) Alexander Berkman.

We had come to the United States less than two years earlier, lived briefly in Miami, and then left that city in search of jobs and a life away from right-wing fellow Cubans. We were exiles from Castro's Cuba. My family, like the majority of working-class families in 1950s Cuba, had welcomed the revolution on January 1, 1959. Members of my extended family ranged from liberal to socialist in their political identity and political past. Within the family there were sympathies for Antonio Guiteras and his Joven Cuba movement in the 1930s, for Ramón Grau and Carlos Prío's Auténticos in the 1940s (they were a disappointment due to their corruption), and for the ethical Ortodoxos in the 1950s (my uncle Rufino would listen to Eduardo Chibás on the radio). We were also practicing but liberal Catholics, although my youngest aunt, the actress Gladys Anreus, was into Santería. Overall, the family was anti-Batista, anti-Americano (of the US variety), and anticommunist (of the Stalinist variety, the one most available in pre-1959 Cuba). So it was natural that they hid weapons, students, and publications during Batista's reign in the mid- to late 1950s. When the revolution triumphed, they were ecstatic. The early enthusiasm for Castro's revolution started to wane when he declared himself a Marxist-Leninist after the Bay of Pigs. ("The problem wasn't Marx, it was the ideas of that nasty *calvito* Lenin," my grandmother would say.) Disillusionment grew as independent labor unions

23

ceased to exist and homosexuals were persecuted, the newspaper *Revolución* was taken away from independent socialist Carlos Franqui, Castro supported the invasion of Czechoslovakia in the summer of 1968, and the poet Heberto Padilla was forced to make a public confession at the Writers and Artists Union in 1970. The Cuban road to utopia had become dystopic.

On August 19, 1970, we boarded one of the "freedom flights" sponsored by President Lyndon B. Johnson. We were out of there. Half the family stayed behind for a variety of reasons, both personal and political. As the plane took off, my grandmother looked out the window and said to me: "You will return. I probably won't, so let me look at those greens and blues and keep them in my mind forever."

And here we were in December 1972, our first winter in New Jersey. Like good tropical folk, we were not prepared for the cold. My mother was working in a factory (Magnus Organs, in Linden), my aunt Dinorah was a receptionist for a Cuban surgeon, my aunt Nereyda was home struggling with the early stages of sclerodermia and muscular dystrophy, and my grandmother, as usual, was running the household and taking care of me when I was not in school (PS#22). We had very little money; we walked a lot, used coupons, received free food from the local Catholic charities, and bought our clothes and furniture used and piecemeal at the Salvation Army. And above all, we were not ready for winter, physically or psychologically. It would take us forever to get dressed (thermal long johns, always) and step out into the cold.

What I am about to narrate happened shortly before Christmas and on a weekday. Classes were over, and I was home with my grandmother and my ill aunt. My mother and my other aunt were at work. We had saved enough money to buy some yucca, rice and beans, plenty of Spanish nougat (Sanchiz Mira), and a nice bottle of Rioja. There was not enough for pork or Guinea hens or turkey, but there was enough to buy two fresh chickens. That morning at breakfast my grandmother had announced that we were going to *la placita*—the open-air market in Peterstown, the Italian neighborhood in Elizabeth—and we were going to buy two fresh chickens, which for her meant alive and kicking. We were going to bring them home and kill them and roast them for Noche Buena, Christmas Eve dinner. I was excited and nervous. In Cuba we did this all the time. But that was Cuba, our homeland; we knew the ropes there, we knew what to do. What about here? I started to mention this to my grandmother, but she placed her hand on my right shoulder and told me to hurry and finish my breakfast, because we had to go. Getting dressed was an ordeal and stepping out the front door was another. The wind hit our faces and as we stepped out she said, "Este frío está del carajo. Me cago en tu madre Fidel."

We walked one long block of Florida Street, where we lived, up to Elizabeth Avenue, and from there a block and a half to the corner of Third Street to take the number 30 bus to la placita. We had exact change to get there (15 cents for me each way, 30 cents for my grandmother each way) and $12.00 to buy two chickens. And not a penny more. Waiting for the bus at the corner seemed like an eternity. The wind was fierce and the temperature had to be in the low thirties. She grabbed my left hand in its blue and red mitten (Salvation Army special) and squeezed it. She assured me that the bus was coming and that patience was a virtue. The bus arrived and we got in half frozen. The trip took a little less than twenty minutes and we got off in front of the Harmonia bank on Elizabeth Avenue and Seventh Street. We had barely warmed up and here we were back on the cold and windy streets. We walked a little over two blocks into la placita and made our way to the live poultry store. As we entered, the stench of feathers and chicken shit hit my nostrils and made me gag. But it was warm and it wasn't windy, even if it smelled.

My grandmother gave me instructions to speak in English to the old man behind the counter. I told him in my new and heavily accented language that she wanted two hens, one white and the other black-and-white, that she wanted them fat and that she wanted to pick them out herself and take them home alive. The old man behind the counter smiled at me, then at her and said to me, "That's fine, kid. Your grandma is just like the old Italian women. Like my Nonna, God rest her soul."

He gestured at my grandmother and guided her to the chicken cage, opened the gate and let her in. She entered. Feathers flew and chickens squawked as my grandmother made her way through the birds, picking them up and feeling their weight. First she found the speckled one, then the white one. She grabbed them by their legs with their heads upside down and walked out of the cage. The old man followed her saying out loud that she was a real pro. Then he took them from her and weighed them. They were $12.75 total. My grandmother and I looked at each other, wondering where we could find the extra 75 cents.

The old man realized we were short 75 cents and he asked me, "How do you say grandma in Spanish?" "Abuela," I said.

"Abuela," he said, "it's okay, it's only $12.00." She paid him with a discreet smile on her face, never losing her composure and dignity. Before I knew it we were standing on a corner braving the wind and cold with two chickens sticking their heads out of a large paper bag with handles.

The bus arrived and we got in. We sat right in the front, on the right side of the bus. We shared the side seat with a rather large older woman, who was dressed very properly and wore a great deal of makeup. The bus had not advanced more than three or four blocks when she poked me and asked, pointing to the large bag between my left leg and my grandmother's right leg, "And what are those live animals doing on this bus?"

I looked. The two chickens were sticking their heads out of the top of the bag. I ignored her and started to think to myself, oh God, now we are in trouble, we are going to have to get off the bus or they are going to take those two chickens from us. Oh God, this is not going to turn out right.

The large woman ignored the fact that I was ignoring her and spoke directly to the bus driver: "There are live animals on this bus. There are chickens on this bus. It's not hygienic, it goes against regulations from the Board of Health."

The driver pulled the bus over to the side and stopped. He turned around and spoke directly to me. "Kid, you are going to have to get off the bus with the old lady. You cannot bring live animals on the bus. It breaks all kinds of codes, Board of Health, Transportation Department."

I proceeded to translate all of this to my grandmother, who listened calmly. My grandmother's right hand reached into the bag and she pulled out a chicken; with lightning speed, almost before any of us could realize what she was doing, she twisted the neck of the white chicken with her bare hand and dropped its lifeless body into the bag. A similar but even faster motion disposed of the black-and-white speckled bird. I looked up and around and saw the startled faces of the other passengers—they had just witnessed the assassination of two birds in front of their very eyes by an old, thin, wrinkled woman dressed in black.

My grandmother looked at me and stated simply, "Dile al guagüero que ya no hay pollos vivos en la guagua."

"Mister," I said to the bus driver, "there are no more live chickens on the bus." The bus driver had witnessed the way my grandmother had dispatched the chickens. His face was frozen in stupefaction. It took a second for him to snap out of it.

"Okay, kid, the chickens are definitely not alive on this bus anymore. You can stay."

The bus started to move. We would be home in less than twenty minutes. The chickens on the bus were dead, and we were on the bus keeping warm, not outside, being devoured by the cold and the wind.

Note

"Chickens on the Bus," by Alejandro Anreus, is reprinted from *I Am Aztlán: The Personal Essay in Chicano Studies* (Los Angeles: UCLA Chicano Studies Research Center Press, 2004) and from *Aztlán: A Journal of Chicano Studies* 32, no. 1 (2007).

Home/Work

Research Note

Chon A. Noriega

Men should sing with their heads thrown back, with their mouths wide open and their eyes shut. Fill your lungs, so they can hear you at the pasture's farther end.

—Américo Paredes, *"With His Pistol in His Hand":*
A Border Ballad and Its Hero

Perhaps don Américo was wrong, men should *not* sing with their heads thrown back, with their mouths wide open, and their eyes shut. In the pasture's farther end, another story echoes. . . .

—Chon A. Noriega, *Shot in America: Television, the State,*
and the Rise of Chicano Cinema

On a recent trip to Chicago, I encountered a most unusual set of artifacts that challenges my own challenge from the quotation above. I will write about these artifacts momentarily, but first I want to provide some context. In my book about the rise of Chicano cinema, I had sought "the irony of knowing more than your own story" in order to render a more complicated account of how minorities first gained access to film and television. To me, that history was filled with paradox, irony, and ambivalence, whereas Américo Paredes presented the archetypal study of Chicano resistance through a masculine expressive form, the corrido. Paredes was none other than the father of Chicano studies, and what he had to say about the corrido—and resistance more generally—seemed to be all about my own father. I knew that story all too well, and so I looked elsewhere. Besides, as I confessed in the acknowledgments, I could not sing. . . .

While I stand by my original research, and my challenge of Paredes, I have begun to wonder if perhaps I was wrong, too. In other words, if the history I wrote was filled with paradox, irony, and ambivalence, then the same must be true of the historian himself. In fact, as I noted at several points in my book, it was often difficult to draw clear boundaries between historian and history: there were certain events I simply could not narrate as a historian and so on these points I remained silent. And I acknowledged this. These silences were self-conscious attempts to honor and yet contain my participation as an advocate and activist within the historical narrative I was telling. I would have to write about this part of my intellectual life in another context.

But there was another, more profound silence within my book that spoke to a relationship outside the book's subject matter. This relationship had to do with the person who inspired my ongoing intellectual quest: my father. He did so in a way that drove me to approach all things as a life-and-death struggle. But he also wrote poetry. And how he could sing, throwing his head back and filling his lungs, so that he could be heard at the neighborhood's farther end . . . much to the horror of my sister. In Miami, where we grew up, corridos and rancheras stood out, calling attention to our difference from the Cuban and Anglo neighbors

In January 2002 I discovered a new archive in Chicago: my sister Reni's collection of our father's Mexican LPs. As a child I had fixated on the album covers, the most intriguing of which showed Antonio Aguilar kneeling over his dead horse, pistol raised, and head thrown back, singing a corrido, of course (fig. 1). My father, who listened to these albums every weekend, informed me somewhat tongue-in-cheek that in Mexico all songs were love songs and the objects of these songs were either horses or women, but mostly horses. He taught himself to play guitar and sing his favorite love songs, and when he played, I would always request that he sing my favorite song of all, "Cucurrucucú Paloma." Most summers our family returned to his hometown of Alamogordo, New Mexico, where my father would sing a corrido to and about his own father, Gavino Noriega. I now suspect he had modified another corrido, "Gabino Barrera," from the Aguilar album with the dead horse.

While I have carried the image of these albums with me to this day, I had long since let go of them as objects. So it was a surprise to find them in my sister's living room, especially since she never quite identified with our Mexican patrimony. Nevertheless, she had made a point of preserving these albums, even if she never listened to them, could not understand

CORRIDOS : ANTONIO AGUILAR

GABINO BARRERA
Y 11 EXITOS MAS

153

musart

Figure 1. Album cover of Gabino Barrera y 11 Exitos Más *by Antonio Aguilar.*

them, and had even forgotten she had taken possession of them. My sister shared my own commitment to the archive, where one collects first and asks questions later. Now, with the objects in my hands again, we began asking questions about our father that ended up providing some answers about ourselves.

The albums can be divided into two periods. The first group was purchased in the early 1960s, apparently in the two years between my birth and that of my sister. The singers are male and exemplify postrevolutionary masculine ideals in Mexico: Jorge Negrete, Pedro Infante, Antonio Aguilar, Javier Solis, and Los Tres Ases. Solis clearly served as the model for my father's singing voice. I imagine my father felt considerable cultural dislocation and isolation in Miami and that these singers provided a connection with his sense of self as a "Mexican." If so, that connection was an ironic one on at least two levels. First, from what I can gather, my father's taste in music during the 1950s ran much more toward country and western and rock 'n roll. Indeed, he loved to sing Hank Williams and Johnny Cash songs, and he wore heavy black-rimmed glasses that affected a "Buddy Holly" look. Second, the imprints for these albums came from Miami-based companies; the very place that created a sense of cultural isolation also served as a gateway for the music that eased that isolation.

At the time, my father was a reporter covering the Latin American beat for the Associated Press. But after a few close calls during the Cuban Missile Crisis, he realized that the political upheaval in Latin America was too dangerous for a new father. And so he left journalism for a career in public relations (fig. 2). He also left behind his Hemingway-esque aspirations to become a writer. But he clung to love songs that helped define what it meant to be Mexican after the revolution.

Former Sports Editor Takes PR Position

Saturnino Noriega, f o r m e r Florida state radio tv editor for the Associated Press, has been named senior account executive of the Gerald Schwartz Agency, Miami Beach public relations firm.

Noriega, who was with the AP for two and one-half years, was sports editor of the Alamogordo Daily News prior to serving in the United States Army for two years.

He has traveled extensively in Mexico and the Caribbean and will direct the Latin American division of the Schwartz Agency.

SATURNINO NOREIGA

Figure 2. Article from Alamogordo Daily News (New Mexico) c. 1963.

In 1972 my father was promoted and transferred to the regional office of a trade association in Chicago. We entered the middle class in a dramatic fashion, moving into Hemingway's suburban hometown, Oak Park. The second group of albums was purchased in 1978 and 1979, a period during which my parents divorced, my father lost his job, and I left home. The singers are female and are fewer in number: Lola Beltrán and Maria de Lourdes. Sometimes the songs are the same, songs about a person who would rather suffer, accept blame, and even be lied to than be alone. Only now that person was a woman, at least in song. In this period, my father and I attended a performance by Antonio Aguilar at a sports arena in Chicago. Aguilar rode his horse from one end of the arena to the other, singing corridos about crossing the border to a new and uncertain life. It was as if the album cover had come to life in the heroic moments just before the horse would be shot. In such moments, sombrero in hand and head thrown back, a man could survive anything. My father, who endured and struggled against rather explicit racism from his employers before losing his job altogether, slowly built his own business over the next two decades. I was one of his first employees. He also rebuilt his life, as did my mother. Last year, he retired and returned to Alamogordo, building his own house, although his second wife drove the tractor.

The value of the archive is not always what one would expect. I remember everything. And I have pictures, too. But these artifacts have challenged such certainties, bringing a nuanced and more compassionate understanding of my father and his impact on my life. Sitting in my sister's living room, we listened to each of these albums, some nearly forty years old, while I translated the lyrics. Our father's spirit was in the room—in us—whereas before it had been the room, the neighborhood, the universe. His history was now ours, too, rather than being the thing that had created and stood between us in our need for each other.

After we had listened to the albums, and my sister promised to burn them into CDs for me, we put on a formative album from our youth—a collection of disco hits—and spent the next hour dancing with Reni's five-year-old daughter, Anna. My nephew Martin, two years older than his sister, peered in from the hallway, embarrassed by our dancing. Decades from now Anna and Martin may re-encounter that album and reclaim a bit of the past in each other. They need each other, and someday they will need to understand why (figs. 3 and 4).

This essay is a research note because it signals a profound and still-emerging change in my scholarship. I wanted to write about the personal

Figure 3. Chon and Reni, around ages seven and five. Photo by Saturnino Noriega.

basis for that change insofar as it relates to my object of study and the historical method. For the past decade, my personal history has functioned as a structuring subtext or as an allegory informing my research. As such, the archive allowed me to confront my past as an object—or as a set of artifacts—that I could isolate, understand, narrate, and thereby master. That is one reason why I remained silent when I encountered myself as a political actor within my own historical narrative. I seemed to be all over the place:

Figure 4. Anna and Martin, ages five and seven. Photo by Reni Celeste.

writer, allegory, and actor. This conundrum of our place within our own work and the world is the intellectual's dark side. We cannot bring light to this place—the fantasy of enlightenment being that the mind can free itself from the body and its past—but we can bring understanding and compassion to the darkness. This editor's commentary is a note—a tone, a sounding, a key of an instrument—that serves as one way in which I can sing for my father.

Postscript (2020)

"Research Note" is a personal reflection on my *Shot in America: Television, the State, and the Rise of Chicano Cinema* (2000), one that stands in contrast to the more disciplinary concerns of the book itself vis-à-vis the study of film and television texts, industry regulation and media reform, and Chicano culture and history. This personal reflection was prompted by a visit with my sister in early 2002. We listened to our father's Mexican albums, which he had purchased in the early 1960s, when we lived in Miami, and the late 1970s, after we moved to Chicago. This experience led me to come to terms with how "my personal history has functioned as a structuring subtext or as an allegory informing my research." What I did not bring into this essay directly were the facts that my sister had been fighting stage 4 breast cancer for four years and that her mortality was very much on our minds as we connected with our shared past. Instead, I gestured to the dynamic at work between my niece and nephew at that time and their need later on to be able to understand how their own bond was formed by histories big and small.

In writing such a research note, I sought to situate film and television studies within a larger cultural framework—which does not happen as much as one would expect—and to access that framework through consumer culture located in the home. (Here, Spanish-language LP albums that connected my father with his own upbringing in Alamogordo.) The book itself situated early Chicano media reform and film production within the regulatory framework of the television industry. In doing so, I located the personal outside the disciplinary dialogue the book attempted—between cinema and media studies and Chicano studies—rather than collapse everything around my identity, or, rather, around the declaration of an identity as equivalent to an epistemology. Don't get me wrong. I was not disavowing identity, nor was I denying its epistemological stakes, but I did think it was important to maintain some analytical distinctions in order to realize the dialogic potential of interdisciplinary work. People cannot be meaningfully reduced to social or psychological abstractions (the "I am" of identity) or to a theory of knowledge (the "I think" of epistemology), even if these provide insights into certain tendencies, intentions, and social moorings.

In the nearly two decades since I wrote "Research Note," both my sister and father have passed away. I live with their absence, but I also hold their memories above ground. Although they connect me to my own past and make looking ahead more meaningful, there remains an absence that can be neither overcome nor overturned. And that dual experience is quite different than what I wrote about in "Research Note." The personal can be a useful tool in making meaning within academic research, whether the source for the "personal" resides in the scholar's memory, personal possessions, or the archive. But the personal is also a unique experience with no other meaning than simply that of existence itself. Photographs haunt and taunt this sense of the personal, or what Albert Camus called the absurd. These indexes of a past time demand social meaning and reorient personal memory toward that goal, yet they also stand as evidence that memory remains elusive.

The first time I ever visited Los Angeles was to visit my sister, who lived one block north of Hollywood Boulevard. You could see the Fredericks of Hollywood store from her front porch, the mannequins dressed in nurse erotica. It was 1982. I had just taken a three-day bus ride from Morelia, Michoacán, to downtown Los Angeles. Halfway through the taxi ride to Hollywood, I explained that the meter had just hit the exact amount that I had in my pocket. The driver turned it off and continued to drive me to my sister's apartment so that we could continue talking. Reni was not home yet, so I struck up a conversation with the landlord. When he told me the rent, I asked how in the world anyone would agree to pay such an outrageous amount. "They're here to live the dream, man."

My sister was beautiful, and even more so in photographs, no matter the photographer. She never took a bad one. I used to joke that she was living her life like a California postcard. The photographs only proved my point—and she had lots of photographs. Reni, who changed her name from Renee, had fled our home in Chicago, barely completing high school. In Los Angeles she took classes at California State University, Northridge, and worked at various entry-level clerical jobs. I had dropped out of college to travel for that year, first across Europe and then in Mexico. Visiting Reni was the closest thing I had to going home at that time in my life.

One week later, leaving Los Angeles on a bus to visit my best friend in North Carolina, I spent the first night looking out the window at a lightning storm as we passed through the desert. Slowly I became aware of my own reflection, first as an overlay on the landscape, then as someone I had been running away from. I smiled and knew things would be different from that point onward. In those days, nothing happened fast, least of all the relationship between Reni and me, which unfolded slowly across the country. Over the years we would continue to come home to each other, in Santa Cruz, San Francisco, New York City, Baltimore, Albuquerque, Chicago, New Haven, and even in Los Angeles again—this time my home.

Reni canceled her last trip to Los Angeles in late summer 2004, and instead I flew to New Haven, where she taught at Yale University. I spent two weeks on that visit, then returned throughout the fall. She lived with metastatic breast cancer for almost seven years, refusing to consider herself a terminal patient. She completed a PhD, wrote two books, raised her children, and lived the dream until she died on Tuesday, December 7, 2004.

Shortly after my grandfather died in the late 1970s, I came across my dad in his study one night. He was sitting at his desk looking inward. He turned to me and said, "I'm on the front line now. My father isn't out there ahead of me anymore. It's just me and death." My father knew how to sum things up in an axiomatic, yet also poetic way:

"Be right, be wrong, but be definite!"

"If you are going faster than them, they can't hit you from behind."

"You must have a philosophy, otherwise you are not a person."

"Be careful, people here don't like Mexicans."

"Don't let the bastards get you down!"

My father grew up in in a large working-class family near the US-Mexico border. He loved and adored his "twin" sister, Toby, whose beauty he later saw in my own sister. With a high school degree he went on to become a journalist for the Associated Press who covered the Cuban Revolution, a public relations executive, a "business man," a mayoral candidate in Chicago, and, in off-hours, a poet, painter, dancer, and singer. We would watch football together on weekends and then go outside and toss the football back and forth in an empty field until it was too dark. And he enrolled the two of us in ballet lessons at the Ruth Page Academy. He was driven and easy going, righteous while also inclined toward the absurd. We were, he always said, "Mexican." But it never seemed that way in Mexico.

I now have my father's extensive papers, photographs, and books, including seven tiny paperbacks, published in 1907, which his father had given him as a child. The title of each begins *An Evening With* and concludes with the author's name: Burns, Tennyson, Irving, Lamb, Thackeray, Hawthorne, Longfellow. Reading them, he saw a world outside the sawmills and apple orchards where his family worked, and he moved toward that world.

Two photos, two worlds, each insistently unknowable to the other. From 1955: a stylish eighteen-year-old trickster and cub reporter, set against the expansive landscape of southern New Mexico. From 1962: a father holding his toddler son in Miami, Florida. One memory deep within my body. Before I knew my name, I knew him. He'd settle me across his chest as he took an afternoon nap, my body cradled by one arm, my back gently stroked by the other. Face down on a smooth and warm surface, rising and falling on the steady breath and heartbeat of the new world in which I have appeared. The world loves me. And I sleep.

On April 15, 2019, my father watched Notre Dame burn from his television in Alamogordo. Visiting the church in the 1970s had been a defining moment for him—a first trip to the City of Lights, an encounter with deep history still living, and an inspiration for him to continue living large as a citizen of the world. And there it was, engulfed in flames. The next morning his wife called in tears to tell me that he had died in his sleep.

One year later, I've been thinking of my father, Notre Dame, a world that lives within its history, and one that also burns to the ground. I've wanted to call him so that we could talk about the novel coronavirus, a phrase that would amuse him: "I want to read that novel." I wonder how he would be responding to the threat, and, secretly, I want him to reassure me that I will be okay, we will be okay, that from the ashes new inspirations will form.

Note

"Research Note," by Chon A. Noriega, is reprinted from *I Am Aztlán: The Personal Essay in Chicano Studies* (Los Angeles: UCLA Chicano Studies Research Center Press, 2004) and from *Aztlán: A Journal of Chicano Studies* 27, no. 2 (2002).

Beyond the Cinema of the Other, or Toward Another Cinema

Frances Negrón-Muntaner

For the past three years, "Beyond the Cinema of the Other, or Toward Another Cinema" has been fittingly nomadic. Several journals and anthologies have almost published it, but a last-minute act of God or censorship has allowed the original text to survive only as spoken words on half-forgetful ears. And perhaps the only two reasons to disrupt this state of affairs by its publication is the puzzling impact of such unthreatening words on certain gatekeepers, and the quiet testimony this simple address provides about the mutability of purpose and truth.

The text was originally written in Spanish as part of a panel presentation organized by filmmaker Ana María García at the San Juan CinemaFest, during October of 1995. The panel opened up the discussion for "Made in the U.S.A.," a sampling of works by Puerto Rican US-based filmmakers.

At the time of enunciation, these words were greeted with some bewilderment and a degree of apprehension, in part because I accompanied them with images of previous films, culminating in a three-minute clip of *Brincando el charco*, representing several female couples in different phases of a sex tease. At the time, the moderator broke the silence by asking, *"Están en shock, ¿no?"* The audience responded with laughter. Unfortunately, reason bars us from packaging a multimedia presentation for current readers; hence here are the words, not surprisingly translated into English.

Homecomings

During the seven years spanning my first professional film, *AIDS in the Barrio* (1989), to my last, *Homeless Diaries* (1995), I have been invited on multiple occasions to recount the process through which I have become a Puerto Rican filmmaker in the United States. A mouthful, no doubt, and not something you are born into. The "answer" to this inquiry has mutated, transformed, and resignified itself so many times, that it has taken the form of a story. Like all stories that are repeated in different places and for diverse audiences, the story can't always be, nor mean, the same thing. Due to the increasing tediousness of the biographical on occasions like this, I would prefer to speak to you today about a proposed film practice, not as a function of identity but as a space of possibility. Possibilities that may not always be realizable, not even agreeable to everyone, but perhaps simply available to some spectators, or one person's life. Cinema has often been a plane ticket to places that I never wanted to go, but that is the only true risk of this proposal.

Given my continuous transit between diverse geographic, sexual, and creative localities, the cinematic space can enact a resignification of home and partially serve as its witness. The house-space of cinema certainly comes with twisted porches, doors leading to pleasure or hell, lots of people, lots of noise, and also with a deafening silence (perhaps that is my room of nightmares), but ultimately stands as people are free to wander from room to room. For the house of cinema is an invitation to occupy (un)common seats, regardless of where one physically rests at any given moment. Because film is nothing if not a provocation to travel and, hence, a possibility for encounters, displacements, seductions not real. Because those of us who continuously go through it have the maddening habit of carrying many keys, although most do not correspond to any doors in particular, and even if they did, we wouldn't use them since safety is another house of cinematic illusion.

The house trope emerges from the critical response to *Brincando el charco: Portrait of a Puerto Rican*, and the subsequent videos, *Puerto Rican ID* (a meditation on one Puerto Rican's relationship with American TV), and *Homeless Diaries* (a dialogue with several homeless advocates from north Philadelphia). The trope comes to life after arriving in Puerto Rico to show *Brincando el charco*, and one of my first exchanges with a local journalist ends in the following way: "Welcome home, if we can talk about home after seeing your film." A comment that triggered another memory, where a spectator in an academic screening in New England proposed that in *Brincando el charco*, home is an unresolved, fundamental, and politically charged problem because the film does not articulate a clear position regarding the political as a national project. But this is not so much a problem as an alternative proposition. In *Brincando el charco*, home is closer to what Caribbean and African American writer Audre Lorde called "the very house of difference" than a political metanarrative. In this sense, my cinematic proposition is one that tends toward questions and critical ambiguities, where objectivity is constituted through and within a debate among different positions, and not in the authority of a single version.

Challenging home—that heterogeneity not contained in the categories of nation, race, class, ethnicity, and identity—is part of creating communities where both dialogue and cacophony are possible, particularly when one must acknowledge that the notion of home itself is not easily discardable for subjects whose positions as daughters, lovers, lesbians, colonized, and migrants have precisely resulted in the potentially productive trauma of being forced to move away from home. Just as for the anorexic, her only obsession is to eat; for those who feel that they have no home, there is no other desire but to find one, even when it has been in the process of inhabiting the chronotope of homelessness, that a more inclusive and democratic notion of community has been produced, lived, and enjoyed.

Contradictorily, the fact that one may become obsessed with reaching home does not entail that the traveler actually wants to, or can, reach it. One can fall in love with the pain that offers symbolic centrality, however fleeting, thus avoiding more healing possibilities. From this, the nomad's tent, the ancestral cave, the letter's ink postscript, the open spaces, the borders, become enticing tropes to think about divergent notions of community, as well as divergent ways of seeing and seeking pleasures. But also, these tropes can have devastating results when instead of symbolic, empowering strategies, these constitute policies imposed by some groups over others. This last observation was my most important lesson in videotaping *Homeless Diaries*. For the activists featured in this video diary, many of whom were literally homeless, facing the cold and the rats—real and symbolic—the most transgressive trope is not their condition, but their potential becoming as owners of a concrete house: a house hopefully made out of solid materials, in a clean and drug-free neighborhood with running water, gas, and electricity.

In *Brincando el charco*, the problematization of home stems from the exclusion of at least four communities from the island's nationalist imagination: Afro–Puerto Ricans, homosexuals, lesbians, and US-born Puerto Ricans. In the insistence of representing those voices and bodies, I proposed a continuous questioning of the construction of home as the everyday practice of tolerance and a rupture with Puerto Rican dominant filmmaking. But mostly, cinema became a symbolic attempt to return "home" after a period of engaging in a filmmaking practice rooted in the "other," a method motivated by a political desire of finding a place as an ethnic subject in the United States. This last conceptualization was an alternative to understanding my stay in the United States as a form of exile—the condition in which the present is mortgaged to a future that will never be the past one yearns for—and to imagine new solidarities with multiple communities. The ethnification of my political location, which is nothing but a way of seeing and inhabiting the world as a decentered participant rather than as a protagonist, has been a crucial part of my critical position challenging totalizing discourses. However, due to my class and ethnic background, the cinema of the other became a cinema about certain Puerto Ricans in the United States. Puerto Ricans tendentiously concentrated in poor neighborhoods, and whose cultural practices are often coopted as symbols of resistance by writers, filmmakers, and academics, who, however, enjoy a privileged distance from the everyday lives of the people who live in these communities.

Although the above-mentioned proposal can help create class alliances to contest authoritarian apparatuses of representation, it is no less true that it could also have politically problematic effects, particularly if these interventions don't have a degree of reflexivity in their structure. The fact that middle-class Puerto Ricans and Islanders are the ones usually interpolated to represent the "other" Puerto Ricans has resulted, with few exceptions, in a cinema where "Puerto Ricanness" is equivalent with "otherness" itself. Ironically, this is a cinema that locates those who practice it in a position of power as spokespeople of communities that ultimately continue to have limited access to self-representation. The strong nationalist inflection of this work also constitutes a silencing of many Puerto Ricans whose cultural practices, pleasures, and perspectives are neither represented nor acknowledged, except as pathologies. In a broader context, this tendency also works by displacing the relatively privileged position of the filmmaker (even if symbolically peripheral) to that of the economically marginal of the represented subject. This discursive operation does very little to transform the positioning of the represented subject, or even facilitate a critical reflection about the differences and hierarchies involved in any context where Puerto Ricans meet.

In critiquing the Puerto Rican cinema of the Other, which is fundamentally also a self-criticism, I do not want to suggest that this type of intervention may not have an important strategic value. *AIDS in the Barrio*, for example, was the first independent film with Puerto Rican producers and directors that proposed an antihomophobic discourse in relation to the AIDS epidemic. It also cleared a few frames for the representation of gay Puerto Rican voices and bodies. In this sense, this kind of intervention is part of creating spaces where the challenge is not simply the representation of subaltern subjects, but of proposing other narrative modes for representing these subjects.

Responding to the problematic aspects of *AIDS in the Barrio*, especially on the realist premise of representation of the "other" Puerto Rican, *Brincando el charco* constructs a lesbian character, distant from the island, residing in a body intersected by contradictory discourses. Many have read this as a transparently autobiographical gesture, attempting to suggest that the film is eccentric and, therefore, an easily discardable provocation. The only truly autobiographical aspect in the film, however, relates to my shared desire with the protagonist of multiplying the travel routes, the various ways one can come and go, without being forced to exclusively dwell within the house of the national. A conceptualization that, I believe, tends to subvert the multiple possibilities of the "Puerto Rican" sign.

Without doubt, I wanted *Brincando el charco* to provoke some type of polemic. At the same time, although the film invites the spectator to a dialogue, it also fears it. In the last instance, I expected the film to answer the question of whether it is possible to return home, or at least to return to some houses in common. The answer is that, without doubt, it is possible to travel home through film, not as a cinema of the other, but another cinema. A film practice that unceremoniously sends the nostalgia of a paternalistic, racist, and classist nineteenth century to a mausoleum (or museum) and destroys the notion that every Puerto Rican's life should be a duel to death with the evils forces of colonialism (as if these were exterior to our own practice). Ultimately, a radically contemporary cinema capable of addressing those radical needs and desires that we hear today shouting in a whisper, but that before long will come down, shattering all the wine glasses, even those kept under lock and key.

Once I abandoned the paternal home, the possibilities of dwelling multiplied, even as nostalgia has clearly overtaken me. Because of this, I will leave you with the possibility of yet another cinema: a surprising one. To define it more, from the authority that the podium and the university confers, would no doubt constitute a violent act.

Epilogue

Since facing the not necessarily hostile, yet silent, University of Puerto Rico classroom in 1995, I have been engaged in productions that elastically expand or even bypass the question of home. Moving to South Florida in 1997 took care of much of my physical alienation: no more English only, cold winters, pale faces, or Quaker restraint. Two plane hours from Puerto Rico and three from the Big Apple, the island of Miami Beach could well be the center of one universe.

But there is something more. Photographing *The Splendid Little War*, a two-hour film on the context and impact of the Spanish-American War (1895–1917), I traveled to the Philippines, Puerto Rico, and Guam looking for a broader community, and found it, alas, no more friendly or familiar than New York, Los Angeles, or Miami. In some cases, I traveled more than nine thousand miles to search for alternative images to those solemnly preserved at the Library of Congress, only to find a ripped-out copy of *Harper's History of the Spanish-American War*. In some ways, searching for the authenticity of place seemed to be an excuse for the lack of imagination at home. Seeking what is lacking in the United States brought me face to face to what is here already, what one hundred years of colonialism and massive displacement from and to the US has created. In other words, there is part of here there, and here part of there, but in the transit that is time, their coming together on one plane is fortuitous.

Note

"Beyond the Cinema of the Other, or Toward Another Cinema," by Frances Negrón-Mutaner, is reprinted from *I Am Aztlán: The Personal Essay in Chicano Studies* (Los Angeles: UCLA Chicano Studies Research Center Press, 2004) and from *Aztlán: A Journal of Chicano Studies* 24, no. 2 (1999).

Afrofuturism/Chicanafuturism
Fictive Kin

Catherine S. Ramírez

I open this essay with a confession: I was a nerd when I was a kid and I expressed my nerdiness most clearly as a science fiction fan. I stood in line for hours to see *Return of the Jedi* the day it opened. Ewoks notwithstanding, I truly enjoyed this film. I also spent many an afternoon in my parents' backyard with my sisters, friends, and cousins reenacting scenes from our favorite movies and TV shows. We pulled apart transistor radios and stuffed their entrails into our socks to mimic the Bionic Woman, and we held a fraying tennis racket over our faces to play the role of her formidable nemesis, the fembot. A rusty shopping cart, boosted from a supermarket parking lot, doubled as the Millennium Falcon and an old *olla* my mother had used for cooking beans was transformed into Darth Vader's helmet.

Nobody told us that girls, much less Mexican girls, weren't supposed to like science fiction. Undeniably, few if any of the characters in the mainstream science fiction films and television programs of the 1970s and early 1980s looked like us. As the African American science fiction writer Octavia E. Butler pointed out, *Star Wars* featured "every kind of alien . . . but only one kind of human—white ones" (Beal 1986, 17). Sadly, only Ricardo Montalbán's Khan and *Blade Runner*'s Gaff, played by our homie Edward James Olmos, resembled us. Moreover, there was no mistaking me for any of the good guys—in the strictest sense of "guy." Yet, despite the genre's androcentrism and overwhelming whiteness, I found pleasure and meaning in science fiction. It beckoned me to imagine a world—indeed a universe—beyond the freeways, strip malls, and smog-alert days of my Southern California childhood.

More than mere escapism, science fiction can prompt us to recognize and rethink the status quo by depicting an alternative world, be it a parallel universe, distant future, or revised past. Good science fiction re-presents the present or past, albeit with a twist. It tweaks what we take to be reality or history and in doing so exposes its constructedness. For this reason, the genre has proven fertile ground for a number of black and feminist writers, artists, and musicians, from Edgar Arceneaux to Marion Zimmer Bradley. These innovative cultural workers have transformed what was once considered the domain of geeky white boys into a rich, exciting, and politically charged medium for the interrogation of ideology, identity, historiography, and epistemology.

• • •

Science fiction lends itself easily to stories by and about people of African descent in the New World. As cultural critic Mark Dery has noted, "African Americans, in a very real sense, are the descendants of alien abductees; they inhabit a sci-fi nightmare in which unseen but no less impassable force fields of intolerance frustrate their movements; official histories undo what has been done; and technology is too often brought to bear on black bodies (branding, forced sterilization, the Tuskegee experiment, and tasers come readily to mind)" (1993, 736). Works of literature, film, art, and music that address the relationship of black people to science, technology, and humanism have been grouped beneath the rubric of Afrofuturism.[1] These texts use science fiction themes, such as abduction, slavery, displacement, and alienation, to renarrate the past, present, and future of the African diaspora.

Butler's *Parable of the Sower* was the first Afrofuturist work I read, and in the mid-1990s it rekindled my passion for science fiction, which I had abandoned in an effort to be cool once I started high school. This 1995 novel offers a fairly common sci-fi scenario: it is set in the year 2024 in a Southern California plagued by drought, pollution, and economic crisis. However, the protagonist, Lauren Olamina, is like no other I had encountered in science fiction, or in any other literary genre for that matter. She is an African American teenager afflicted with "hyperempathy," a condition that causes her to experience others' physical sensations as if they were her own. After a gang of marauders kills her family and destroys her home and community, she heads north in search of water and employment. Along the way, she picks up other refugees, some of whom are fugitive slaves.

Slavery—past and present—figures prominently in many of Butler's novels. As she travels north, Lauren bears a strong resemblance to Harriet

Tubman and refers to her group as "the crew of a modern underground railroad" (Butler 1995, 268). The protagonist of Butler's 1979 time-travel novel, *Kindred*, is a young African American who is catapulted from her home in Pasadena in the late twentieth century to a plantation in antebellum Maryland. *Wild Seed* (1980) is about a three-hundred-year-old West African woman with superhuman powers who is brought to North America as a slave in the late seventeenth century. And in *Dawn* (1987), aliens abduct the black heroine with the intention of repopulating a postapocalyptic Earth by breeding with her and their other human captives.

These novels represent only a portion of Butler's impressive oeuvre. Before her untimely death in 2006 at the age of fifty-eight, she had just published her thirteenth book. She had also won a MacArthur fellowship and the prestigious Hugo and Nebula awards. The best of speculative fiction (an umbrella term that encompasses science fiction and fantasy), her novels and short stories simultaneously present the new and the familiar. They are about upheaval, migration, estrangement, tactical subjectivity, coalition, and survival, themes that resonate in narratives about African American life and culture.[2] I have found them, along with works by Samuel R. Delany, Deltron 3030, Nalo Hopkinson, Walter Mosley, and Sun Ra (to list just a handful of writers and musicians), to be effective tools for teaching the history of the African diaspora in North America, linking theories of race, class, gender, and sexuality, and elucidating the relationship of African Americans and other people of color to the discourses of modernity.

• • •

The concept of Chicanafuturism, which I introduced in *Aztlán* in 2004, borrows from theories of Afrofuturism (see Ramírez 2004). Chicanafuturism explores the ways that new and everyday technologies, including their detritus, transform Mexican American life and culture. It questions the promises of science, technology, and humanism for Chicanas, Chicanos, and other people of color. And like Afrofuturism, which reflects diasporic experience, Chicanafuturism articulates colonial and postcolonial histories of *indigenismo, mestizaje,* hegemony, and survival.

While it is indebted to Afrofuturism, the concept of Chicanafuturism was also inspired by the work of New Mexican artist Marion C. Martinez. I first saw Martinez's dazzling sculptures and wall hangings at the show *Cyber Arte: Tradition Meets Technology*, held at the Museum of International Folk Art in Santa Fe in 2001. The Catholic images she fashioned from discarded computer components, like circuit boards, disks, wires, and chips, prompted me to rethink the relationship of Chicana/o cultural identity and cultural production to science, technology, and progress.

Martinez's artwork illuminates the dynamism and malleability of cultural products and practices as it exposes the impact of science and technology on the people of the upper Río Grande Valley. She has found inspiration not only at a dump at Los Alamos National Laboratory (the origin of some of the materials that have ended up in her pieces) but also from New Mexico's esteemed *santo* tradition and from pre-Columbian Mesoamerican imagery. Yet, where *santos* (saints and other Catholic icons) have historically been carved from wood and those colossal Olmec heads were sculpted from stone, her self-labeled "mixed-tech" (think *Mixtec*) media wall hangings and "AzTechna" (a play on *Aztec*) brooches are made of machine parts.[3] These works simultaneously speak of New Mexico's unique history as a dumping ground for high-tech trash, including radioactive waste, and the planet's growing pile of so-called e-waste.[4]

Instead of applauding science and technology or condemning them altogether, Martinez's work shows how they have transformed Native American and Hispanic life and culture—and how one self-described "Indio-Hispanic" woman has transformed some of the tools of science and technology. Like black people, especially black women, Chicanas, Chicanos, and Native Americans are usually disassociated from science and technology, signifiers of civilization, rationality, and progress. At the same time, many Chicanas, Chicanos, and Native Americans have been injured or killed by and/or for science and technology. Here, I'm thinking of forced sterilizations, environmental racism, and Jared M. Diamond's (1997) provocative argument about the important role guns, germs, and steel played in the European colonization of the New World. All too often, we are linked to savagery, carnality, intuition, and passion, and we are fixed in a primitive and racialized past. The future, in contrast, is generally imagined as white, as many of the science fiction movies and TV shows of my childhood made evident. More recently, information technologies such as the internet have prompted some cultural critics to celebrate the present and imminent future as "placeless, raceless [and] bodiless" (Nelson 2002, 1). Already, people of color have been erased from the future, just as many of us were excised from narratives of the past and remain hidden from view in the barrios, ghettoes, reservations, and prisons of the present.

By appropriating the imagery of science and technology, Chicanafuturist works disrupt age-old racist and sexist binaries that exclude Chicanas and Chicanos from visions of the future. Examples include Yolanda M.

López's 1988 logo for the Chicana feminist organization Mujeres Activas en Letras y Cambio Social, which depicts a pre-Columbian goddess at a desktop computer; Alma López's 2006 update, *La Luchadora*, in which a young, athletic brown woman cradles a laptop; and the collaborative projects of the MeChicano Alliance of Space Artists (M.A.S.A.) (fig. 1).[5] At the same time, some of the most powerful Chicanafuturist works, such as Martinez's santos and Guillermo Gómez-Peña and Roberto Sifuentes's performances as El Naftazteca and El Cybervato, throw into question the link between science, technology, civilization, and progress.[6]

In addition, Chicanafuturism interrogates definitions of the human. El Teatro Campesino's *acto Los Vendidos*, first performed in 1967 and thus one of the earliest examples of Chicanafuturism, offers a more expansive definition of "human" as it criticizes racist and classist perceptions of Chicanos and Mexicans, especially Mexican workers, as automatons. Similarly, Gloria Anzaldúa's 1987 theory of "alien" consciousness endeavors to undo the legacies of patriarchy, homophobia, and white supremacy in the United States by rejecting Enlightenment epistemology and ontology, as represented in great part by empiricism and the Cartesian subject.[7]

Finally, Chicanafuturism defamiliarizes the familiar. Like good science fiction, it brings into relief that which is generally taken for granted, such as tradition, history, or the norm, including normative gender and

Figure 1. Luis Valderas, detail of logo for MeChicano Alliance of Space Artists, 2007. Reproduced by permission of the artist.

sexuality. Martinez's Catholic icons distort the santo tradition of which they are still a part. Set in the near future in the border region between the independent nation of Aztlán and Gringolandia (the former United States of America), Cherríe Moraga's play *The Hungry Woman: A Mexican Medea* (2001) reinterprets ancient Greek and Mesoamerican myths as well as the promises and pitfalls of Chicano cultural nationalism. And Laura Molina's 2004 painting *Amor Alien* (fig. 2) offers a sci-fi riff on mid-twentieth-century Mexican calendar art. Like Anzaldúa's theory, it points to the alien as a symbol for Chicana and Latina sexuality.[8]

Taken as a whole, these works show that science fiction is just as well suited for Chicanas and Chicanos as it is for African Americans. Some, like *Amor Alien*, are clearly science fiction. Yet for others, such as *Los Vendidos* and Anzaldúa's *Borderlands/La Frontera*, the connection to science fiction is probably less apparent at first. Theories of Afrofuturism have taught me to see cultural products that would not necessarily be classified as science or science fiction, like the music of Parliament and Midnight Star, as, or at the very least through the lens of, science and science fiction. These theories have inspired me to ask: What happens to Chicana/o texts when we read them as science fiction? To Chicana/o cultural identity? And to the concepts of science, technology, civilization, progress, modernity, and the human? These are the questions Chicanafuturism offers and confronts.

• • •

I no longer hide my passion for science fiction, and I have been able to channel it into a course I've developed on black speculative fiction. My students and I discuss a variety of texts, media, and concepts, such as the front and back covers of Earth Wind & Fire's 1977 album *All 'n All*, Jewelle Gomez's *The Gilda Stories* (1991), Evelyn Brooks Higginbotham's (1992) feminist theorization of the metalanguage of race, Zola Maseko's 1998 film *The Life and Times of Sara Baartman: The Hottentot Venus*, and Stuart Hall's (1994) configuration of the two vectors of a diasporic black cultural identity. Each year there are new works to teach and I have a hard time deciding how to rearrange the syllabus so that I can squeeze in just a little bit more. Nonetheless, I'm repeatedly asked by colleagues if my students and I have enough to talk about in my course. I bristle when I hear this question, in great part because I believe that it's motivated by the racist assumption that black people have no connection to science, technology, and science fiction.

Figure 2. Laura Molina, Amor Alien, 2004. Oil, fluorescent enamel, and metallic powder on canvas, 49 x 37 inches. Reproduced by permission of the artist.

Although most of my students enjoy the readings, especially the fiction, I've decided that I must change this course radically if I'm going to continue to teach it. During the first weeks of the quarter, the course introduces the students, many of whom are juniors and seniors and the majority of whom are white, to the concepts of modernity and humanism. Among other things, we discuss the Atlantic slave trade, *Plessy v. Ferguson*, eugenics, and the Tuskegee experiment. I believe that many of my students benefit from my lectures and our discussions and that the works we study are more than simple entertainment. However, I've grown increasingly uncomfortable delivering lectures on the objectification and abjection of black bodies in a classroom in which there's a pronounced absence of black students, a visible reality at the University of California in the wake of the passage of Proposition 209. Unable to resolve this paradox singlehandedly and in the immediate future, I've decided to change the focus of the course. Instead of emphasizing black speculative fiction, the course will take a more compara-tive and polycultural approach. We'll study black speculative fiction and theories of Afrofuturism alongside Sherman Alexie's 2007 time-travel novel *Flight*, Karen Tei Yamashita's magical realist tale *Tropic of Orange* (1997), William Gibson's post-9/11 technothriller *Pattern Recognition* (2004), and Alfonso Cuaron's 2006 film adaptation of P. D. James's dystopian novel *The Children of Men* (1992). In addition, we'll read science fiction from the so-called developing world, a site of booming offshore industrialization and technological experimentation in the early twenty-first century. I realize that by widening the course's perspective, I'll lose the specificity that I worked hard to hone over the years. Moreover, I understand that altering the focus of the course won't make more students of color appear out of thin air. Still, I maintain hope that the course's new focus will highlight the importance and expanding influence of Afrofuturism and the ties that bind the peoples of the aptly named New and Old Worlds.

Notes

"Afrofuturism/Chicanafuturism: Fictive Kin," by Catherine S. Ramírez, is reprinted from *Aztlán: A Journal of Chicano Studies* 33, no. 1 (2008).

1. I take my definition of *Afrofuturism* from http://www.afrofuturism.net/ and the special issue of *Social Text* on Afrofuturism, in particular Alondra Nelson's introduction, "Future Texts" (2002).

2. A "tactical subjectivity" is dynamic and flexible as opposed to fixed or essential. It refers to an active and self-conscious process of identification rather than to a static and given identity. Feminist scholar Chela Sandoval coined this term in her landmark essay "U.S. Third World Feminism: The Theory and Method of Oppositional Consciousness in the Postmodern World" (1991).

3. For more information regarding Martinez's mixed-tech media works and AzTechna accessories, see http://www.marionmartinez.com/home.php.

4. A misleading term if ever there was one, *e-waste* does not refer to spam (electronic junk mail) or the virtual in any way. Rather, it refers to discarded information technology tools such as computers and cell phones, neither of which decompose rapidly or safely.

5. According to its mission statement, the MeChicano Alliance of Space Artists seeks to "establish an awareness of outer space as an integral part of the Chicano(a) ModernMythos/Reality/Iconography." The first M.A.S.A. show, *Project:M.A.S.A. #1*, took place at the Gallista Gallery in San Antonio, Texas, in October 2005. More recently, M.A.S.A.'s third annual exhibit opened at San Antonio's Centro Cultural Aztlán on September 14, 2007. For more information about M.A.S.A., see http://www.projectmasa.com/index.html.

6. Regarding Gómez-Peña and Sifuentes's performances as El Naftazteca and El Cybervato, see Foster (2002).

7. Regarding Anzaldúa's theory of alien consciousness, see Anzaldúa (1987). For an extended discussion of this theory and its relationship to science fiction, especially Butler's work, see Ramírez (2002).

8. *The Hungry Woman* received its first staged reading in 1995 at the Berkeley Repertory Theater in Berkeley, California (Moraga 2001, 5). See Ramírez Berg (1989) for a reading of mainstream science fiction films that collapse the alien with the Hispanic immigrant and/or Third World mother.

Works Cited

Alexie, Sherman. 2007. *Flight.* New York: Black Cat.

Anzaldúa, Gloria. 1987. *Borderlands/La Frontera: The New Mestiza.* San Francisco: Aunt Lute.

Beal, Frances M. 1986. "Black Scholar Interview with Octavia Butler: Black Women and the Science Fiction Genre." *Black Scholar* 17, no. 2: 14–18.

Butler, Octavia E. 1979. *Kindred.* Boston: Beacon.

———. 1980. *Wild Seed.* New York: Popular Library.

———. 1987. *Dawn.* New York: Popular Library.

———. 1995. *Parable of the Sower.* London: Women's Press.

Dery, Mark. 1993. "Black to the Future: Interviews with Samuel R. Delany, Greg Tate, and Tricia Rose." *South Atlantic Quarterly* 92, no. 4: 735–78.

Diamond, Jared M. 1997. *Guns, Germs, and Steel: The Fates of Human Societies.* New York: W. W. Norton.

Foster, Thomas. 2002. "Cyber-Aztecs and Cholo-Punks: Guillermo Gómez-Peña's Five-Worlds Theory." *PMLA* 117, no. 1: 43–67.

Gibson, William. 2004. *Pattern Recognition.* New York: Penguin.

Gomez, Jewelle. 1991. *The Gilda Stories.* Ithaca, NY: Firebrand.

Hall, Stuart. 1994. "Cultural Identity and Diaspora." In *Colonial Discourse and Post-Colonial Theory: A Reader,* edited by Patrick Williams and Laura Chrisman, 392–401. New York: Columbia University Press.

Higginbotham, Evelyn Brooks. 1992. "African-American Women's History and the Metalanguage of Race." *Signs: Journal of Women in Culture and Society* 17, no. 2: 251–74.

James, P. D. 1992. *The Children of Men*. New York: Knopf.

Moraga, Cherríe. 2001. *The Hungry Woman*. Albuquerque: West End Press.

Nelson, Alondra. 2002. "Introduction: Future Texts." *Social Text* 20, no. 2: 1–15.

Ramírez, Catherine S. 2002. "Cyborg Feminism: The Science Fiction of Octavia E. Butler and Gloria Anzaldúa." In *Reload: Rethinking Women + Cyberculture*, edited by Mary Flanagan and Austin Booth, 374–402. Cambridge, MA: MIT Press.

———. 2004. "Deus ex Machina: Tradition, Technology, and the Chicanafuturist Art of Marion C. Martinez." *Aztlán: A Journal of Chicano Studies* 29, no. 2: 55–92.

Ramírez Berg, Charles. 1989. "Immigrants, Aliens, and Extraterrestrials: Science Fiction's Alien 'Other' as (Among *Other* Things) New Hispanic Imagery." *CineAction!* 18 (Fall): 3–17.

Sandoval, Chela. 1991. "U.S. Third World Feminism: The Theory and Method of Oppositional Consciousness in the Postmodern World." *Genders* 10 (Spring): 1–24.

Yamashita, Karen Tei. 1997. *Tropic of Orange*. Minneapolis: Coffee House Press.

Entre Familia

A Poetics of Remembrance

Testimonial Memory as Resistance and Repression

Vincent Pérez

To remember is not only the act of not forgetting but the act of not being forgotten, just as remembering the past as utopian cultural terrain reveals the very conditions of cultural dislocation that made a necessity of retrospective communitarian idealization.

—Genaro M. Padilla, *My History, Not Yours*

I came to Comala because I was told that my father, a certain Pedro Páramo, was living there. My mother told me so, and I promised her I would come to see him as soon as she died. . . . She told me, "Don't ask him for anything that isn't ours. Just for what he should have given me and didn't. Make him pay for the way he forgot us."

—Juan Rulfo, *Pedro Páramo*

Chicano literary and historical studies have increasingly focused attention on Mexican American autobiography. Since 1988, when a special issue of *The Americas Review* entitled "United States Hispanic Autobiography" appeared, commentators have examined its status as a distinct genre and explored the socioideological and cultural dimensions of its nineteenth- and twentieth-century texts.[1] Since many of Chicano literature's foundational narratives are autobiographies, or fictions in large measure autobiographical, critics of Mexican American writing have always had to wrestle with the nature of autobiographical texts.[2] At the same time, Luis Leal's pathbreaking work in Chicano literary criticism has directed his successors toward the archaeological endeavor of recovering that vast catalog of Mexican American autobiographical narratives that have remained unpublished or unavailable to a wide audience.[3] Genaro Padilla's *My History, Not Yours* follows both critical paths. Not only does he proclaim the need for "the archival recovery, editing, translation, and publication of this body of foundational literary discourse," which in his own case revolves around that set of Mexican American texts, most still unpublished, collected during the 1870s by the California historian Hubert H. Bancroft, but Padilla also demands, from himself and others, "critical and interpretive activity that shall establish the discursive genealogy (its continuities as well as discontinuities) of our literary traditions" (1993, 7).

Drawing on the work of Padilla and other scholars of historical and autobiographical works, I would like to examine Francisco Róbles Pérez's "Memorias," an unpublished journal of personal reminiscences, written between 1990 and 1992, by a Mexican American immigrant.[4] Born in 1908 in the state of Zacatecas, Mexico, Pérez is a former farm laborer. He is also my paternal grandfather. The 250-page manuscript, seventy pages of which have been transcribed from the original handwriting and translated from the Spanish, recounts his childhood on a hacienda in Mexico, his emigration at the age of thirteen to the United States, and his youth as a farmworker in Southern California (figs. 1 and 2). I would like to amplify Padilla's work by examining not only the nostalgic cast of my grandfather's account but also a second family narrative that "Memorias" effectively suppresses—a narrative that foregrounds class and gender conflicts in turn-of-the-century Mexican hacienda society.

My interest in this project developed in a rather unorthodox fashion. While transcribing my grandfather's manuscript, quite by chance I became involved in a clash between two branches of my family (figs. 3 and 4), which took place at the funeral of my "Aunt" Isabel "Chavela" Róbles.[5] The source of the conflict was a second version of Pérez history offered by the Róbleses, a group of relatives whose genealogy from the later nineteenth century to the present is closely interwoven with the Pérez family line. Largely suppressed in my family until comments at Chavela's funeral dramatically brought it to light, the Róbles narrative led me to question the ideological contradictions, rhetorical strategies, and sociohistorical particularities of "Memorias." In this essay I will first show how certain counterhegemonic socioideological articulations embedded in nostalgic memory make "Memorias" a perfect example of Padilla's model. My second and broader objective, however, is to show that as Padilla carries out his project to restore the dignity and integrity

Figure 1. Francisco Róbles Pérez acquired this document from the Mexican Consulate in Los Angeles in 1929 at age twenty-one, having lived in the United States as an undocumented alien for eight years. He used it in lieu of a birth certificate or United States visa to apply for residency status. Although the document states that he emigrated in September 1922, according to "Memorias" he arrived in 1921 at age thirteen.

Figure 2. Francisco Róbles Pérez at age twenty-three with his two eldest children, Esther and Juan, at Long Beach, California, in 1931.

The Pérez Family Tree

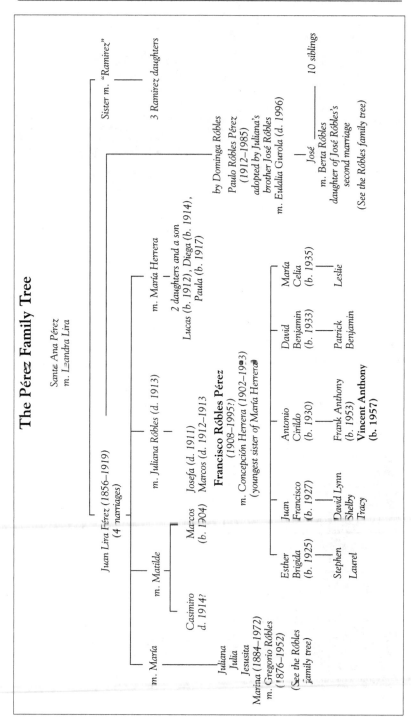

Figure 3. The Pérez family tree.

of the lives of early Mexican American autobiographers, and to extend the Chicano literary canon into the nineteenth century, he almost inevitably resuppresses underlying class and gender contradictions in California (Mexican) hacienda society—a suppression most notable in his account of the Mexican American politician, rancher, and author Mariano Guadalupe Vallejo.

Padilla proposes a sociohistorical reading of autobiographies that refuses to treat reductively that range of cultural and ideological meanings that his groundbreaking study displays in these texts. *My History, Not Yours* urges contemporary Chicano critics not to dismiss nineteenth-century Mexican American autobiographies simply because, as the products of a social elite dispossessed by Anglo-American conquest and colonialism, their authors often nostalgically embrace early Mexican hacienda society instead of providing examples of "heroic narrative resistance" (1993, 39). Padilla argues that when colonized by the United States after the United States–Mexican War of 1846–1848, Mexicans "immediately gave utterance to the threat of social erasure" at the hands of a foreign culture and imposed political system (4). Critics dealing with narratives of that era must "examine the various ways in which autobiographical expression emerged from social rupture and was formed within a matrix of dislocation, fear, and uncertainty" (10). Calling their works "narratives of dispossession," Padilla convincingly suggests that "nostalgia for an earlier world produced not a noncritical reaction to loss, but an oppositional response to displacement, albeit a response often deeply mediated by a language of accommodation" (x).

My History, Not Yours thus uncovers a "retrospective narrative habit" in nineteenth-century Mexican American autobiographies that "goes beyond reconstructing an individual life." Instead, such a life "is measured within a communitarian configuration and against the disruption of identity as identity and is situated within an imagined cultural community of the past" (232). For the Vallejo family, for example, the wealthiest and most powerful in pre-1848 "alta California," US annexation of Mexico's northern region meant economic dispossession and disenfranchisement. This economic and political disempowerment under Anglo-American hegemony brought rapid cultural fragmentation and displacement for the entire Mexican American population. As Padilla remarks about Vallejo's five-volume historical narrative, "Recuerdos históricos y personales tocante a la alta California" (Personal and historical remembrances of alta California) (1875), "the autobiographical act, therefore, becomes

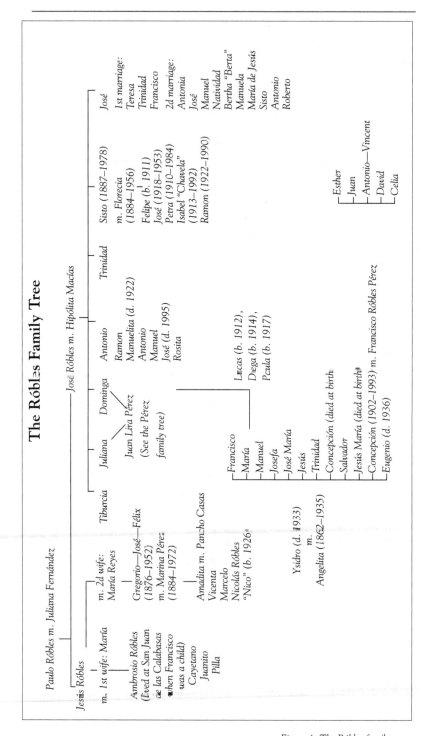

Figure 4. The Róbles family tree.

a tense ritual of gathering and sorting the relics of the communal past, narratively reifying the cultural legacy while rearranging the national one, proclaiming a desire to become an American but doing so in a language and discourse of opposition" (89).

Following Padilla's paradigm, I attend first to my grandfather's nostalgic idealization of hacienda life in prerevolutionary Mexico. Rather than mark this aspect of the text with an ideological label, however, I will, as Padilla's nuanced readings of Mexican American autobiographies propose, measure the utopian aspects of my grandfather's account against 1) his dislocation and dispossession as a child, buffeted by the social upheaval of the Mexican Revolution, and 2) the economic exploitation and sociocultural fragmentation he experienced as a Mexican immigrant laborer in the United States. As in many Mexican immigrant narratives and nineteenth-century Mexican American autobiographies, nostalgia for an "idealized and unobtainable" past serves a fundamental oppositional function in "Memorias," certainly enacting an imaginative communion with the narrator's lost family and community, but also articulating "resistance to cultural evisceration" in the United States. Or as Padilla puts it, nostalgia serves "the reintegrative psychic and social need for sustaining an idea of the past and for fixing a version of history within a cultural text that would mark historical presence in the face of erasure" (16).

My next level of analysis, however, responds to my accidental encounter with the Róbles narrative to show that while correct in defending early Mexican American autobiographies from the charge of indulging in the "hacienda syndrome," Padilla's model obscures social contradictions in those foundational life stories by male and/or upper-class members of pre-1848 California (Mexican) society.[6] Within my own family, the Róbles's oral narrative turned my grandfather's text into a terrain of intense contestation, challenging his nostalgic memory in ways that cannot be contained or elaborated by Padilla's theoretical framework. As I evaluate Padilla's usefulness for understanding my grandfather's complex deployment of nostalgia, the recovered Róbles counterhistory, which foregrounds women's narratives and declares my great-grandfather's role as a hacienda manager in the repressive Porfirian hacienda economy, inevitably moves to the foreground. Recovering the suppressed, antinostalgic counterversion of Dominga Róbles—who according to her family narrative was raped by her brother-in-law (my grandfather's father), Juan Lira Pérez, in 1912—not only rehistoricizes my grandfather's representation of his father's life, but like Rosaura Sánchez's recent analysis of class and gender discourses in the California testimonios, challenges Padilla's "close" readings of early Mexican American autobiographies.

My interest in these foundational narratives obviously constitutes part of a larger genealogical project to uncover an unclear family and community history. But further, though my own family's narrative is no more representative of the Mexican American past than any other Chicano family's, I have found that investigating my own background has helped me better negotiate the history of Mexican American society as a whole. My essay in this way seeks to bridge Mexican American oral narratives and historical literary scholarship. Peeling back the layers of my family's Chicano and Mexicano history has, for instance, strongly convinced me that whether narrated by my grandfather, by other Mexican American grandparents and families, by Chicano fiction writers, or by Mexican American historians, the recovery of our past remains incomplete, often suppressed, and untranscribed. Like members of the Buendía clan, who struggle for more than a century to read and translate Melquíades's encoded parchments in Gabriel García Márquez's *One Hundred Years of Solitude* (1967), we have only begun to decipher our history and escape the labyrinthine "city of mirrors." Though such contemporary works as Alejandro Morales's historical novels, Ernesto Galarza's autobiography *Barrio Boy* (1971), and Chicana writings that deconstruct and historicize Chicano/Mexicano patriarchy stand as exceptions, too many of our writers seem unengaged by the conflictive power relations to be found in our not so distant Mexican (hacienda) social history.[7] As we have searched for our historical origins, our Mexican cultural legacy that has been objectified, denigrated, or destroyed by a hegemonic United States culture ever since the annexation of northern Mexico in 1848, too often we have read our *abuelos'* (grandparents) stories uncritically or failed to pursue these histories wherever they may lead. Just as so many autobiographies by our nineteenth-century ancestors reify a pre-American communal religiocultural inheritance in the face of cultural rupture and dispossession, so too, in the interest of recovering our history, have some of our most informed writers and critics placed their faith in a utopian vision of a harmonious Mexican cultural and spiritual homeland.[8] Even Padilla, though he foregrounds the constructed, even fictional, character of all Mexican American autobiography, himself evades, but cannot help but evoke, the profound ideological contradictions, arising from nostalgic desire, in these nineteenth-century texts.

My History, Not Yours shows that while Mexican history has been reified in these autobiographical accounts, they nevertheless represent an honorable Mexican American historical and cultural legacy preserved for, and available to, later generations. What is missing from his model is an explanation of how and why, in sociohistorical terms, key aspects of our history were mythologized or suppressed. Having recovered a part of the encoded "parchments" and embraced it as our own, we must now decipher, interpret, and historicize the remainder of the text. By looking at my grandfather's "Memorias" and the family clash that called them into question—set in the imaginative space of the Mexican hacienda—I hope to begin carrying out this task.

Nostalgia and Resistance

My father had three nieces, named Ramirez, who were distinguished, older women in their forties, all unmarried. They were couturiers. They owned a fashion shop in the commercial zone downtown, where they sold expensive, custom-made dresses for young women and suits for men. Jerez was the [commercial] center for the entire outlying hacienda community, and so their shop was the only one of its kind for thirty kilometers or more around the town. These women belonged to high society . . . and lived in a mansion—surrounded by bougainvillea—with electricity, a garden with beautiful plants, and a swimming pool. You'll probably ask how they had a pool in the center of town, but I'm one step ahead of you. In that part of Jerez, there was a stream called the Rio Chiquito, which passed close to their mansion, and two kilometers away was the Rio Grande. But let's return for a moment to the house. My father and I were often invited to go and dine with these sisters. You see, my family had all of the same luxuries as they had during the 1890–1912 period. The Ramirez sisters were one of the illustrious families [of Jerez] that have now passed into history, but I remember them as a part of my own family, of whom I am very, very proud. . . .

The disturbers of the peace, that is, the revolutionaries, wouldn't leave my father alone. They wanted to assassinate him. Many times he escaped by the skin of his teeth. Other times he hid in wells . . . we finally escaped from Jerez under the cover of night by burro—one for each of us—so that our loyal Mexican "brethren," who one day were our employees and we the employers, could not detect us. . . . So departed a citizen of Jerez who was at one time a descendant of the most prosperous and landed hacendados in the entire valley of Zacatecas. . . . We left all of our property behind; it was many, many years before I slept in a bed again.

—Francisco Róbles Pérez, "Memorias"

> Domination and suppression, the reality of the group's material and social condition, is often narratively occluded, or transformed into a life in an imaginary pre-American past through which aristocratic pretense, genealogical invention, and political self-deceit articulate resistance in language often ideologically deaf to itself.
>
> —Genaro M. Padilla, *My History, Not Yours*

I began to delve into my family's history when, as an undergraduate, I went to Mexico for two years to study Latin American literature. Prior to my visit, I had recognized that I could not reveal certain legends about my Mexican ancestors to my Chicano university friends without risking undermining my own cultural authenticity as a working-class Chicano. I often secretly questioned the genealogical lore narrated by some of my Chicano college friends—not the humble origins of their *antepasados* (ancestors) nor their families' suffering as immigrants and laborers in the United States, but the romantic representation of their ancestors' role in the Mexican Revolution (1910–20), invariably as peasant combatants. I understood that many of my Mexican American friends were, like my own family, descended from *los de abajo* (people of the lower classes)—to use the title of Mariano Azuela's novel of the Mexican Revolution. But after I began to read modern Mexican literature and to develop a clearer understanding of the hacienda—the foundational socioeconomic institution in Mexican history—I felt that we had, as a group, become alienated from our history.[9] When speaking with my Chicano friends or family members, I either held my peace about my grandfather's obscure past or revised my history. Rather than acknowledge my grandparents' unspoken pain and profound ambivalence about the revolution and its aftermath, I portrayed my paternal grandfather, who emigrated from Mexico in 1921, as an impoverished *campesino* (farmworker) whose family had sympathized with Pancho Villa's revolutionary insurrectionists.[10]

This romantic narrative of origins was not entirely a fabrication; like most Mexicans of his generation, my grandfather embraced the romantic Villa legend and idolized Francisco Madero, the liberal Constitutionalist political leader who helped topple the regime of Porfirio Díaz in 1911. But my omissions marked the unconscious ideological content of my family's genealogy, omissions also found in some of the Chicano literary and historical studies I had read up to that time. These, like many recent works, designated the inception of Mexican American history as either

the "great migration" to the United States during the 1900–30 period or
the military defeat of Mexico in 1848 (for Texas, 1836).[11] Privileging the
modern Mexican American social experience, they rarely delved into the
Mexican period in the Southwest—when a semi-feudal and patriarchal
hacienda (rancho) system dominated the region—or the prerevolutionary nineteenth-century hacienda era in Mexico. Rather than imagining
links between Mexican historical models and the Mexican American
experience, or applying the borderlands paradigm to the realm of history, many instead constructed boundaries between the early period and
the modern.[12] This contradiction became more apparent when I visited
Mexico to attend classes at UNAM (Autonomous National University
of Mexico). While studying there, I first read the fictions of such modern
Mexican authors as Juan Rulfo (*Pedro Páramo*, 1955) and José Revueltas
(*El luto humano* [Human Mourning], 1943). Long before the poets and
writers of the Chicano movement began their project to recover, revitalize, and embrace our Mexican cultural origins, these earlier writers had
deconstructed the Mexican national mythologies and ideologies surrounding both the revolution and the prerevolutionary (hacienda) period. The
narratives and myths I had sought out as a Mexican American college
student participating in the struggle to contest and expand mainstream
US histories had been rigorously interrogated by Mexican writers, artists,
and scholars. Rulfo, for example, carried out a definitive critique of the
Mexican myth of origins, demonstrating how the hacienda, as a founding
nineteenth-century institution and particularly its identification with
a tradition of *caciquismo*, determined the direction and outcome of the
Mexican Revolution. Revueltas's earlier novel debunked the mythology
of the revolution itself, portraying it as a peasant movement ultimately
betrayed by state bureaucrats in thrall to conservative political and business interests. Rather than discovering a stable originary "homeland,"
which, when I was in my twenties, I still believed was possible, I found
in Mexico a society marked by contradictions and almost unfathomable
complexity—one still struggling to come to terms with its own history
and "lost" origins. Speaking of the development of Latin American
history, Carlos Fuentes remarked that "the Utopia of foundation was
exploited, degraded, and finally assassinated by the epic of history, activity, commerce, and crime," a sentiment that my readings at that time
underscored.[13] The engagement with the past by Mexican and other Latin
American writers achieved its apotheosis in Rulfo's fiction and García
Márquez's *One Hundred Years of Solitude* (1967), the latter work indebted

to both Rulfo and Revueltas, and thus one that speaks to Mexican and Chicano history as well as to the more general Spanish American past.

Though García Márquez, Rulfo, Revueltas, Fuentes, or even Faulkner did not hesitate to delve into the labyrinthine convolutions of historical memory—where Rulfo and Faulkner felt the most at home—I have encountered in some Chicano literary and historical narratives a reluctance to embark on critical genealogical inquiry into the early Mexican (American) past. Our historical condition as an oppressed minority demands that we document and analyze the contemporary period, yet these circumstances can also limit our historical and imaginative vision. Even in my own research I find myself drawing back from certain investigative paths, denying myself the critical freedom needed to approach the "truths" about history. (In an earlier version of this very essay I unintentionally (re)suppressed the story of the rape of Dominga Róbles and thus downplayed my great-grandfather's role in the hacienda economy.) And as "Memorias" implicitly demonstrates, many members of my family, and particularly my grandparents, have been displeased to find me using my education, which they made possible, to retrieve and expose long-buried secrets.

Chicano writers and historians have not only (un)consciously suppressed and nostalgically mythologized distant Mexican American history but also marginalized it in their attempt to address urgent contemporary cultural and political issues. In a remarkable interview, one of our most accomplished fiction writers, Tomás Rivera, dismisses the need to conceptualize, let alone interrogate, a Mexican American historical consciousness rooted in an earlier Mexican period:

> I don't really feel that I have a strong relationship with [Mexican culture]. . . . I read the Mexican classics . . . [and] I felt a strong affinity to [them]. When I visited Mexico, it reinforced that feeling. Then I began to realize that I'm not a Mexican. All of these feelings are a result of learning, not of growing up in Mexico with all *its* problems, *its* history, *its* beauty, and all *its* affinities. I thought, "It's not really mine. I know [Mexico] as mine, now, because I've learned it. I don't actually have it, nor have I lived it." After that I had to come back and say this is reality right here. . . . The fact is that if I had not gotten a college education I would know very little about Mexico. (Bruce-Novoa 1980, 152–53)

These remarks, which capture the fundamental historical and cultural paradox that Mexican Americans as a group have lived, at one level recall Richard Rodriguez's well-known renunciation of the "private" Mexican side of his cultural identity in his *Hunger of Memory: The Education of Richard Rodriguez* (1984). Even though in much of his writing Rivera mounts a sustained materialist critique of hegemonic ideology, while Rodriguez embraces a middle-class assimilationist ethic, I would suggest that both writers arrive at a similar *cultural* impasse precisely because they do not retrieve and draw upon the multiple and contending (suppressed) histories that make up the Mexican American historical consciousness. Though Rivera's cultural politics are antithetical to Rodriguez's, both authors seek to establish rigid cultural, as well as chronological, boundaries between Mexico and the United States, rather than imagining Chicano history and subjectivity as spaces marked by the pervasive presence of contradiction and discontinuity. Rivera's novel *And the Earth Did Not Devour Him* (1971) does recover a communal farmworker cultural memory, but neither he nor Rodriguez thematizes Mexican (American) origins and ancestry.

My genealogical research attempts just such a recuperative project, and in fact, my grandfather's memoirs are themselves the result of the investigation into my family's history I began fifteen years ago while studying in Mexico. While a graduate student in the late 1980s, I began a series of taped interviews with my grandfather, which over the course of six years developed into a full-length written autobiography. Though I had not imagined, nor do I believe today, that as an assimilated Mexican American child growing up in a working-class suburb of Los Angeles I had lost part of my history or culture, these lengthy interviews were my opportunity to explore my family's Mexican past as well as to establish a closer relationship with my grandfather in the language of his forebears. I could not have known how the conflicted genealogy they would bring to light would continue to weigh on the lives and consciences of family members.

A critic of Faulkner once remarked that all of the author's major characters "enter the fiction trailing behind them clouds of familial and regional qualifiers . . . the grandparents, parents, and siblings, the hill country or bottom land or tidewater, whose cumulative significance is the indispensable background of identity" (Karl 1988, 133–34). Similarly, I found that certain (over)determining historical qualifiers—which in *Absalom, Absalom!* reach back into distant family and community memory—also determine contemporary Mexican American subjectivity and culture. Juan Preciado, the Mexican campesino in Rulfo's *Pedro Páramo*, returns to the rural village where his mother grew up to search for his father and lost origins; Quentin Compson, tormented and obsessed with the past, attempts to recover the history of the United States South in Faulkner's novel. In the same fashion, Mexican Americans today carry on our shoulders and in our conscience the sum of the "combined memories" of our families and communities. For the same holds true in Mexican American society as Faulkner observed in the south: "There is no such thing as *was*. . . . Time [history] is not a fixed condition, time [history] is in a way the sum of the combined intelligences of all men who breathe at that moment" (1932, 179). Yet, for Mexican Americans, the collective memory of our communities is rooted not only in a twentieth-century urban or rural United States context but inevitably in the hacienda and rancho social economy of prerevolutionary Mexico and the nineteenth-century Southwest.

Since I could visit my grandfather only twice a year, on one occasion I asked him to begin writing down the stories of his life in Mexico and as an immigrant. Thirty-five notebooks, filled with Spanish prose written in the stilted style of a child and carefully numbered to avoid chronological confusion, have been the result. Noting that his education "was only three years in primary school" (3), my grandfather repeatedly apologizes for his "poor orthography and grammar." And yet he is proud of his acquired knowledge, drawn from his lifelong experience in the real world in Mexico and later in the United States. "My philosophy is my own—I didn't go to any university," he states early in the narrative. "What I'm saying I've compiled from a long and bumpy journey over the face of our mother Earth" (26). Although I have estimated that the edited manuscript will be 250 pages, the final version may be longer. I have not translated many of the post-1936 era notebooks, nor have I determined precisely how the hours of tape-recorded interviews—which complement the written account—will be integrated into the text.

I also recorded hours of interviews with my paternal grandmother, Concepción Herrera Pérez—which I am incorporating into a written family narrative—who, in keeping with her reputation for shrewd family diplomacy and unlike my grandfather, measured each word that she spoke with the painstaking care of a politician. (I later learned the reasons for her reticence, see below.) In what initially struck me as a deliberate refusal to grant me entry into the vaults of family history, she skirted events that I suspected were crucial to our family's narrative of origins. I felt like an ethnographer trying to wrest critical anthropological information from an unwilling or suspicious interlocutor. The analogy of an outsider may seem an odd one to apply to my relationship with my grandmother, but it illustrates my ignorance, ten years ago, of my family's history and particularly the women's stories in our narrative of origins. By retrieving one woman's account from a longstanding patriarchal tradition of family legend and lore, I hope in this essay to begin filling in some of the tradition's gaps and omissions. For all of my grandfather's candor in narrating his childhood experience of hacienda society, it displaced more effectively than my grandmother's reticence a side of our early history that Chavela's funeral would only coincidentally bring to light. Since the patriarchal myth is rooted in sociohistorical reality, it must be examined for what it can tell us not only about the Mexican American historical consciousness but about the role of the hacienda in the formation of this consciousness.

Though I first encouraged my grandfather to write his story, and I now serve as its translator and editor, the journal itself is entirely my grandfather's work.[14] It begins with his childhood in the prerevolutionary period, which he portrays as a pastoral and idyllic life in the hacienda communities outside of Jerez, where his father worked. Though born in 1908, my grandfather nostalgically reconstructs the Porfirian hacienda period of the late nineteenth century. The text ends with the account of his attempt to rear five young children on farmworker wages during the United States' depression. "Memorias" thus spans roughly thirty years of Mexican and Mexican American history.

My grandfather, Francisco, was the son of a bookkeeper named Juan Lira Pérez, a business associate from the 1880s until 1913 of a group of landowning *hacendados* (ranchers and landowners) near the city of Zacatecas in central Mexico. Though born into relative privilege in an era of socioeconomic polarization that set the *hacendado* elite apart from the masses of campesinos and laborers, my grandfather's comfortable early circumstances were shortlived. Orphaned at eleven, he was forced to fend for himself during a time of social and economic upheaval.[15] Emigrating to Southern California in 1921, he worked for more than fifty years as a ranch laborer and field hand. Forty-two years were spent at Rancho Sespe, a 6,000-acre citrus ranch owned by the Spalding sports equipment manufacturing family in Ventura County. My grandfather had a number of agricultural occupations at this ranch:

> I picked fruit for twenty years, then, as a gardener, planted vegetables
> and flowers and trees. . . . I once helped dynamite a mountain on which

the owner built a cabin; and for two years I worked with an agronomy engineer to build a nine-hole golf course, which Mister Keith Spalding had ordered. (40)

My grandfather and his wife reared a family in the ranch's workers' camp, Sespe Village, where 150 Mexican families lived.[16] Unable to return to Mexico and reclaim his father's land and status because of the civil war and its economic aftermath, my grandfather remained within the ranks of agricultural laborers in a country where Mexicans were not only cultural outsiders, but were exploited as laborers and excluded as racial others. His family's fall from the Mexican upper class due to the war's disruption of the hacienda economy left my grandfather with a dual class identity. He could thus sing the praises of the revolutionary leader Villa, yet also revile him as a bandit who had disenfranchised Lira Pérez and forced young Francisco to leave his homeland for good. Similarly, he could nostalgically recount the heroics of the martyred Constitutionalist leader Madero, yet with pride list the modernizing accomplishments of the dictator Díaz, whom Madero toppled.

In the early sections of "Memorias," my grandfather imaginatively reconstructs the life of that fifty-seven-year-old established businessman and accountant who was his father. In these early passages and elsewhere, my grandfather harks back to life in a "harmonious" rural community in a prerevolutionary and "colonial" Mexico.[17] He was born in 1908, on the eve of the civil war, to "Don Juan Lira Pérez and Doña Juliana Róbles de Pérez," in the "beautiful small town of Jerez, in the state of Zacatecas" (1). "Direct descendants of the seventeenth-century Spanish pioneers and founders of Jerez," both his parents had deep roots in that region. My grandfather remembers his father saying once that his own "father, Santa Ana Pérez, and uncles were descended from the original founders and settlers of the town" (2). "Memorias" thus forges a genealogical link between Lira Pérez and the Spanish colonial settlers of Mexico. Assuming that the locality's first settlers had been "conquistadors," my grandfather concludes, despite a vast chronological discrepancy, that his own "grandfather" must have come from Spain. He points out that the town's name may have been "inspired by the town of Jerez de la Frontera in southern Spain" (2).[18] This Spanish link reappears at the time of my uncles' and my father's births, for these light-haired infants are cited as proof that the blood "from my Mexican ancestors, descendants of the [Spanish] *gachupines*, continues" (32).

On the surface, these passages seem to reflect little more than those contradictory racial and class biases rooted in the Spanish conquest and colonial domination of Mexico's indigenous peoples that are still widespread in Mexico to this day. Rather than acknowledging his *mestizo* (Spanish/Indian) cultural and ethnic heritage, my grandfather, steeped in his father's Hispano-centric nineteenth-century mores, which denigrate indigenous origins, claims his descent from the "racially pure" Spanish conquerors.[19] As Jesús Flores Olague points out, although in the sixteenth century "the presence of diverse racial groups was one characteristic of the [Zacatecan] mining centers, . . . the permanent relationship established between these groups . . . exhibited the presence of one dominant group: the *mestizo*" (1996, 83). Even without taking into account the various groups of Chichimeca Indians in that region conquered by the Spanish, "numerous groups of indigenous Mexicans, Tarascans, and Tlaxcaltecans—who accompanied the Spaniards in their expeditions and participated in the pacification of the Indians who inhabited the region—formed part of the new settler population around the Zacatecan mines" (89–90). However indirectly, my grandfather acknowledges this Indian and mestizo history through his use of the word *gachupin*, a term for *Spaniard* that can be used pejoratively. Its use in the above quote suggests the narrator's (un)conscious desire for cultural distinction from the Spanish conquerors as well as his identification with the region's Indian and *mestizo* population.

Other sociocultural motivations and forces contribute to this problematical aspect of my grandfather's autobiography. His nostalgia for a legendary Mexican (Spanish) world, and more specifically his construction through memory of a childhood and youth spent within this "mythic" hacienda past, are examples of what Padilla has called the author's "epistemological ground of subjectivity" (1993, 158). Like other early Mexican American autobiographers, my grandfather sets this pre-American cultural and social originary ground of being and memory against the nightmare of Mexican life under the Anglo-American sociocultural regime.

Let me briefly explain how my grandfather's effort to reclaim his origins leads me to Padilla's theoretical model. Coming six years after the death of his mother, Juliana Róbles Pérez, and definitively marking the end of his hacienda childhood and the start of his hardscrabble existence as a *descalzo* (barefoot waif), the death of his father is the defining moment of my grandfather's life. Nostalgic desire is thus interwoven with retrospective longing. As a boy orphaned at an early age and forced to support himself at various jobs before making his way the United States, my grandfather wished to embrace a father and a community that he knew only in childhood. By retrieving his father's myth from the social and familial ruins of the revolutionary period, my grandfather's testimonial remembrance reenacts the short-lived relationship that his father's unexpected death in 1919 abruptly ended. But, if we accept orphanhood as a figuration embodying deeper sociohistorical and cultural forces, the death of Lira Pérez can also stand as that traumatic moment of social and cultural rupture that Padilla identifies as key to understanding the Mexican American autobiographical and historical consciousness. In the figure of the descalzo, my grandfather alluded to his suddenly precarious socioeconomic status:

> The person writing this [account] was a descalzo, because the first shoes that I owned were bought sometime in 1910. Since my feet grew fast, I couldn't use them for very long. I didn't own another pair until I crossed the United States border in 1921. Someone bought me a secondhand pair there for twenty-five cents, but they were too big for me. When I put them on without socks and walked, my feet sweated and slipped. The noise they made when I crossed the border at Juárez made me think that someone was following me. When I recall this event, it now seems both curious and fitting to me that I write it down, so that you know where Don Francisco came from. (15)

My grandfather used *descalzo* not only to capture his desperate situation when he crossed the border at El Paso, but also the many sociocultural and class-bound "ideological" transitions he was forced to make since then.[20] The first shift was from membership in the "high" society of the Mexican rancher class to the status of a homeless orphan at the height of the revolution. The second took him from his life as a servant for a wealthy Mexican family in the city of Torreón to that of an impoverished, displaced immigrant laborer in a foreign country.

But, as the above passage suggests, for my grandfather descalzo also had a tragicomic and picaresque quality to it, for unlike most Mexican immigrant autobiographies, my grandfather shared with early nineteenth-century Mexican American writers the distant remembrance of an actual "upper class" hacienda past. According to family history, Lira Pérez had by the late nineteenth century become a relatively successful accountant, managing the affairs and finances of several local haciendas: large cattle and livestock ranches owned by the elite of central Zacatecas. Though not a hacendado himself, by the turn of the century he had apparently prospered enough to be closely identified with this privileged class. Orphanhood thus functions in my grandfather's account at two discursive levels. On the one hand, it represents his abrupt separation from his father's financially secure world, and soon after from the Mexican culture of his ancestors. The descalzo is, therefore, a prince in disguise. (Though he had only a third-grade education, my grandfather sometimes set his "high" cultural status against the lower-class background of the farm laborers with whom he worked at Rancho Sespe. The community in turn acknowledged this background respectfully, selecting him to several local public positions.) On the other hand, "Memorias" is obviously an immigrant narrative as well, which charts the narrator's struggles as a destitute Mexican laborer in what he increasingly came to view as a materialistic society overtly hostile to Mexicans. At this level, orphanhood signifies his cultural and socioeconomic alienation as a marginalized and exploited immigrant in the United States. He will thus always be a descalzo.

The contestatory Róbles narrative will expose certain sociohistorical deceptions in this notion of orphanhood as well as in the construction of Porfirian hacienda society in "Memorias." For the moment, though, let us consider the usefulness of Padilla's paradigm for understanding this figure and "Memorias" in total. Padilla has established that early Mexican American autobiographies and modern Mexican immigrant autobiographical narratives exhibit a "consciousness split by contending sociocultural regimes" (1993, 51). Much like W. E. B. Dubois's concept of the double "self," this "double-consciousness" originates in that moment when the Mexican American author's pre-American religiocultural identity comes under the dominating influence of an Anglo-American sociocultural regime. For the nineteenth-century Mexicans living in what was once northern Mexico and is now the Southwest United States, this moment came violently with the 1848 American military victory over Mexico and the annexation of its northern region. As my grandfather's memoir and other narratives of Mexican emigration show, an equally sharp cultural break has taken place among twentieth-century Mexican immigrants. Symbolized by the border crossing, this modern rupture results from both the forced emigration from the "homeland" and the inevitable cultural accommodation that Mexican immigrants have had to make in a country with fundamentally different sociocultural traditions.

All of the many studies examining Mexican immigration to the United States agree that a huge number of immigrants arrived during this century's first three decades. Mario Barrera, for example, cites an estimate that by 1928 more than one-tenth of Mexico's population had moved to the United States (1979, 68). More recently, David G. Gutiérrez writes that "although immigration and demographic statistics for [the] era are notoriously inaccurate, most scholars concur that at least one million, and possibly as many as a million and a half Mexican immigrants entered the United States between 1890 and 1929" (1995, 40). In accounting for this large-scale migration, Barrera notes that while the political upheavals created by the Mexican Revolution caused a great many to emigrate—particularly "those who happened to be on the losing side at a given moment"—economic and social factors were perhaps more significant, for "a large number of agricultural workers during this time were displaced from the land as the process of [Porfirian] modernization was ruthlessly pursued" (1979, 68). Furthermore, between 1875 and 1910, the Mexican population increased by approximately 50 percent. As Friedrich Katz explains, "the number of laborers available to central Mexican haciendas greatly increased . . . as the massive expropriations . . . created a new landless proletariat, which the limited industry in most parts of central Mexico could not absorb" (Katz as quoted in Barrera 1979, 68).

In *My History, Not Yours*, Padilla examines the dramatic break in socio-cultural self-consciousness portrayed in late nineteenth-century Mexican American autobiographies—one typically represented in twentieth-century Mexican immigrant autobiographical narratives by the border crossing. Refusing to dismiss early California "Hispano" texts as politically and ideologically self-deceiving, he views their nostalgic impulse as a complex narrative strategy with a hidden counterdiscursive objective. As we shall see in my grandfather's narrative, though admittedly shot through with ideological, cultural, and historiographic contradictions, this strategy sustains the Mexican American autobiographer's pre-American and communitarian cultural identity in the face of threats from Anglo-American social institutions. Viewed in this light, my grandfather's efforts to link himself to Spanish colonial forebears invokes the powerful cultural presence of his Mexican ancestors. Such a legacy grants my grandfather, and his largely assimilated Mexican American children, grandchildren, and great-grandchildren, a cultural identity in the face of "orphanhood" in Mexico and the United States.

Like the nineteenth-century Mexican American California autobiographers who measure the past according to their "present" socioeconomic and cultural dilemmas, my grandfather foregrounded his struggles with poverty, displacement, and "slavelike" experiences as an immigrant farmworker. Without seeking pity and in an understated tone, he relates the brutal, inhuman work and his own felt status in the United States as a victim, a commodity, and a deracinated and alienated figure apparently without hope or future. "Memorias" identifies three forces of rigid exclusion and severe abuse during the 1930s: the exploitation of Mexican agricultural laborers by American ranchers, the suppression of Mexican efforts to organize a union, and the racial segregation that farmworkers endured at every level of society.[21] Taken together, these forces constitute my grandfather's depression-era economic, sociocultural, and personal plight.

Grandfather's account of his participation in a labor union strike in Placentia in 1936 epitomizes this precarious and alienated condition—as well as his efforts to lift himself and those around him above the impoverished status of farmworkers:

> I joined a society of united Mexican workers and started to work on its behalf. We fought to defend the human, civic, and economic rights of Mexican agricultural workers. But we were a small group, perhaps forty in number, and none of us was educated nor had funds to sustain the organization. We asked ten cents in dues from each worker's paycheck. We eventually called a strike to try to improve our lives, but it was in vain. We lost after two months. Many of the strikers were thrown in jail and others were physically abused on the picket line. In one confrontation, the police used tear gas against us. In this struggle, [the ranchers] had no respect for women or children. Our only recourse was the Mexican Consulate in Los Angeles, but [the ranchers] later blocked our communication with this office. (33)

In her history of the Southern California communities of San Juan Capistrano and Santa Ana, Lisabeth Haas provides an account of this 1936 strike. Haas's reconstruction of the violent response by ranchers and police closely parallels my grandfather's remembrance of events. As she puts it, "attacks on the barrio . . . [reflected] the way in which race politics fortified coercive labor structures. Vigilantes attacked participants in the nightly strike meetings in each barrio, sometimes using tear gas. On July 7 during a meeting of 115 Mexican men, women, and children in Placentia, 'one hundred ranchers drove up . . . each . . . armed with a new axe handle'" (208). My grandfather's oral story, as told to me during an interview, of his narrow escape from armed attackers who broke up a union meeting in Placentia supports the following description in Haas's book:

79

On the single evening of July 10, vigilantes smashed the windows of a meeting place in Anaheim while the meeting was in progress, disrupted a large meeting in La Habra, and broke up a smaller one in Placentia, where they hurled twenty tear gas bombs into the room and wielded clubs against those who ran out. Barrio residents said they could not sleep because the tear gas filled their homes. The sheriff had already issued a "shoot to kill" order against the strikers, thus implicitly giving license to vigilante activity. (208)

My grandfather's activism reflects the widespread labor unrest during the 1930s among Mexican and Mexican American workers in California. During that time, a series of strikes and labor-related protests by Mexican and Mexican American laborers ravaged the state's agriculture industry (Gutiérrez 1995, 102, 106). "Well over 160 major strikes occurred between 1933 and 1937 alone" (101). As Rodolfo Acuña notes, "given the industrialization of agriculture, the exploitation of Mexican labor, and the abuses of the contract labor system, conflict would have occurred without the depression; the events of 1929 merely intensified the struggle" (1988, 209).

My grandfather's account endorses the view that Mexican and Mexican American labor strife during this period "often took the form of organized race conflict" (Gutiérrez 1995, 100). Because of his role as a union activist, my grandfather and other Mexican organizers were blacklisted by Orange County ranchers. Forced to move his family to Ventura County, some fifty-five miles away, he was soon hired to pick grapefruit, for twenty-eight cents an hour, near the town of Fillmore. (He contacted Gregorio Róbles, his brother-in-law, who, along with other Róbles family members, had made his way to Fillmore several years earlier.) Grandfather recalled that the foreman at Rancho Sespe asked him where he had moved from. When he said Orange County, the foreman asked if he was a striker. My grandfather, of course, said no: "If I had said yes, they wouldn't have given me work . . . and at that time I had four children to support and feed, all of school age with the exception of the youngest, who was three" (42).

During the 1960s, when the United Farm Workers began organizing workers at Rancho Sespe, my grandfather voiced support but refused to join the new union. Not only had his youthful experience as an organizer—as well as his concern for the livelihood of his wife and five children—made him cautious, but in 1941 he had narrowly managed to keep his job and (company) home during a mass firing and eviction of striking farmworkers at Sespe. In that strike, at least 80 percent of the Mexican and Mexican American families in the village were left homeless; ranch owners removed their possessions and left them on the side of the highway one mile away. My father, who was eleven at the time, recalled seeing these displaced families, whose children were his friends, waiting with their few possessions on the road as it rained. The strike occurred throughout Ventura County, and eventually over 6,000 workers and their families were evicted from company housing (Menchaca 1995, 87).

Martha Menchaca provides an account of the events of 1941 in her study of Mexican Americans in Santa Paula, a town located five miles from Rancho Sespe. As she explains, "the coalition of [Ventura County agricultural] unions . . . crippled the county's lemon industry because the walkout prevented the harvesting, packing, and distribution of all citrus. In essence, there was a complete work stoppage because the harvesters, packers, and canners were all on strike" (84). After threatening to evict the strikers if the strikers did not return to work, "the growers carried out their [threat] . . . a devastating experience for the workers especially since many of them had resided on the ranches for two or three generations" (87). As my father recollected, though some of the strikers made their way back to Sespe, the mass eviction transformed the small workers' community in Fillmore—particularly with the arrival of many "Okie" agricultural workers to replace the strikers.

A second encounter after my grandfather's arrival in Sespe in 1936 underscored for him that, although his location had changed, his social position as a Mexican remained the same:

> After we settled into our little house in the workers' camp at Rancho Sespe—the last great hacienda in California—I met an American rancher and foreman whose property bordered the camp. He introduced himself, then said to me, "I hope that your family, especially your children, respect my property and don't trespass beyond that wire fence." He added these humiliating words: "Any individual who doesn't own a piece of land, or at least, a home in which to live, is not worthy of being a citizen of any country." We were thus eating the bitter bread of the exiled. (35)

For my grandfather, these two exchanges with American ranchers captured something crucial about his life. "Why was man born?" he asked. "To struggle, just as birds were born to fly." To remain steadfast in the face of unjust suffering formed a defining component of Francisco's

81

existence as a farmworker during the 1930s. His description of himself at twenty-seven as "ambitious, genial, self-confident, humorous, and above all, hardworking" (34) makes it clear that my grandfather felt more than up to that struggle.

And yet, as Esther Pérez Doran, Francisco's daughter and eldest child, and my aunt, wrote in 1965 for a college class, life in Sespe Village continually tested the Pérez family's strength, spirit, and resilience. According to Esther, the village community lived under a "feudal system" completely dominated by the ranch owner, Keith Spalding. Esther juxtaposes this North American hacendado first to her own family's impoverished status and meager living conditions in the farmworker camp and then to her father's brutal work as a laborer:

> Once a month the lord and master, the owner of Rancho Sespe, would make his rounds on horseback and look down at his "peasants." An "edict" would first go out to the village stating when Mr. Spalding would arrive so that we could prepare by watering our beautiful yards and by putting on our best Sunday clothes. But I made it a point never to appear to show any interest in this event, in this wealthy man who was the giver of all things in Sespe. I already knew better; I had seen my father, black with dust and soaked with perspiration, come home from picking lemons and oranges after a hot day. For this backbreaking work he was paid the great sum of a couple of dollars a day and allowed to rent a three-room house without heat, without indoor water, and without indoor plumbing (the homes were very cold and damp; in fact, I am still trying to get warm after all those cold years). My mother worked in the ranch's packing house at Sespe, where the pay was worse; later, my brothers also worked picking fruit. At Sespe, the Mexican community had a life without any hope for the future. I hated the people who were responsible for this, who made my father and mother work so hard for a crust of bread and a dried tortilla. But my father showed that while a man's body may be economically bound, his spirit is not; although he had only a third-grade education, he read avidly and passed this habit along to his children.[22]

For the white community of Fillmore, education translated into opportunity and hope. Within the racialized space of the Spalding hacienda for Mexican Americans, however, a high school education did little to change one's status and circumstances. Esther relates her own efforts, after finishing high school, to obtain an office position as a clerk at the rancho:

> I had gotten straight A's as a student, which helped me realize my dream of going to nursing school. In high school I had also taken courses in

typing, bookkeeping, and shorthand. I did very well in these classes, and my bookkeeping teacher recommended me to work in Rancho Sespe's payroll office. I interviewed and was not accepted. Later, I learned that a white girl who had not finished high school was given the job. My family was very upset by this rejection. . . . Several years later, I was visiting my family in Sespe after graduating from nursing school. The same man who had refused me the job came by to see my father. He saw me carrying my new uniforms. He was surprised, and congratulated me on graduating. He remarked, "Now you can take care of me when I get sick." Although I said it to myself, my response was, "You can drop dead!"

My grandfather's idealization of a mythic Mexican homeland founded on the imagined pastoral terrain of rural Zacatecas, therefore, not only represents a spiritual solidarity with the farmworker immigrant community sharing his origins but also stands as a defense against the perpetual "threat of social erasure" by colonizing United States sociocultural and economic institutions (Padilla 1993, 6). His imaginative return to the pre-American pastoral environment of his *abuelos* (grandparents) and his ancestor's hacienda society must be understood in relation to Esther's descriptions, the earlier comments like the rancher's, and the accounts of the 1936 and 1941 strikes. This nostalgic recuperation reaffirms cultural and genealogical continuity in the face of my grandfather's forced separation from that world as a child, and his continued alienation from both Mexican and American society as an adult. It thus forms the foundation of his children's Mexican American cultural identity within the racially hostile environment described above.

Just as his orphanhood may be read as a figuration for the cultural fragmentation of all Mexican immigrants in the United States, the reconstituted topography of rural Zacatecas stands as the originary "epistemological ground" of his cultural subjectivity. Situated "exactly in the center of the Mexican Republic" (2), the Zacatecas region where he was born is for my grandfather the geographic and cultural "heartland" of the nation. As descendants of its Spanish settlers, he and his father are thus "native sons" of a region which, according to popular sentiment in Mexico to this day, embodies the Mexican national character. When recalling his visit to the city of Zacatecas shortly after his family was forced to leave Jerez in early 1914, my grandfather asks the reader's patience as he not only "describes the topography of that great capital" but also strategically conflates this topography with Mexico's Spanish colonial history. "The city was founded in 1600 after the Spaniards discovered silver there," he explained. "It is situated in a small valley surrounded by mountains. The most prominent is the 'Bufa' mountain, which contains the richest silver mine ever discovered on the American continent" (5). Accounts of early Zacatecas illuminate the origins of the city as a mining center. As Enrique Semo explains, "on September 8, [1546,] a small detachment of Spanish soldiers, headed by Juan Tolosa, discovered the deposits of what has since been known as Cerro de la Bufa (Zacatecas). The exploitation of these deposits, carried out under very difficult conditions . . . quickly fulfilled all expectations" (1993, 73). King Philip II granted the mining town of Zacatecas the title of "city" on October 17, 1585. Three years later, the king and the Council of the Indies added to this official title the words "noble and loyal" and granted the city a coat of arms. As stated in the royal enactment, the inhabitants of Zacatecas had "served [the King] with faithfulness and care, and defended the city from the Chichimeca Indians . . . as well as [serving] through the benefits accorded by the silver mines on its outskirts, from which have been, and continue to be, derived much wealth" (Flores 1996, 90). By the turn of the century, Zacatecas [became] the third largest city in the country." A description from 1620 mentions "more than 1,000 European families, and a total of 40,000 inhabitants; the city [also] had 25 large *haciendas de beneficio* [livestock haciendas]" (Semo 1993, 73).

What my grandfather did not identify was the actual status of these great mines—symbolized by the prominent Bufa Mountain in the center of the city of Zacatecas—at the end of the Porfirian period. In their study of economic dependency, Fernando Enrique Cardoso and Enzo Faletto (1979) illustrate how the Mexican mining industry exemplified the late nineteenth-century dilemmas of underdevelopment throughout Latin America. While acknowledging that during the thirty-five-year reign of Díaz (1876–1911), "Mexico recovered much of its economic dynamism thanks chiefly to renewed exploitation of its silver wealth," Cardoso also notes that by 1914, when my grandfather saw the Bufa for the first time, three-quarters of Mexico's mines "belonged to foreigners" (105). My grand-father's mythic, pastoral, and communal vision of Zacatecas shows no sign of the enormous concentration of property in the hands of politicians, foreign speculators, and surveying companies, which Cardoso finds characteristic of the time (106).[23] Nor did he mention here the conflictive nature of the earlier colonial period. As Semo writes, "the handful of Basques who embarked on the risky exploitation of the Bufa mine represented the beginnings of a silver aristocracy who appropriated virtually all of the

North's resources. Within a few years [after the founding of the mines], they owned large agricultural and cattle properties and commercial and mining enterprises, and they financed, with their own means, expeditions of discovery and conquest" (1993, 74).

Similarly, the complex early history of the hacienda in Zacatecas does not find a place in my grandfather's account. During the eighteenth century the hacienda system in Zacatecas went through a period of consolidation. In the late seventeenth century, property owners took advantage of new laws passed by the Crown to acquire lands that belonged to Indians. These laws "were a means of justifying the growth and development of large areas of land, confining Indians to smaller and smaller space, and controlling [Indians] economically and socially—along with castes and mestizos—so that they would not be able to acquire more land" (Flores 1996, 88). The Indian population became "condemned to dependency on the agrarian structure determined by the hacienda [system], which as it grew increasingly stronger converted them into peons, renters, and later, tenant farmers and salaried laborers" (88–89). By justifying abuses against Indians and lower-class mestizos, and particularly the illegal occupation and plunder of lands, the laws thus contributed to the formation of the feudalistic hacienda system, which lasted into the twentieth century.

For my grandfather, his Spanish ancestors, the Mexican "heartland," and the outlying terrain of his mining and hacienda society together established a heroic, legendary, and prosperous Mexican past, rather than a photograph of disjuncture and exploitation. Other references to prerevolutionary Jerez added to his portrait of a land populated by descendants of illustrious Spanish founders. Especially powerful were his memories of his father, the principal inhabitant of that "colonial" and late nineteenth-century world. Since my grandfather left the hacienda community at age six, stopped regularly attending school at seven, and became orphaned at eleven, his memories of the "prerevolutionary" period probably derived from stories heard as a child from his father. My interviews with my grandfather and the text of "Memorias" suggest that his knowledge of early Mexican history came primarily, though not exclusively, from the same source. Not surprisingly, then, his memories of his father were inseparable from his romantic representation of the outlying hacienda terrain of Jerez—a town situated forty miles from the capital.

Nor did his father simply embody familial origins; in fact, as Pérez patriarch, his overshadowing figure participated in that genealogical and sociocultural rootedness in Mexico that my grandfather traces back to its

Mexican (Spanish) colonial "founders." Though my grandfather enjoyed reading imaginative writing, I do not think he had ever read Juan Rulfo or any of the other modern or nineteenth-century Latin American historical novelists. And though detective fiction and the science fiction of Jules Verne delighted him, he did not seem fond of sweeping historical or epic narrative. (He once told me that Don Quixote had not impressed him because he considered it "fantasy.") Nevertheless, my grandfather often described hacienda society in a manner reminiscent of Juan Rulfo's mythic rendering. At the opening of Rulfo's novel *Pedro Páramo*, for example, when asked which lands near a central Mexican rural town belong to a local hacendado, a peasant answers with a series of admonitory questions: "See that mountain, the one that looks like a pig's bladder? Good, now look over there. See the ridge of that mountain? Now look over here. See that mountain way off there? Well, all that's the Media Luna, everything you see. And it all belongs to Pedro Páramo" (1955, 4). The mountain described is Cerro de la Bufa itself, said by some to resemble a bloated animal bladder, which is located near Rulfo's native community in the bordering state of Jalisco. In much the same way as Rulfo's novel, my grandfather noted that in "colonial" times "people of property didn't measure their property in hectares, parcels, or plots, but rather by how far their vision reached; once these men began to dedicate themselves to the raising of sheep and other livestock, within the course of years, they counted herds in the thousands, if not millions" (2). Here, and in many other places as well, my grandfather grants a larger-than-life quality to that Mexican colonial history that Rulfo both refracts and deconstructs. And yet, these renderings of the mythic dimensions of the founding Zacatecan haciendas find support in historical accounts. Semo cites a 1579 report by the *alcalde* mayor of Zacatecas, Hernando Vargas, which states that in the Valley of Aguascalientes, the granary of the Zacatecan mining industry, "more than 100,000 cows and 200,000 sheep and 10,000 mares grazed between the town of San Juan [del Río] and Querétaro, which are seven leagues apart" (1993, 73). In keeping with this portrait of a bountiful hacienda landscape, San Juan de las Calabasas, the hacienda community where my grandfather spent much of his childhood, was his "beloved native village," a place where "everything was the color of roses and all of the food was sweet" (14). The imaginary geocultural terrain of central Mexico stands in sharp opposition to my grandfather's later cultural uprootedness, permanent forced exile, and "slavelike" experience as a farm laborer. Hacienda life in Jerez was a carefree "vacation" or "adventure," the rural landscape symbolizing the innocence and expansive freedom of childhood.

And in the center of this pastoral landscape stand the boy and his father, whose close relationship, rooted irrevocably in the nineteenth-century hacienda world, is conveyed through brief and poignant remembrances of childhood. Early in "Memorias" my grandfather remembers

> asking my father, when I was four or five, the following question: "Tell me how many tortillas I have eaten in my entire life." My father answered, "I'd say about a hundred." Wouldn't you agree that such childish questions, though silly, are at the same time philosophical? (5)

In this way, the landscape of the hacienda contains within it not only communitarian rootedness but also familial intimacy between father and son. Of course, other relatives inhabit this world as well, providing background on the maternal side of my grandfather's family and complementing the emphasis in "Memorias" on patriarchal lineage. His maternal grandparents, ghostly presences in the narrative, lived in a hacienda village near Jerez and took care of him while his father worked. By proudly providing elaborate nineteenth-century names of these abuelos, Don Ambrosio Róbles (who in fact was his grandfather Don José Róbles's nephew) and Doña Hipólita Macías Róbles (his grandmother), he reasserts cultural continuity and familial pride in the face of their total erasure from the United States historical ledger. He insists on carrying such a name forward himself, often referring to himself in "Memorias" as "Don" Francisco, the title his father always affectionately used and thus a constant reminder of his father's love and perhaps even of the writer's "upper class" hacienda ancestors.

As for his own mother Juliana, daughter of Don José Róbles and Doña Hipólita, my grandfather says that he doesn't remember her at all. She died in 1913, soon after giving birth to her third child; thus the only "mother" my grandfather knew was Doña Hipólita. (In the following section I will address the central roles Juliana and her younger sister Dominga play in "Memorias.") As if to claim for his mother and her parents the same nobility he posited for his father's ancestors, my grandfather asserts that Doña Hipólita and the Róbleses "were from a proud family with deep roots in Zacatecas, and though I never knew my mother, I use her family name as a part of my own" (30).[24]

Mexican customs, traditions, and events such as weddings and funerals are also set within the hacienda's retrospective geographic space. Like the landscape, these practices affirm as well the communitarian and familial qualities of my grandfather's pre-American cultural environment. Hacienda weddings, for instance, were "grand events" in which "all families and friends in the community cooperated" (28). The food preparations were highly communal. Some families

> would prepare a cow for the celebration's meal, others two lambs, three pigs, and a few goats—this, of course, doesn't include the dozens of chickens. As for tortillas, no fewer than ten women were grinding corn and making tortillas before and during the celebration. Not only family members came, but the whole community, without any need for invitations. A second party took place the day after, a *tornaboda*, with music and more music and dancing. (28)

This communal and nostalgic vision of Mexican hacienda society is closely linked to that self-contradictory "rupture" of crossing the US–Mexican border. In a telling passage about listening to a record by his favorite opera singer, Mario Lanza, my grandfather reflected on his ancestral Mexican hacienda community and its Spanish colonial past:

> I feel content in my journey through this life that I did something for my family and that I continue being the "trunk" of the future family tree, [following] those Spanish pioneers who one day gave us a language and a religion—even though, as Bernal Díaz del Castillo said [in his account of the Spanish conquest of Mexico], they came with the cross and the sword. (37)

Although the last line momentarily acknowledges that buried, contradictory historical reality of the Mexican (Spanish) colonial mythos, which the Róbles counternarrative will foreground, "Memorias" elsewhere elides prerevolutionary social conflict. Dwelling on the work's ahistorical projection of an impossibly harmonious communal past, however, is less fruitful than placing it within the wider context of my grandfather's life as a deracinated Mexican who, after seventy years in the "belly of the monster," to use Jose Martí's description of life as an Hispanic in the United States, still viewed himself and his American-born descendants as displaced "migrants" and "orphans" regrettably alienated from Mexican culture and history. Recording his Mexican (Spanish) colonial heritage was his way of bequeathing to his immediate family and Chicano descendants a connection to a heroic and noble past.

Not simply aristocratic pretense or genealogical self-invention, then, my grandfather's nostalgic desire for a mythic Spanish colonial world was a socially empowering reassertion of cultural continuity and pride, in the face of deeply felt cultural displacement and fragmentation. "With my hand on my chest, Don Francisco is writing this history," he announces early in the narrative, "the descalzo who one day crossed the Río Grande somewhere near El Paso with his rags on his head—and I am not at all ashamed to say this, because it is the truth" (3). Rejecting the shame that US cultural and economic formations seek to force upon his Mexican American descendants and community, he implicitly urges his Mexican American readers to follow him in shedding their internalized "American" habits. More important, by juxtaposing his status as an orphaned descalzo with his action as Don Francisco, writing the "history" of the family, my grandfather assures that his "nostalgic" narrative must be read in the light of his later US experience of alienation and exploitation.

While specific memories of his father were interwoven throughout my grandfather's vision of hacienda society, other pre-American passages placed his father within the more mundane world of day-to-day affairs. Though described throughout the narrative as a businessman who worked most of his life as an accountant for hacendados, Lira Pérez in fact operated several other businesses after his departure from Jerez. At one point he bought and sold animal bones, a product he acquired from the livestock haciendas of central Mexico. (Wool, hides, tallow, horsehair, and bones—along with meat—were standard products of livestock haciendas.) Grandfather remembered accompanying his father more than once to examine train cars filled with bones, which his father was selling or purchasing. After leaving Jerez, for a time Lira Pérez also owned a butcher shop.

As "the only trained business administrator in that region," before his displacement from Jerez, Lira Pérez had apparently prospered in the hacienda economy: "He was educated at the university in the state capital in business administration, [and] since he was fifty-two-years old when I was born, I imagine that he must have already practiced his profession for more than thirty years by then" (6). Following this chronology, Lira Pérez would therefore have begun his career in 1878, two years after the rise of Porfirio Díaz, the dictator whose name is synonymous with the period of the "modern" hacienda, and with the widespread socioeconomic injustices and repressions this quasifeudalistic economy brought about. Although Díaz met opposition throughout the 1880s in Zacatecas, "the consolida-tion of the Porfirista regime, which was initiated with the assassination [in 1886] of the last dissident [General Trinidad García de la Cadena], . . . culminated [in the state] in 1888, when Jesús Aréchiga became governor" (Flores 1996, 139). Díaz's thirty-five-year reign is a complicated period. He has been credited with "industrializing" the hacienda system and thus

Figure 5. Juan Lira Pérez (standing at right in dark sombrero) with two of his sons, from far right, Francisco and Marcos in Jerez, Mexico, on Independence Day, September 1912.

bringing modern capitalism to a predominantly rural society. In his analysis of early twentieth-century Mexican emigration to the United States, Acuña explains that Díaz's policies "encouraged the industrialization of agriculture, mining, and transportation, which led to the uprooting of the Mexican peasants, many of whom moved northward" (1988, 147). Modernization under Díaz, in short, led to the demise of the communal village and commercialization of the hacienda. And yet, as Cardoso points out, for Díaz "the old hacienda system remained the most effective means of keeping the peasants submissive," therefore he "needed its support" (1979, 107). Lira Pérez's career thus spanned the Díaz period of hacienda dominance from 1880 to 1911.[25] Or as my grandfather proudly announced, in his father's youth "the great haciendas and latifundios began to be formed . . . and that was exactly where my father first began to practice his profession" (11).

The single extant photograph of Lira Pérez was taken in September 1912, during Independence Day celebrations in Jerez (fig. 5). He was fifty-six, a tall, well-dressed, gaunt man who appears to be of higher socioeconomic status than the townsfolk around him. While the aged campesino at the extreme left and most of the others in the photograph wear sombreros made of straw, my great-grandfather's sombrero appears to be made of felt and displays embroidery on its rim. Dark and weatherworn, his expression stern, he stands in front of what appears to be a patriotic parade, grasping the reins of a wagon drawn by three white horses and decorated with Mexican banners and flags. Though actually well to the right, Lira Pérez seems to be at the center of this photograph of his community's most important public celebration, while the man in the middle of the photo may be the son (or perhaps a relative or foreman) of Don Jacinto Carlos, a hacendado who employed Lira Pérez. The lower-class folk in the audience behind these two men seem to squeeze into the photograph's frame. At the picture's extreme right stand Lira Pérez's two young sons. My grandfather Francisco, age four or five and dressed in the white clothes of Mexican campesinos, holds his hand before his face. Marcos, his older half-brother, stares like his father directly into the camera.

I have often imagined how this photograph survived the events of the ten years that followed—not only the chaos of the revolution itself, but the family's forced departure from Jerez in early 1914, their journey during the civil war, the death of Lira Pérez in 1919, and the subsequent orphanhood and emigration of Francisco. Since my grandfather could not have carried the photograph with him when he emigrated in 1921, a Herrera or perhaps Róbles relative from Jerez must have transported it when those families also emigrated (see family tree).

By writing his memoirs, my grandfather tried to grant "textual permanence" to his father's life and his own (Padilla 1993, 4), thus bequeathing to his Mexican American descendants the foundational narrative of their familial and cultural origins. At another level, though, he struggled with the need to resist those material and economic forces that had led to his fragmented cultural condition in the United States. Though often eliding the social conflicts of the pre-American past, "Memorias" therefore participates, however deeply mediated by a language of nostalgic reflection, in that critical discourse that Ramón Saldívar has identified in modern Chicano narratives. Notwithstanding its suppressions, if judged first as an immigrant narrative, my grandfather's autobiography joins with other oppositional autobiographical works, such as Ernesto Galarza's *Barrio Boy* (1971), to explore what Ramón Saldívar has termed the "imaginary ways in which historical men and women live out their lives in a class society, and how the values, concepts, and ideas purveyed by the mainstream, American culture that tie them to their social functions seek to prevent them from a true knowledge of society as a whole" (1990, 6). But another layer of the palimpsest of history in "Memorias" remains to be peeled back.

91

As the Róbles family narrative will reveal, my grandfather's representation of Mexican hacienda society both records and obscures its underlying socioeconomic and cultural formations.

Chavela's Funeral

> It's just incredible. It just does not explain. Or perhaps that's it: they don't explain and we are not supposed to know. We have a few old mouth-to-mouth tales; we exhume from old trunks and boxes and drawers letters without salutation or signature, in which men and women who once lived and breathed are now merely initials or nicknames. . . . [The people] are there, yet something is missing; they are like a chemical formula exhumed along with the letters from that forgotten chest, carefully, the paper old and faded and falling to pieces, the writing faded, almost indecipherable, yet meaningful, familiar in shape and sense, the name and presence of volatile and sentient forces.
>
> —William Faulkner, *Absalom, Absalom!*

> Fictions and the fiction-making process are a central constituent of the truth of any life as it is lived and of any art devoted to the presentation of that life.
>
> —Paul John Eakin, *Fictions in Autobiography*

> The genealogist needs history to dispel the chimeras of the origin, somewhat in the manner of the pious philosopher who needs a doctor to exorcise the shadow of his soul. He must be able to recognize the events of history, its jolts, its surprises, its unsteady victories and unpalatable defeats—the basis of all beginnings, atavisms, and heredities.
>
> —Michel Foucault, "Nietzsche, Genealogy, History"

An incident that caused an unexpected shift in my recuperating and interpreting "Memorias" offers a cautionary reminder of what recent critics of autobiographical and historical narratives have termed the "impulse to self-invention" (Couser, 1989, 19).[26] Certainly, what happened at a relative's funeral underscores Padilla's emphasis on the "centrality of thick socio-historicized readings of formative Mexican American (autobiographical) narratives and the historical particularities of their production" (1993, xi). One could even see this event as an example of what Padilla calls "discontinuity" in the discursive genealogy of Chicano literary traditions (7). More important, though, the funeral encounter I will now discuss strongly suggests that readings—including Padilla's—of early Mexican American autobiographies must be self-critically aware of their own suppressions. As the Róbles family helped to reveal, my grandfather's nostalgic desire worked to conceal iniquities and social conflicts buried deep in his father's hacienda past. To insure that such powerful, shaping forces do not remain unexamined, scholars who recover and interpret autobiographical and historical narratives by individuals whose "voices have not merely been forgotten . . . but suppressed" (xi) must be constantly aware of the issue of fictionality in these texts and must also delve critically into representations of pre-American history. The nostalgic impulse in Mexican American autobiographies is certainly the product of sociocultural rupture and fragmentation, but as Padilla himself has suggested, this impulse constructs a "master" narrative designed to suppress much of what does not conform to the author's idealized projection of the past. Nor does recognizing and retrieving such textual sublimations and contradictions necessarily undermine the obvious need to restore the dignity and integrity of these early autobiographers' lives. In fact, this restoration can be enhanced by foregrounding those submerged power relations so often inherent in the social manifestations of these lives.

At a time when I was beginning to transcribe my grandfather's manuscript, a strange occurrence at a cemetery revealed more about my grandfather's relation to his past and his sense of self-identity than I had to that point been prepared to grasp. When Aunt Chavela was laid to rest in July 1992, the myth of my grandfather's father, drawn in part from the Independence Day photograph, was figuratively exhumed. The funeral was held in Santa Paula, a rural community north of Los Angeles and not far from Fillmore, the town where my grandfather and his wife had reared their children. After attending the service, my parents and I followed the procession to the small cemetery where Chavela would be buried. Members of both sides of my grandfather's family, the Pérezes and Róbleses, were present, some Róbles relatives having come from as far away as central Mexico to pay their respect to a woman who had emigrated from their community some fifty years earlier. A priest read a prayer over the open grave, and my parents and I passed by Chavela's casket. After the prayer, we greeted members of both sides of my grandfather's family, some of whom were as unfamiliar to my father as to me. My father stopped to greet Nicolas Róbles (Nico) and his family—some other Róbleses, he later informed me, that he had not seen in twenty years. A younger couple, who introduced themselves as my father's cousins, but whom my father had never met, stopped for a short conversation.

While my father was engaged with them, I left to speak with other members of my family. When I returned a few minutes later, I was startled to find myself in the midst of an uncomfortably loud argument, one made all the more improbable by the circumstances and locale. My parents later told me that, after introducing herself, the woman launched into a tirade in Spanish against the Pérez family and especially against Juan Lira Pérez, who had been dead for eighty years. When I arrived, the woman was dramatically waving her finger in my father's face. That my father and his siblings, all American-born, neither knew their grandfather nor, with the exception of my Aunt Esther, took any interest in their dead ancestors, made this confrontation all the more baffling. Hearing the commotion, others gathered near us, watching in astonishment and dread: here was a person without shame, or any respect for family, their countenances seemed to say. Face-to-face with my father, our cousin attacked the moral character of the Pérez patriarch and, by association, that of the four succeeding male generations, including my own. The spitefulness of the woman's colloquial Spanish cannot be captured in a literal translation. In effect, she called our long-deceased founding patriarch a "philandering criminal" who in prerevolutionary Zacatecas left a trail of hate and misery in his sinister wake. This, she claimed, was Lira Pérez's contribution to a trusting friendship between the two families that went back to the last century. Concluding her complaint with a string of curses, she informed her stunned audience that the Pérez family's cherished mythologized grandfather had at the age of fifty-six raped Dominga Róbles, his wife's older sister (who for a short period in 1912 had come to live with the couple while my great-grandmother Juliana was recovering from childbirth). Her accusations left everyone speechless. (Later I learned that the product of that crime, Paulo Róbles Pérez—half-brother and cousin to my grandfather—was adopted and reared by Dominga's brother, José.)

My grandfather, whose nostalgic and heartfelt remembrance of his father had created Lira Pérez's ennobling reputation and legend in our family, but whose stories make only passing reference to the Róbles complaint, had apparently been wary of just such a clash. Immediately after the cemetery service, he quietly left without speaking to any of the Róbleses. My father, like his four siblings, never knew his paternal grandfather. Though not likely to take insults without responding in kind, in deference to Chavela and others in attendance, my father listened to the woman's complaint without answering. Like many others at the funeral, he was dumbfounded by the curious spectacle, that, as we later learned, centered on a series of events that occurred in 1912 and 1913 in Jerez.

The forty-five-year-old woman before us, Berta Róbles, was José Róbles's daughter—but she was also a Róbles by *marriage,* having wed Paulo's son José Pérez (her second cousin).[27] Eighty-some years after Lira Pérez's transgression, on the occasion of the gathering of two branches of my grandfather's family, she now sought retribution. According to the Róbles account, as divulged by Berta and later supported by other Róbles relatives, the Róbles family hoped that the illegitimate Paulo would be legally recognized by his father, but the boy was spurned and he and his mother barred from claiming any inheritance upon the death of Lira Pérez.[28] Growing up in the family of his mother, the child suffered the stigma of a confused identity as the bastard child of a man who was detested by those forced to rear the boy. Nor has my grandfather ever acknowledged the kinship. As if keenly aware of the Róbles's dispossession, in "Memorias" my grandfather proclaims his privileged status as "primogenitor," the legitimate firstborn son with inheritance rights to his father's property in Jerez (2).[29] My grandfather had even gone to a funeral in Santa Paula, California (where many Róbleses settled) also attended by his half-brother Paulo, but as one of my aunts later recalled, when directed to meet the elderly man, my grandfather answered, "I don't have any brother."

The figure of Don Juan Lira Pérez, though embodying honorable and even heroic "roots" in my own family's tales, served quite a different function in the Róbles family narrative. The legend of the rape and the father's repudiation of his child, passed down through several generations and carried to the United States when they emigrated, became a central metaphor and theme in the mythos of their family's historical origins. To this day, in their family narrative, Lira Pérez signifies not honor, origins, and ancestry, but rather those intangible historical and social forces, bound to the feudalistic hacienda economy, which contributed to the Róbles family's betrayal and suffering in Mexico and later exodus to the United States.

Leaving us to gather ourselves at the edge of Chavela's grave, Berta and her husband then departed, but the story was not yet finished. Nico, another Róbles "cousin," who in the fifty years that he had lived and worked alongside the Pérez family had never spoken a word to any of us about our founding patriarch, then pulled my father aside. As if wishing to dispel any misplaced belief that Berta's remarks might simply be the unfounded "hysterics" of an angry *mujer,* he calmly told my father that the Róbles family had shown great self-restraint in dealing with the matter of the rape at that time. Though more discreet than Berta, Nico's final message was all the more startling for its brevity. Underscoring the historical injustice that Lira Pérez had, for them, clearly come to personify, he said, "your grandfather did something awful . . . y lo hubieran podido matar. . . . They [the Róbleses] could have killed him for what he did . . . they could have killed your grandfather for what he did to that girl"—words all the more chilling because Lira Pérez was Nico's grandfather .

Before I propose a resolution to the questions that arose from this incident, I should first briefly reconstruct those events occurring between 1912 and 1914 that my grandfather and Berta have so differently described. I begin with the obvious: that part of the Róbles family has remained angry with the Pérez family for almost ninety years, as a result of events involving my grandfather's father two years prior to his departure from the town of his birth. In a manner different from my grandfather's usual sentimental bent, the account of this time in "Memorias" stresses Lira Pérez's precarious political position. Though the local sociopolitical circumstances of the forced flight are not intimated, my grandfather indicates that as an associate of the hacienda elite his father was viewed as an enemy of the insurgents and that he left his ancestral home because soldiers were planning to execute him. (As I will explain in the next section, Lira Pérez paid protection money to the insurrectionists for a time; but in early 1914, perhaps a few months before the April 2 Battle of Torreón, his agreement with the rebels fell apart.)

The legend of his 1914 flight, which had fascinated and disturbed me as a college student, as well as the less than heroic reasons for the exodus, I can now see are plainly inscribed in the margins of my grandfather's memoirs. My earlier desire to reconstruct an ideologically acceptable version of my past had led me to dismiss these passages as youthful "adventures," largely extraneous to my grandfather's romantic narrative of origins. In his account of events in early 1914, my grandfather describes how his father hid in a well for three days without food while the soldiers searching for him sacked and burned his property at San Juan de las Calabasas. Several of Lira Pérez's employers had been executed by the insurrectionists. The haciendas where his father had been employed for more than three decades were raided and burned. Stories by members of my grandmother's family, the Herreras—who lived on the nearby Tesorero and Víboras haciendas—recount pitched battles between troops and rebel soldiers on the hacienda grounds. Salvador Herrera—Concepción Pérez's eldest brother and a man who lived to be ninety-seven—described these engagements in a tape-recorded interview with Esther. He recalled soldiers from opposing sides screaming epithets at each other in the midst of a battle at Tesorero. His wife, Jesusita, remembered the battle as having occurred in and around the hacienda chapel. (Salvador and Concepción's sister, María, became Lira Pérez's fourth wife and bore a child by him in 1912. Though Concepción was ten years older than her husband and therefore likely to be more familiar with Lira Pérez's life and reputation in Jerez, my grandmother never mentioned his name to anyone. When I asked her for information about him during an interview, she said she knew nothing.)

Before escaping from the town, my great-grandfather, according to the myth written by his son, only narrowly evaded his pursuers. When the fallen patriarch emerged from his last hiding place, he escaped with his six-year-old son under the cover of night. What now strikes me in this section of my grandfather's otherwise nostalgic reconstruction of his childhood is his lasting resentment that "when the revolutionaries, those blood brothers of ours, arrived in Jerez, they executed people and they forced many others to flee. . . . They wanted to kill my father, too. Many times he escaped by the skin of his teeth . . . a week later we all escaped through the mountains by burro, one for each of us" (4).[30]

The image of his father escaping in the dark is my grandfather's sharpest memory of this journey through the mountains, and although Lira Pérez lived for another five years and my grandfather remained in Mexico for two more after his death, this childhood trauma—the originary moment of separation from his ancestral Mexican community—serves in "Memorias" as what Padilla names the point of sociocultural rupture in the Mexican American autobiographical and historical consciousness. By fixating on the image of his father on that night, my grandfather cannot but nostalgically push aside the humiliating details of the previous days. Eighty years after his father's inglorious retreat, my grandfather remembers the tall figure in front of him on that night, restored imaginatively to an honored position within the idealized cultural geography of his settler ancestors. "There, fleeing from his ancestral home," my grandfather writes, "went an honorable and productive citizen . . . who at one time was a descendant of the most prosperous and propertied hacendados in the entire valley of Jerez" (4). Neither his father's exile, nor his own permanent displacement, can be viewed by my grandfather except in the light of the mythic hacienda past. His is the elite class perspective of a child whose secure and comfortable world was overturned by a ragtag group of peons. The peasant soldiers who sought his father, he suggests, were actually using their newfound power for short-term gain. As my grandfather ironically explains, "we left at night so that our loyal Mexican 'brethren,' people who one day were our employees and we the employers, couldn't detect us" (4).

We have come a long way from the family narratives of some Chicanos whose *antepasados* were said to have ridden a "raid or two" with Pancho Villa—but we must go further. As I would later learn from my Aunt Esther, who met and spoke with Berta, the Róbles family believes that when Juliana, my grandfather's mother, was pregnant in 1912–13 with her third child, she was cared for in her home by her older sister Dominga. The Róbles family charges that Lira Pérez raped his sister-in-law and then renounced his illegitimate son Paulo, primarily for legal and business reasons. Esther believed that the relationship was consensual, one that Lira Pérez broke off. According to the Róbles narrative, astute accountant that he was, Lira Pérez may have realized that legally recognizing the male child would create a web of financial difficulties for his other sons and family in Jerez. Yet, this suggests that if Lira Pérez had only supported and acknowledged the boy, the accusations of rape would perhaps have been forgotten. Obviously, he did not foresee his forced departure from the town a year or so later. He may even have been forced to leave before the child was born.

But this was not the end of the tale that Lira Pérez, while in Jerez, had written for himself. The fierce nostalgia that imbues my grandfather's account of the escape from town also obscures and suppresses yet another side of his father's life during the 1912–14 period: a secret relationship with a woman named María Herrera (my grandmother's elder sister), who would later become his fourth wife, but who at this time lived with her family twenty miles from Jerez at the hacienda known as Víboras. (After Francisco's father's death in 1919, María and her siblings were extremely important to Francisco; her family took care of him, and, as mentioned earlier, he eventually married María's youngest sister, Concepción.) As my grandfather perhaps unintentionally acknowledged in a tape-recorded interview in 1987, when his father left Jerez in early 1914 on short notice, he took Francisco, his mistress/wife María, and their two children—a boy named Lucas, born in 1912, and a baby girl named Diega, born a few months before the family's flight. Although "Memorias" does not mention María as part of Lira Pérez's life in Jerez, in this interview María appears in my grandfather's description of their 1914 journey. After they left the mountains, they boarded a train, but were forced to ride on its roof because it was filled with soldiers on their way north to do battle with Villista and Maderista rebels. The episode recalls the train rides described in Galarza's *Barrio Boy*, whose early chapters are also set at the height of the revolution. My grandfather remembered María sitting on the curved roof at night, holding on to Diega, struggling to keep herself and the baby from falling off the shaking train. Clearly contradicting this taped recollection, "Memorias" instead states vaguely that it was "during his father's stay" in Torreón, where he lived on and off between early 1914 and his death, that both Lucas and Diega were born. By suggesting that Lira Pérez met María after leaving Jerez, the text erases the secret affair with María. Since this third relationship means that between 1912 and 1914 Lira Pérez had four children by three women—Paulo by Dominga Róbles; Lucas and Diega by María Herrera; and Marcos II, who died in infancy in 1913, by his wife Juliana (see family tree)—Berta's impassioned complaint at the funeral becomes all the more credible and compelling. And yet, although María could presumably have been blamed for Dominga's abandonment by Lira Pérez, the Róbles family narrative doesn't mention her at all, suggesting that the Róbles accusation centers upon Lira Pérez's abuse of Dominga, rather than his decision, if this is in fact what occurred, to take María, rather than Dominga, with him.

The Róbles narrative instead draws other conclusions from the events of this time. Both Dominga and Juliana died at a young age, Juliana in 1913 and Dominga, who was at least fifteen years older than her sister, in 1922. Esther, who for a time mistakenly believed that Dominga had died in 1916, once joked that the aging patriarch may have poisoned these sisters to extricate himself from the legal and personal morass he had created; and while this theory is chronologically impossible in the case of Dominga, I obviously have no way of determining the complete truth of Lira Pérez's complex relationship with the Róbleses. As Galarza, quoting Henry Adams, cites in the epigraph of *Barrio Boy*, "the memory was all that mattered" for the Róbleses. Yet my aunt's passing remarks do perhaps throw added light on the origins of the Róbles narrative, for as Berta's and Nico's comments insinuate, the Róbles family may have excoriated Lira Pérez not only for his rape of Dominga and repudiation of Paulo, but also for the deaths of both sisters at an early age. Juliana apparently died of natural causes while recovering from childbirth. After losing their second daughter Dominga nine years later in 1922, however, the Róbles family may have concluded that any of their daughters who came in contact with Lira Pérez would meet a tragic end—or perhaps that the Pérezes simply brought tragedy to the family. I have not yet determined with any certainty the class status or political sympathies of the Róbleses when they lived near Jerez. Though certainly not associated with the hacendado elite, it is not clear they were impoverished campesinos. Many did not leave Mexico until the 1950s.

By preventing further contact between the Pérez and Róbles families, the revolution settled the issue of the illegitimate child—or so it seemed. For my purposes, the appearance of insurrectionists in Jerez in 1913 serves two important functions. First, by destroying Lira Pérez's career, dispossessing him of his property, and forcing him into permanent exile, it gave him the comeuppance the Róbles family believes he deserved for his treatment of their daughters and perhaps for his decades-long role in the hacienda caste system. This financial ruin explains my grandfather's socioeconomic and cultural "orphanhood." Had his father not left Jerez nor lost his property, my grandfather probably would not have needed to emigrate to the United States. Second, the civil war ensured that the mystery of Lira Pérez's relationship to the Róbles family would not be fully revealed for many decades. The Róbleses never had the opportunity to confront the despised founding father of one line of their family, nor because many of them remained in Mexico until after World War II—his immediate heirs. Though eighty years had passed, Chavela's funeral offered the Róbleses an occasion to meet the descendants of Don Lira Pérez, who, owing to their own unique construction of the past, knew almost nothing of the other side of their patriarch's life and reputation.

I have only recently learned from Esther what is perhaps the most tragic irony in my family narrative. My grandfather always blamed his mother's death in 1913 on her sister Dominga! Refusing to imagine his father as anything but heroic, he came to view this older sister as a wily temptress and seducer of a distinguished and reluctant patriarch. According to this improbable twist, my grandfather's bedridden mother died of a "broken heart" brought on by the shock of her own sister's betrayal. Not only does this turn of plot make for a dramatic denouement to the family narrative; in this way my grandfather transferred the blame for Lira Pérez's apparent crimes onto the Róbles family, thus allowing him to embrace a long-dead father and mother by salvaging untarnished memories of them from the chaos of family history—his most ambitious narrative sleight of hand.

The Maderista Rebellions

In the dining hall of the workers' camp at Rancho Sespe, I heard a [Mexican] "bracero," a plebeian, make the following comment while he ate: "One must eat the gringo's food, but one should throw the plate in his face." I leave this statement to your critical judgment. In difficult times, all things are acceptable. . . .

All of this is a part of a past that is filled with memories and not a few sufferings, but today I am proud for having surmounted them. . . . I was a child in Mexico, then a youth in the United States, a man, a mature man, and now I am an old man. . . . I am so old I already have one foot in the "other world." And what more than this is the inheritance of mankind? Today I am content that the maker of the infinite universe has granted me and my family the divine grace of living for so many years.

—Francisco R. Pérez, "Memorias"

Memory—how we remember and what we choose to remember, since we cannot remember everything—is intimately tied to a culturally organized discursive habitat.

—Genaro M. Padilla, *My History, Not Yours*

After Chavela's funeral, what struck me about my grandfather's text was not just its evasion of the Róbles complaint and nostalgic aggrandizement of Lira Pérez, but the multitude of absences, silences, gaps, and suppressions that now seemed to determine the narrative's representation of family history. The series of tales through which my family came to imagine its historical origins and cultural identity had been constructed on the buried ruins of the anti-nostalgic Róbles counterhistory and this "other" history might be said to signify more than the forgotten grievance of a single family. It represented as well the displaced histories of groups marginalized within Mexican society itself—such as women, Indians, and campesinos—who were systematically victimized by the feudalistic hacienda system and institutionally erased from the historical record. By focusing narrowly on the modern period without acknowledging the "trailing" historical qualifiers that Mexican Americans carry with us, some Chicano literary and historical studies unintentionally construct nineteenth-century (hacienda) history like my own family genealogy. In the interest of recovering our buried Mexican (American) past, they overlook the complexity, contradiction, and discontinuity inherent in this nineteenth-century social experience, thereby erasing our historical links to the hacienda as a social and cultural institution. Berta's complaint, which transgressed the traditional Mexican codes of respect and honor paid to elders and ancestors, provoked key questions about Chicano origins and history that my earlier readings of historical narratives had raised but not yet fully distilled.

The Róbles family narrative illuminates, from the perspective of the invisible victims of the Porfirian hacienda system, the class-based social contradictions as well as the gender-defined conflicts in hacienda society that formed the roots of the civil war and revolution, but that my grandfather's nostalgic idealization of his father's life effectively suppressed. My grandfather alludes to his father's local political predicament and forced exile, but his single reference to the events leading up to the 1913 "well" episode is tellingly brief—a brevity that elides the painfully sublimated reality of the family's exodus: the Constitutionalist forces who gained ascendancy in rural Zacatecas in 1913 wished to put Lira Pérez to death because of his association with the *patrónes* (bosses) in the region.

The rebellions recounted in "Memorias" occurred in the summer of 1913. Since my grandfather was only five years old at the time, his interpretation of the political landscape within which these violent clashes took place must have come from stories told by his father until his death in 1919. Over the years since then, these stories, like all of the others in "Memorias," were subject to the vagaries of memory. Gore Vidal (1995) characterizes memory as a palimpsest: one never remembers an actual event, but rather one's earlier remembrance of the event, until late in life one has only memories of earlier remembrances of earlier recollections, and so forth. Like other contemporary writers of historical fiction both in the United States and Latin America, E. L. Doctorow (1993) too rejects the notion that imagination and memory are ever independent of each other.

By drawing from the historical scholarship on the period, however, one may sketch a picture of the turbulent political events that shaped the lives of Francisco and his father. The violence in Jerez was one of a multitude of lesser uprisings throughout the rural region around the capital occurring during mid-1913, skirmishes that preceded by a year the major battles between Federal troops and northern (Villista) and local revolutionary forces in the cities of Torreón and Zacatecas. The actions were carried out by groups that were a part of the early Madero movement—the first phase of the Madero Revolution in Zacatecas—a movement that came to prominence in the state two years earlier. The Maderistas opposed the Díaz dictatorship and began armed activities to end the regime in the border region of Zacatecas and Durango in February 1911. Led by José Luis Moya, Pánfilo Natera, Martín Triana, and Trinidad Cervantes, the Maderistas sought a transformation of the political system and a role in the governmental decision-making process (Flores 1996, 157). "The immediate effects of the Madero Revolution in the [region] were limited: the removal from office of the governor and his replacement by one who fully represented the cause of Maderismo . . . and the replacement of various functionaries in the occupied regions by revolutionary officers" (157). Although Zacatecan Maderistas claimed that the 1911 Ciudad Juárez agreement, which ended the Díaz regime, did not change the political structure of the Mexican government, up to the summer of 1911 none of the Maderista groups in Zacatecas espoused any ideas other than those set forth by Maderismo (157).

Even before the February 1913 coup that ended the Madero presidency, the Zacatecan Maderistas were disappointed with the Madero presidency. By the time the president was assassinated, opposition to the government was widespread throughout the region and expressed in the form of rebellions and banditry (158). And while the official state political apparatus recognized the new administration of Victoriano Huerta, local functionaries with Maderista ties, who held either civil posts or positions in the rural forces, immediately rebelled (158). Led by Natera—the greatest Zacatecan hero of the revolution, whose giant bronze statue today stands atop the Bufa alongside that of Villa—the Maderista militants began armed actions to carry out the Constitutionalist revolution. Their forces quickly took control of most of the state. At this point, Lira Pérez's status as an associate of the hacendados marked him as an opponent of local, perhaps newly recruited rebels in Jerez. Some of the insurrectionists he faced could well have been former peons recruited from the very haciendas where he had worked for more than three decades.

The objective of the "second phase of the Madero revolution" in Zacatecas was the end of *cacicazgo*. Hacienda society, whose contradictions Porfirian modernization and industrialization amplified, was controlled for generations by *caciques* (local landowners or bosses), who wielded absolute power over peons, servants, and tenants. Even before the well-known depredations of the hacienda system under the Díaz dictatorship, in its mid-nineteenth-century manifestation, cacicazgo meant serfdom for the great majority of Mexican citizens. Speaking at the Mexican constitutional convention of 1856, the same year that Lira Pérez was born, reformer Ponciano Arriaga denounced the injustices of the landowning and peonage structure:

> The rich Mexican landowner . . . or the majordomo who represents him, may be compared to a feudal lord of the Middle Ages. On his domain, with more or less formality, he makes laws and executes them; administers justice and exercises civil powers; imposes taxes and fines; has jails, chains, and jailers; inflicts punishments and tortures, monopolizes trade and forbids any other business than that of his estate to be carried on without his consent. As a rule the judges and other public officials on these estates are the landowner's servants or tenants; they are henchmen incapable of acting freely, impartially, or justly, or of enforcing any law other than the absolute will of the master. (1993, 97)

As mentioned earlier, the economic policies enacted under Díaz aggravated these contradictions. The second phase of the Madero movement thus constituted a social revolution with more radical goals than those of the first phase. Not only did diverse sectors of the Zacatecan population participate in the movement, but, in seeking an end to *cacicazgo*, they "radicalized the substance of [earlier] demands, which now included substantial changes in rural and mining work conditions, higher living standards, a redefinition of the structure of private property . . . and a desire for more effective, honest, and respectful government administrations" (Flores 1996, 156).

In the summer of 1913, Zacatecan Constitutionalist forces responded to Huerta's coup by carrying out reprisals and other military actions against groups identified with the hacienda system—"landlords, *caciques*, Federals, sometimes clerics, and Spaniards (though rarely Americans)" (Knight 1986, 42). Accounts of these revolts in northern Zacatecas capture what probably happened in nearby Jerez, where Lira Pérez was employed:

> [Justo] Avila, a small rancher at odds with the Lobatos hacienda, raised the latter's peons in revolt, recruiting 500 men. . . . Lobatos was a hacienda with an absentee owner and, more important, a notoriously harsh *administrador*. Other properties suffered: the huge, Spanish-owned El Saucillo, near Rincón de Ramos, was sacked; peons were reported to have taken over estates at Pinos, to the east, where the *rurales* had mutinied. Soon, towns became targets. At the mines of Los Tocayos the entreaties of the miners' wives prevented the triumphant rebels from dynamiting the company building; at Sombrerete, the *jefe* and his men held off the rebels for a while, but finally the town was taken and sacked. (43)

Rural grievances and recruitment were all-important in these uprisings (43). Since landowners and caciques had exploited their peons, servants, and tenants, Constitutionalist recruitment among the ranks of hacienda laborers in Zacatecas continued apace throughout early 1913. By the summer of 1913, the Constitutionalist army had grown to a point where "the governors and military commanders of Zacatecas, San Luis and Coahuila admitted that they could not police beyond the major cities, and they urged landowners to undertake their own defense" (45). Executions and other reprisals against officials, landowners, and merchants were common. Yet some smaller towns and villages, choosing to acknowledge the defeat of the Federals, "gave up appealing for troops and made terms with the rebels instead" (45). Lira Pérez attempted this strategy. His brother-in-law Salvador Herrera told Esther that Francisco's father made an agreement with the rebels in Jerez, paying money to them in return for a guarantee of his safety.

The Federal withdrawal from the countryside during the summer of 1913 was paralleled by a general exodus of middle- and upper-class groups (45). His agreement broken in the fall of 1913, Lira Perez's life was in peril. Pursued by Maderista soldiers, he next found himself among the thousands of "well-to-do" refugees fleeing to the major cities of the northeast (45). He made his way to Torreón, where he hoped his anonymity, as well as the city's geographic distance from Jerez, would provide a measure of protection. (Instead, with the arrival of Pancho Villa's Division of the North only a few months later, in March 1914, Torreón would be the site of one of the bloodiest battles of the revolution, witnessed by Lira Pérez and his family. Later, in August, Natera's Zacatecan forces joined up with Villa's army to lay siege to the city of Zacatecas, killing 6,000 Federal troops in three days.)

By the end of 1913, the Zacatecan Constitutionalists controlled most of the state, with the exception of the capital, where the Huertistas remained in power (Flores 1996, 158). The haciendas surrounding Jerez were "left in the hands of overseers or of peons, sharecroppers and villagers, and most of the smaller towns in the region were stripped of their *caciques*, officials and elite families" (Knight 1986, 46). Lira Pérez's exile thus represents the widespread and random nature of the process of military and political dissolution in Mexico during 1913–14. As Knight explains:

> Historians of the Revolution are wont to trace its advance with an eye on the major cities. But their fall came at the end of a long sequence, beginning with the mountains and remote hamlets, then the villages and scattered mining camps, finally the provincial towns and state capitals. The major revolutionary armies of the north, it is true, advanced on Mexico City in 1914 in a roughly progressive, geographical fashion.

> But long before—and also while—this advance took place, there was a complementary revolutionary advance which cannot be mapped, save metaphorically. This took the form, not of a tide sweeping the country, but rather of an insidiously rising water level, which first inundated the rural areas . . . and finally swamped [the cities] to cover the face of the earth like Noah's flood. (46)

By the beginning of 1914, Lira Pérez's situation was desperate. Now in his late fifties, he had several young children to provide for as well as a son by a previous marriage fighting in the Federal Army. Though freed from the Maderista threat in Jerez, he was now a refugee bereft of property and a means of employment. When by chance he landed in Torreón in time to witness one of the great battles of the civil war, he too must have felt helpless before the flood.

Orphans of History

> I do not buy all the myths of the tribe into which I was born. . . . I will not glorify those aspects of my culture which have injured me and which have injured me in the name of protecting me.
>
> —Gloria Anzaldúa, *Borderlands/La Frontera*

The further information that Berta Róbles provided in her definitive deconstruction of the Pérez patriarchal legend—a dismantling completed by my family's knowledge of Lira Pérez's affair with María Herrera as well as the political context provided above—suggests that my grandfather's father abused his privileged status in Jerez not only to violate the young Róbles daughter sexually but also to evade responsibility for his actions. In the male-dominated, economically polarized hacienda world, Lira Pérez's elite peers may well have viewed his actions as an "indiscretion." The marginalized status of women in nineteenth-century Mexico would certainly support this view. Describing the condition of women in Mexico City during this period, Sylvia Marina Arrom observes that

> the pater familias exercised his authority without restraints, unencumbered by tradition or competing power; he completely controlled his wife's legal acts, property and person, being able to claim her domestic services, obedience and sexual fidelity (although the double standard granted him sexual freedom); he made all important decisions to enforce his will upon its members using whatever means he deemed necessary. (quoted in Griswold del Castillo 1989, 86)

As Lira Pérez's story demonstrates, an important aspect of the ideal of patriarchal authority in Mexico involved the subordinate position of women, one defined by tradition. Richard Griswold del Castillo explains:

> In the Iberian Catholic and the pre-Columbian traditions, women were supposed to accept absolute male authority in the household. Spanish laws, including the *Siete Partidas*, frequently described the relationship between husband and wife in monarchical terms. . . . Men were the "rulers," women the "subjects"; husbands were the "absolute monarchs" of the "nation" of the family. (88)

The feudalistic social structure of the Porfirian hacienda system, controlled by patriarchs who passed their property and *patrón* status on to the eldest son, intensified the subordination and exploitation of female peons, servants, and tenants. By depicting the rapes committed by the cacique Páramo as well as by his teenage son, Miguel, Rulfo's *Pedro Páramo* foregrounds the crisis of abused campesino women under the hacienda system.

When local Maderistas rebelled in the summer of 1913, Lira Pérez's "indiscretion" was likely only one of the many moral transgressions held against the Jerez hacendados and their associates. I have learned from interviews with other family members that Dominga must have been at least twenty-five years younger than Lira Pérez, and while my relatives today refuse to discuss the topic, the evidence seems convincing that Lira Pérez raped Dominga. Only such an action would account fully for Berta's outburst and Nico's comment at the funeral, as well as the other corroborating stories that I have subsequently gathered.[31]

The silencing of Dominga's voice in my family history emblematizes that elaborate suppression of submerged power relations and social antagonisms found in many of the early Mexican American autobiographies. In such texts, nostalgia for an idealized past is often the narrator's dominant self-fashioning technique. Though a highly subjective narrative constructed by deeply interested individuals over three generations, Berta's anti-nostalgic denunciation of the Pérez patriarch lays bare fundamental class and gender conflicts buried deep within the imaginary pastoral sociocultural terrain of "Memorias." Lira Pérez's elite class status before the civil war, a position bolstered by the capitalist modernization of the Mexican hacienda economy under the Díaz regime, probably would have protected him from any accusation by the Róbles family, apparently people of a lower, though not necessarily peasant, class whose own economic situation worsened considerably during the war. Working for hacendados for more than thirty years would have ensured for my grandfather's father the protection of those men who for decades had wielded political and economic authority in the region. Even a university-educated crony of the hacendados, however, could not in 1912 have foreseen the uprisings in Jerez only a year later, let alone the coming social upheaval.

Padilla's study of early Mexican American autobiographies has informed my attempts to describe the range of contradictory socio-ideological and cultural meanings inscribed in my grandfather's autobiography. Padilla adroitly positions Mexican American autobiographies in relation to their authors' sociohistorical and cultural condition under Anglo-American domination. He also demonstrates the complex strategies by which they forge an identity for themselves out of their marginalized lives. Valuable not only as foundational Mexican American literary texts, the heroic, self-told stories of formerly unknown Mexican American writers also disclose the monumental injustice Mexican American society has suffered through the exclusion of Chicano works from mainstream American literary and cultural discourse. Beginning as early as 1848, the sustained institutional suppression of such works within the context of US sociocultural domination suggests how great a challenge critics and theorists of Mexican American literature face as they conduct their recuperative and interpretive projects. My History, Not Yours is the culmination of a substantial body of research and criticism on Mexican American autobiography. To those who would dismiss the writings of these early autobiographers for their presumed "hacienda syndrome," Padilla replies with a distinctly historicized sense of the complex imbrication of these autobiographers' private and public struggles as Mexican American "orphans" in a land that was once their cultural, spiritual, and geographic home. Rosaura Sánchez's recent scholarship on nineteenth-century Mexican American writing follows in the path created by Padilla's retrieval project and particularly the historicist impetus that informs it. Yet Sánchez's work expands on Padilla's theoretical paradigm as well as on his treatment of the socio-ideological and political context of the Californio narratives. As Sánchez puts it, her study is "rooted in cultural politics" and thus considers "cultural production as inseparable from structural and agential relations." For that reason, it "takes on and examines the issue of representation by a subaltern population within the context of relations of production, social restructuring, and collective agency" (1995, x). Because Sánchez offers a more comprehensive study of that body of testimonials by Californios collected by Bancroft in the

1870s, and takes Padilla's historicist premises an important step forward through its dialectical analysis grounded in feminist, postcolonial, and especially Marxist theory, her work will prove to be indispensable to the future study of nineteenth-century Mexican American literature.[32]

Sánchez's aim in *Telling Identities* may be said to parallel my own. As Berta Róbles's narrative powerfully suggests, such historicizing as Padilla's may still leave the voices of other victims and orphans of history suppressed. They must no longer be silenced. Although the story of Dominga Róbles has been elaborately sublimated within my own family consciousness for more than eighty years, her distant voice, if not yet fully retrieved, has finally been acknowledged. Berta's dramatic statement at the funeral, as well as the other family secrets presented in this essay, should thus remind scholars intent on recovering marginalized texts and establishing the discursive genealogy of suppressed (Chicano) literary traditions that the powerfully disruptive autobiographical impulse to self-invention is always at work. The same may be said of many historiographic texts. Her confrontation with my grandfather's narrative, and her implicit challenge to Padilla's autobiography model has a more fundamental purpose as well. Just as her story has profoundly influenced my own interpretation of my grandfather's text, as students of Mexican American autobiography, literature, and history, we must recognize and identify the omissions, inaccuracies, misrepresentations, and lies—both conscious and unconscious—in other foundational Mexican American narratives if we wish to move toward a version of history closer to the "truth" than we can ever approach through "close" readings of Mexican American autobiographies and other historical works. As I've suggested, Sánchez's research on the California testimonies has already begun to move Chicano autobiography and historical studies in this productive direction. Engaging the socio-ideological suppressions of nineteenth-century autobiographers, and particularly their pre-American nostalgic sublimations, will help scholars both recuperate and critique how their subjects represent the existential and cultural dilemmas of their fragmented existence. Though Berta's disclosure does not necessarily provide a more representative version of the Mexican American past, it certainly reveals the remarkable energy of my grandfather's retrospective desire, after a life in exile as a cultural "orphan" torn between Mexico and the United States, to resist his community's "present" sociocultural erasure and fragmentation by imaginatively restoring and tenaciously repressing the social reality of his Mexican ancestors.

Padilla notes that Mariano Guadalupe Vallejo's autobiography operates as a eulogy to a Mexican "social and cultural subjectivity stranded in the past over and against a colonized subjectivity accommodating and acquiescent toward an American social formation that had exploited and displaced [Mexicans]" (1993, 87). Like many modern Mexican immigrant narrators, Vallejo and other nineteenth-century Mexican American authors write from the cultural perspective of a marginalized community dislocated and excluded by colonizing American institutions. Just as my grandfather's orphanhood symbolizes his immigrant community's sociocultural break with the past *and* a continued alienation from both Mexico and the United States, Vallejo and early autobiographers write as culturally and economically deracinated *huérfanos* (orphans), compelled to reconstruct in narrative an earlier "heroic" world that American society has denigrated, destroyed, or simply forgotten. Undeniably, like Vallejo and other early autobiographers, my grandfather struggled in his writings to negotiate his "bicultural" status in the United States without rejecting Anglo-American culture in toto. My grandfather honored this country, and he was in turn very proud of being an American citizen. As a Mexican exploited and dispossessed by United States social formations, however, he also resisted this political and sociocultural hegemony. Along with the family of Dominga Róbles, a true orphan of history, we can only wish that my grandfather had also been capable of speaking to similar repressions in the hacienda sociocultural economy of his Mexican forebears. His nostalgic recovery of his father's life story today instructs others who continue to pursue the recuperation of our Chicano origins.

Epilogue

> On the second day, a sail drew near, nearer, and picked me up at last. It was the devious-cruising Rachel, that in her retracing search after her missing children, only found another orphan.
>
> —Herman Melville, Moby Dick

Since October 17, 1994, when my grandfather left on a trip to Mexico, my family has received no word from him, nor any other information that would tell us what may have happened to him or whether he is still alive. A missing person's report was filed with the US and Mexican police, and the disappearance was publicized in several newspapers in Los Angeles and along the United States–Mexican border. In late 1994, the Ventura County Police Department informed us that my grandfather did arrive on October 17 at the Los Angeles bus depot downtown, where he purchased a ticket to the Mexican border city of Tijuana. The police, however, could not determine whether he boarded the bus that would have taken him to Mexico. Just as the California and Mexican authorities have been confounded by this case, my family has been frustrated in its efforts to find out what may have become of my grandfather. Our relatives in central and northern Mexico have heard nothing from him; hospitals, funeral homes, and public institutions that we have contacted in Mexico and the United States have no record of his admittance; media announcements of his disappearance ultimately yielded no rewarding clues. After almost five years of exasperation and grief, we have grown resigned to the likelihood that the circumstances of his death will remain a mystery. On the anniversary of his departure later this year, we will hold a memorial service to honor my grandfather.

When he boarded a bus in Fillmore, California, at a location just down the road from where, as a young farmworker seeking employment at the Sespe Ranch, he had arrived sixty years earlier, my grandfather was not carrying any luggage and, as he was wont to do in his old age, probably had no identification. He was eighty-six years old, underweight, and in poor health. His adopted community of more than half a century must have seemed strangely different from the town that he had first seen in his youth. After his wife died, he lived alone in a tract house that he never considered his true home because it was "far away" (five miles) from the Mexican community at Sespe Village where he had reared his children and where, against their wishes, he continued to live until 1970. Beginning in the late 1940s, the children had all left the village for Los Angeles; his grandchildren and great-grandchildren, all of them assimilated and urban, were now further removed from their patriarch's Mexican rural community and culture.

Some would probably never know what the workers' camp at Sespe meant to my grandfather. The Mexican village, built above the banks of a river and set amid citrus and avocado orchards as well as eucalyptus and oak trees, had once been a thriving and self-sustaining community filled with well-tended homes and productive gardens—a place where for decades the language, customs, and culture of Mexico were practiced and maintained in the midst of an Anglo-dominated environment that was hostile toward and exploitative of Mexicans. My grandfather was proud of the town and of the people who had been a part of it. When he first arrived there, he knew that the village, from its houses to its trees and flowers, was owned by the Spalding family, and that Mexican workers and their families could be evicted on short notice at the whim of its owners.[33] Yet its rural and pastoral qualities must have attracted my grandfather from the outset, perhaps reminding him of his secure and idyllic hacienda childhood alongside his father and grandmother Hipólita at San Juan de las Calabasas near Jerez. My Aunt Esther's version of her childhood at Sespe supports this very characterization of the physical setting of the rancho. Though Esther is elsewhere highly critical of the feudal nature of ranch society, she describes its physical setting nostalgically in her essay as a "little paradise that was surrounded on three sides by lemon and orange orchards and completely isolated from the American community five miles away . . . a place where the skies were clear, the air fresh, the nearby mountains high and majestic, and the river that bordered the village a haven for a man and his three growing sons."

Until it was demolished five years ago, Sespe Village remained a functioning workers' camp for Mexican agricultural laborers and their families. One year before the camp was razed, my parents, grandparents, and I visited the town for the last time. Access to the village was the same as it had been fifty years earlier, a bumpy dirt road whose entrance was barely visible from the highway and which wound for a half mile through a thick grove of orange and avocado trees and then along the Sespe River to the dusty outskirts of the town. Amid the 150 shotgun houses in disrepair and decay, we found the house where my father and his brothers and sisters spent their childhoods. My grandparents and my father were upset and disappointed at the condition of the dilapidated house, and especially the growth of weeds and vegetation engulfing it and the other homes. My father recalled this home, and the Mexican village of his youth, in a manner reminiscent of his father's own nostalgic recollection of the bountiful hacienda landscape where Juan Lira Pérez had lived.

Though most of its full-time residents had already deserted Sespe Village, as we drove through the town we met an old man, Pancho Casas, Nico's brother-in-law and a close friend of my grandfather, whose family had lived in the camp since the time of my grandfather's arrival in 1936. Pancho had been evicted from Sespe for participating in the 1941 strike; he returned to the village several years later. Knowing that the last inhabitants of the workers' camp were young immigrants from Mexico, I was astonished at meeting, at that late date, a distant relative and an original resident from my grandfather's generation. I half-expected other ghosts from my grandfather's past to appear—perhaps, as I now reflect on that visit, his lost half-brother Paulo, whose distant cousins (Nico and his siblings) had lived in Sespe Village from the 1920s through the 1960s. But, as it turned out, Mr. Casas was at that moment preparing to move. His departure marked the end of my family's decades-long residence in Sespe Village. Although the history of the community was erased from the official record, it lives in the collective memory of Sespe's Chicano descendants.

Chronology: The Life of Francisco Róbles Pérez

1908   Born in Jerez, Zacatecas, Mexico, to Juan Lira Pérez and Juliana Róbles Pérez.

1911   Thirty-five year reign of Porfirio Díaz ends.

1912   Half-brother/cousin Paulo Róbles Pérez and half-brother Lucas Herrera Pérez born in Jerez.

1908–13   Childhood in Jerez and San Juan de las Calabasas.

1913   Mother dies. Maderista rebels take Jerez.

1914   Half-sister Diega Herrera Pérez born. Civil War breaks out throughout rural Zacatecas. Flees with father and step-mother María Herrera. In Coahuila, father and son witness the Battle of Torreón.

1914–17   Moves with father throughout north-central Mexico. Francisco attends school to the third grade.

1917   Half-sister Paula Herrera Pérez born in Torreón.

1919   Father dies in Gómez Palacios, Durango. Francisco works as a servant for a wealthy family.

1920   Works as a servant for a North American dentist in Gómez Palacios.

1921   Emigrates to the United States with the Herrera family, in-laws to his father.

1922   Dominga Róbles dies in Jerez.

1923   Works as a farm laborer in Orange County, California. Lives with the Herrera family.

1924   Marries Concepción Herrera in Whittier, California.

1925   Daughter Esther Brígida Herrera Pérez born in Placentia.

1927   Son Juan Francisco Herrera Pérez born in Placentia.

1930   Son Antonio Cirildo Herrera Pérez born in Placentia.

1933   Son David Herrera Pérez born in Placentia.

1936   Citrus workers strike in Orange County.

1935   Blacklisted by ranchers for organizing Mexican agricultural workers, Francisco is forced to leave Orange County. Moves family to Ventura County. Takes a job as a farm laborer at Rancho Sespe, owned by the Spalding sports equipment manufacturing family.

1937	Daughter María Celia Herrera Pérez born in Sespe Village.
1935–77	Works for the Spalding family at Rancho Sespe.
1957	Grandson Vincent Anthony Pérez born.
1977	Retires from job at Rancho Sespe.
1985	Begins taped narration of his autobiography to grandson Vincent. Paulo Róbles Pérez dies in Jerez, Mexico.
1990	Begins work on a written autobiography.
1992	Funeral of Isabel "Chavela" Róbles.
1994	Leaves on trip to Mexico. Reported missing and believed dead by family.

Postscript (2020)

My own fondest childhood memories are of visiting my grandparents when they still lived in the village as well as later on, when they resided in Fillmore, the nearby town also set amid citrus farms, where my grandmother had separately bought a home. After my grandfather retired from Rancho Sespe in 1973, he worked for eight years as the caretaker at another ranch, owned by the Vantree family and situated on the Sespe River at the entrance to Sespe Canyon, a mile or so from town. My grandfather tended the ranch's garden and stables and lived in a small guest house built at the edge of the river—really a tiny frame cabin with only a fireplace for heat—where we often visited. In 1979, winter storms turned the river into a torrent, washing away the cabin. A few years later, when the Vantree ranch house burned to the ground, my grandfather finally returned to live with his wife in Fillmore. Some of us wondered why he had chosen to live and work at another ranch after he had retired, under the authority of yet another wealthy rancher. I now see that it was not only because my grandfather enjoyed the tasks and pleasures of ranch life but also because he missed Sespe.

My grandfather loved Rancho Sespe not only because it was his home and workplace for almost four decades, the place where he and his wife Concepción raised their children and where his family's sweat and tears had commingled with soil. Nor can his attachment be explained entirely by either the socioeconomic circumstances that geographically constrained his life as a farm worker or his desire to return imaginatively to the mythic agrarian landscape of his childhood in rural Zacatecas. He also loved Rancho Sespe—which he always called the last great hacienda in California—because it reproduced for him the agrarian (hacienda) social order that his father Juan Lira Pérez had known in Mexico. Though always exploitative, and often brutally so, in its treatment of its Mexican laborers, as Esther and my father vividly remember, Rancho Sespe also offered my grandfather a traditional agrarian space of social stability, and hence a measure of Mexican ethnic cultural coherence, that he had not formerly experienced as an immigrant farm worker in the United States. This sense of space and stability may explain why my grandfather never spoke ill of Mr. Spalding, whom he liked and respected. (It took the writing of this narrative for me to understand and accept my grandfather's affection for a figure whom my father and aunt despised.) Within the limits of Rancho Sespe's racialized social hierarchy, which prohibited union organizing among its largely Mexican work force, my grandfather knew that he would have a secure job and small home in the Mexican Village where he could raise his children without the arduous trials of migrant farm worker life. In return, Mr. Spalding had a loyal worker for life. Hence my grandfather found solace as a displaced Mexican immigrant not only by nostalgically remembering the ancestral agrarian society that he and his family had once known in Mexico but also by adopting as a home a similar paternalistic agrarian space in the United States. The paternalistic bond between Mr. Spalding and my grandfather, strengthened by my grandfather's fierce identification with Rancho Sespe over a span of decades, was never broken. Mr. Spalding was buried on a hill overlooking his beloved ranch, where his most trusted Mexican employee, my grandfather, dug his grave, set his headstone, and poured the cement for his tomb. In contrast to my grandfather's affective bond with his patron, to this day, for my own father, Mr. Spalding's headstone stands as a monument to the Mexican American community's long-aggrieved social condition under Rancho Sespe's semifeudal labor system.

My grandfather's immersion in the social world of the hacienda, his irrevocable attachment to the premodern rural landscape of his childhood, symbolizes the proximity of the semifeudal and agrarian past of the imagined Mexican American national community. His life as an immigrant buffeted by civil and social turmoil similarly registered that convulsive transformation of Mexican agrarian society generated by the forces of modernity in the late nineteenth and early twentieth centuries. This journey from the precapitalist rural "third" world to the modern industrial capitalist "first" world has, of course, been the historical patrimony of immigrants from other populations in other regions throughout the modern era. Though compelled by socioeconomic circumstances to return to a semifeudal social landscape that he would eventually adopt as his home, my grandfather's life journey in this sense captured the struggles of all agrarian populations from traditional cultures plunged into the industrial capitalist "first" world by the modernizing forces of history.

The collective history of Mexican Americans—their collective memory—is rooted in the agrarian cultural geography of prerevolutionary Mexico and the Spanish colonial Southwest. Many early Mexican (American) hacienda writings illustrate the historical immediacy of this inheritance. In these works, the hacienda memory-place resonates with charged meaning as a socially fraught symbol of Mexican (American) identity and origins. Set against a racialized US sociopolitical landscape, the hacienda delineates in these texts an emergent Mexican (American) subjectivity struggling ambiguously against the threat of discursive erasure and material loss. More generally, the hacienda as memory-place serves as a symbolic resolution to social contradictions resulting from the cataclysmic decline of Mexican (American) agrarian ranch society in the late nineteenth and early twentieth centuries, a decline driven by the expansion of (US) industrial capitalism. Though González and Raleigh's *Caballero* (1996) stands as a notable exception by overtly identifying the hacienda's social contradictions, in the texts I have examined, the hacienda as memory-place works to cement history and memory together into an iconic monument to the past, burying contrary memories in the project to (re)constitute an enabling Mexican (American) historical subjectivity. Hacienda narratives, however, cannot evade the silenced voices of the Mexican past buried deep within the semifeudal agrarian landscape they describe. The ambiguous symbolic meaning of the hacienda as a Mexican American site of memory thus serves as an eloquent illustration of Pierre Nora's conception of memory-places as "fleeting incursions of the sacred [past] into a disenchanted [modern] world; vestiges of parochial loyalties in a society that is busily effacing all parochialisms; de facto differentiations in a society that levels on principle; signs of recognition and group affiliation in a society that tends to recognize only individuals" (1996, 7).

Despite such dissonances and ambiguities within Mexican American cultural memory, scholars and students of the Mexican American past must also remember the hacienda, seeing in it a sign of sociohistorical differences as well as commonality within the imagined Mexican American national community, a sign of the range of cultural identities, rooted in a foundational colonial past, that have emerged through time from disparate sociocultural and economic processes.

116

Notes

This essay, originally titled "Heroes and Orphans of the Hacienda: Narratives of a Mexican American Family," by Vincent Pérez, is reprinted from *I Am Aztlán: The Personal Essay in Chicano Studies* (Los Angeles: UCLA Chicano Studies Research Center Press, 2004) and from *Aztlán: A Journal of Chicano Studies* 24, no. 1 (1999).

This essay is excerpted from "Heroes and Orphans: Testimonial Memory as Resistance and Repression in Francisco Róbles Pérez's 'Memories,'" which appeared in *Biography* 20, no 1 (1997). An earlier version of this article was presented in December 1994 at the Recovery Project Conference.

I would like to acknowledge the help and support of my aunt, Esther Pérez Doran in the writing of this essay. The daughter and eldest child of Francisco Róbles Pérez, and the first Pérez of her generation to attend college, Esther is today a marriage, family, and child counselor and a clinical specialist in psychiatric nursing. She is employed at the Los Angeles Veterans Administration Medical Center's Post-Traumatic Stress Disorder Unit. Without her love, inspiration, knowledge, and guidance, the truths that I have tried to bring to light in this article could not have been recovered.

1. Two studies of Mexican American autobiography, both of which draw upon previous research on the nineteenth-century origins of Chicano literature, are Genaro M. Padilla's *My History, Not Yours*, and Rosaura Sánchez's *Telling Identities: The California Testimonies*. Padilla's model provides the discursive framework for my analysis of modern Mexican American immigrant autobiography. For two recent articles that engage issues linked to Padilla's discussion, see Rebolledo (1990) and Goldman (1992). The first studies to deal specifically with Chicano autobiography as a genre are Márquez 1984, Padilla 1984, and Saldívar 1985.

2. See Saldívar 1990 and 1985, particularly chapter seven. Following Bruce-Novoa's (1990) assessment of recent developments in Chicano literary theory and particularly works by Ramón Saldívar and José David Saldívar, my examination of Mexican American autobiography takes as its underlying critical assumptions the need for "dialectical analysis that takes history into consideration as another text," and the idea "that true dialectical thought is always self-critical" (Bruce-Novoa 1990, 171).

3. The "Recovering the United States Hispanic Literary Heritage" project, under the direction of Nicolás Kanellos at the University of Houston, has been at the forefront of this recuperative endeavor. See Gutiérrez (1993) and Gonzáles-Berry (1996) for anthologies of critical essays collected and published through this project.

4. Francisco Róbles Pérez's "Memorias" is an unpublished manuscript. All subsequent paginations refer to the seventy-page text that I have compiled from my transcription of two notebooks from the original handwritten manuscript. All translations of this text are mine.

5. Though called "aunt" by my father, Isabel "Chavela" Róbles was actually my grandfather's first cousin, the niece of Juliana Róbles and first cousin of Berta Róbles (see fig. 4).

6. Raymund A. Paredes uses this term to highlight sociocultural and ideological contradictions in writings by early New Mexican "Hispano" writers, and to call attention to what he views as the works' "contrived and derivative romanticism" (1982, 52–53).

7. For Chicana feminist approaches to Chicano/Mexicano culture and history that intersect my analysis of the Róbles critique of Mexicano patriarchy, see the distinguished body of writings produced over the past ten years by Rosaura Sánchez (1995), Norma Alarcón (1993), Gloria Anzaldúa (1987), Ana Castillo (1994), Cherríe Moraga (1983), María Herrera-Sobek (1990), Tey Diana Rebolledo (1993), and Adelaida R. del Castillo (1990). Because of the Chicana's position within a patriarchal society, many Chicana writers are keenly attuned to the historical and ideological issues that I raise throughout this article. Their writings have in turn helped me to interpret and historicize my grandfather's narrative. Yet, at the same time, several Chicana cultural critics have posited a unitary Mexican homeland and therefore apparently created ideologically self-contradictory texts. As Padilla has explained, "Anzaldúa and other recent Chicano/a autobiographers, although recognizing themselves as occupying a social space of multiple identities, speak another (contradictory?) desire for a unitary and collective cultural economy imagined in the past, or on the other side of the border" (1993, 238).

8. For an analysis of this question as it has arisen in Chicano poetry, see Pérez-Torres (1995), chapters two and three.

9. Sociologist Mario Barrera notes the diverse socioeconomic origins of early twentieth-century Mexican emigrants to the United States: "The background of the immigrants prior to migrating is a little explored topic. The impression most writers have is that the immigrants during this period were largely agricultural workers in Mexico, notwithstanding the fact that the Mexican Revolution of 1910–20 also caused people of higher occupational categories to migrate. Still, there are indications that the immigrants were not necessarily representative of the largely rural, agricultural population in Mexico at that time" (1979, 67). Barrera cites a 1944 survey in San Bernardino, California, of men who had come to the United States from Mexico in the early part of the century, which indicated that only about a third of them had been engaged in hacienda work in Mexico.

10. Doroteo Arango (Francisco "Pancho" Villa) (1877–1922) was the legendary general of the famous Division of the North, which sought to overthrow the Mexican government beginning in 1913. In March to April of 1914, in the town of Torreón, Coahuila, my grandfather and his father crossed paths with Villa's army, as they were caught in "the most grueling and bloody contest in the long annals of the Mexican Revolution" (Knight 1986, 143) "Memorias" describes the artillery and infantry siege by Villa's Constitutionalist army from the perspective of a child barricaded in a house with his family. After days of explosions that included, according to my grandfather, the destruction of a nearby train filled with ammunition, and several days more of street fighting, the battle ended with the Villistas victorious. My grandfather and his family emerged from their house to search for food and water. "In the street there were mountains of dead bodies," my grandfather writes, "both soldiers and their horses, thousands of dead piled on each other in the streets, all shot and covered with blood . . . the plumes of smoke and soot made the sky

look yellow, because all of the *fincas* (ranches) near the town had been burned and all of the businesses and stores in town had been sacked and burned in just a few days" (17). As John Reed observes in his first-hand account of the battle, after the fighting ended there were "vultures gorging themselves on dead horses; the prolific executions of prisoners, the faint smell of corpses and the rising smoke of dozens of funeral pyres" (Reed as quoted in Knight 1986, 143). While my grandfather walked through a street near his house, he discovered a revolver. He recalled dragging the gun home to give to his father. Grandfather's most vivid memory of this event is of his father, after seeing the gift, angrily throwing it outside. He admonished his son harshly for drawing attention to their family during a dangerous time.

11. See, for example, Ramón Saldívar (1990) and José David Saldívar (1991). For historical studies that examine Mexican American history but do not foreground links to the Mexican period in the Southwest, see Acuña (1988) and De Leon (1982). Though delving critically into Mexican hacienda society in Texas, Montejano (1987) focuses on Mexican American dispossession after the United States takeover. Of the book-length histories written by Mexican American scholars, only Ramón A. Gutiérrez (1991) and Armando C. Alonzo (1998) delve at length into the history of the Mexican period.

12. Ramón Gutiérrez examined how Chicano historiography has traditionally structured the past in a recent lecture at the University of Texas at Austin. He identified five "typologies" based on the ideological perspective of the historian and the period chosen as the "inception" of Chicano history. According to Gutiérrez, the "bourgeois" version selects 30,000 BC as the point of origin; the "proletarian," 1910; the "internal colonial," 1848; the "Feminist," 1519; and the "conjunctural or postmodernist," 1836. The "proletarian" model, according to Gutiérrez, dominates the written record, demonstrating that Chicano historical scholarship has been governed and defined by studies of the modern period. See his "Time, Space, and Becoming: Narratives of Chicano History," a lecture presented at the University of Texas at Austin, March 11, 1999.

13. Quoted in Martin (1989, 260–61).

14. I will refer to "Memorias" throughout as an autobiography rather than as a *testimonio* (testimonial). The collaborative nature of my genealogical project implies, however, that my grandfather's account may also be classified as a testimonial. Rosaura Sánchez has distinguished testimonials from autobiographies by identifying their collaborative and mediated qualities. According to Sánchez, while autobiography "offers a self-generated/agential discursive construction of 'self' within particular social spaces," the testimonial is the product of a collaboration involving an interviewer/editor. The production of the testimonial is "mediated and filtered through a second, more powerful agency" so that its narrating voice "is othered in terms of production as well as at the discursive level." In works of this type, "narrating agency . . . is thus not simply that of the speaking subject but also that of the editing and writing subject" (1995, 8). Both the "production" and recuperation of "Memorias" are obviously mediated by my own involvement as an interviewer, editor, critic—as well as a relative of the interviewee. The final manuscript will, for instance, include transcribed oral responses to questions posed to my grandfather during tape-recorded interviews.

119

15. The scale of this social upheaval and its impact on the Southwest United States are suggested by Meier and Ribera (1993) in their history of Mexican Americans:

> The 1910 revolution, a period of incredible violence and confusion, directly affected the Southwest. Out of fifteen million Mexicans, an estimated one million lost their lives in the decade of revolution, and there was a large-scale displacement of people. Thousands fled from the countryside into the larger towns and cities of Mexico; at the same time other thousands fled northward to the United States. No one knows precisely how many Mexicans were involved in this great exodus; one estimate holds that more than one million Mexicans crossed over into the Southwest between 1910 and 1920. (108–9).

As for my grandfather, "Memorias" suggests that he was abandoned. Any blood relatives of his father had apparently remained in Jerez during the revolution, and the war prevented communication with them. My grandfather mentions a sister (mother of the three Ramirez daughters), but she is spoken of only in passing. Except for several half-siblings, no other living Pérez blood relatives are identified in the text. As I mentioned earlier, another family, the Herreras, in-laws to my grandfather's father and also from Jerez, were extremely important to my grandfather after Lira Pérez died in 1919—in fact, Francisco came to the United States with the Herreras. However, he did not consider them "family"; he always felt like an outsider and "orphan" among them. Lira Pérez apparently married the last of his four wives, María Herrera, by whom he had three children, after he settled in Torreón in 1914, but he had his first child by her, named Lucas, in 1912, while he was married to Juliana Róbles. (It is also possible that both my family and the Róbleses are a year off on the date of Juliana's death; if she died in 1912 rather than 1913, Lira Pérez could perhaps have married María just after his wife died and then had Lucas later that year.) The reason my grandfather felt "abandoned" by his Herrera in-laws was because, two years after his father's death, his step-mother María, rather than embracing her husband's son as a family member (he had been supporting himself as a servant for two years), instead handed him a train ticket to the United States and "gave" him to her brothers who were then preparing to emigrate. She and her own children never emigrated. (My Aunt Esther believes that María sent Francisco to the United States so that only she and her children would be able to claim Lira Pérez's property in Jerez.) So, although my grandfather was by definition an orphan when he journeyed to the United States, he came here with members of the Herrera family and therefore was not alone and abandoned. Though not mentioned by name in "Memorias," one of the Herreras must have been the person who bought him a pair of shoes at the border (in Mexico he wore only *huaraches*, or sandals). Francisco eventually lived with the Herreras in California for several years, and in 1924 married María's youngest sister, Concepción. "Memorias" states that when my grandfather arrived in 1921 at the Herrera home in Yorba Linda, he had to explain to them who he was. In the middle of a celebration, someone asked for quiet, and, pointing at Francisco, asked, "And who is he?"

16. For a description of Sespe Village, see the epilogue of this article.

17. I use "colonial" in quotes because colonialism actually ended in 1821 with Mexican independence from Spain; Lira Pérez was born in 1856.

18. Jerez de la Frontera, the Andalusian town famous for its sherry wine, was the birthplace of Álvar Núñez Cabeza de Vaca (1490–1560), the first Spaniard to explore a large region of North America. Fernández and Favata explain that Cabeza de Vaca's account of his journey, *La relación* (1542), is one of the first Spanish descriptions of the New World that "calls for a compassionate and tolerant policy toward the natives of the Western Hemisphere" (1993, 11).

19. The subjugation of the indigenous peoples of Mexico during the colonial period took on a distinctly modern (i.e., positivist) cast during the era in which Lira Pérez prospered as a business associate of the Zacatecan hacendados. As Meier and Ribera (1993) observe, between 1880 and 1910:

> The economic policies of the government were promoted by a group of positivists, who planned and worked for a modern, scientifically run Mexico which [they believed] would take its rightful place in the world. They accepted that certain races were less advanced because of heredity and environment; they believed that Indians and their culture were inferior and therefore not a sound base on which to build a modern Mexico. In the name of progress they set out to Europeanize Mexico's Indians, partly as a result of positivist ideas. . . . Indians were brutally hounded, and many were sold into virtual slavery to large landowners. (104)

20. My grandfather foregrounded his alienation from Anglo-American as well as Mexican society and therefore contradicts recent theoretical projections of a transcultural subject who easily traverses cultural borders. Several passages in "Memorias," however, suggest that my grandfather recognized in Mexican American cultural formations a new bicultural subject who occupied a borderlands space. In what may well be one of the earliest written references to a distinctive "Chicano" language and culture, my grandfather recalled one of his first encounters, as a Mexican immigrant, with "pochis" (acculturated, or "faded," Mexicans). On Sundays in 1922, the Mexican American community in Whittier, California, would gather for social events. As my grandfather explained,

> It was there that I made a few friends, two of whom were young *pochas* born in the United States, Rosa and Luisa. One day while we were talking, one of them asked me, "Oye, por qué no nos tritéas?" (Hey, why don't ya treat us?) To which I answered, "Y eso, qué es?" (What do you mean?) The other said, "Pues, que nos des una raspada o una goma." (Well, buy us a snow cone or some gum.) What they meant to say, of course, was "una copa de hielo raspado" (a cup of shaved ice) and "un paquete de chicle" (a pack of gum). The two spoke very poor Spanish. The pochos also called automobiles *carruchas*. The following week, I went out on my first date with Rosa. We went to a *borlote*, which is the word the pochos used for "dance." (22)

Although one might expect my grandfather to have labeled the culture of the "pochos" inferior to his "aristocratic" Mexican hacienda culture, he didn't judge the Americanized "pochos" for their cultural hybridity and even befriended them and their families.

121

21. In a passage that links my grandfather's sense of cultural superiority over Anglo-Americans—because of his "aristocratic" Mexican childhood—to the racism faced by Mexican Americans of that period, "Memorias" depicts the efforts of Mexican immigrants in the late 1930s to attend a movie at a local segregated theater in Fillmore, California:

> In the movie theater in town, which is still in business today, the racists segregated us from the whites. This, after we had worked perhaps sixty hours during the week—and six days a week. They did the same to the Mexican children; there was a separate school for them. We, of course, protested both of these actions. As we told the whites, we paid money for these services like anyone else in town. . . . In any case, the "theater" was a cheap little shack filled with "white fleas" compared to the theaters in my own country. I came from a culture where even the burros sang opera! You see, almost every large town in Mexico has an opera house, quite unlike the United States. (36)

22. Keith Spalding, the multimillionaire co-owner of the Spalding Corporation and hacendado of Rancho Sespe, died in 1963. He left $3,000 in his will to my grandfather, who had been a loyal worker at the ranch for nearly thirty years.

23. According to Acuña:

> By 1910, foreign investors controlled 76 percent of all corporations [in Mexico], 95 percent of mining, 89 percent of industry, 100 percent of oil, and 96 percent of agriculture. The United States owned 38 percent of this investment, Britain 29 percent, and France 27 percent [and] in contrast, 97.1 percent of the families in [the state of] Guanajuato were without land, 96.2 percent in Jalisco, 99.5 percent in Mexico (state), and 99.3 percent in Puebla. (1988, 149–50)

24. Elsewhere in "Memorias," my grandfather used the same phrasing to describe the Pérez side of his family, and as my Aunt Esther told me in a telephone call in May 1995, he always signed his name Francisco Róbles Pérez. In the same conversation, Esther told me that, although my grandfather only briefly mentioned these Róbles forebears in "Memorias," she believes he was as "proud" of the Róbles ancestors as of the Pérez. Nonetheless, the emphasis throughout the early part of "Memorias," the only section in which my grandfather discussed his origins, is on the nobility of the Pérez line. Based on my conversations with him and Esther, I don't think this was entirely conscious, however. As I've pointed out, the only mother he ever knew was the Róbles "matriarch," Doña Hipólita, and "Memorias" clearly shows that he has fond memories of life with her. His remembrances of the Róbles grandparents—conveyed in "Memorias" as well as in conversations with me and with Esther—were completely removed from the Róbles-Pérez clash later initiated by Lira Pérez, and rekindled in 1992 by Berta Róbles. Esther's recollection of her father's castigation of Dominga, when considered alongside Francisco's refusal to acknowledge Paulo at a funeral in 1984, as well as the subsequent revelations brought to light by the Róbles narrative, have led me to conclude that my grandfather must have viewed Paulo as a bastard and interloper—and a legitimate member of *neither* side of his family. Though Paulo was in fact a closer "blood" relative

than half-brother, since their mothers, Juliana and Dominga, were sisters, from my grandfather's perspective, as he expressed it once to Esther, Dominga was to blame for a great many of his father's troubles and most significantly the death of Juliana; this would explain why she is set apart in "Memorias," and in his conversations with family members, from his cherished memories of the Róbles "matriarch."

25. Following his father's example, my grandfather portrays Díaz in a flattering light. He is described in several passages as a benevolent dictator and national hero. The revolutionaries who rose up against Díaz and this dictator's legacy, says grandfather, thus "fought against a government that was unique in the history of Mexico . . . one which had maintained the country at the high social and economic level of the other great nations in the western world at that time" (4). Not surprisingly, Casimiro—Lira Pérez's first son, the product of his second marriage, to Matilde—joined the Federal Army to fight against the Maderista and Villista insurrections.

26. See Adams (1990), Eakin (1985), and Couser (1989). Couser has summarized the development in recent autobiography studies in the wake of the structuralist and poststructuralist critiques of the subject:

> The trend in autobiography studies has been to erode the distinction between fiction and nonfiction and to deconstruct the apparent relation between the self and its textual embodiment. . . . Autobiography, then, is seen not as produced by a preexistent self but as producing a provisional and contingent one. Indeed, that self is seen as bound and (pre)determined by the constraints of the linguistic resources and narrative tropes available to the "author." (19)

27. Though Paulo later adopted Pérez as his legal name, he was reared by the Róbleses and never had contact with members of the Pérez family. So, while Berta Róbles married a "Pérez," she wed into a family known by her own as Róbles.

28. In his last will and testament, Lira Pérez names as his "only heirs" four sons (including Francisco), two daughters, and his fourth wife, María Herrera, who was also his executor. My translation of part of the will reads as follows:

> In the city of Gómez Palacios, in the house on North Morelos Street, on the thirteenth day of May 1919, in the presence of the witnesses Mr. Don Filemón Turado and Mr. Don Antonio Correa, I state that, being gravely ill, and feeling that I am on the brink of death, it is necessary to set forth the following terms [of my will]. . . .
>
> I am the owner of a house in Jerez, Zacatecas. The house is comprised of a corner room, bedroom, kitchen, hall, living room, corral, and waterwheel/well. [I own] two tracts of land in San Juan de las Calabasas and a granary in the same location. The granary [is situated] on a smaller piece of land toward the south, but since I do not have the [proper] papers before me, I cannot specify the measurements [of any of these properties].
>
> It is my wish to leave as my only heirs my wife María Herrera and my children, named Casimiro Pérez, Marcos Pérez, Francisco Pérez, Lucas Pérez, [and] Diega and Paula Pérez. I assign to my wife the role of guardian and administrator [of my estate], whose function will be to divide the shares [of my property] in equal parts, in a manner that she is best able to carry out.

With nothing more to express, I conclude the present private disposition [of my will]. Since I have no other recourse and am in a foreign region, I have not written this document in the proper legal manner before a Notary Public.

29. Although he had two elder half-brothers, the oldest, Casimiro, disappeared in 1914 while serving in the Federal Army, and may have died in one of the battles of that year, while the second, Marcos, the one in the photo, was incapacitated by mental illness and drug addiction during adolescence. My grandfather told me that in 1913, while on leave, Casimiro returned to ask his father for his portion of his inheritance. Lira Pérez sold a tract of land and gave Casimiro the money from the sale. The story from my grandfather is that Casimiro believed he would be killed in the civil war and wanted to spend his inheritance. It seems very likely that he *was* killed in one of the battles of 1914—possibly in Torreón, where his father was living. If Casimiro had ever returned to Jerez after 1921, my grandfather would have learned of it through his younger half-siblings or perhaps through María Herrera's family. As for Marcos, if he had gone with Lira Pérez when he was forced to leave Jerez, my grandfather probably would have mentioned it. Apparently, Marcos was later brought to his father in Torreón. Marcos is mentioned in "Memorias" for his odd behavior as a teenager in Torreón—namely, public nudity and petty crime. The last we hear of this half-brother is when my grandfather, leaving in 1921 to go to the United States, says goodbye to him at the train station. My grandfather says the Herrera family never knew what became of Marcos; the story I have heard is that he left town when still a teenager and wasn't heard from again.

30. A number of parallels between my grandfather's childhood and the life of the Mexican novelist Juan Rulfo stand out. Though born ten years after my grandfather in 1918, Rulfo was from the state of Jalisco, which borders Zacatecas. (The name "La Bufa," the mountain landmark near the city of Zacatecas described in my grandfather's account, comes from the hill's resemblance to an animal's bladder—an allusion used in the Rulfo quote [see page 27]). Both writers were born into the upper class, and both were orphaned as young children during the civil war. Rulfo's hometown, Apulco, was sacked and burned by armed insurgents, and his father was murdered in 1923 while fleeing. According to some scholars, Rulfo's father was killed by peasant insurrectionists, though in an interview the author denied knowing who was responsible. *Pedro Páramo*, Rulfo's nostalgic re-creation of the hacienda community of his childhood, addresses orphanhood and "origins" as central themes. A more remarkable coincidence is Rulfo's family name. After his mother died in 1927, Rulfo was taken in by her relatives in Mexico City, who required that he use their name—Pérez (the author's full name was Juan Pérez Rulfo).

31. Two stories that provide circumstantial evidence are my grandfather's narrative of Lira Pérez's forced flight due to his expected execution by local insurrectionists, some of whom could have been Róbleses, and his suggestion that Dominga Róbles was responsible not only for her relationship with his father but also for his mother's death. The latter narrative tells us that my grandfather may well have always known about the Róbles complaint and perhaps of the rape accusation. His claim that Dominga caused Juliana's death may have been a response to the rape

accusation. This also makes it easier to see why he could never acknowledge Paulo as his half-brother.

32. Sánchez discusses but does not foreground the suppressions and exclusions in the Californio testimonios. Her study argues that the nineteenth-century world of Alta California "was not an idyllic 'pastoral' society," but rather a "labor-intensive . . . economy with a largely 'unfree' labor force made up of Indian men and women whose ancestors had lived on those lands for generations" (1995, 168). Thus, all Californios, according to Sánchez, do not get equal time in the testimonials. "The nonpropertied classes and what [Hubert] Bancroft calls the plebeian 'humble *ranchero*' are largely absent or mentioned only in passing. Significantly, the Indians are very visible as the Other of the Californios. . . . In every case, representation [in the testimonials] follows the ideological perspectives of dominant segments of the Californio population, perspectives often at odds with those of other factions, given regional and social divisions of Californio society (10).

33. According to my father, Anthony Pérez, during one week in 1941, 80 percent of the families in Sespe were evicted because of their involvement with a labor strike against the Spalding-owned ranch. See Menchaca (1995, 83–89).

Works Cited

Acuña, Rodolfo. 1988. *Occupied America: A History of Chicanos*. New York: HarperCollins.

Adams, Timothy Dow. 1990. *Telling Lies in Modern American Autobiography*. Chapel Hill: University of North Carolina Press.

Alarcón, Norma. 1989. *The Sexuality of Latinas*. Berkeley: Third Woman Press.

———. 1991. "The Theoretical Subject(s) of This Bridge Called My Back." In *Criticism in the Borderlands: Studies in Chicano Literature, Culture, and Ideology*, edited by Héctor Calderón and José David Saldívar, 28–39. Durham, NC: Duke University Press.

———, ed. 1993. *Chicana Critical Issues*. Berkeley: Third Woman Press.

Alonzo, Armando C. 1998. *Tejano Legacy: Rancheros and Settlers in South Texas, 1734–1900*. Albuquerque: University of New Mexico Press.

The Americas Review: A Review of Hispanic Literature and Art of the USA 16, no. 3–4 (Fall–Winter 1988). Special issue on "United States Hispanic Autobiography."

Anzaldúa, Gloria. 1987. *Borderlands/La Frontera: The New Mestiza*. San Francisco: Spinsters/Aunt Lute.

Arriaga, Ponciano. 1993. "The Dispossessed of Rural Mexico." In *Latin America, Conflict and Creation: A Historical Reader*, edited by E. Bradford Burns. Englewood Cliffs, NJ: Prentice Hall.

Barrera, Mario. 1979. *Race and Class in the Southwest: A Theory of Racial Inequality*. South Bend, IN: University of Notre Dame Press.

———. 1990. *Retrospace: Collected Essays on Chicano Literature*. Houston: Arte Público.

Bruce-Novoa, Juan, ed. 1980. *Chicano Authors: Inquiry by Interview*. Austin: University of Texas Press.

Cardoso, Fernando Henrique, and Enzo Faletto. 1979. *Dependency and Development in Latin America*, translated by Marjory Muttingly Urquidi. Berkeley: University of California Press.

Castillo, Ana. 1994. *Massacre of the Dreamers: Essays on Xicanisma*. Albuquerque: University of New Mexico Press.

Couser, G. Thomas. 1989. *Altered Egos: Authority in American Autobiography*. New York: Oxford University Press.

del Castillo, Adelaida R., ed. 1990. *Between Borders: Essays on Mexicana/Chicana History*. Encino, CA: Floricanto Press.

De León, Arnoldo. 1982. *The Tejano Community, 1836–1900*. Dallas: Southern Methodist University Press.

Doctorow, E. L. 1993. *Jack London, Hemingway, and the Constitution: Selected Essays, 1977–1992*. New York: Random House.

Doran, Esther Pérez. 1965. "Death in the Mexican American Community." Unpublished essay.

Eakin, Paul John. 1985. *Fictions in Autobiography: Studies in the Art of Self-Invention*. Princeton, NJ: Princeton University Press.

Faulkner, William. [1932] 1959. *Light in August*. New York: Random House.

———. [1936] 1972. *Absalom, Absalom!* New York: Vintage.

Fernández, José B., and Martin A. Favata. [1542] 1993. Introduction to *The Account: Álvar Núñez Cabeza de Vaca's Relación*. Houston: Arte Público.

Flores Olague, Jesús, Mercedes de Vega, Sandra Kuntz Ficker, and Laura del Alizal. 1996. *Breve Historia de Zacatecas*. Mexico D. F.: El Colegio de México.

Foucault, Michel. 1977. *Language, Counter-Memory, Practice: Selected Essays and Interviews*, edited by Donald F. Bouchard. Ithaca, NY: Cornell University Press.

Galarza, Ernesto. [1971] 1986. *Barrio Boy*. Notre Dame, IN: University of Notre Dame Press.

García Márquez, Gabriel. [1970] 1991. *One Hundred Years of Solitude*. New York: HarperCollins.

Goldman, Anne. 1992. "'I Yam What I Yam': Cooking, Culture, and Colonialism." In *De/Colonizing the Subject: Politics and Gender in Women's Autobiographical Practice*, edited by Sidonie Smith and Julia Watson, 170–82. Minneapolis: University of Minnesota Press.

Gonzáles-Berry, Erlinda, and Chuck Tatum, ed. 1996. *Recovering the United States Hispanic Literary Heritage*. Houston: Arte Público.

González, Jovita, and Eve Raleigh. 1996. *Caballero: A Historical Novel*. College Station: Texas A&M University Press.

Griswold del Castillo, Richard. 1989. "Patriarchy and the Status of Women in the Late Nineteenth-Century Southwest." In *The Mexican and Mexican American Experience in the 19th Century*, edited by Jamie E. Rodriguez O. Tempe, AZ: Bilingual Press.

Gutiérrez, David G. 1995. *Walls and Mirrors: Mexican Americans, Mexican Immigrants, and the Politics of Ethnicity*. Berkeley: University of California Press.

Gutiérrez, Ramón A. 1991. *When Jesus Came, the Corn Mothers Went Away: Marriage, Sexuality, and Power in New Mexico, 1500–1846*. Stanford: Stanford University Press.

Gutiérrez, Ramón A., and Genaro Padilla, ed. 1993. *Recovering the United States Hispanic Literary Heritage*. Houston: Arte Público.

Haas, Lisabeth. 1995. *Conquests and Historical Identities in California, 1769–1936*. Berkeley: University of California Press.

Herrera-Sobek, Maria, and Helena Viramontes, eds. 1996. *Chicana Creativity and Criticism: New Frontiers in American Literature*. Albuquerque: University of New Mexico Press.

Karl, Frederick. 1988. *William Faulkner: A Biography*. New York: Knopf.

Knight, Alan. 1986. *The Mexican Revolution, Volume 2: Counter-revolution and Reconstruction*. Lincoln: University of Nebraska Press.

Leal, Luis. 1973. "Mexican American Literature: A Historical Perspective." *Revista Chicano-Riqueña* I, 1: 32–44. Reprinted in *Modern Chicano Writers: A Collection of Critical Essays*, edited by Joseph Sommers and Tomás Ybarra-Frausto, 18–30. New York: Prentice-Hall, 1979.

Márquez, Antonio C. 1984. "Richard Rodriguez' *Hunger of Memory* and the Poetics of Experience." *Arizona Quarterly* 39, no. 4: 130–41.

Martí, José. 1975. *Inside the Monster: Writings on the United States and American Imperialism*, edited by Phillip S. Foner, translated by Elinor Randall. New York: Monthly Review Press.

Martin, Gerald. 1989. *Journeys through the Labryinth: Latin American Fiction in the Twentieth Century*. New York: Verso.

Meier, Matt S., and Feliciano Ribera. 1993. *Mexican Americans/American Mexicans: From Conquistadors to Chicanos*. New York: Farrar, Straus & Giroux.

Menchaca, Martha. 1995. *The Mexican Outsiders: A Community History of Marginalization and Discrimination in California*. Austin: University of Texas Press.

Montejano, David. 1987. *Anglos and Mexicans in the Making of Texas, 1836–1986*. Austin: University of Texas Press.

Moraga, Cherrie. 1983. *Loving in the War Years: Lo que nunca pasó por sus labios*. Boston: South End Press.

Moraga, Cherríe, and Gloria Anzaldua, eds. 1981. *This Bridge Called My Back: Writings by Radical Women of Color*. Watertown, Pennsylvania: Persephone Press.

Nora, Pierre. 1996. "General Introduction: Between Memory and History." In *Realms of Memory: Rethinking the French Past*, edited by Pierre Nora, vol. 1: *Conflicts and Divisions*, 1–20. Translated by Arthur Goldhammer. New York: Columbia University Press

Padilla, Genaro M. 1993. *My History, Not Yours: The Formation of Mexican American Autobiography*. Madison: University of Wisconsin Press.

———. 1984. "Self as Cultural Metaphor in Acosta's *The Autobiography of a Brown Buffalo*." *Journal of General Education* 35: 242–58.

Paredes, Raymund A. 1982. "The Evolution of Chicano Literature." In *Three American Literatures*, edited by Houston A. Baker Jr., 33–79. New York: Modern Language Association.

Pérez-Torres, Rafael. 1995. *Movements in Chicano Poetry: Against Myths, Against Margins*. New York: Cambridge University Press.

Rebolledo, Tey Diana. 1990. "Narrative Strategies of Resistance in Hispana Writing." *Journal of Narrative Technique* 20, no. 2 (Spring): 134–46.

———. 1995. *Women Singing in the Snow: A Cultural Analysis of Chicana Literature*. Tucson: University of Arizona Press.

Rebolledo, Tey Diana, and Eliana S. Rivero. 1993. Introduction to *Infinite Divisions: An Anthology of Chicana Literature*, edited by Rebolledo and Rivero. Tucson: University of Arizona Press.

Revueltas, José. [1943] 1990. *Human Mourning* [E luto humano], trans. Roberto Crespi. Minneapolis: University of Minneapolis Press.

Rulfo, Juan. [1955] 1987. *Pedro Páramo*. New York: Grove.

Saldivar, Jose David. 1991. *The Dialectics of Our America: Genealogy, Cultural Critique, and Literary History*. Durham, NC: Duke University Press.

Saldívar, Ramón. 1990. *Chicano Narrative: The Dialectics of Difference*. Madison: University of Wisconsin Press.

———. 1985. "Ideologies of the Self: Chicano Autobiography." *Diacritics* (Fall): 25–34.

Sánchez, Rosaura. 1995. *Telling Identities: The Californio Testimonios*. Minneapolis: University of Minnesota Press.

Semo, Enrique. 1993. *The History of Capitalism in Mexico: Its Origins, 1521–1763*. Austin: University of Texas Press.

Vallejo, Mariano Guadalupe. 1994. "Recuerdos históricos y personales tocante a la Alta California de Mariano Guadalupe Vallejo." In *Nineteenth Century Californio Testimonials*, edited by Rosaura Sánchez, Beatrice Pita, and Bárbara Reyes, 138–43. San Diego: Crítica Monograph.

Vidal, Gore. 1995. *Palimpsest: A Memoir*. New York: Random House.

The Measure of a Cock
Mexican Cockfighting, Culture, and Masculinity

Jerry Garcia

> I don't want to play a macho! What does that word mean? See, a macho
> has no questions. A macho is self-assured. He has no doubts . . . When I
> say macho, I see my grandfather, a man: good, kind, gentle, and strong.
> He was a macho. He raised fighting cocks.
>
> —Rick Najera, *The Pain of the Macho*

I have no memory of the first time I saw my father measuring his cock. I
remain, however, keenly aware that at a young age I was initiated into a
world of manliness unlike any other. Often, I would watch in amazement
as my father held and caressed the red bobbing head in his hands. As I
recall those adolescent years I remain curious about the fixation my father
had as he deliberately, tenderly, and with subtle care stroked and admired
his cock. There were times when I saw him place his salivating mouth
over the head and run his lips back and forth along the shaft as if trying
to will it to new life. This ritual, almost religious in nature, of checking
for hardness, softness, strength, and weakness, became a familiar practice.
I found it strange, even as an adolescent, that someone would pay such
attention to this symbol of masculinity. As I came of age, I soon realized
that Mexican culture valued strong, courageous, aggressive, and virile men
and that the cock represented these traits. Thus, in my childhood, the
cock became a master symbol of manliness and of characteristics valued by
Mexican culture. It became clear that my father had a deep psychological
identification with his cock, a bond that appeared obsessive. My intent is
not to make ethical arguments for or against my father's behavior, but to

focus on this experience and to question why some men, Mexican men in particular, are overly devoted to their cocks. I hope it is evident that I am speaking of the cocks used in cockfights, or *peleas de gallos*, as my father calls them. The double entendre is difficult to avoid, as it is relevant and important in discussing Mexican men and cockfights.[1]

Historians, anthropologists, sociologists, and scholars from other fields have, intentionally or unintentionally, largely ignored Mexican culture and cockfighting. This study is an attempt to fill this void and is based on my personal experiences growing up in a cockfighting family in the Pacific Northwest, on interviews with other sources from a similar background, and on the relevant existing scholarship on cockfighting.

First introduced into North America in the early colonial era, cockfighting continues to serve an important but controversial role in Mexican culture within the United States. Spain and its colonial subjects introduced the sport to regions of Latin America and to what is now known as the American Southwest, where it has continued to flourish as a culturally important tradition in Mexican American communities. The British meanwhile introduced cockfighting along the Eastern Seaboard, from where it spread to the American South. Today, in 2004, cockfights persist in the United States even though most states impose severe penalties on individuals arrested in conjunction with cockfighting, and there is a well-vocalized public contempt for the sport.

People of Mexican origin, a historically marginalized ethnic group in the United States, have tried to maintain a strong sense of their culture despite extensive efforts by US society at deculturalization. The willingness of ethnic Mexicans to engage in illegal activity through active participation in, and support of, cockfighting can be seen as an attempt to minimize and resist this deculturalization and marginalization. This resistance may manifest itself in a distinctive form of masculinity outwardly expressed through cockfighting. Mexican cockfighting may also be encouraging transnationalism as Mexicans negotiate their marginalization on both sides of the border. For all these reasons, cockfighting plays a unique and significant role within the Mexican community in the United States. At the same time, it stands as one of the cultural barriers between people of Mexican origin and mainstream US society. If this conflict is to be resolved, there is a need to better understand the underlying reasons for the persistence in selected communities of this usually illegal and always ethically controversial sport.

Of Gallos and Galleros

Cockfighting is considered one of the oldest organized forms of recreation. Its origins can be traced to Southeast Asia, to around 3000 BC with the domestication of the chicken (McCaghy and Neal 1973, 15).[2] Admiration for and even adoration of the *Gallus sonneratii* unquestionably reaches far into antiquity. The gamecock was an object of worship among the Babylonians, ancient Syrians, and Greeks. In Rome it was idealized as a symbol of courage in battle, and Roman authorities in Gaul minted coins bearing a representation of a Gaulish helmet with a cock on its crest (Ingersoll 1923, 45). In fact, it is with the Romans that the notion of "blood sport" emerges (Plass 1995).

In the Christian era, some scholars attribute the first comments on the deeper meaning of the cockfight to St. Augustine (AD 354–430), who asked, "Why do cocks fight and why are men so fascinated by cockfights?" (1942, 49). Although St. Augustine was writing on a larger theme, in *De ordine* (About order) he nonetheless touched upon some fundamental elements of cockfighting that have perplexed scholars to the present. St. Augustine describes witnessing a cockfight in a barnyard, and says that he and his companions were drawn to the spectacle. In the end he asks:

> Why do all cocks behave this way? Why do they fight for the sake of supremacy of the hens subject to them? Why did the very beauty of the fight draw us aside from this higher study for a while, and onto the pleasure of the spectacle? What is there in us that searches out many things beyond the reach of the senses? And on the other hand, what is it that is grasped by the beckoning of the senses themselves? (51)

Although not universal, cockfighting flourished in many parts of the world. There appears to be no record, however, of game fowl (chicken) in the Americas before the arrival of Europeans. Nevertheless, Alfred Crosby, in *The Columbian Exchange*, does refer to a "type" of chicken in existence before colonization:

> The acceptance of a pre-Columbian American chicken probably also means acceptance of pre-Columbian trans-Pacific contacts with areas where the chicken was first domesticated. Whatever the truth may be, there is no doubt that most of the chickens in America by 1600 were of European descent. (1972, 95–96)

Whether or not the indigenous people had chickens, there is no doubt that they were familiar with blood sports. Scholars have studied sport, competition, and violence among indigenous tribes of pre-Columbian America, most notably the Aztecs, and have compared them to the sports of other ancient cultures, such as the Roman. For example, Inga Clendinnen in *Aztecs* relates that "the Mexica male self was constructed in competition" and that most men lived in a precarious position, especially those from the warrior class who were constantly challenged (1991, 142). Although not a sport in the traditional sense, gladiatorial sacrifices were conducted throughout the Aztec empire and provided spectacles for entire cities. In most cases those being sacrificed were captured warriors or nobles:

> The captive was taken to the round sacrificial stone, where he was painted with stripes. He was given four cudgels to throw, a shield, and a sword with its obsidian blades replaced by feathers. After drinking octli, he fought warriors—several, if he was a great warrior. First he fought four warriors of the military orders in a row—two jaguars and two eagles—and if he triumphed, then he fought a left-handed warrior. He fought until he was felled, whereupon he was stretched on his back, his chest was cut open, and his heart was torn out and dedicated to the sun. Then the body was flayed, and the priests wore the skin. (Hassig 1988, 200–2)

Another competitive sport in Mesoamerica that has gained some attention is the "ballgame." It is believed to have been first played in the Olmec civilization around 1500 BC. The game was usually played for ceremonial purposes, to resolve conflicts, or for gambling, and at times became a game of death. Several detailed paintings and stone carvings from Mesoamerica depict entire teams being decapitated after losing to an opponent (Carrasco 1998, 179–80).

The people of Mesoamerica were thus well accustomed to violent competitions and sports and the participation of the public in such events. This tradition found new expression in the sport of cockfighting, introduced into the Americas after the European conquest and colonization. Like the Balinese cockfighting examined by anthropologist Clifford Geertz (1972, 101), Mexican cockfighting can be seen as a continuation of a cultural past in which sport often involved a blood offering or even human sacrifice.

Cockfighting came to the Western Hemisphere and eventually to what is now the American Southwest via conquest and colonization by Spain and England in the fifteenth and sixteenth centuries. The European conquest of the Americas brought not only violence and destruction but also a resettling of the region. This resettling was coupled with a restructuring of society, a process of cultural modification that varied depending on the intent of the colonizer. By the late colonial period in the Americas, various forms of European culture and entertainment had found their way into the daily lives of those living in the conquered territories. The sport of cockfighting was one aspect of this societal transformation.

Space constraints prevent a detailed comparison of the different forms of cockfighting introduced by the English and Spanish. However, it is interesting to note that the English introduced gaff fighting, using an instrument that resembles a rapier with a sharpened point and a round body. The American gaff fight requires that one gaff be tied to each leg of the cock. The Spanish and Mexicans brought in a tradition of "slasher" or knife fights, with a blade resembling a curved single-edged razor blade tied to the cock's leg. Both forms are popular in the United States, but Mexican cockfighters have traditionally favored the knife, quite possibly because it increases the risk and somewhat neutralizes the level of skill, creating the possibility of an upset by a less-skilled cock.

Cockfighting flourished throughout Latin America and the Caribbean in such places as Mexico, Venezuela, Cuba, the Dominican Republic, and Haiti. By the early nineteenth century, gambling associated with cockfighting was well entrenched in Mexico. In fact, some sources claim that the infamous General Antonio López de Santa Anna was addicted to cockfighting and opium (Wasserman 2000, 17).

In *Cocks and Bulls in Caracas*, Olga Briceño provides a colorful description of a cockfight in Venezuela during the early twentieth century:

> The audience consisted of country people in their Sunday best, muleteers, vagabonds, and sprinkle of respectable men in hunting clothes. . . . There were not more than ten country women, for women do not enjoy that kind of occasion. . . . The rival cocks faced each other, their combs erect. As their owners had done, they eyed each other for a moment before attacking in a savage moment. . . . The old man soothed his cock with a mother's tenderness, whispering in its ear between the rounds as he wiped blood from its head . . . The old man took a mouthful of vinegar and standing near the bird spurted it over the injury, in an attempt to bring it to. (1945, 138–40)

Cuba has also sustained a vibrant cockfighting culture. In fact, some of the earliest documented cockfights in the Americas took place on the island. Cockfighting in prerevolutionary Cuba was not only a form of popular culture in which all social groups participated but also a source of income for the government:

> Cockfighting, also supervised as a government monopoly, was next to the lottery in general gambling favor. All degrees of people, including

the poorest farmers, not a few priests, and royal officials as high as an occasional captain general, had been raising, training, and fighting cocks ever since early in the sixteenth century. During some prosperous and feverish years mains [cockfights] were held at several public and official pits almost daily. High and low, black and white crowded into the enclosure, elbowing, sweating, shouting, and betting. Thousands of dollars were bet upon each occasion while the government, which placed a small tax upon each pair of birds set in the ring, thus obtained about fifteen thousand dollars annually. (Bradley 1941, 266)

Cockfighting became so popular in Cuba that when it was banned for ten years in the late nineteenth century, José Míguel Gómez ran for president on a platform that included lifting the ban. He kept his promise when he became president in the early twentieth century (397–98).

As cockfighting increased in popularity throughout the Americas it created a sense of identity for individuals and countries. After Haiti gained independence in 1804 it embraced the cock as a symbol, thus following the lead of France, which had adopted the rooster as a symbol of its revolution in the late eighteenth century (Wucker 1999, 13). In Haiti and the Dominican Republic, which share the island of Hispaniola, cockfighting not only remains a passion but also has come to symbolize each country's nationalistic fervor and their historic rivalry. The cockfight has been used metaphorically to describe politicians and their sometimes adversarial relationships, as Michele Wucker writes in *Why the Cocks Fight*:

On one level, the scraggly fighting rooster makes sense as a politician's symbol: politics, after all, is a battle of strategy, endurance, and aggression played out on a national stage. It inspires the same emotion and scheming that the cockfight does in spectators and gamblers. Look closer, however, and the political rooster dissolves into other images with entirely different meanings in religion and daily life. In other contexts, the rooster of aggression becomes a bird of sustenance, a symbol of the dawn and new beginning, and, most important, a guardian of territory. (10–11)

Thus, the cock in Haitian and Dominican cultures not only represents independence but also remains a potent political symbol that resonates in both countries.

The United States inherited the practice of cockfighting from Mexico—after its conquest of Mexico's northern territories—as well as directly from Europe. American cockfighting was most widespread in the colonial and early modern era, when it was not yet considered deviant or illegal (Scott 1983).

> By the nineteenth century the first formal complaints against cockfighting
> in the United States emerged. In the 1820s and 1830s various states were
> considering anti-cockfighting bills. Registered complaints were most pro-
> nounced in the North. Letters to the editor proclaimed that "cockfighting
> was unfriendly to morals, occasioned idleness, fraud, gambling, profane
> swearing, and hardened the heart against the feelings of humanity." (123)

The first state to outlaw cockfighting was Pennsylvania, in 1830
(McCaghy and Neal 1973, 559). Today, in 2004, all but two states prohibit
cockfighting, on the principle that the fights are inhumane and cruel to
animals. The sport remains legal only in Louisiana and New Mexico, home
to many established back-road pits (Kilborn 2000). Oklahoma banned
cockfighting in 2002, but legal challenges have been filed and the fights
continue. All states allow the breeding of gamecocks, which are often
exported to states where fighting is legal despite federal law prohibiting
interstate transport of fighting birds. Despite the laws passed against it,
the sport continues underground and remains a popular form of culture or
subculture in various parts of the country. It is particularly entrenched in
rural America, but it is not unheard of in urban areas, as recent cockfighting
raids in New York City attest (Chivers 2000; Kilborn 2000; Ross 2003).

To my knowledge there is no published literature on cockfighting
in the Pacific Northwest, where my case study is set. However, we can
assume that cockfighting emerged in the region, mostly likely around the
turn of the nineteenth century, as a result of European and American
settlement. European colonization of the Pacific Northwest was mainly by
non-Spaniards, and with some exceptions that have been noted by scholars, Spanish culture did not consolidate itself in this region. Cockfighting
therefore was principally with the gaff, traditionally preferred by European
Americans, rather than with the knife, which was chiefly used by Spaniards and eventually Mexicans in what is today the American Southwest.
However, exceptions can be found, and my father and uncle began their
cockfighting careers using the gaff.

Mexican Masculinity and Cockfighting

Of cocks and men . . . this phrase from Geertz's seminal essay "Deep Play:
Notes on the Balinese Cockfight" (1972) comes to mind as I reconstruct
visions of the cockfights I attended as a child, as well as those I still occasionally see. Attendance at a cockfight leaves little doubt that this sport is
a space created, regulated, and dominated by men. Indeed, the picture is
one of unabashed masculine sexuality: the sensuous dance of the two cocks,

mirrored by the similar movements of their human handlers, and the frenzy of the spectators, all within the confines of a pit fifteen feet in diameter. Men gather in a corner drinking and talking of an upcoming fight, while others huddle around a cock, admiring it, in awe of its power. Mexicans often refer to the gamecock as a *gallo,* and this term is also used metaphorically to describe someone who exemplifies Mexican manhood. Although no sexual act is performed, there is no mistaking the aura of masculinity, sex, and sexuality that hangs over the cockfighting pit.

At the same time, within this exclusively male-to-male preserve, an element of homoeroticism can be seen at play. To begin with, the cockfight arena is, as Varda Burstyn argues in *The Rites of Men,* an example of homosociality, or the desire and custom of men to be in male company exclusively (1999, 294n41). It goes beyond that, though, to encompass an experience and spectacle of intense physical interaction between males of two species that can indeed be described as homoerotic. This interaction begins with an intense male-to-male "gaze" that has also been noted in other sporting arenas. For example, it has been chronicled that in the late nineteenth century homoeroticism may have inspired the sporting male-to-male gaze, providing a nonverbal language of desire. This gaze is evident at the beginning of any boxing match, as the two boxers stand face-to-face within inches of each other. In the cockfight, the human handlers use this male-to-male gaze in an attempt to intimidate before the fight begins.

In some ways the cockfight can be interpreted as a homoerotic dance between the cocks themselves, between the two human handlers, and between cock and man. The highly charged atmosphere and the symbolism involved in sustaining the cock's life by sucking, blowing, caressing, and stroking create a great web of homoeroticism. I described this intimacy between my father and his cock at the beginning of this paper. These techniques are almost universal, and though only meant to resuscitate a gamecock, they partially explain why cockfighting has often been associated with sexuality. Another example of this interplay is described in *The Day of the Locust*:

> When the dwarf [Abe] gathered the red up, its neck had begun to droop and it was a mass of blood and matted feathers. . . . He spit into its gaping beak and took the comb between his lips and sucked the blood back into it. The red began to regain its fury. . . . Abe, moaning softly, smoothed its feathers and licked its eyes clean, then took its whole head in his mouth. The red was finished, however. It couldn't even hold its neck straight. (West 1969, 154)

What makes all this unusual is that it takes place within a Mexican working-class environment that is usually linked with homophobic men. Is it possible, as Dundes suggests, that in cockfighting one proves his maleness by feminizing the opponent (1994, 250–51)?

The sport of cockfighting is not exclusively male. But women are underrepresented and are usually relegated to spectator status, and they are not intimately involved in handling the cock. The gamecock "handler" and the "cockpit" are roles and spaces generally reserved for males.[3] This is largely true across cockfighting cultures. Geertz, in his study of Balinese cockfighting, observed that women were discouraged from attending cockfights. Wucker, writing of cockfighting on Hispaniola, reports that cockfighting is a male ritual in the region but, ironically, "the most enduring Dominican legends of strength and redemption are female" (1999, 7). According to my uncle, in his more than fifty years of cockfighting he has never seen a Mexican female "handler." Although he has witnessed Anglo women performing this task, he says it is a rare occurrence.[4]

This domain is for the interaction of man and man, cock and man, cock and cock. Both the gamecock and the cockfighting man have been described as the embodiment of courage, commitment, dominance, and aggressiveness. In Bali, Geertz notes, "*Sabung*, the word for cock, is used metaphorically to mean 'hero,' 'warrior,' champion,' 'man of parts,' 'lady killer,' or 'tough guy'" (1972, 99). A cock without these virtues is considered impotent. According to some social scientists, Mexicans' manliness is often compared to that of roosters: "The better man is the one who can drink more, defend himself best, have more sex relations, and have more sons born by his wife" (Madsen 1973, 22). If the cock and the cockfight can be considered an extension of Mexican masculinity, the reverse is also true. For the cock to be considered aggressive and domineering, it has to be "handled" by a man who possesses the same qualities. Thus masculinity becomes an important element of the cockfight, whether actually displayed by the man or imagined for the rooster.

Scholarship examining Mexican masculinity is in short supply and some of what has been done is deeply flawed. Critics have examined both old and recent scholarship on masculinity and its expression among ethnic Mexicans residing in the United States. For example, the concept of machismo, which is actually inherent in most cultures, is strongly associated with Mexican and other Latino men. Américo Paredes writes that the characteristics of machismo are "the outrageous boast, a distinct phallic symbolism, the identification of a man with the male animal, and the ambivalence toward women—varying from an abject and tearful posture to brutal disdain" (1993, 215). Another scholar observes:

> *Machismo* has been used by scholars and authors to describe male asser-
> tiveness and control over everything from nature to society. In its most
> succinct form, machismo is defined as a template for male behavior that
> reifies aggression and domination as uniquely male attributes and reproj-
> ects them to every area of culture. The behavioral traits most commonly
> associated with machismo include hypermasculine bravado and posturing,
> willingness to confront physically any perceived slight, domination of
> women and other men through act and language, drinking to excess,
> sexual conquest, and siring children. (Klein 2000)

Alfredo Mirandé, in *Hombres y Machos* (1997), and Alan Klein, in his insightful article "Dueling Machos: Masculinity and Sport in Mexican Base-ball" (2000), shed some light on the origins of the equation of machismo with Mexican masculinity. According to their studies, the person most responsible for the fusion is essayist and poet Octavio Paz in *The Labyrinth of Solitude* (1950). Klein observes that *Labyrinth* contained "a definition of masculinity that wed psychoanalytic elements with history":

> The original conquest of Aztec forebears by conquistadors was seen, by
> Paz, as so traumatic as to imprint itself on all subsequent generations.
> Overall Spanish brutality toward Aztecs was converted into the sexual
> act of raping Aztec women, and with it came the implication that Aztec
> men were unable to prevent it." (Klein 2000, 68–69)

Mirandé argues in similar fashion:

> Native men developed an overly masculine and aggressive response in
> order to compensate for deeply felt feelings of powerlessness and weak-
> ness. Machismo, then, is nothing more than a futile attempt to mask a
> profound sense of impotence, powerlessness, and ineptitude, an expression
> of weakness and a sense of inferiority. (1997, 36)

Some scholars have described Mexican working-class masculin-ity as a "protest masculinity" that responds to economic disadvantage. According to this theory, Mexican males who feel inferior because they lack economic mobility or political clout conceal those feelings behind a substantial display of power and virility (36). Baca Zinn considers this point in her article "Chicano Men and Masculinity." While acknowledging that male dominance does exist among Chicanos, she contends that the culture argument is oversimplified: "Research suggests that in the realm of marital decision making, egalitarianism is far more prevalent than macho dominance" (1982, 29–43).

Other scholars, such Lionel Cantú, have argued that examining Chicano masculinity through the lens of studies conducted on males in Latin American distorts the reality of Chicanos and, more important, represents Chicano culture "as if it were fixed or static" (2000, 227). Along these same lines, he maintains, studying Chicano sex roles from the perspective of the machismo/*marianismo* model found in traditional or mainstream analysis perpetuates stereotypes of Latino culture (228). Finally, Cantú asserts that "the static and monolithic definition of the Mexican 'macho' is problematic both in its failure to capture the diverse social locations of Mexican men and in its assumption that Mexican gender identities transcend time" (228).

As can be seen, the conceptualization of masculinity for ethnic Mexicans, as for other men of color, has been problematic. What does appear true is that Mexican men do not fit into a traditional or stereotypical form of masculinity, but exhibit multiple forms, as R. W. Connell has observed:

> It follows that in multicultural societies such as the contemporary United States there are likely to be multiple definitions of masculinity. . . . There are for instance differences in the expression of masculinity between Latino and Anglo men in the United States. . . . The meaning of masculinity in working-class life is different from the meaning in middle-class life, not to mention among the very rich and the very poor. (1996, 208)

I agree with Connell's assessment that ethnic Mexicans in the United States exhibit various forms of masculinity. I would argue that those who participate in the underground and illegal sport of cockfighting are challenging hegemonic masculinity, which Connell defines as "the configuration of gender practice which embodies the currently accepted answer to the problem of legitimacy or patriarchy, which guarantees the dominant position of men and the subordination of women" (1995, 77). Or, put another way, nonhegemonic masculinities are "subordinated by the ruling, or 'hegemonic,' masculinity of Western white, hetereosexual, middle-class men" (Cantú 2000, 226).

One can see a parallel in the behavior of some black males in American society who adopt the "cool pose," defined by Majors and Billson as "a ritualized form of masculinity that entails behaviors, scripts, physical posturing" (1992, 2–3). This is also thought to be a coping mechanism that provides "a means to show the dominant culture that the black male is strong, proud, and can survive, regardless of what may have been done to harm or limit him" (Majors 1990, 111). Like African Americans, ethnic Mexicans living in the United States occupy a marginalized status, one shaped by political and cultural exclusion and economic discrimination as well as by the concept of "otherness" based on race and ethnicity (Connell 1995, 79–80). By challenging hegemonic masculinity, cockfighting, I argue, is a form of "resistance masculinity" by which Mexican men assert their own masculine values based on a traditional sport. Like the "cool pose," it is a survival mechanism that empowers the Mexican male; "it eases the worry and pain of blocked opportunities" (Majors 1992, 5). And through the cockfight, Mexican males construct a masculine identity that garners respect within the Mexican family and local Mexican community, even though it does not live up to the ideal form of masculinity established in the dominant culture.

"Resistance masculinity" does have some limitations, however. For example, scholars argue that public displays of masculinity or machismo are not only a form of resistance against class and race oppression, but also a means of oppressing women. Hondagneu-Sotelo and Messner state that "gender is commonly viewed as . . . an effect of the dominant class and/or race relations [and] what is obscured, or even drops out of sight, is the feminist observation that masculinity itself is a form of domination over women" (2000, 68). Some of these limitations emerged when I interviewed various individuals for this project and they will be illustrated in the following case study. Nevertheless, the sport of Mexican cockfighting provides an opportunity to examine ethnic Mexicans within a sphere rarely seen by the majority of the public, and it offers investigators an unusual opportunity to observe displays of masculinity within this realm.

Cockfighting in the Pacific Northwest: A Case Study

Investigating Mexican cockfighting in the United States requires one to navigate the blurred boundaries of Mexican and Mexican American ethnicity and culture. Most of my life experiences have taken place in the Pacific Northwest, almost two thousand miles from the US-Mexican border. The Pacific Northwest has a long history of Spanish, Mexican, and Chicano influences, yet it remains detached from what many Chicana/o studies scholars consider the cultural center of Mexicanness, namely the US-Mexico border region.[5] As a result, Mexicans and Mexican Americans who live in the Pacific Northwest and other regions outside the Southwest have had to cope with distance and the lack of a "critical mass" of Mexicans locally, making their experiences diverse. Nonetheless, I agree with Adelaida del Castillo when she writes, "The affinity between things

Mexican and Mexican American/Chicano has a basis in common history, border space, culture, and language long renewed by migration and immigration, which more recently has come to signify the mexicanization of the United States" (1996, 207). In addition, the concept of borders has changed in the last twenty years and no longer refers simply to the political boundaries between countries. The new conceptualization of borders encompasses illusory and metaphoric constructions of demarcations, borderlands, and "borderlessness." I submit that Mexicans living in the Pacific Northwest exist in a similar multidimensional space. Even here, Mexican culture thrives with the continued renewal of traditional values and customs through immigration/migration and through the activities of those Mexican Americans who cling to their Mexican heritage.

The co-existence of the Mexican and Mexican American communities within these various border constructs has obscured many of their cultural differences. Offsetting this are the counter-pressures for Mexican acculturation and assimilation to the dominant society. For example, in order to survive in the United States, my father has had to acculturate economically as a laborer. Despite this workplace assimilation, however, and the fact that he is a naturalized US citizen, my father maintains primary relations with his own ethnic group and has only secondary interaction with individuals and institutions of the dominant culture (fig. 1). Some sociologists have called this process "selective acculturation" (Portes and Rumbaut 1996, 250–51).

This selective acculturation partially explains why Mexican culture remains intact among those who engage in cockfighting at the level of my elders. First-generation immigrants such as my father and uncle find in the cockfight a cultural cocoon to protect them from alienation, domination, and isolation within American society and culture. It is thus the equivalent of the "cool pose" discussed earlier. My father and uncle take part in this tradition as a means of maintaining their cultural identity as Mexicans, part of which includes the notion of machismo and masculinity, an important aspect of Mexican cockfighting.

My father and his brother are cockfighters, or *galleros*, par excellence. They display the near-obsessive behavior toward their cocks that Geertz described among Balinese cockfighters:

> Balinese men, or any large majority of Balinese men, spend an enormous amount of time with their favorites, grooming them, feeding them, discussing them, trying them out against one another, or just gazing at them with a mixture of rapt admiration and dreamy self-absorption. (1972, 99–100)

Figure 1. The author's father, R. Garcia, with his first car, a Ford Crown Victoria, in Granger, Washington, 1956. Photo taken by his brother R. Garcia. Garcia family photo collection.

As a child and as an adult I witnessed similar behavior. At family functions my father and uncle would discuss their favorite cocks, training and care of the birds, game strategy, and upcoming matches. These gatherings often featured impromptu friendly matches in the front yard or a challenge from a rival appearing unannounced, as happened on a number of occasions. My father's and uncle's time away from home increasingly included tending to their gamecocks for an upcoming season of cockfights. It is important to note that within my working-class Mexican family, cockfighting was never seen as deviant or barbaric. My mother never complained about its cruelty, only that my father spent too much time and money on it. On numerous occasions my mother complained of the depletion of family income and, to a certain degree, of neglect by my father. When I interviewed my aunt she expressed no alarm about the treatment of gamecocks or her husband's participation in a sport deemed inhumane, low-life, and criminal. Like many Mexicans, she had a relative who was involved with cockfighting long before she met my uncle and so she was familiar with the sport.[6]

Very early I came to the realization that my father and uncle were not simply spectators. Instead, they were actually men of prominence and importance in the cockfighting world. By the time I had reached the age of twelve my father and uncle had garnered the respect and admiration of fellow *galleros* and aficionados of the sport. Although today it is illegal in all but two states, cockfighting has its own promotional magazines with thousands of subscribers. The most prominent of these are *Gamecock* and *Grit and Steel*, with one lesser-known publication called *The Feathered Warrior*. In fact, my father and uncle were once featured in an issue of *Gamecock* for having won a significant number of their cockfights.[7] In the cockfighting world this is the equivalent of being featured in *Sports Illustrated*, and it is considered quite an honor.

When the daily lives of my father and uncle are juxtaposed with their status as respected cockfighters, a stark contrast emerges. They were born three years apart in a place called El Rancho de Agua Fresca, on the outskirts of Monterrey, Mexico. You will not find this community on any map; in fact, when I interviewed my uncle he was uncertain whether it still existed. Growing up, I always enjoyed hearing this name and knowing that it was also my place of origin. There is a certain mystical and divine quality to the sound of the name, and I want to believe that it is an actual place. More likely, however, El Rancho de Agua Fresca was simply a few houses located in a rural site with a fresh-water well, as my uncle put it, and has long since disappeared or turned into a ghost town. Nonetheless, that was the place my father and uncle left when they emigrated from Mexico to Texas in the late 1940s. As Mexican immigrants, they survived by moving frequently within Texas in search of farmwork. At the age of about twelve, my uncle was paid $2.50 per day, he recalls. By the early 1950s my father and uncle and their families began another long migration, this time to the Northwest. They followed long-established migration routes that took them through Montana, where they worked sugar beets, then to Idaho to pick potatoes, and finally to the Yakima Valley in Washington, where they worked sugar beets, hops, and potato crops.

Their motivation for this arduous journey was economic. Texas growers tended to pay wages by the day; in the Northwest, however, growers paid laborers by the hour. In the early 1950s, when my father and uncle arrived in the Northwest, the prevailing wage for a farm laborer was $1.00

per hour, a significant income for a family of migrant workers. Because they were both immigrants and undereducated, the two brothers worked as farm laborers for most of their lives, along with their families. Although my father and uncle eventually went from unskilled to semi-skilled work and finally to skilled blue-collar positions, and were generally well respected in the community, they never received the admiration or respect on the job that they achieved as cockfighters and breeders. Thus, the cockfight became a world of acceptance and success for my uncle and father, a place where each became a clear winner, and where they could display their self-worth, have a sense of accomplishment, and practice a nontraditional form of masculinity.

Racial discrimination was another aspect of the exclusion experienced by my father and uncle in their relations with the dominant culture. For example, my uncle elaborates on how they were regarded as they migrated to various communities in West Texas to pick cotton:

> There were many Mexicans, but it was mostly Anglo people living in this region. I will never forget that we once went to the movies and after getting my popcorn and soda I went to sit in the center of the theater. Shortly after, a young white girl poked me on the shoulder and said, "You are not supposed to sit here. You are supposed to sit up there in the balcony." In those days we did not know our rights and we did as we were told.

Both my father and uncle recall a significant change in treatment after leaving for the Northwest, where they did not experience the overt forms of racism and discrimination they were subjected to in Texas. Other Mexican American migrants who came to the Northwest during the same period have made similar statements. The only explanation I have to offer for this variation in treatment between regions is the small number of Mexicans in the Northwest at the time. Without a critical mass of Mexicans, Mexican culture posed no threat to the dominant culture. It might also be argued that still fresh in the minds of many Anglo families and growers were the Mexican braceros who came to the Northwest during World War II to harvest their crops.

My uncle became interested in cockfighting at a very early age, having attended his first cockfight at the age of about four or five in Mexico during a fiesta (fig. 2):

> I don't know who in the hell took me, but they used to make a few fights during fiestas near Monterrey in Nuevo Leon. I remember, like in a dream, when they used to fight those chickens. I think that is why I have this in

Figure 2. The author's uncle, R. Garcia, holds one of his first roosters, a young McClanahan. The photograph was taken circa 1953 at the Crewport Labor Camp in Granger, Washington. Garcia family photo collection.

my blood. I was about fourteen when I fought my first rooster. It was a gaff fight. I actually won my first fight against an old timer. I guess this is why I got hooked. However, I don't think I got real serious about cockfighting until after I got married at age twenty and was making enough money. At this time I had maybe four roosters. Right now I have over two hundred that I breed and fight.

My uncle introduced my father to cockfighting. By the time my father entered the sport my uncle already had a decade of experience as a breeder and handler. According to my uncle, when he and my father arrived in the Pacific Northwest, Anglos were the dominant cockfighters in the region, though that changed as more Mexicans arrived. My uncle mentioned that within the region an economic cross-section of society participated in cockfighting, but I sense that he may have derived this impression from observing the sport as practiced by Anglos in other areas of the country. Among Anglos, it is clear that cockfighting does appeal to a wide socioeconomic circle. The sport's various trade magazines as well as the (limited) scholarship on the topic and statistical data gleaned from surveys provide evidence that a cross-section of US society participates in cockfighting. However, among Mexicans, working-class males dominate cockfighting in the Pacific Northwest, with very little representation from other socioeconomic groups. While very few surveys on cockfighters have been done, either in the United States or in Mexico, a 1991 survey of cockfighting in the United States found most cockfighters to be

> white male Protestants from small communities or rural areas in the general southern region of the United States, who were likely to have grown up in similar localities. They were usually married, had slightly more children than the national average, with a median age of 42, and an average educational attainment of high school graduation or 1 to 2 years of college. For the most part, they were skilled craftsmen, managers, or owners of small businesses. (Bryant and Li 1991, 199–202)

In contrast to this socioeconomic diversity, my observations at Mexican cockfights and discussions with Mexican cockfighters suggest they have similar rural backgrounds and occupational levels, although because of regional differences Mexicans residing in eastern Washington tend to be in agricultural occupations. Furthermore, at the two dozen fights I have attended, Chicano (as opposed to Mexican) males were noticeably absent, and the few who attended were there as spectators.

My uncle further observed that Mexican immigration to the Pacific Northwest changed not only the ethnic makeup of cockfighting there but also the very nature of the fight. When my family arrived in the region in the 1950s cockfighting was primarily done with the American gaff. However, as Mexicans began arriving and supplanting Anglo cockfighters, they introduced the Mexican knife described earlier. This surprised me, since I was under the impression that my father and uncle had always fought with the knife. However, my uncle remembers that it was a difficult transition—switching instruments of death—and at first he could not accept the change. In fact, my uncle and father had no experience using the Mexican knife and had to have others show them how to tie it on a rooster's spur. Using a Mexican knife demands a tremendous amount of care and skill from both trainer and handler. Because the knife is razor-sharp, one wrong move can slice off a human finger or slash a wrist. In comparison to the American gaff, the Mexican knife also changes the dynamics of the fight. With the gaff, a well-bred and conditioned game-cock has a clear advantage. The Mexican knife diminishes this advantage due to its "slashing" capacity and the amount of damage it can inflict in a short time. If they wished to continue fighting cocks, my uncle recalls, he and my father had to modify their approach and adapt to the Mexican knife, since it was the preferred style of the Mexican cockfighters coming into the region. Ultimately he and my father did adapt, and by the late 1980s and early 1990s they were still considered the most successful cockfighters in the region.[8]

In my discussions with my father and particularly with my uncle, neither displays much modesty about his cockfighting abilities. My uncle, when discussing his skills as a master breeder, demonstrates the confidence one would expect from a successful cockfighter with fifty years of experi-ence. He is self-assured and states without hesitation that he and his brother raise and fight the best cocks in the Northwest. He also states that he continues to prefer the American gaff fight and compares a gamecock fighting with a gaff to a boxer. "We breed our cocks to have some stamina and power and remain kicking like a boxer, but with the knife it's just one or two 'flys' and one is a winner and the other a loser." I have witnessed numerous cockfights that use the Mexican knife: most end rather quickly, with one cock mortally wounded or killed. With the gaff, by contrast, fights can last for thirty minutes or longer and oftentimes a handler will pull a cock before it is killed.

My father and uncle were both concerned with the public image of the Mexican cockfighter. However, they tended to disagree with that image somewhat. In fact, my uncle became defensive when I posed a question regarding cockfighting and machismo:

> A Mexicano who fights roosters is any goddamn Mexicano. He doesn't have to be no macho. The cockfighter wishes for his roosters to be macho, but he doesn't have to be. The songs about cockfighters I think are just pretend, that is not the reality. A man can never be as brave as rooster.

Later, after I explained to my uncle that I have seen him and my father display forms of machismo, he told me that cockfighters must maintain a certain mystique about themselves. In his estimation, a gamecock is only as good as its breeder and handler, and both bird and human must have an air of confidence and toughness. These contradictory statements are not difficult to understand, given the unsavory image of cockfighting in the media. Furthermore, it also reinforces my argument that the arena of cockfighting provides ethnic Mexicans a sense of control over their lives.

To further explore the interplay between cockfighting and Mexican culture, I have examined my family's rural background in Mexico, and interviewed other *galleros* of similar origins to gauge similarities or differences in culture continuity. Juan Gómez-Quiñones explored the meaning of culture, stating, "Culture is a central concept in all societies and one that encompasses the customs, values, attitudes, ideas, patterns of social behavior and arts common to members of a group. Culture, ethnicity, identity, language, history, nationhood, and nationality are all related" (1979, 55). Almost all of the *galleros*, including my father and uncle, practiced a traditional form of Mexican culture, with its most prominent element being a hierarchal structure. Men are the heads of the households, the main breadwinners and powerbrokers, while women have the roles of mother, homemaker, nurturer, and child bearer.

I was raised in this traditional family structure. My father, although dominant, was not domineering; nonetheless, the notion of machismo remained strong in my family, and it shaped my own masculinity during my adolescent years. My father played a major role until my fourteenth year, when my parents divorced. Thereafter, my mother became the primary role model and I gained much of my identity from her. Cockfighting reinforced a patriarchal notion of masculinity in my family, suggesting another limitation to the concept of "resistance masculinity." For example, although this study argues that some ethnic Mexicans use cockfighting as a form of liberation, other scholars have argued against such a view, stating, "in foregrounding the oppression of men by men, [some] studies risk portraying aggressive, even misogynist, gender displays primarily as liberatory forms of resistance against class and racial oppression" while ignoring that masculinity itself is domination over women (Hondagneu-Sotelo and Messner 2000, 69–70). Furthermore, although my relationship with my father was not antagonistic, I had decided that I would seek respectability outside of the cockfighting world.

I had sensed early on that my father might be grooming me to follow in his footsteps and carry on the cockfighting tradition in our family. At a very early age he allowed me to attend cockfights, witness the training sessions, and sit in on discussions with my uncle—in other words, to be present in a very adult-oriented sport. I recall one incident that speaks to this point. As a young teenager I had accompanied my father and uncle to a large cockfighting derby. In an attempt to give me a sense of belonging and acquaint me with some of the intricacies of cockfighting, my father put me in charge of handling the gaff/knife case. I took this responsibility very seriously, for the case carried all the necessary instruments of destruction needed to win the derby. I proudly followed my father, carrying the case, and at the right moments I opened it so my father could retrieve a gaff or knife. Sometime during the match someone yelled either *policía!* or *la migra!*, signaling a raid by the police or the immigration service or both. It really didn't matter which, since either word brought pandemonium to this illegal sport, where police raids were a constant threat. In most cases these fights took place in remote secret locations known only to the participants within the "circle of trust." In this instance men and gamecocks scattered, but I remained to protect the sacred gaff/knife case and a deputy sheriff apprehended me. My father, seeing his son in police custody, came forward and took full responsibility. In the end my father was fined and had to hire an attorney to retrieve the weapons case, which had been confiscated. I, in turn, had to testify in court about why I was carrying a case full of gaffs and knives. This turned out to be my rite of passage, in which I indirectly earned membership in the underground world of cockfighting.

A Mexican cockfight can take place anywhere that men gather (fig. 3). They can be spontaneous events. For example, because my father and uncle are well-known cockfighters, they are constantly being challenged by new arrivals, possibly up-and-coming *galleros* or others who hold a grudge from a fight lost long ago. In one particular "grudge match," several Mexicanos arrived at my father's home while we were enjoying a barbecue, and the usual challenge ensued. These matches are somewhat unusual because they involve only one fight with, in most instances, a sizeable wager. Mexican cockfighting is conducted for two purposes: first, to determine who has the finest cocks, and second, for financial gain. I have attended cockfights in which the wager amounted to thousands of dollars. Typically two types of betting take place: one in the center between the owners of the cocks, and others on the side among the spectators. Although betting can be more complicated in other cultures, such as in Bali, at Mexican cockfights the system is relatively simple. Rarely are odds given: both the center and outside bets are straight up. However, the center bet tends to be the larger and normally involves a number of supporters pooling their resources. The outside bets, made on a one-to-one basis among the spectators, are usually smaller.

The grudge match I witnessed involved a center bet determined by the principals without side bets being conducted. To an outsider it may appear

Figure. 3. A typical cockfight in the Pacific Northwest, 2001. The two roosters are Bonanza Black breeds out of Okalahoma, also known as the gallo negro. The spectators are predominantly male. Photo taken by R. Garcia. Garcia family photo collection.

that the cockfight, because of its illegal status, has no rules or etiquette. However, it is self-regulated and structured by the participants, and rules of engagement and etiquette are strict. Betting makes it more complicated. For brevity, let me just say that on this day a dispute over the rules turned into a shouting match between a dozen or so cockfighters that almost led to violence—always a danger in a grudge match because of the inflated egos at stake. The bravado of the cockfight, and of the *galleros* themselves, can at times reach the absurd rhetorical level of an argument about who possesses the largest *cojones* (balls). The danger, of course, is that masculinity will be expressed through behavior in which men inflict violence upon themselves and others. Emulating their cocks, they do their utmost to avoid showing tameness, meekness, or a lack of balls. I watched my father in the midst of this dispute, wondering whether I myself would be pulled into this surreal event. As my father and the other cockfighter came closer to each other, it seemed as if they had become the cocks. Their words were reminiscent of the sounds cocks make as they battle and their body language resembled that of cocks ready to plunge in for the kill. In this case, however, cooler heads prevailed, a draw was declared, and the challengers left without serious incident.

At another cockfight in which my father's cock was pitted against another Mexican cock, the fight began, as they all do, with the two male handlers in the middle of the pit, slowly dancing with their cocks in their hands, inciting the birds by allowing them to "bill" at each other. This makes the cocks aggressive and signals that the action is about to begin. However, as I watched my father's opponent handling his cock, I noticed a pistol tucked under his belt. After the match I asked my father about this, and his explanation, although simplistic, speaks to the essential symbolism of cockfighting. The pistol, according to him, was simply an element of bravado. Mexican cockfighters carry weapons to intimidate their opponents and to display bravery, and a few fights later, I saw a pistol tucked under my father's belt.

In retrospect, these incidents seem typical of cockfights. Cockfighting, like any other sport, can have its unsavory elements and moments, but most individuals involved are there to simply enjoy the sport. I have seen heated discussions and disagreements at cockfights, but never have they escalated into physical violence between people, an observation substantiated by my uncle. Moreover, my father and uncle have always been respected for their fairness and incorruptibility, so unpleasant incidents were rare.

Nevertheless, cases have been recorded where violence and shootings have occurred. For example, in Wapato, Washington, several men were shot and one killed while attending a cockfight. From the newspaper account it is difficult to determine whether this incident involved cockfighters or spectators and whether the dispute was over cockfighting or something unrelated. According to the *Seattle Post-Intelligencer* (2001), "Detectives believe the shooting occurred as the result of 'some long-standing hostilities' between [Noe] Sanchez and others at the cockfight." Again, this example serves to illustrate the complexities of my argument regarding "resistance masculinity." It is apparent that in this case masculinity was expressed through violence. Furthermore, displays of masculinity at these matches can transcend the boundaries of cockfighting and spill over into private space, intersecting not only with race and class differences but also with gender. In other words, ethnic Mexicans display multiple forms of masculinity: on the one hand, these can help them resist their marginalization in US society, but on the other, these create a paradox in which Mexicans become the oppressors within their communities.

Yet bravado is an inherent element of the cockfight, particularly at the more formal events in which a *gallero* may be fighting six or eight cocks in one day. My father was a master of bravado and intimidation in the fighting pit, channeling this through the cock itself. He was the handler, while my uncle was the master breeder of the cocks. Each role is significant in its own right, but the handler metaphorically embodies the manliness that needs to be transferred to the cock in order to maintain the cock's fierceness. At the beginning of the paper I described a scene in which my father appeared to be performing a sexual act, but in fact was only tending one of his cocks during a lull in a fight. During such lulls, handlers inspect their cocks for any injuries and use a number of techniques to motivate the bird to fight on with increasing aggressiveness—attention and intimacy that creates an unusual bond between man and cock. Examples of such techniques can be seen in observations of an East Timorese cockfight:

> As the handler inspects his charge for wounds, any sign of glumness provokes gleeful howls from the rival's supporters. The others hold their peace. To revive an injured champion, a handler spruces up the comb, jowls, and fleshy flaps surrounding the ears and may even blow water into the bird's mouth. Each handler has his own favorite methods for effecting recovery. One man I noticed plucked out a tail feather and stuck it down the bird's throat. Another rubbed his charge's back and thighs, stretched its legs, and blew into its open beak. A third, suspecting perhaps a ruptured lung, sucked blood from the stricken creature's mouth. Blowing on the head is also held by some handlers to be efficacious. (Hicks 2001)

The relationship is similar to the one between a boxer and his trainer, although that bond lacks the intimacy a handler shows a cock. My father and uncle each spoke of the need to display a strong sense of confidence while in the pit. My father believes that the gamecock can sense this confidence and will in turn display similar qualities:

> The handler must enter the pit not showing any fear. The rooster does not know fear so the handler cannot fear the other handler. If the handler is not confident this will help the rooster lose.

Elements of masculinity as defined by Mexican culture are kept alive within the arena of the cockfight. They then manifest themselves throughout the community in both negative and positive forms; for example, the aggressiveness and bravado of a cockfight can carry over into general public space, where negative forms of machismo, such as fistfights, are displayed. On the other hand, Mexican males who see masculinity as a positive mechanism for overcoming discriminatory structural forces in the United States display forms of assertiveness, responsibility, and selflessness. As a result, the cockfight becomes the means by which Mexican males are able to create a space of their own in a world far from their origins and, in some way, slow down the process of assimilation. This "resistance masculinity" thus becomes a defensive mechanism against the devaluation of Mexican culture.

This dynamic was very evident within my own family. My father, having lived in the United States for over fifty years, could easily slip back into Mexico without missing a cultural beat. After five decades in the United States he has remained culturally Mexican, and the same can be said of my uncle. Their commonalities consist of an intense interest in cockfighting and continued association with like-minded Mexican men. Although by strict definition my father is a US citizen of Mexican ancestry, because of his naturalization some fifty years ago, he nonetheless remains culturally a Mexicano. By this I mean that he practices a culture that is imbued with his Mexican heritage. He has continued speaking Spanish, socializes frequently with other Mexicans, and maintains ethnic awareness and loyalty—key criteria of Mexican cultural identification, according to Moore and Pachon (1985, 130–31). This is not to say, however, that assimilation forces have not affected my family's first generation. For example, my father and uncle speak both Spanish and English, but read and write only English. This is explained by the limited formal education they received while in Mexico and the United States; for all practical purposes, my elders were *forced* to learn how to read and write only in English. My uncle even admits that his literacy skills in English and Spanish are limited, which is common among first-generation immigrants.

As successful cockfighters, my father and uncle enjoy a sense of accomplishment and respect they could not easily obtain otherwise, given the realities of their position in US society. Cockfighting publications have featured them, individuals seek their advice on all facets of the sport, and within the Mexican community they are honored with the title of "Don," a term that recognizes them as important elders. Thus, for my elders and others, the sport of cockfighting transcends the arena itself and creates a parallel world for its participants. Like *fútbol*, baseball, bullfighting, and the *charreada* (rodeo/variety show), cockfighting is as much about culture and identity as it is about the sport itself. These national pastimes provide participants and spectators a space to practice their culture of origin without ridicule or shame. For Mexican cockfighters, the beloved sport is a connection to their Mexicanness and to a land left behind.

Conclusion

As my uncle stated, "We will keep fighting roosters until the very end. It's in our blood." Historians, sociologists, and anthropologists who have studied cockfighting throughout the world would recognize these words. This devotion to cockfighting is what makes the sport appealing and intriguing as a subject of study. For the Mexican men who breed, train, and fight cocks, the sport appears to have a meaning that reaches beyond watching two roosters battle to the death. Although money and betting are crucial elements, they do not fully explain the devotion displayed by my father and uncle.

Cockfighting in the Mexican community in the United States has a long history. For rural Mexican males in this country, maintenance of the cockfighting tradition has created a buffer against assimilation by providing a gendered space for displays of masculinity. The masculinity on display couples elements of traditional Mexican masculinity with a form of resistance masculinity, and carries over from the sport into the larger Mexican community. Cockfighting, at least for those men I have described in this article, has provided a sense of community and cultural continuity in a place far distant from their place of origin. Considering the limited opportunities and structural barriers that my father and uncle encountered, cockfighting has allowed them to experience a kind of economic and social upward mobility that their working class status in mainstream society did not provide or allow. Lastly, when I see my father's cock matched up against an opponent's cock, I can see that it has an equalizing effect. In the cockfighting pit, it is all about skill and aggressiveness; place of origin, socioeconomic background, race, and ethnicity are effectively neutralized.

In the end, my father was not adamant, forceful, or even concerned when my interest waned and I decided to be a spectator and not a cockfighter. As a second-generation Chicano, I have had opportunities not afforded to my father or uncle, and thus I have been able to challenge oppression and discrimination in other ways. In hindsight, my father may have seen cockfighting as an old tradition that he did not want his children to follow, just as he insisted that his children break the cycle of poverty. Still, there are days I realize that when my father and uncle finally stop fighting gamecocks a family tradition will end.

Postscript (2020)

When this essay was published in *I Am Aztlán* in 2004, cockfighting was still legal in two states, Louisiana and New Mexico, and it was the subject of litigation in Oklahoma (see page 135). Cockfighting is now illegal in all states.

Notes

"The Measure of a Cock: Mexican Cockfighting, Culture, and Masculinity," by Jerry Garcia, is reprinted from *I Am Aztlán: The Personal Essay in Chicano Studies* (Los Angeles: UCLA Chicano Studies Research Center Press, 2004).

I began this essay in the fall of 2001 and subsequently presented a portion of it at the III Congreso Internacional de Literatura de Chicana in Malaga, Spain, in May 2002. I want to thank Sharon Bird, Iowa State University Department of Sociology, for the many discussions we had on masculinity and for her insightful suggestions on fine-tuning this essay. Also, I thank Sidner Larson, director of the American Indian Studies Program at Iowa State University, and Andrejs Plakans, chair of the History Department at Iowa State University, for their support and editorial suggestions. A word of thanks to the anonymous peer reviewers at *Aztlán* for their helpful suggestions and comments. Cathy Sunshine, the copyeditor at the UCLA Chicano Studies Research Center Press, worked her magic throughout this paper. Finally, to my father and uncle—thanks for the unique childhood experiences that continue to resonate with me and for keeping many aspects of our culture alive.

    1. In choosing among the various terms describing Mexicans in the United States, I make use of David G. Gutíerrez's definitions (1993, 520n1). In this essay, when I speak of *Mexican Americans* I am referring to American citizens of Mexican descent, regardless of their length of residence in the United States. The term *Chicano* refers to persons of Mexican descent who used that term as a self-referent during the 1960s and 1970s. I use the term *Mexican immigrants* when referring to citizens of Mexico residing in the United States. Although all of these groups historically have recognized important distinctions among themselves, all have been subject to varying degrees of prejudice and discrimination in the United States, regardless of their formal citizenship status. Thus, when referring to the combined population of all persons of Mexican ancestry or descent living in the United States, I employ the term *ethnic Mexicans*.

2. See also Dundes (1994) and Scott (1983).

3. The handler, formerly called a *setter* or *setter-to*, is supposed have expert knowledge of preparing cocks for battle and handling them during the actual fights. For terms associated with cockfighting see Scott (1983, 188–93).

4. Statements in this essay attributed to my uncle were obtained in an interview I did with him on January 3, 2003. My father and uncle are still active cockfighters and to protect their identities I cannot use their names or disclose their whereabouts. After all, this is an illegal sport.

5. There remains a paucity of literature on the Mexican diaspora in the Pacific Northwest. Further discussion on ethnic Mexicans in this region can be found in Maldonado and Garcia (2001, 1–7). For insight into the Spanish exploration of the Pacific Northwest see Weber (1992), and for additional readings on the origins of Mexicans in the Pacific Northwest see Gamboa and Baun (1995).

6. I interviewed my aunt and uncle on January 9, 2003.

7. Under normal circumstances I would provide a citation to the issue of *Gamecock* in which my elders appeared. However, for security purposes I am unable to provide any information that could reveal the identities of my father and uncle.

8. For an excellent description of a cockfight see Clifford Geertz's article (1972) on Balinese cockfighting. The Mexican cockfight and rules of engagement are similar to the Balinese.

Works Cited

Baca Zinn, Maxine. 1982. "Chicano Men and Masculinity." *Journal of Ethnic Studies* 10, no. 2: 29–43.

Bradley, Hugh. 1941. *Havana: Cinderella's City*. New York: Doubleday, Doran.

Bryant, Clifton D., and Li Li. 1991. "A Statistical Value Profile of Cockfighters." *Sociology and Social Research* 75, no. 4: 199–209.

Briceño, Olga. 1945. *Cocks and Bulls in Caracas: How We Live in Venezuela*. Boston: Houghton Mifflin.

Burstyn, Varda. 1999. *The Rites of Men: Manhood, Politics, and the Culture of Sport*. Toronto: University of Toronto Press.

Cantú, Lionel. 2000. "*Entre Hombres*/Between Men: Latino Masculinities and Homosexualities." In *Gay Masculinities*, edited by Peter Nardi. Thousand Oaks, CA: Sage Publications.

Carrasco, David, with Scott Sessions. 1998. *Daily Life of the Aztec: People of the Sun and Earth*. Westport, CT: Greenwood Press.

Chivers, C. J. 2000. "Police Storm Cockfighting Tournament in a Derelict Bronx Theatre." *New York Times*, June 5.

Clendinnen, Inga. 1991. *Aztecs: An Interpretation*. Cambridge: Cambridge University Press.

Connell, R. W. 1996. "Teaching the Boys: New Research on Masculinity, and Gender Strategies for Schools." *Teachers College Record* 98, no. 2: 208.

———. 1995. *Masculinities*. Berkeley and Los Angeles: University of California Press.

Crosby, Alfred W. Jr. 1972. *The Columbian Exchange: Biological and Cultural Consequences of 1492*. Westport, CT: Greenwood Press.

del Castillo, Adelaida R. 1996. "Gender and Its Discontinuities in Male/Female Domestic Relations: Mexicans in Cross-Cultural Context." In *Chicanas/Chicanos at the Crossroads: Social, Economic, and Political Change*, edited by David R. Maciel and Isidro D. Ortiz. Tucson: University of Arizona Press.

Dundes, Alan. 1994. *The Cockfight: A Casebook*. Madison: University of Wisconsin Press.

Gamboa, Erasmo, and Carolyn M. Baun. 1995. *Nosotros: The Hispanic People of Oregon, Essays and Collections*. Portland: Oregon Council for the Humanities.

Geertz, Clifford. 1972. "Deep Play: Notes on the Balinese Cockfight." *Daedalus: Journal of the American Academy of Arts and Sciences* 101, no. 1: 1–37. Reprinted in *The Cockfight: A Casebook*, edited by Alan Dundes. Madison: University of Wisconsin Press, 1994.

Gómez-Quiñones, Juan. 1979. "Toward a Concept of Culture." In *Modern Chicano Writers: A Collection of Critical Essays*, edited by Joseph Sommers and Tomás Ybarra-Frausto. Upper Saddle River, NJ: Prentice Hall.

Gutiérrez, David G. 1993. "Significant to Whom? Mexican Americans and the History of the American West." *Western Historical Quarterly* 24, no. 4: 519–39.

Hassig, Ross. 1988. *Aztec Warfare: Imperial Expansion and Political Control*. Norman: University of Oklahoma Press.

Hicks, David. 2001. "Blood and Feathers: Masculine Identity in East Timorese Cockfighting." *World and I*, January. http://www.etan.org/et2001a/january/07-13/07blood.htm.

Hondagneu-Sotelo, Pierrette, and Michael A. Messner. 2000. "Gender Displays and Men's Power: The 'New Man' and the Mexican Immigrant Man." In *Gender Through the Prism of Difference*, 2nd ed., edited by Maxine Baca Zinn, Pierrette Hondagneu-Sotelo, and Michael A. Messner. Boston: Allyn and Bacon.

Ingersoll, Ernest. 1923. *Birds in Legend, Fable, and Folklore*. New York: Longman's, Green.

Kilborn, T. 2000. "In Enclaves of Rural America, a Cockfighting Industry Thrives." *New York Times*, June 6.

Klein, Alan M. 2000. "Dueling Machos: Masculinity and Sport in Mexican Baseball." In *Masculinities, Gender Relations, and Sport*, edited by Jim McKay, Michael A. Messner, and Donald F. Sabo. London: Sage Publications.

Madsen, William. 1973. *Mexican Americans of South Texas*. New York: Holt, Rinehart, and Winston.

Majors, Richard. 1990. "Cool Pose: Black Masculinity and Sports." In *Sport, Men, and Gender Order: Critical Feminist Perspectives*, edited by Michael A. Messner and Donald F. Sabo. Champaign, IL: Human Kinetics Books.

Majors, Richard, and Janet Mancini Billson. 1992. *Cool Pose: The Dilemmas of Black Manhood in America*. New York: Lexington Books.

Maldonado, Carlos S., and Gilberto Garcia. 2001. *The Chicano Experience in the Northwest*, 2d ed. Dubuque, IA: Kendall/Hunt.

McCaghy, H., and Arthur G. Neal. 1973. "The Fraternity of Cockfighters: Ethical Embellishments of an Illegal Sport." *Journal of Popular Culture* 8, no. 3: 557–69.

Mirandé, Alfredo. 1997. *Hombres y Machos: Masculinity and Latino Culture*. Boulder, CO: Westview.

Moore, Joan, and Harry Pachon. 1985. *Hispanics in the United States*. Upper Saddle River, NJ: Prentice Hall.

Najera, Rick. 1997. *The Pain of the Macho and Other Plays*. Houston: Arte Público.

Paredes, Américo. 1993. *Folklore and Culture on the Texas-Mexican Border*. Austin: University of Texas, Center for Mexican American Studies.

Paz, Octavio. 1950. *El laberinto de la soledad*. Mexico City: Cuadernos Americanos.

Plass, Paul. 1995. *The Game of Death in Ancient Rome: Arena Sport and Political Suicide*. Madison: University of Wisconsin Press.

Portes, Alejandro, and Rubén G. Rumbaut. 1996. *Immigrant America: A Portrait*. Berkeley and Los Angeles: University of California Press.

Ross, Brian. 2001. "Roosters with Razors: Cockfighting Still Legal in Three States, Gambling Persists." ABC News website, March 30.

Scott, George Ryley. 1983. *The History of Cockfighting*. Hindhead, Surrey, UK: Saiga.

Seattle Post–Intelligencer. 2001. "Victim Likely Had Been Bystander at Shooting." December 5.

St. Augustine, Bishop of Hippo. 1942. *Divine Providence and the Problem of Evil: A Translation of St. Augustine's De Ordine*, translated by Robert P. Russell. New York: Cosmopolitan Science and Art Service.

Wasserman, Mark. 2000. *Everyday Life and Politics in Nineteenth Century Mexico: Men, Women, and War*. Albuquerque: University of New Mexico Press.

Weber, David J. 1992. *The Spanish Frontier in North America*. New Haven, CT: Yale University Press.

West, Nathaniel. 1969. "California Cockfight." In *The Day of the Locust*. New York: New Direction Books.

Wucker, Michele. 1999. *Why the Cocks Fight: Dominicans, Haitians, and the Struggle for Hispaniola*. New York: Hill and Wang.

Remembrance of Raymond Moreno, Founding Member of the Group Workshop

Renee M. Moreno

In the preface to her book *Silent Dancing: A Partial Remembrance of a Puerto Rican Childhood*, Judith Ortiz Cofer writes, "As one gets older, childhood years are often conveniently consolidated into one perfect summer's afternoon. The events can be projected on a light blue screen; the hurtful parts can be edited out, and the moments of joy brought in sharp focus to the foreground. It is our show. But with all that on the cutting room floor, what remains to tell?" (1990, 11). Ortiz Cofer thus suggests that while capturing "moments of joy," one must also confront the painful, even troubling parts of an untold narrative.

This essay recovers an untold story of my father, Chicano artist and labor activist Raymond Moreno. Born June 16, 1932, he was married to my mother, Florence Davis, and was the father of eight children. He was only forty years old when he was killed in a car accident on September 22, 1972, leaving his young wife and family. The oldest of the eight siblings was only seventeen when he died; the youngest was five. In remembering my father, I have often vacillated between romantic notions of him as an artist and labor activist—doing the creative and difficult work of making life better for his family and community—and anger that he left this world so young. As a result of his death, I experienced considerable pain and confusion in my life, both as a child and as an adult. The narrative of my life was broken, as happens when one experiences the death of a young parent (Bowlby 1969, 8). To deal with this pain, I started to collect the stories and histories of his life, along with my own recollections and those of my family members, in order to work through old grief and to begin putting the pieces of a "broken narrative" back together. Ortiz Cofer also raises the question of the pieces of a narrative left on the "cutting room floor" and renders "speakable" (Morrison 1989) what may have been left unspoken—as were the events surrounding my father's death. The question, after all, is a rhetorical one, and there is much that remains to be told.

My father's death certificate and other "objective" records report in stark detail how he died, but this was only one small piece of a complex life story. When I asked for more details about the hows and whys of my father's death, my mother Florence and my sister Dolores filled in the unspoken narrative and "rip[ped] that veil drawn over 'proceedings too terrible to relate'" (Morrison 1990, 302). My process of transformation and, eventually, healing from these traumatic events included embracing the painful parts of his narrative, which I recount later in this essay. My father also left a corpus of artwork created as a result of his collaboration with other artists who formed an arts collective known as the Group Workshop. Much of this artwork hung in our home for years, slipping into the backdrop of our daily lives, before I started to ask questions about his activities and engagement in the nascent Chicano arts movement, the labor movement, and the Chicano movement in Denver, Colorado. This artwork was telling a story, I realized, and it represented yet another unspoken, uninterpreted narrative of his life.

Contextualizing his work brings up several issues, given that the focus of Chicano art scholarship tends to be on artists from California or Texas. The objective seems simple: to write my father and the artists he worked with into the master narrative of Chicano art and to give them a chance to be evaluated among other Chicana/o artists who created artwork during the 1960s and 1970s. Yet the task is a complicated one. When I was exploring his importance as an artist, his work with labor, and his role in the Chicano arts movement in Denver, I relied on the help of informants—his fellow artists and activists, his co-workers and union brothers, people who labored alongside my father in their workaday lives. Many of them recall the unique contributions that he made as an artist and positively recall his personal attributes and character. When I met the artist and muralist Carlotta Espinoza in 2010, almost forty years after my father's death, she remarked that it was as if the ghost of my father had walked through her door. Certain facial expressions that I made during our interview reminded her of him. My father was a tall man who stood just over six feet, and according to Espinoza, I sat like him, even slumped in the chair and crossed my arms and legs like him. Another informant, Willie Ray Montoya (2008), said that he missed my father more at the present time than he had in all the years since my father's death. Montoya had often wondered how my father would have counseled him about various paths his life had taken, certain decisions he had made for good or for bad. Several times during our conversation, he wondered aloud, "What would Ray have done had he lived longer?" This suggests to me that many people, both friends and fellow artists, were traumatized by his passing and that his death had marked them in significant ways. My father's friends and colleagues missed and longed for him, evoking some of the grief I had experienced as a child and as an adult.

To mediate my grief, I relied on my training as a scholar to trace my father's story. I went to archives, both formal and informal, to seek him out. Especially useful was the Denver Public Library's Western History and Genealogy collection, whose general index documents the history of Denver. Organized under headings like "Chicano Arts Organizations" and "Chicano Theater," the collection references historical newspaper articles, clipping files, and much more. In this way, I was able to follow an archival trail to document the "official" history of the Group Workshop. This enabled me to learn about my father's creative activities with other artists, such as exhibitions by the Group Workshop artists, and their work in the Denver arts community, such as the effort to establish a cultural arts center on the predominately Chicano Westside (Marvel 1970). The archive also revealed details of his union activities (Colorado Labor Advocate 1972, 1).

However, as Eduardo Galeano observes, "History books are not supposed to be subjective" (1991, 120), and a certain anxiety of legitimacy has always surrounded my telling of my father's story. Throughout this essay, I reference scholars and artists who have worked through their own anxiety of legitimacy, including Galeano (1991), Rina Benmayor (1987), Sonia Saldívar-Hull (2000), Robin D. G. Kelley (1993), and others. Their work, much like my father's, is created both inside and outside institutional spaces and calls attention to working folk doing ordinary and extraordinary things in their everyday lives. Like my efforts to establish an "official history," their scholarship helps legitimize my father's story and recognizes that history is not always found in the places we expect. This task of recovering lost histories contributes to a larger historical vision of society. By culling through lost histories of everyday people doing important work in art and social movements, we begin to build a different story of American history, one that includes subjectivity as a frame of reference. As Galeano goes on to observe,

> I mentioned this [subjectivity] to José Coronel Urtecho: in this book I'm writing, however you look at it, backwards or forwards, in the light or against it, my loves and quarrels can be seen at a single glance.
>
> And on the banks of the San Juan River, the old poet told me that there is no fucking reason to pay attention to the fanatics of objectivity:
>
> *"Don't worry,"* he said to me. *"That's how it should be. Those who make objectivity a religion are liars. They are scared of human pain. They don't want to be objective, it's a lie: they want to be objects, so as not to suffer."* (1991, 120, emphasis in original)

History, according to Galeano, is a process of constructing narratives and contextualizing them into lived experiences. As he writes in the historical narrative *Memory of Fire* (1985), his life is reflected and explained in the writing: "what had happened was happening, happening all around," and writing was a way to strike out and embrace (120). The stories he hears make him "replace" himself in the larger historical narrative. Confronting the sum of his experiences—his subjectivity—is necessary to Galeano's act of writing histories, which in turn write his own life. My own subjectivity, similarly, enables me to place myself and my lived experiences (as a Chicana and scholar, and as the daughter of a labor activist and Chicano artist) within larger frameworks of history, culture, and society. My own subjectivity reveals why telling a story can perform certain kinds of interventions. Storytelling has allowed me to understand the particular circumstances of my father's life and the contributions he made to his community and society, and also to embrace the painful aspects of his death.

Re-membering a Broken Narrative

On the day he died, my father and some co-workers left work at lunch and headed to a bar in lower downtown Denver, a chic spot now but in those days rather seedy. When they came back to work at the meatpacking plant, a foreman noticed their intoxication and suspended them for the day. They left and returned downtown to continue drinking. As they were returning to the packinghouse to retrieve their cars and go home, my father lost control of the car, which struck the railing of a bridge. He was the only one severely injured in the accident; he sustained lethal head injuries as a result of the impact and died a short time later.

His unexpected passing devastated our family. We struggled to put the pieces of our shattered lives together again and to mend the narrative of a family. Being so young, I found it difficult to articulate exactly what I was feeling, and I remember succumbing to undirected rage or pain when words failed me. Having no language to express the intensity of my grief, I used whatever strategies I could to make my life feel whole. When we were expected to return to school less than two weeks after his death, I feigned illness to stay at home. When my faked illnesses were discovered and I was forced to return, I invented new strategies. I also remember clearly my frustration at not being able to communicate with the adults around me, who supposedly knew more than I did but who were dealing with their own pain and trying to make sense of the loss. Death, I came to realize, is inevitable, but death at such a young age seemed so unnatural that I struggled throughout most of my life to understand exactly what my father's death might mean. In the process, I came to know that understanding his death meant "re-membering" his life (Morrison 1987).

A veteran labor leader, my father was a longtime member of the Amalgamated Meat Cutters and Butcher Workmen Local P-85. By the time of his death, he had served his union as a steward, vice president, and assistant chief steward (Colorado Labor Advocate 1972, 1). His service no doubt reflected his profound distaste for injustice and his identification with the dispossessed and marginalized members of society. As a child growing up in the rural community of Brighton, Colorado, he would see signs hanging in windows which read "No dogs, farm animals or Mexicans allowed." His painting *Posadas 1969* (fig. 1), I am convinced, is a comment on the injustices that Chicanos were experiencing in the late 1960s; the painting depicts people suffering abuse at the hands of the police and other authorities, abuse that could be particularly brutal in Denver. (Denver police, as documented by Ernesto Vigil [1999], carried out surveillance on citizens independent of the FBI and enlisted a vast network of informants who were paid to attend political gatherings and report back to their police handlers. In fact, many one-time activists requested their "police surveillance files" under the Freedom of Information Act when these became publicly available. In one of the FOIA requests in Corky Gonzales's archive, there are pages of blacked-out names of informants who regularly attended meetings at the Crusade for Justice and reported to the police.)

The son of an immigrant, my father was also allied with the struggles of Mexican migrant farmworkers. My older sisters experienced their own initiation in popular struggle when they picketed and leafleted on behalf of the United Farm Workers (UFW) outside Safeway supermarkets during the most intense moments of this movement. My father's struggle was also for quality of life—more humane working conditions, better wages for workers who might otherwise be exploited. The 1960s and 1970s were

Figure 1. Raymond Moreno, Posadas 1969, *1969. Oil on canvas. Image courtesy of Carlos Santistevan.*

Figure 2. Raymond Moreno, untitled painting of the Virgin, date unknown. Oil on canvas. Slide courtesy of Carlos Santistevan.

decades in which ordinary men, women, and young people—like my father and my sisters—were moved to express their grievances and to participate in grassroots social movements, such as the UFW and the unions. Growing up in a union family, my sister Sharon confided, gives one an open mind and opens one's eyes to things that otherwise may go unnoticed. She remembers fondly Christmas breakfasts at the CIO union hall in Denver, to which our whole family was invited. An untitled painting, reprinted from a slide photograph in Carlos Santistevan's archive, may have been painted as a result of our father's work with the UFW and his union (fig. 2). The whereabouts of the original painting is unknown, although I suspect that it may reside in a private archive. At the end of the day, the work of recovering the narratives of forgotten artists requires painstaking research, culling through archives or dusty, unorganized papers that someone thought important to save. Thank God for the hoarders, I often argue, because without them we might not be able to connect the lives of working people to a larger historical narrative.

But even those recovered details do not tell the whole story. My mother confided to me that the packinghouse was a "horrendous" place to work and that alcohol abuse may have provided my father a way to cope with the indignities of such work, just as his participation in his union was a coping strategy—hope and destruction coexisting. Alisea McLeod's dissertation, "Living Detroit" (1998), similarly narrates stories of alcoholism and drug abuse at assembly plants in Detroit; for these workers, substance abuse was a way to endure the boring, humiliating, even life-robbing aspects of assembly work. Very few strategies exist to invest workers with a sense of dignity in work that is not meant to be dignified or fulfilling. At the same time, I do not want to suggest that drinking alcohol as a respite from work is necessarily an illness. My partner Georg often reminds me of the differences between American and European views on alcohol: Americans view alcohol consumption from a puritanical, Christian perspective that too often denies bodily pleasures, while Europeans value the social space of the pub or Biergarten or Stammtisch (literally the "regular table") as a place to unwind, talk, and socialize. My dad and his friends and comrades also participated in the social aspects of drinking. How could they not? They were artists, after all, who looked to social spaces to create and engage in "talk."

My older sister Dolores connected my mother's part of the story to even more interesting issues. Shortly before my father's death, a plan to close the packinghouse came to light. My father's union worked to keep it open. "Can you imagine the stress he was under!" Dolores asked. "What would have happened to our family if Dad had been laid off?" Less than ten years after his death, management began to lay off and fire workers, which the union asserted was in violation of their contract; about three years later, the meatpacking plant did shut down (Rocky Mountain News 1981, 7; 1984, 16). The closing of the plant had profound and lasting implications, adding to social distress in our community and reshaping it in ways that have been documented by social historians in other settings where plants have closed (Davis 1994). Dolores also mentioned another aspect of my father's death that many of us had overlooked: my grandfather, Epifanio Moreno, had said something to her about my father not getting his car fixed. The gas pedal kept sticking, according to my grandfather, and he and my sister believed this may have contributed to the accident.

In the days following his death, many people visited our family, wanting to help however they could or simply wanting to express their grief. My father's fellow artist and union brother, Pete Suminez, wrote a poem in one of my father's sketchbooks that captured my father's humanity:

> The Lord called out as you made that turn.
> Ray, I need you now.
> So you left.
> Alone you went to meet him. Even though you weren't finished here,
> but you were like that.
> When someone needed you, you were there.
> Now you paint for God.
> He gave you forty years to learn. You did well here on earth.
> You captured the hearts of your fellow man.
> You wove a fabric of love and humility in the hearts of those you met.
> All those great workers in heaven must be proud.
> You are good enough to sit and show your originality to them.
> Good luck Ray, and may God in his wisdom find suitable tasks for
> your talents.

The poem is a narrative for my father's family, and in the intervening years it has become a fitting tribute to his life's work as an artist and an activist. Parts of the poem were inscribed on his cemetery marker.

The Group Workshop

During his short life, my father was a productive artist. Through interviews and archival work, I learned that he was one of four artists who formed the Denver collective known as the Group Workshop, which flourished during the late 1960s and early 1970s. In addition to my father, the Group Workshop included Bob Crespin, Carlotta Espinoza, and Ray Espinoza. These three men and one woman were factory workers, office workers, and teachers, all working-class; none of them worked full-time as an artist. Yet they managed to set up a center for artistic collaboration and representation, exhibiting the spirit of cooperation and coalition building that marked the era. Denver art critic Barbara Haddad took note:

> If you happen to be in the neighborhood of the Exodus, at 28 E. 28th Ave. to be exact, you may come upon the most-unusual innovation of the current art scene. Called "The Group Workshop," it is a promising attempt by some young Spanish Americans to establish an interracial art center.

> While news of such a development might be expected to evoke good wishes, a figurative pat on the back and then casual dismissal, the big surprise at the workshop is that much of the art is far too vigorous to be patronized. A few works on view are better than some being featured in commercial galleries. (1968, 16)

The purpose of the Group Workshop was to give artists a chance to develop, to exhibit, and to collaborate with each other. At the time, few spaces existed in Denver where Chicano artists could show their work, and the founding of the Group Workshop was influenced by the activist spirit of the time. The Group Workshop artists had a significant, though "loose," connection to Rodolfo "Corky" Gonzales's Crusade for Justice, according to Willie Ray Montoya (2011). Indeed, my father and Corky grew up together. According to Montoya (2011), Corky and his brothers Fred and Al lived in the same Eastside neighborhood as my father, and they all knew each other as children. Gonzales's archive has recently become available at the Denver Public Library, Western History Collection. One document, titled "Proposal for the Crusade for Justice Cultural Arts Center," sets forth the plans for an art center:

> The [center] will offer workshops in art, drama, history, and writing. The Crusade through its art workshop will also be working toward creating opportunities for young artists to be able to display their work. Currently, ten artists [who included the Group Workshop artists] meet regularly to discuss the Mexican emphasis of their work. Many of these artists are accomplished painters and sculptors, all have the desire to continue to create while also wanting to teach others. *These artists have had little success in Denver, being able to show their art work in local galleries.* This lack of success in their work being shown has hindered their own development. Included in this proposal will be opportunities for periodic art shows as well as public performances of drama groups at times to be held simultaneously so that various artists get an opportunity for public exposure. (Gonzales 1967, 5, emphasis mine)

Although the Group Workshop was independent of the Crusade for Justice, their activities sometimes intersected. The library archive contains various playbills showing that Group Workshop artists were often featured when a play was performed at the Crusade for Justice building, which was an important gathering spot for the Chicano community. One playbill in my possession, from Carlos Santistevan's archive, shows a concurrent art exhibition when a play was performed at the Crusade for Justice. While my father and the other artists were supportive of the Crusade for Justice, occasionally participating in demonstrations, my father understood that artists were a "valuable piece of the larger revolution"—an opinion Gonzales appeared to share. "The artists," according to Montoya (2011), had "opinions of their own, and your dad's was that of the working man."

Ray Espinoza (2011) reports that he and Carlotta met my father at Denver's Emily Griffith Opportunity School, a place where adults could take classes and advance their skills. My father, according to my mother, had been looking for studio space, and he thought that Ray and Carlotta could share the rent. Carlotta knew Bob Crespin, who also took classes at the Opportunity School, and invited him to join them.

Walter Green, who taught at the Opportunity School, was a locally and nationally recognized artist. He was also the founder of the Colorado Water Colorist Association, of which Moreno was also an active member.

> Ray [Moreno] studied at Emily Griffith Opportunity School in Denver under [Walter] Green for ten years, until the instructor thought [Moreno] had learned all [Green] could teach him. Entirely different from all of Colorado's artists, Ray was in a class all his own. If his work was to be compared for style, one would have to say that he had a little of the genius of Rufino Tamayo, Toulouse Lautrec, and Pablo Picasso. (Espinoza 1977, 11)

In addition to his work at the Opportunity School, Green exhibited throughout Colorado and maintained a studio in the mountains (Arneill 1959; Rocky Mountain News 1956). There my father and his colleagues from the Group Workshop and the Colorado Water Colorist Association would spend weekends painting and collaborating. Green's connection to Moreno is important on a couple of levels. First, it demonstrates that Chicano artists were by no means shaped only by the Chicano movement of the 1960s and 1970s, as influential as it was on their development and visibility as artists. Second, artists like Raymond Moreno were having conversations with other artists not only across class and ethnic/racial differences, but also across time, as evident in Espinoza's observations about Moreno's connections to Tamayo, Picasso, and Lautrec.

My interviews with Ray Espinoza (2011) and Carlotta Espinoza (2010) confirm that Chicano artists were not working in a vacuum but were in fact reaching out to other artists. In Group Workshop meetings, the artists would often challenge each other to create, picking out a reproduction by one of the Old Masters in order to copy it or reenvision it to suit their purposes. They also collaborated with other local artists, including Vance Kirkland, the noted Denver painter. Carlotta Espinoza states, "Denver was a small city at the time. Artists knew one another. Ray Espinoza introduced me to [other artists like] Vance Kirkland, and [Moreno] also knew him" (2010).

My father's corpus of artwork, some of which is featured here, needs to be recognized and evaluated—not only in the context in which it was created, namely the Chicano movement, the Chicano arts movement, and the labor movement of the 1960s and 1970s, but also in the context of today's Chicano art. Where does Moreno rank among artists of his time? What influence did he have on the artists with whom he worked, and on the generation of artists who came after him? What about those who see his work now and evaluate and learn from it? A central question has to do with how we collect narratives of artists like Moreno, who worked at their art and left a body of work for other generations of viewers. What does it mean to reevaluate and resurrect an artist in order to place him within the master narrative of Chicano art—and even for his daughter to do it?

Such questions need to asked, given that the stories of many artists across the country who created art at different moments have been forgotten or eclipsed by the stories of better-known artists. Or perhaps their stories have been overlooked because we most often associate Chicano art with places that have large populations of Chicanos, like California or Texas (Gaspar de Alba 1998). Although a great deal of scholarship, including published catalogs for national exhibitions, has elevated Chicano art to the mainstream, it has done so only for some artists and in some parts of the country, California being the most prominent (Griswold del Castillo, McKenna, and Yarbro-Bejarano 1991; Malagamba-Ansótegui et al. 2006; Pérez 2007). Less is known about artists from areas with smaller, but nevertheless active, Chicano communities, and their connection to the Chicano movement and Chicano art master narrative has been largely overlooked. Lack of representation from these smaller communities has been noted before, starting with the CARA exhibit. As Gaspar de Alba reports, the exhibition was "criticized in all ten cities it . . . toured" (1998, 188). One viewer complained, "What the exhibit lacks, perhaps, is more representation of Colorado artists." Another wrote, "Zoot suits and pachucos were born in El Paso's Segundo Barrio. San Antonio had the first arts group. But visit the [CARA] exhibit, and you'd think it all happened in California" (188).

Artists who were my father's contemporaries in Denver went on to experience highs and lows in their careers. In the years following the Group Workshop, they struggled to make a living as artists, and some may have even stepped backwards in their artistic development due to isolation and lack of recognition. While we need to recover as many stories as we can, my father's story, given his work in popular social movements of the day, is particularly compelling and instructive. It is working folks like my father whose stories may ultimately shape another narrative of Chicano art.

Denver artist Carlos Fresquez (2009) told me that seeing my father's artwork reminds him of the "timelessness of art." To Fresquez, Moreno's art "feels contemporary" even though much of the work is decades old. Reflected in the artwork, Fresquez says, is "Moreno's intelligence" and his "hipness and style." Such observations from a working artist validate the long hours that my father spent developing his craft and add to the folklore surrounding his short but prolific life.

Wynton Marsalis, the jazz musician, has said that "the thing about art is, it is always now" (2006). He states,

> Charlie Parker would be great if he came today and played the same exact stuff he played. He would still be a genius. So I have to pay my respects to music. . . . There's been a lot of cats who really spent hours at the craft. That's the thing. I feel a lot of times our music is tied up in serious folklore. And the musicians add to that. . . . People have got to understand that you must learn the craft of the music. The art form has a craft. (Marsalis 1992, 337–39)

It can be argued that assiduous attention to the craft and "paying respects" to what other artists (be they visual artists or musicians) have done before are important components of the development and genius of artistic work—traits that will cross time and space, difference and particularity.

In interviews, Moreno's friends and fellow artists have often remarked that he was ahead of the curve (much like Parker), not only in terms of the artwork he created but also in his life perspective—what one might even term "his style." I would also underscore that this style, evident in his photo (fig. 3), was born of "the daily indignities of the factory [and] utopian visions of a life free of difficult wage work" (Kelley 1993, 75). Writing of African Americans, Robin D. G. Kelley argues,

> For members of a class whose long workdays were spent in backbreaking, low-paid wage work in settings pervaded by racism, the places where they played were more than relatively free spaces in which to articulate griev- ances and dreams. They were places that enabled African Americans to take back their bodies, to recuperate, to be together. (75)

Figure 3. Raymond Moreno. Image courtesy of the author.

Similarly, the Group Workshop, as Ray Espinoza (2011) has commented, "was a place where the artists could play, experiment, enjoy each one another's company, and support each other." Willie Ray Montoya recalls that "Ray saw art in everything. Even in something like boxing. He was listening to music [like jazz] that many of us would discover only later" (2008) (fig. 4).

My father's friends recall him as a hardworking artist who painstakingly attended to his craft. He would often wake up in the wee hours of the morning to paint before leaving for his job at the Cudahy meatpacking plant in the nearby neighborhood of Elyria. The toil of that job, which Willie Ray Montoya describes as going into a "dungeon of death and blood and guts" (2008), must have made creating art seem almost like a purification—or at the very least a reminder of what his life's work really was. Leaving the factory in the afternoon, Moreno would head to the Group Workshop to create with his fellow artists and enjoy the community so necessary for artists if they are to flourish and develop.

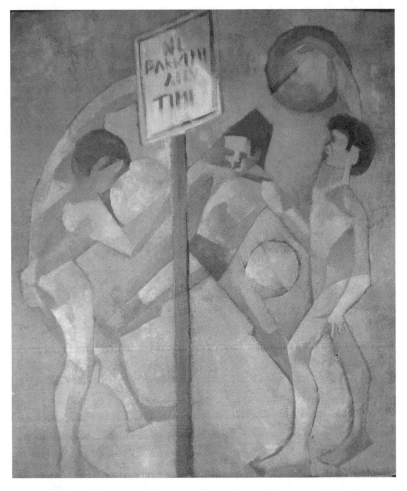

Figure 4. Raymond Moreno, untitled painting, date unknown. Oil on canvas. Image courtesy of Carlos Santistevan.

A Painting Never Finished

Unpacking grief through storytelling or seeking to understand the circum-stances surrounding a death might seem like an exercise in confronting private pain before an impersonal audience. I am sure that my choice to relate specific circumstances of my father's death may distress members of my family who have made peace with their grief. But the story of the last moments of his life, which reveal the creative and self-destructive forces that coexisted in him, helps flesh out the sum of his being, which makes him more human, more sympathetic, and ultimately more complicated. Embracing my father's story, including facts that cause pain, has not only helped me heal from this traumatic event; it has helped reveal who my father really was in his life outside the factory floor. It enables us to place his personal story in the context of larger social issues. Yet his narrative remains incomplete, despite my best effort to re-member it.

The answer to the question that Ortiz Cofer proposes at the beginning of this essay also lies in imagination and art. Ortiz Cofer's "partial remembrances," where she "track[s] an image from picture to meaning to text" (Morrison 1990, 305), instills in her "confidence in the power of art to discover meaning and truth in ordinary events" (Cofer 1990, 13). Similarly, the poem my father's friend wrote for him and the events that I have narrated and learned from others are clues in "re-membering" the pieces of my father's narrative, which was broken upon his death. Reading the poem years later, I realize that it sums up his best quality, which was his generosity and his ability to affect others through his work and his art. The stories told by my mother, my sister, and my father's fellow artists and co-workers show the stresses he and other workers faced as they connected the personal to the social and produced highly creative work amid circumstances that negated creativity and freedom.

Furthermore, in writing imaginatively about my partial remembrances, I develop my father's narrative that the poem began and my informants continued. On my perfect summer's afternoon, my dad is painting, an activity that he named his "ninth child." He is mixing paints, working on some canvas, with an unfiltered Camel cigarette perched on his lip. His friends and fellow artists report that he would paint a canvas over and over and over again; the painting would transform from one day to the next as he worked on it. For him, a painting was never finished. The sunlight is streaming in through a window on one of those glorious sunny days in Denver, a memory that often caused me to curse living in the perpetual gray of the Midwest when I was in graduate school. The stereo console with the "Arc de Triomphe" detailing plays Horace Silver's "Song for My Father" (1963). The smell of India ink and turpentine permeates the air, and crayon bits stain the cement floor of his studio, which was at various times located in a rented storefront where the Group Workshop painted together, in the basement of our own house, and on the upper floor of the Crusade for Justice building. In his time on this earth, my father walked with grace, which enabled him to accomplish his life's work, fulfilling his artistic vision and his duty as a working man and artist.

In the opening pages of *The Book of Embraces*, Eduardo Galeano defines the verb *recordar*: "To remember, from the Latin *re-cordis*, to pass back through the heart" (1991, 11). Many events in his history book are remembered in this way, and in my own life and in the context of my own struggles, events and memories about my father have been similarly re-membered and passed back through my heart.

Notes

"Remembrance of Raymond Moreno, Founding Member of the Group Workshop," by Renee M. Moreno, is reprinted from *Aztlán: A Journal of Chicano Studies* 36, no. 2 (2011).

This work was made possible by generous funding from Colorado Humanities and from the California State University–Northridge College of Humanities, Graduate Studies, Research and International Programs, and Department of Chicana and Chicano Studies.

Works Cited

Arneill, Anne. 1959. "Studio Thoroughly Fulfills Artist's Ambition." *Denver Post Roundup*, September 20, 31.

Benmayor, Rina. 1987. "For Every Story There Is Another Story Which Stands Before It." In *Stories to Live By: Continuity and Change in Three Generations of Puerto Rican Women*. New York: Centro de Estudios Puertorriqueños.

Bowlby, John. 1969. *Attachment and Loss*. New York: Basic Books.

Cofer, Judith Ortiz. 1990. *Silent Dancing: A Partial Remembrance of a Puerto Rican Childhood*. Houston: Arte Público.

Colorado Labor Advocate. 1972. "Ray Moreno Dies in Car Accident." October 6, 1.

Davis, Mike. 1994. "The Sky Falls on Compton." *The Nation*, September 19, 268–71.

Espinoza, Carlotta. 2010. Interview by author, Denver, May 7.

Espinoza, Ray. 1977. "Brown Artists of Our Time: Chicano Art and Artists." Unpublished manuscript. Denver.

———. 2011. Interview by author, Denver, February 21.

Fresquez, Carlos. 2009. Interview by author, Denver, March 3.

Galeano, Eduardo. 1985. *Memory of Fire: Genesis*. Translated by Cedric Belfrage. New York: Pantheon.

———. 1991. *The Book of Embraces*. Translated by Cedric Belfrage. New York: Norton.

Gaspar de Alba, Alicia. 1998. *Chicano Art Inside/outside the Master's House: Cultural Politics and the CARA Exhibition*. Austin: University of Texas Press.

Gonzales, Rodolfo "Corky." 1967. "Proposal for the Crusade for Justice Cultural Arts Center." Series 4: Crusade for Justice, Box 1, FF60, Rodolfo "Corky" Gonzales Papers, Western History Collection, Denver Public Library.

Griswold del Castillo, Richard, Teresa McKenna, and Yvonne Yarbro-Bejarano, eds. 1991. *Chicano Art: Resistance and Affirmation, 1965–1985*. Los Angeles: Wight Art Gallery, University of California.

Haddad, Barbara. 1968. "Unusual Innovation Scene of Surprises in Level of Talent." *Denver Post Roundup*, April 28, 16–17.

Kelley, Robin D. G. 1993. "'We Are Not What We Seem': Rethinking Black Working-Class Opposition in the Jim Crow South." *Journal of American History* 80, no. 1: 75–113.

Malagamba-Ansótegui, Amelia, with Gilberto Cárdenas, Miki Garcia, Ramón Rivera-Servera, José Manuel Valenzuela Arce, and Tomás Ybarra-Frausto. 2006. *Caras Vemos, Corazones No Sabemos/Faces Seen, Hearts Unknown: The Human Landscape of Mexican Migration*. Exhibition catalog. South Bend, IN: Snite Museum of Art, University of Notre Dame.

Marsalis, Wynton. 1992. Interview by Ben Sidran. In *Talking Jazz: An Illustrated Oral History*. Petaluma, CA: Pomegranate Artbooks.

———. 2006. Interview by Ben Sidran. In *Talking Jazz: An Oral History*. CD 1–3, vol. 1: *Trumpet*. New York: Unlimited Media.

Marvel, Bill. 1970. "Viva Centro Cultural! Hispano Art Fiesta." *Rocky Mountain News*, April 29, 3.

McLeod, Alisea Charmain. 1998. "Living Detroit (on the Edge of Disorder): Time and Space in the Twentieth Century." PhD diss., University of Michigan.

Montoya, Willie Ray. 2008. Interview by author, Denver, April 4.

———. 2011. Telephone interview by author, Los Angeles, May 11.

Morrison, Toni. 1987. *Beloved*. New York: Knopf.

———. 1989. "Unspeakable Things Unspoken: The Afro-American Presence in American Literature." *Michigan Quarterly Review* 28, no. 1: 1–34.

———. 1990. "The Site of Memory." In *Out There: Marginalization and Contemporary Cultures*, edited by Russell Ferguson, Martha Gever, Trinh T. Minh-ha, and Cornel West, 299–305. New York: New Museum of Contemporary Art.

Pérez, Laura Elisa. 2007. *Chicana Art: The Politics of Spiritual and Aesthetic Altarities*. Durham, NC: Duke University Press.

Rocky Mountain News. 1956. "Walt Green to Exhibit Water Color Paintings." February 16, 18.

———. 1981. "Meatpackers Fired." November 28, 7.

———. 1984. "Jury Rules on Plant Closing." February 18, 16.

Saldívar-Hull, Sonia. 2000. *Feminism on the Border: Chicana Gender Politics and Literature*. Berkeley: University of California Press.

Vigil, Ernesto. 1999. *The Crusade for Justice: Chicano Militancy and the Government's War on Dissent*. Madison: University of Wisconsin Press.

La Memoria de Nuestra Tierra: Colorado

Judith F. Baca

My mural for the Denver International Airport, entitled *La Memoria de Nuestra Tierra*, is of a personal nature. My grandparents came from Mexico to La Junta, Colorado, during the Mexican Revolution. They followed the course traveled by thousands of other Mexican families from Chihuahua to the United States through the historic northern territories of Mexico (Texas, New Mexico, Colorado) via the "Ellis Island" of the southwest, El Paso. It is a story that has been little chronicled and one for which I was anxious to create a visual record. Over the years working as a muralist, I had told many stories of communities across the United States but never my own.

My mother was born in La Junta, educated in Colorado's segregated school system, and raised in its segregated housing in the 1920s and 1930s. A few years ago, she returned to La Junta, for a high school reunion, for the first time in many years. There she visited her father's grave, only to find that the segment of the graveyard designated for Mexicans had not been maintained for many years (fig.1). After much searching among the fallen gravestones, she found her father's grave. He was buried in a junkyard of old, unmarked stones and loose dirt while the rest of the graveyard was green and well maintained. Not finding recourse with the local authorities, who remained steadfast in their refusals to rectify the situation, she was successful in petitioning the governor of Colorado to remedy the segregated graveyard of her hometown. Due to my mother's insistence, the governor mandated preservation and maintenance for my grandfather's grave and those of the other Mexicans who were buried in the Mexican section of the La Junta cemetery.

The simple reality that even in death the bodies of racially different people were separated moved me to create an artwork that would give

177

Figure 1. Ortencia Ferrari Baca searches for her father's grave along the borders of the cemetery in the unmaintained area. Image courtesy of the author.

dignity to the mestizo's story and the stories of countless others who toiled in the mines, fields, and railroads of Colorado. I wanted not only to tell the forgotten stories of people who, like birds or water, traveled back and forth across the land freely before there was a line that distinguished which side you were from, but also to speak to our shared human condition as temporary residents of the earth.

My great-grandfather, as family mythology recites, had water rights and delivered water with a wagon to residents of the area. His Spanish bright-green eyes and red hair distinguished him, as did his large horses. He is also buried in the La Junta graveyard. Perhaps my ancestors being planted in Colorado's soil caused me to wonder what was recorded there in the granules of dirt, where I believe the memory of the land might reside (figs. 2–4).

In a sense this mural is an excavation of the Chicana/os complexity as an indigenous people and of their multiple identities as Spaniards, Africans, and Asians, living among newly immigrated Irish, Greek, and Italian peoples. The making of this work was a re-membering of their histories. By revealing what is hidden, through pictorial iconography of the land, this mural is a kind of Mayan map not really intended to guide your path, but instead to tell you about the road.

In the La Junta Museum, my research located photographs of railroad workers of the region and of my grandfather, which became important to

Figures 2-4. Memorial service at the Baca family gravesite with its new head-stone. Images courtesy of the author.

the narrative aspect of the work. I conducted interviews with many from the region and lead a workshop with University of Southern Colorado students on the region's history. Students brought photos and personal narratives of their family history in Colorado, which provided me with valuable insight for this work. I visited seven local high schools and spoke with the young people, and met with scholars and archivists.

Stored in boxes in a garage in Pueblo, I found a priceless photo by Juan Espinosa, photographer and founder of *El Diario de la Gente*, Boulder, Colorado, of an important meeting between Corky Gonzales of the Colorado Crusade for Justice and César Chávez of the United Farm Workers. This photo was taken at the moment of the agreement to bring the grape boycott to Colorado and became the basis of the mesas in my mural.

I also learned of the Luis Maria Baca land grant, with my family's name, which inspired many more questions and lead to further research beyond the mural. The origin of so many creeks and streams, could the Luis Maria Baca land grant be where my great-grandfather Seferino Baca's water rights originated? One corner of this land is also the site of the Sand Creek massacre of the Cheyenne people, today unjustly marked by a town named for the Colonel Chivington who carried out the brutal attack on women and children. No record exists of a man named Silos Soule who would not attack the Cheyenne and was killed by the townspeople for his resistance to the orders.

In 1998, as a master artist in residence with the Role of the Arts in Civic Dialogue at Harvard University, I was afforded the time to work with interns on the development of a web portion of the mural and to continue my research. There I designed a collision of the landscapes my grandparents crossed from Hidalgo de Parral to Colorado by horse-drawn cart, train, and on foot, escaping the troops who wanted to enlist my grandfather Teodoro Baca into Pancho Villa's army. In a basement studio at Harvard, I spent the summer painting the landscapes of Chihuahua, New Mexico's Mesa Verde, the Rio Grande, and finally the Arkansas River as if seen from the different eye levels of my grandparents as they made the journey. I painted "los Caminantes" walking on water with their small child to provide an alternate view of immigrants from those so often broadcast in the media, images of people scattering like small insects from crowded trucks.

Teodoro Baca owned land and a store with established routes to the north to gain important supplies for that region of Mexico. The simultaneous robbery of my grandmother at the family store and of my grandfather on the train going to replace supplies from previous robberies pushed them to leave everything behind to go north. When they finally arrived in Juarez, they heard that Pancho Villa's men were only a day behind them. So, they decided to cross. They must have found the town filled with the thousands of refugees that history records there at that time. They traveled to Seferino Baca and settled at the base of the Purgatory River, facing Kansas in a bitter cold place to which my grandmother would never become accustomed.

With the use of computer technology, I have incorporated these images and documents into the mural (fig. 5). The landscape imagery was hand-painted at a small scale and then scanned into the computer at a very high resolution for inclusion into the mural. *La Memoria de Nuestra Tierra* combines a meticulously hand-painted landscape with historic photographs

Figure 5. Judith F. Baca, detail of La Memoria de Nuestra Tierra: Colorado *(The Memory of Our Land: Colorado), 2000. Hand-painted and digitally generated mural on aluminum substrate, 10 × 55 feet. Image courtesy of SPARC.*

in a seamless blend imprinted upon the holographic-like surface of a metallic coated substrate (fig. 5).

The final work is a breakthrough in digital murals, printed digitally on a bronze-colored aluminum ten feet by fifty feet in length and installed in the Jeppeson central terminal of the Denver International Airport. The work is also stored digitally, existing as an interactive website at www. judybaca.com, so is entirely reproducible should it be damaged. The mural was completed in the UCLA-SPARC Digital/Mural Lab in 2000 and is currently on permanent display at the Denver International Airport.

It is in the making of this artwork that my family mythology and that of so many others is finding substance in place.

Note

"*La Memoria de Nuestra Tierra: Colorado*," by Judith F. Baca, is reprinted from *Aztlán: A Journal of Chicano Studies* 30, no. 1 (2005).

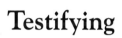

Testifying

Activist Latina Lesbian Publishing

esto no tiene nombre and *conmoción*

tatiana de la tierra

> ***esto no tiene nombre:*** *this has no name: the way a look says desire, the way love spirals into DNA, the way dancing happens with one finger, the way that sisterhood travels, the way in which we walk with certainty even when there's not a word to stake a claim. ¿Qué quieres? What is your desire? esto.*

> —de la tierra, "Las Sinvergüenzas"

From 1991 until 1996, two Latina lesbian magazines, *esto no tiene nombre* (this has no name) and *conmoción* (commotion + in motion) were published. I was one of the founders and editors of both of these periodicals. For the sake of herstory and with the intent of exposing and analyzing the reality and implications of publishing these magazines, I unearthed three boxes that contain the archives of *esto* and *conmoción*.

The files are messy and incomplete. The story that unfolds will be detailed with the raw materials that created it, including documents from the archives and the magazines themselves, as well as interviews with key people and my own perception and memory of the events, geography, politics, and "characters" involved. This is not an impartial narrative, though I do intend to be as factually accurate as possible and it will be easy for the reader to distinguish between fact and interpretation. I don't expect that everyone who was engaged with *esto* and *conmoción* will agree with or even appreciate my point of view. Still, I was at the center of these publications from the beginning until the end, and I am the holder of the archives.

I think this is a story that needs to be told—we really did create history with the act of publishing. We left documents behind, we added to the Latina lesbian body of work, and we did so, in my opinion, with a rawness and vibrancy that had not existed to date and has not been repeated since within the world of Latina lesbian literary expression.

This story begins in Miami, Florida, circa 1991.

I remember reading a classified ad in *New Times*, a weekly entertainment paper. It went something like this: "Latina lesbians, let's get together." Close to twenty of us congregated one Saturday afternoon in someone's hot and crowded living room. We voiced our need to be together as Latinas and as lesbians, to have barbecues, to have positive reinforcement for our existence. We wanted to be able to talk in Spanish among our own. Many of us did not connect with the white lesbian organizations and were deemed invisible and/or undesirable by our own families. Some were in the closet. We passed around a piece of paper and put our names and telephone numbers on it. It seemed like the Beginning of Something Good.

We never met again.

Las Salamandras de Ambiente

Months later, I heard about a new Latina lesbian group that was started by Angie and Ena. The word spread and soon Everyone made the scene, including many of the same ones who attended the other meeting. It was obvious to all of us that there was a great need for a Latina lesbian organization. As far as we knew, such a group had never existed in Miami. While there had always been a teeming Latina lesbian presence in the gay and lesbian bars and probably on every street in Miami, there had not been an official, public declaration that united sexual and ethnic identity. The weekly meetings were being held in a room in a warehouse district that had been converted into "women's space." By the time I got there, the group had been meeting for several months and was due for a party. I phoned every lesbian on the list from the original classified ad meeting to tell them about the party. One of them, Margarita, offered to pick me up and I agreed, not realizing that it was a Date.

The party was a smash. It took place at Ena and Isabel's large, fancy house in Hialeah. Salsa music blasted, ham croquetas and pasteles de guayaba were eaten up, Spanish was spoken, and everyone was decked out to the hilt, Latin style. I think all of us knew that the group was really happening, that it would be long-lasting and fruitful. I got a ride back home from someone else, as Margarita terrified me. She was a loud, obnoxious, Cuban old-time butch who was so forthright in her sexual energy that I didn't know how to respond to her.

Soon after, the group had a name—Las Salamandras de Ambiente. "De ambiente" is Latin queer code for "in the life." And salamanders were, according to research conducted by Vanessa and Patricia, amphibians whose reproduction was female-centered. Female salamanders hatched eggs without any male intervention and, thus, were "lesbians." In addition, they were blessed with the mythical ability to live in fire. Therefore, salamanders were not only lesbians, they were hardy survivors. The name was happily adopted. Later, Vanessa and Patricia discovered that their initial research was flawed and that the "lesbian" reptile was a close cousin to the salamander. But it was too late—Las Salamandras de Ambiente had already been baptized by all of its members. Angie designed the group's logo, two lusty salamanders encircling a palm tree within a triangle.

Las Salamandras reflected the diversity of Miami's Latin community. Members were from all over—Cuba, the Dominican Republic, Puerto Rico, Colombia, Mexico, Venezuela, Costa Rica, and Ecuador. We were all immigrants and fluent in Spanish and English. We were of working and middle-class extraction, mostly mulatas and light-skinned, from twenty to forty-something years old. We were students, teachers, accountants, counselors, saleswomen, massage therapists, bank tellers, federal employees, musicians, writers, and housewives. Typical of Latinas, we were family-oriented. The Cuban Salamandras were fierce anti-comunistas. Overall, I would classify the group as "conservative." This was not a flag-waving rabble-rousing ensemble at all, and it was not ever linked with any social movement or "activism" beyond existing as a publicly recognized Latina lesbian organization.

In practical terms, Las Salamandras was a support group that met every Thursday evening at 8:00. We rapped about coming out, about family and lovers, about who we were. We met in each other's apartments at times, though once the group got settled, the meetings were held at the Metropolitan Community Church and, once it opened, at the Lesbian and Gay Community Center in Miami Beach. The true "support" that Las Salamandras offered anyone was questionable, but if you could measure a group's success by the parties, Las Salamandras was over the top. We had parties in each other's homes, at rented halls, at the Unitarian church, at clubs, in celebration of New Year's, Halloween, Valentine's, or whatever—and not one of them was a dud.

Most of us in Las Salamandras were true Miamians: we were born in another country but, in the United States, Miami was our only home. I had lived in Miami most of my life and had completed my undergraduate degree in Gainesville, north Florida. Before moving back to Miami, I had traveled throughout the United States. Several other Salamandras had relocated from Boston and a few other cities in the Northeast. I mention these distinctions because there were noticeable differences between the Miami natives and those who had also resided in other metropolitan areas. Miami Salamandras, it seemed, viewed lesbianism in practical and narrow terms. To be able to live in a fashion that allowed lesbianism to coexist with being a functioning member of family, society, and the workforce was the ultimate goal. Parties on weekends were a plus. But being a lesbian did not include challenging the social construction that kept lesbianism a private matter or exploring beyond the Miami shores. And Miami Latinas, due to culture and geography, were alienated from the Anglo gay and lesbian "community" and its corresponding national concerns and internal politics. I saw Miami, in a sense, as an island unto itself.

Those of us who had lived elsewhere, though, had participated in or at least been exposed to a wider gamut of lesbian culture, including women's bookstores, music festivals, feminist politics, and lesbian herstory and literature. By 1991, I had been "out" for eight years and had gone through my own worldwide lesbian awakening. I was a barefoot traveling lesbian in search of an exotic secret society. I had participated in several Latin American lesbian feminist gatherings, beginning with the first one that was held in Mexico in 1987 (see de la tierra 1988). And I had attended women's gatherings in the United States, including numerous women's music festivals. For years, I had been negotiating my identity within all of these spaces. The lesbians I encountered at home in Colombia and in Latin America were often educated and wealthy daddy's girls whom I could not easily identify with. Besides, I was a Latina from the United States, which put me in a different class altogether. I had been influenced by angry white separatist feminist vegetarian dykes who danced to the goddess's tune, which didn't help me blend in with South American sisters.

In the United States, on the other hand, I was eventually alienated from the whiteness of mainstream culture and allied myself with women of color. I had read and connected with some of the defining literature of the 1980s—*This Bridge Called My Back* (Moraga and Anzaldúa 1981), *Loving in the War Years* (Moraga 1983), *Chicana Lesbians* (Trujillo 1991), and *Compañeras* (Ramos 1994), where I had my first poem, "De ambiente," published. I had also written articles about Latin American lesbians and had begun to compile lists of international Latin lesbian organizations. I was a natural networker and collector of Latina lesbian culture—flyers, books, music, photographs, posters, anything.

I had been Desperately In Search of Latinas for many years, no doubt a search for my own self. After having internalized the ethnic and linguistic self-hatred produced by this country's racism and hatred of Others, I was ready to embrace my own. I don't think this was mutual, though. As I have felt my entire life anywhere that I have ever lived, I also felt alienated from Las Salamandras. I was more Americanized than most, and less fluid in social customs and graces. I could not even speak in public at the time without turning red. And worst of all, I could not dance. I did have nerve, though, and I was creative and persistent, as well as a budding writer, all qualities that led me to join the group's newsletter committee. It was the only place where I could possibly find a niche.

esto no tiene nombre

The first issue, dated 23 September 1991, was a basic black-and-white eighteen-page homegrown publication that was photocopied at Kinko's and sold for $2. We printed fifty copies, and then reprinted another batch. It debuted the evening of yet another sensational Salamandra party. We called it *esto no tiene nombre, revista de lesbianas latinas en Miami* (this has no name, Latina lesbian magazine in Miami) (fig. 1).[1] We literally could not come up with a name, and on the editorial page we wrote, in bold letters, "Necesitamos un nombre" (we need a name). Of course, we liked the double entendre of not having a name, of not being able to name lesbian desire. It insinuated love in the closet. "Esto no tiene nombre" is also an expression of something being beyond words. It was the title of a Puerto Rican comedy TV show that aired in the 1970s. And it was charming, in a way. We could rationalize many things about being poetically nameless, and actually, we did just that. The name grew on us and it was there to stay.

But *esto no tiene nombre* was a source of conflict from the first. The headline on the cover asks, "Debut y ¿Despedida?" (Debut and Farewell?) This was also a play on words: it was the title of a song by Puerto Rican singer Lissette, yet it posed a pertinent question. A few Salamandras were concerned, even before we published anything at all, about the content, the editorial control, and the role that the publication would play in the community. They wanted a simple newsletter, one that would inform about the group's activities, and they wanted the final copy to be approved by the group as a whole before anything was published. But those of us on the editorial committee wanted a magazine, one that would include as many voices as possible. We wanted to publish anything any of us had to say. We

Figure 1. Cover of esto no tiene nombre, *volume 2, number 1 (1992). Image courtesy of the author.*

solicited writings, graphics, and ideas from the group, and these, compiled with our own writings and vision, were the raw materials for the first issue.

On the cover, in Spanish, we published the first editorial, one that acknowledged the conflict that preempted *esto*. "We understand that this is an internal struggle and part of the process of growth in our community. The editorial committee has decided to publish this first volume so that each woman can formulate her own responses." We defended freedom of creativity and expression and asked, "Is our community ready for our magazine? . . . Who has not enjoyed a clitoris, a nipple, a woman's kiss? It would be hypocritical and a form of internalized lesbophobia to exclude these images when they are the basis of our expression." The rest of the newsletter included brief pieces, written by nine Salamandra contributors. It included lots of (bad) poetry, a few very short stories and chronicles, a cartoon, a recipe (for onion rice), advice on natural pesticides, video and book reviews, news and announcements, and "Cuéntame," an anonymous interview that I conducted and edited. The majority of the content was in Spanish and most of the contributors were identified only by first names by their request.

The first issue of *esto* caused a commotion. There was immediate dissent about what we had published. At question was how Las Salamandras was being represented (one had written a first-person narrative about her experience with the group); the graphic use of language (we decided to publish an orgasm in every issue—poetry or prose that celebrated our sexuality); and the Cuéntame interview, where a black Latina talked about her preference for black women and boasted in crude detail about bringing her lovers to orgasm. Her language was strong. It was real. It was us. And by publishing her words, we were being true to our editorial policy, which read in part: "*esto no tiene nombre* publishes materials by Latina lesbians that reflect our diversity and rupture the stereotypes that have been nailed upon us. Our objective is to create a forum for words and images that contribute to the fortitude and pride of our community."

But Las Salamandras did not appreciate our inclusive philosophy. Heated discussions ensued. We met in Caridad's apartment, where Salamandras fumed about the trash we were publishing. Our response was: if it bothers you, write a letter to the editor; let it be a debate among us. We saw *esto* as a forum for discussion within our community. We worked earnestly to produce the second issue of *esto*, despite the controversy. This time, though, we expanded beyond the local network and invited lesbians from Latin America, whom we met when they came into town for an international environmental conference, to contribute writings and to help us spread the word.

The second edition of *esto* was twenty pages, dated 31 January 1992, volume 1, number 2. It was printed on lavender paper, also at Kinko's. The cover had an image of Argentinian rockers Sandra Mihanovich and Celeste Carballo dreamily gazing into each other's eyes, as well as the cute

Salamandra logo. The graphics, created by Patricia, were light-years ahead of the first edition. *Esto* had a clean-cut and orderly look now, with a table of contents, an editorial and contributor's page, letters to the editor, news and announcements, two ads, seven poems, and wide-ranging content. Among the highlights were Amy's essay on death, an interview with a Costa Rican lesbian activist, Vanessa's take on the Latino "disease model" of lesbianism, Patricia's witty crossword puzzle (that required knowledge of Latina and lesbian history and culture), my review of two lesbian sex videos, and the Cuéntame. There were eleven contributors this time, including a poet from Costa Rica and one from Puerto Rico.

Again, *esto* caused an uproar. And, again, it was the sexually explicit material that generated controversy: Margarita's "orgasm," my reviews of the videos *Bathroom Sluts* (1991) and *Dress Up for Daddy* (1991), and the anonymous Cuéntame interview, which denounced feminists and praised tribadism. While these pieces did not even take up two full pages in the publication, they were the focus of a debate that quickly escalated in intensity. Some of the Salamandras felt we had betrayed the group's morality, and they screamed for censorship. We were staunchly opposed to censorship and supported the free expression of ideas and experience by Latina lesbians on any topic. And we were not just free thinkers; we were true lovers of literature and were writers ourselves. We regarded our roles as editors with utmost seriousness—we believed that publishing had the power to transgress invisibility, that we were creating and representing our community along the way, that expressing lesbian sexuality was good and fun and healthy, and that what we were doing was meaningful. We saw internalized homophobia as the real crux of the matter. Several of Las Salamandras were offended by the word "lesbian" on the cover. Many were not "out" publicly and did not intend to be.

But those of us at the core of *esto* were of a different breed. Margarita, who had come to Miami during the Mariel exodus in 1980, had walked the streets of La Habana arm-in-arm with her female lovers in a country where being homosexual was a crime. She lived by laws of her own making. She was, according to the biographical note that we published in every issue of *esto*, "an anti-communist, a Christian, and a lover of women, sexuality, and communication." She was also Eurocentric and thought President Bush and Pinochet were the greatest, and she was one of the strongest characters anyone could ever imagine knowing.

The rest of us were bleeding-heart liberals. Patricia was a Cuban–Puerto Rican with leftist tendencies who had a bachelor's degree in political science. Vanessa, her partner, from Puerto Rico, had studied economics at MIT in Cambridge, where the two had met. Vane and Patri were well read in lesbian literature and well versed in lesbian and liberal discourse, including identity politics, class issues, and environmentalism. They had been involved with the politically active lesbian community in Boston, including the Women's Community Center and lesbian organizations on MIT's campus. They had attended conferences on pornography and on race and ethnicity among lesbians. When we first met, Vane and Patri lived in a house in South Dade, set smack in the middle of a field of tomatoes. They had back-to-the-earth values and envisioned living off the land. I shared many of Vane and Patri's worldviews. And like Margarita, I lived by my own rules. We were, each of us, strong-willed, outspoken, and independent. The four of us were the creators of *esto no tiene nombre*, and even though we were not in complete agreement about the world, we were able to accept that there would be disagreements.

"There's an agreement to our morality in the group"

Las Salamandras was not willing to accept the disagreements, though, and more screaming matches took place. On Sunday afternoon, 8 March 1992, a special meeting was held at the Alice Wainwright Park, practically across the street from Madonna's lavish Miami home. We tape-recorded the meeting and I later transcribed it. Among the verbatim excerpts from this meeting: "There is no need to use derogatory language." "I don't want these words in a magazine I share with my friends." "You think I can show this to my mother? Where do we draw the line?" "If the idea of this group is to give lesbians a positive image, how are we doing that here?" "I don't have a penis. I don't fuck." "What happens in the bedroom shouldn't be published." "You can open up much more with tenderness and sweetness, not by trying to scandalize people." "With all the empowering things to write about, I don't see a place for pornographic reviews." "A pornography book, is that what you want?" "Is this going to be *Playgirl*? *On Our Backs*?" "There's an agreement to our morality in the group." "Would you like your family to look at those words? Is that how you want to be represented?"

During the meeting at the park that Sunday, it was decided that a greater number of Salamandras should become involved in *esto's* editorial process. But by now, outsiders were getting in on the debate, including a Cuban lesbian minister from the Metropolitan Community Church, Mari Castellanos. Many members of Las Salamandras also attended Mari's sermons; some were her "groupies." The Latina lesbian moral majority now had their own Oral

193

Roberts. The official editorial committee consisted of Vanessa Cruz, Patricia Pereira-Pujol, and myself. Margarita Castilla took charge of the accounting from the beginning and was part of the core group. Her name appears in the editorial box as of the second issue, along with Sylvia's name, who never did anything that I can recall. In fact, suddenly people who never had any interest in publishing joined the editorial committee. The "real" editorial committee was joined by six others, including two *esto* contributors and four moral police agents. By March 9, the new, expanded committee had approved sixteen official editorial policies. The Newsletter Committee Document has the word "woman" and "women" scratched out and replaced with "lesbian" and "lesbians." The policies, written originally in English, are presented here just as they appear in the document, misspellings and all:

> Majority rule; No quorum required; The committee is open to any latin lesbian that is in agreement with the editorial policy; The editorial policy is open to discussion and change; All writers must be lesbian; All writers must be latin with the following exceptions—letters to the editor, collaboration with other latin women; The writings may not be oppressive; The writings do not contradict the purpose of the group as stated in the articles of incorporation; The writings do not include profanity or vulgarity for it's own sake or for the purpose to shock or when it is demeaning and oppressive; The writings may be in spanish or in english with the exception that the Editorial Notes presented on the inside cover of the News Letter be written in spanish; There will be no translations of the writings; Preference will be given to issues related to latin lesbian; No editorial changes without the agreement of the author, except for changes related to grammar or syntax; The editorial committee will aspire to present a balance view as to form and content; Authors will have copyright privileges; and Pseudonyms are allowed, however, the Editorial Committee must know who the person submitting the writing is. The right of the person to be anonymous will be respected in all cases.

Two policies were rejected by the majority: "There will be a qualitative standard of good taste and form in presenting the writers views"; and "Writings giving exposure to pornography be not allowed."

A final note appears at the bottom:

> A test of how the approved editorial policies would work was performed by having committee members vote on whether or not the article "Video-View: Las Putas y Los Papis" would be included in a News Letter issue if each of the committee members would apply the approved editorial policies. The article was accepted by a vote of 6 members voting yes to include the article and 4 members voting no.

I remember Vanessa saying that she trusted the process; the members of the editorial committee would come to understand what it meant to publish and they would either naturally eliminate themselves or grow. But of the ten people on this committee, only four were there as "moral police," and they were outnumbered. They cried foul.

Several days later, Las Salamandras held a meeting behind our backs. I was tipped off by a friend. Before the next Thursday night group meeting, and in anticipation of what was to evolve, Vanessa, Patricia, Margarita, and I decided to withdraw from the group. That night, 12 March 1992, we were presented with the following petition written in English, signed by almost every Salamandra, including new "outsiders" and many of the original Salamandras, who were our friends, or so we thought:

To: Editorial Committee "*ESTO NO TIENE NOMBRE*"

We, the undersigned, individually and collectively agree to the following:

1. The content of the newsletter *ESTO NO TIENE NOMBRE* continues to be a source of conflict which greatly distresses all of us. Therefore, we hereby, demand that this newsletter be discontinued, and/or the presumed sponsorship of SALAMANDRAS DE AMBIENTE be withdrawn from any such publication until such a date when the proper mechanisms are set into place to insure that said newsletter is representative and respectful of the consensus, philosophy and standards of this group.

2. We consider that the problems that have ensued from the newsletter are symptomatic of a lack of clarity regarding the position and purpose of SALAMANDRAS DE AMBIENTE and the lack of any structure designed to implement such position and purpose. Therefore, we call for the creation of a task force to study this issue, to design a model and to present and propose their conclusions to the membership at large by a specific date. Said task force will be constituted by volunteer members who are endorsed by a 2/3 majority of the membership to be selected at our next business meeting.

off our backs or *On Our Backs?*

Salamandras: Lizard-like lesbianas who can't take the heat. They stay low to the ground and hump hidden in the shadows of shame. Salamandras are the riff-raff of the race, Christian comemierda pets of the right-wing machine, pious pendejas who become skittish in the presence of potent sinvergüenzas.

—de la tierra, "Las Sinvergüenzas"

We didn't take what happened lightly—it was an ugly scenario, to be stabbed in the back by our own familia, and it was deeply painful, never to be forgotten. Vanessa and Patricia completely shut Las Salamandras out, while Margarita and I occasionally went to meetings and parties. Despite what had happened, Las Salamandras was our main connection to the local Latina lesbian community, and we still had friends among the group. But it was the end of an era.

Getting kicked out of Las Salamandras expanded *esto's* horizon. The way they did what they did—behind closed doors—and that they penned a petition intended to silence us fueled our conviction in publishing. It served as inspiration to continue with *esto*, and it strengthened our bond. By then, Margarita and I were locked in a steamy and passionate relationship, and Vane and Patri were as solid as partners can be. The four of us were in love with each other, and we had a mission: this, which has no name.

We continued with the immediate task at hand: to publish the next issue of *esto*. The spring 1992 edition, volume 1, number 3, came out about six weeks after our rupture with Las Salamandras, and it was markedly different. We ditched Kinko's for a real printer and had a print run of 200, which cost us $150. The final product was a twenty-page glossy magazine with a full-sized black and white photograph of an alluring woman in the woods who looked you right in the eye. (Years later, I was to discover that she wasn't even a lesbian.) The contributors were all local, and the contents were similar to the previous issue. The layout, though, was much more sophisticated, with labryses, lesbian symbols, and kissing women scanned into the background of selected pieces, as well as a variety of fonts, gray and black boxes, and just the right amount of white space. But the real difference was our focus. "Miami" was dropped from the official name, which was now, simply, *esto no tiene nombre, revista de lesbianas latinas*.

There were still remnants from Las Salamandras, though, in the letters to the editor section which was titled "en nuestras mentes" (on our minds). Mari Castellanos, the moral-majority-Cuban-lesbian minister, wrote (in Spanish), a letter that begins by congratulating us for our wonderful, professional-looking magazine and then continues to praise and attack every single one of our contributions. About the controversy, she wrote:

> What confuses me about the magazine is that at times I don't know if I am reading *off our backs* (a national feminist magazine) or *On Our Backs* (a pornographic lesbian magazine). Tatiana's fascination with pornography intrigues me.[2] It is not my place to determine if it is appropriate or not. This should be determined by the group as a whole, by consensus.

This magazine belongs to all of us, right? . . . I don't think this is representative of the values of the group. Oh, the tyranny of minorities! For some people, vulgar language represents a progressive wave against the established order. For others, the use of obscenities only indicates a lack of vocabulary. This definitely does not respect the sensibilities of many and imposes criteria that cause unnecessary friction. To impact society, one needs cutting-edge ideas and valiant positions, not vulgarity.

I responded (in Spanish) by deconstructing several of the offending "vulgar" words, all of which were used within the context of the lesbian sex video reviews that I had written: "singar" (to fuck); "puta" (slut); and "dyke." I defended sexual vocabulary, sexual education, and sexual liberation. They were futile words, though. We would never agree.

The back cover of the magazine announced *esto's* new venture—"la estupenda *esto*-peña" (the stupendous *esto*-club). This was to be a cultural event, to be held the third Sunday of every month, that would feature poetry readings, art exhibits, and the like. It would be a fundraiser for *esto*, as well as a literary/artistic link to the local Latina lesbian community. In the end, though, the *esto*-peña flopped, as would all our local efforts. While we did have supporters in the community, most of the "out" Latina lesbians were somehow associated with Las Salamandras, and a significant number of these women were faithful churchgoers who abided by the moral mood of the time. So while we did have an audience for our events, it was a small one in comparison to the multitudes that turned out for parties. "Literature" did not draw crowds. And there was an undeclared yet palpable boycott of *esto* by Las Salamandras, symptomatic of a mutual bitterness that would endure.

Technically, Las Salamandras had never truly sponsored *esto*. Margarita had fronted the money for the first issue, and since we had no publishing funds to begin with, we had started selling subscriptions, $10 a year for four issues, since the first edition. By the time *esto* had been kicked out of the group, around twenty members of Las Salamandras had subscribed. (Margarita, Vane, Patri, and I had also paid for our own subscriptions.) Margarita had already started the subscription list on a spiral shorthand pad, and she had been keeping a ledger for incoming funds and expenses as of 6 February 1992.

Esto No Tiene Nombre, Inc.

It was clear to us that in order to pursue our vision our efforts would have to have a national focus, not a local one. I had always envisioned a national magazine to begin with, and this turn of events paved our path. We didn't know much about distribution, publicity, or publishing, but we did know that we needed money to do anything at all. Our plan for *esto* involved establishing an existence as a legal entity and associating with an organization that had tax-exempt status so that we could apply for grants. We wanted to be independent, though, with the ability to manage our funds and activities. I consulted with Brenda Stout, an accountant who knew the gay community well, and she put us in contact with Brian Geenty, the director of Lambda Community Center of Greater Miami, Inc. Soon after, Brenda helped us fill out the Articles of Incorporation and Brian, via Lambda, became our fiscal sponsor. Lambda had tax-exempt status but was not active at the time, so it was a perfect match. We hoped eventually to establish tax-exempt status for *esto*, but since this would take a long time, we began by forming this alliance. The terms were simple. We would write grants and if we were awarded funds, Brian would receive them for us and hand them over. Subscriptions and any other funds would be directed to Lambda Community Center and the funds would go directly to *esto*.

We mailed the Articles of Incorporation for Esto No Tiene Nombre, Inc. to the Florida Department of State on May 12, 1992. On May 20 we received a letter requesting that we "provide an English translation for the corporate name." We complied and on June 9, 1992, ESTO NO TIENE NOMBRE, INC., "the English translation of which is 'This Has No Name, Inc.'," became "a corporation organized under the Laws of the State of Florida." The four of us were directors, and Vanessa was the registered agent. Soon, Esto No Tiene Nombre, Inc. had an independent bank account.

Becoming a legal entity was frightening. It was a defining moment for us. We didn't know a thing about corporations. But then, we didn't know a thing about publishing, either. We just did it by examining the ways that other publications seemed to do things and considered that our starting point. Then, we talked about it and came up with our own version. Thus, we created the editorial policy, call for submissions, table of contents, contributor notes, photo releases, and everything else. We made decisions by consensus, which was not always pretty, as we differed in ideology and in our approach to the actual work involved. Still, we worked with great mutual respect.

I remember one dispute about selection of material. Our policy was to publish anything by any Latina lesbian, regardless of point of view, unless we considered the writings "oppressive." In the beginning, we were desperate for enough material to fill the pages, so getting published in *esto* was practically a done deal for anyone who contributed. We did not have much quality control at first, though we did edit and doctor up shoddy writing when possible. Then came the poem in Spanish called "Como una mujer . . . como una rosa" (like a woman, like a rose):

A woman is like a rose: With her soft and delicate lips . . . there is nothing like a woman, only a rose.

The rose is like a woman: With its satin petals so delicious to touch.

The woman is like a rose: With so many mysteries of nature. . . .

There it was, the Latina lesbian cliché from hell. We hated it. I didn't want to publish it. But Margarita was adamant about being true to our all-inclusive policy. After much yelling, policy prevailed over quality and we put it in volume 1, number 3. It was not the first "bad" piece of writing that we published and it wouldn't be the last, but it put our values to test.

We collectively called ourselves "las publicadoras que hacemos todo en esto" (the publishers who do everything in *esto*), yet our fields of responsibility and interest were well defined. I was the networker, the one who maintained the mailing list, whose job it was to Find Stuff to Publish from any Latina lesbian, anywhere in the world. I was also one of the writers in the background; I grew up as a writer with *esto no tiene nombre*. Vanessa was the other writer in the group, a great writer, actually, sharp and creative with wonderful style. She typeset the materials that we all selected as a group, and edited most of the pieces. I don't know where she learned to edit, but she was an excellent editor, with a Zen sensibility in knowing where, exactly, to cut. Patricia was the graphic artist; she taught herself PageMaker and grew more skilled with each edition. It was impressive to witness her skill as a graphic artist evolve, issue by issue. Also worthy of note is that Vane and Patri didn't own a computer at first; they used the Macintosh computers at Miami-Dade Community College for the first four issues. And Margarita kept the books, collected the mail in her private mailbox, sold subscriptions, and proofread the writings in Spanish.

Grants and Golden Opportunitie$

After incorporating, we directed our attention to the next task at hand—grant writing. None of us had ever written or seen a grant proposal before. While we were serious about publishing, writing grant proposals added a new dimension to our commitment. The process forced us to reconsider our vision, to search within for the words that fully portrayed our intent.

The proposals would also put us in the view of a different audience—people who would consider our vision and the products that resulted from it, and who would decide if our project was worthy of their funds. We were not aware of local funding sources and so we prepared ourselves to be assessed on a national level, most likely by individuals far removed from our island in mayami (Miami). We wondered if foundations would understand the unique situation of lesbian immigrants who existed without the support of national organizations, publications, centers, editorial houses, or gatherings, of if they even cared. We knew that we were outside the mainstream of everything white and gay and everything heterosexual and Latino, and that venturing into these territories was inherently risky. But we also thought that it was our best alternative for taking *esto* on the high road. And we knew we were ahead of our time and hoped that astute people would see this and would want to support us. We had heard that Astraea, the National Lesbian Action Foundation in New York City, funded lesbian organizations. We wrote our first proposal for Astraea, which included the following declaration:

> The goal of Esto No Tiene Nombre, Inc. is to foster cultural exchange and all forms of expressions by Latina lesbians. We intend to serve as a vehicle for the dissemination of ideas and information about and from Latina lesbians. We feel it is important to have a space to explore who we are, what we do, what we want, what we think and where we are going. We want to establish a dialogue among ourselves without fear, censure, or having to justify ourselves in order to talk about what is important to us. With *esto no tiene nombre* we want to open minds, provoke discussion, create controversy, break isolation, celebrate the diversity of our communities, provide space where there is none and nurture a passion for our roots.

Astraea believed in us—they awarded *esto* $1,000 in 1992, and $1,000 in 1993, and $2,500 in 1994. Through Astraea we found out about other foundations that supported gay and lesbian nonprofit organizations, and we applied to a few of them. Thus, we were awarded $700 by Open Meadows Foundation on October 6, 1992, and $800 by RESIST on October 23, 1993. These funds would turn out to be absolutely essential to *esto's* evolution, a trajectory that would lead far away from Miami.

"Selling" *esto*

Expanding our network to the point of establishing a national and international presence within our community required lots of legwork and outreach. I was more than happy to take on this responsibility—making connections and converting them into tangible, useful parts of a whole is one of my innate abilities. Key to making *esto* an organic part of the national Latina lesbian community was to go where the Latina lesbians were—sprinkled throughout white lesbian enclaves in the United States and concentrated within Latina lesbian organizations.

In addition to covering routine publishing expenses such as postage, photocopies, office supplies and such, grant moneys permitted us to invest in other areas that we previously could not consider. The expenses were relatively small at first, but they were critical. We placed subscription ads in *Lesbian Connection*, for instance, and a call for submissions in *Poets and Writers*. We paid for an exhibit at the National Latina Lesbian and Gay Conference, held in Houston in 1992. I contacted Latina lesbian organizations such as Lesbianas Unidas in Los Angeles, Mujerio in San Francisco, Ellas in San Antonio, and Las Buenas Amigas in Manhattan. Where possible, *esto* subscription flyers were sent to everyone on each group's mailing list, either directly by us or by the organization itself. I sent flyers to lesbian and gay organizations, archives, and publications in the United States, Mexico, Latin America, and the Caribbean.

It wasn't all about money, though—it was about following any lead that could generate national visibility for *esto*. We needed material to publish, and we needed an audience for the final product. I had had an innate love and understanding of the media since I was young—I had been the features editor of my high school newspaper. I knew that editors appreciated the offbeat, that they had the means to make items of their interest visible, and that, through them, the word would eventually spread. I used the media in any way that I could conjure. I traded my writings, mostly columns, for advertising for *esto* in publications such as *Outlines* in Chicago and *The Fountain* in Miami. I established exchange subscriptions with many gay and lesbian periodicals, from *Sojourner* to *Calyx* to the *Washington Blade*. I contacted bookstores and asked them to place our flyers on their bulletin boards, or to sell *esto* on consignment. I sent sample copies of *esto* to women's presses, such as Kitchen Table Women of Color Press, Naiad, and Firebrand, and requested that they place us on their mailing lists.

I even went on national television myself, for The Cause. The first time was on Telemundo's magazine-format *Contacto* show for a segment called "Cuando su hijo es gay" (when your child is gay). I got my mom to go on the air with me. (There we were, the Radical Lesbian and her Accepting Christian Mother.) The stipulation was that the producers had to mention *esto no tiene nombre* and publicize our contact information, which they did.

And when I was arrested in front of the Colombian consulate in Coral Gables on March 9, 1994, an act that attracted media attention, my immediate concern was how to keep the reporters away from *me* and use them in favor of The Cause. I was the sole counter-demonstrator in a throng of Cubans who were threatening to boycott Colombian products because Colombia was negotiating the sale of petroleum to Cuba. Thousands of Cubans were protesting when I showed up with the Colombian flag, a "Free Cuba" T-shirt, and a "Down with the Cuban Embargo" sign. The crowd attacked me, I fought back, and the police whisked me to jail. It was a highly publicized rally and all the local news stations were there. The melee was filmed for the world to see. I experienced, unwittingly, my fifteen seconds of fame. The image of a dueling tatiana made it to Canada, Mexico, Colombia and back. And since my arrest was the only authentic event of the protest, reporters ambushed me for interviews. I declined—my views on Cuba would not get me anywhere—and offered to give them interviews about Latina lesbians instead.

A few Colombian reporters took me up on it. This is how I ended up on Colombia's national television show, *El Noticiero de las Siete,* and on other national Colombian media: *El Tiempo,* a newspaper (Shanahan 1994); *Revista Semana,* a weekly newsmagazine (1994, my interview appeared right after a piece on Princess Diana, to my aunt's shock); and Caracol, a national radio station (de la tierra 1994). The interviews didn't generate subscriptions, but they presumably had positive effects for queer visibility in Colombia. They also brought me out to all my Colombian relatives, an aftereffect I had somehow overlooked. But my strategy was flawed; I was terrible on screen, very self-conscious and liable to spontaneously say the wrong thing. One day, I finally decided to Just Say No to television. (For an in-depth account of the arrest, see de la tierra 1999a.)

My biggest and most successful campaign in reaching Latina lesbians took place on the phone. I would somehow get the phone number of Some Latina Lesbian Somewhere in the United States, and I would call her. I wanted to know who the local Latina lesbian writers and artists were, where Latina lesbians congregated, what organizations they were involved in, who was good at what, where local information was published, who had the central mailing list—anything that could possibly lead to my being able to obtain either contributions of writings or graphics for the magazine, or new subscribers. I don't know if I was good on the phone or just persistent, but I know that I stayed on the phone for as long as my unknown Latina lesbian victim would permit. Maybe they complied just to get rid of me, but I was able to establish many connections this way and to get my foot in the door of some of the Latina lesbian organizations (all but Las Salamandras, of course, who wouldn't agree to sending *esto* subscription flyers to its mailing list).[3] Eventually, since the world is indeed as small as they say, I would meet in person some of the women to whom I had previously spoken on the phone. Making the scene at conferences and gatherings here and there was another one of my methods of "selling" *esto*. (Unfortunately, though, *esto* was never able to fund any of us for travel.)

Personal contact is the most powerful way to engender trust and commitment to a cause from people. Others can always sense when you truly believe in what you do; the enthusiasm is contagious. I was very focused on soliciting materials for publishing and on selling subscriptions. I would do anything, even unwise things.

Once, I got a phone call from a Cuban lesbian who lived in Miami Beach. She had gotten my phone number from the Telemundo show and she wanted to know more about *esto*. Smelling a possible subscription sale, I volunteered that, next time I was on South Beach, I could stop by her place and show her the magazines. One day, that's exactly what I did. She cracked the door open a bit and checked me out before unhooking the security chain. I walked in and she locked the door, snapping each of the seven deadbolts into place. That's when I noticed that, even though it was the middle of the afternoon, there was no natural light in the house; incandescent bulbs lit the place. The windowpanes were covered with aluminum foil. Each piece of furniture was draped with a white cloth. The woman herself was wearing a housedress akin to a white sheet, and she said incomprehensible things and shook. I pretended that everything was normal, showed her the magazines, and counted the minutes until I could find a way out. She never did subscribe.

"Ask me for your hunger, in Spanish"

We published nine issues of *esto no tiene nombre*, a total of 182 pages, a pile half an inch thick, with the collaboration of sixty-eight contributors. The volumes are slim; they average twenty $8\frac{1}{2}" \times 11"$ pages each. It doesn't seem like much; *esto* was small, by any standard. Yet it was significant—each issue carries its weight proudly, adds pages to the Latina lesbian archives of the future, to the herstorical records of the recent past.

As part of the "research" for this paper, I got in bed with all the issues of *esto no tiene nombre* and read them all over again, cover to cover. I'm not sure why I did this, but I read them in reverse order, beginning with volume 3, number 1, published in 1994, three years after the first edition. I am not an objective reader—each magazine reminded me of the writers and artists who contributed, of the particular circumstances behind the scenes of each edition, of the political topic of the moment, of my love life, my friendships, my health, my dreams. But if I can possibly extract the personal associations that I have with each issue, I can make some general observations about *esto*.

There are noticeable changes from issue to issue. The first major shift begins with the fourth edition (volume 1, number 4, summer 1992) which has an image of Coyolxauhqui, the Aztec moon goddess, on the cover. Miami is suddenly replaced with Aztlán—Chicanas make themselves at home in *esto*. I remember not knowing much about Chicanas until we started publishing their voices. I had read some of the literature and had even traveled to Mexico, but Chicanos were still mythical beings who existed very far away from Miami, Latin America, and the Caribbean. Suddenly, we were publishing writings about the Rodney King beating and the riots that followed, pesticide poisoning and Chicano farmworkers, Chicana writers, Chicana herstorians, and Chicana artists. Puerto Rico and the Northeast also moved into *esto*, as contributors from Boston, Brooklyn, Manhattan, and San Juan joined us. And many of the new contributors brought new languages to *esto*—English and Spanglish. We gave Spanglish an official recognition in this issue's editorial. We wrote (in Spanglish, here translated):

> Our policy is to publish articles in the language that they are submitted. We think we should leave it where people are at. Our Latina lesbian community includes women in the U.S. as well as in Latin America. We cannot say that English or Spanish is the "official" language of our community because this would exclude many. And if the question is being P.C., neither is more correct than the other; both are colonizing languages. In our daily conversations we usually mix both languages. Some things can only be expressed in English or in Spanish: How do you say "empowerment" in Spanish? How do you say "amar" in English? As Latinas from the U.S. and Latin America come together, we will naturally move towards speaking Spanglish. ¡Qué viva el Spanglish! (4)

It's from this issue onward, I think, that *esto* really rocks. Soon after, we had the coolest covers—a photograph of two women in the nude, one with her back to the camera, the other's pubic hair in full bloom (volume 2, number 1); a handsome Cuban butch in a white guayabera (this was Margarita) flirting with a high-heeled femme on a street corner

Figure 2. Cover of esto no tiene nombre, *volume 2, number 2 (1993). Image courtesy of the author.*

in South Beach (volume 2, number 2) (fig. 2); Aztec lesbians bathed in golden moonlight (volume 2, number 3); a Nuyorican salsera at the Michigan Womyn's Music Festival (volume 2, number 4); and a cosmic earth momma emerging from the trunk of a banyan tree (this was me) (volume 3, number 1).

If you read *esto no tiene nombre*, you'll learn about a few of our icons (Sor Juana Inés de la Cruz, Frida Kahlo); about some of our published writers (Nancy Cárdenas, Rosamaria Roffiel, Terri de la Peña, Mariana Romo-Carmona, Carmen de Monteflores, Cherríe Moraga, and Sara Levi Calderón); and about our realities and concerns (identity, desire, politics, international gatherings, building coalitions with women of color, fears, feminism, language, and being in sisterhood with each other).

I have a few favorite pieces from all these pages. I dig Maria Cristina's poem, "Pídeme tu hambre . . . en español" (Ask me for your hunger . . . in Spanish), an erotic play on the accents, diphthongs and peculiarities of the Spanish language. Rosita Libre de Marulanda's "La niña, la puta y la Santa María" (The girl, the whore, and the Santa Maria) analyzes Cristobal Colón's journey to the Americas, concluding that the ship named *La Pinta* was really a puta (whore) in disguise. Teresa Mendoza's poem, "She," honors butch masculinity in a way that only a femme can. There is an insightful interview of photographer Roberta Almerez, "A Mistaken Minority with a Wonder Bread Identity Tows [sic] the Thin Line Between Art, Pornography, and Living Happily Ever After," made all the more interesting by the fact that she interviewed herself (!) under a pseudonym. (We didn't know this at the time.) Rebecca García created some awesome cartoons of "la mujer ideal" (the ideal woman). I love Amy Santos's poem "Biology," and Margarita's poem "Fuiste mía en ese instante" (You belonged to me in that instant), and every single thing Vanessa ever wrote. I also like my mom's contribution, "El regalo" (The gift), about her acceptance and appreciation of being the mother of a lesbian. ("El regalo" was subsequently reprinted in other books and magazines, most recently in *Conversaciones*. See Restrepo 2001.)

Then there was a great compilation of news and gossip about groups, publications, individuals, and international political and cultural happenings that we published in each edition. Compiled by me and/or Patricia and/or Lori Cardona, this section was filled with many tiny bits of information about Latina lesbians and gays in the United States and in Latin America and Mexico. Valuable for reflecting the political climate and issues of the time, this section had a variety of incarnations and, thus, various names: "Estamos en todas partes" (We are everywhere); "Eventos, anuncios, noticias y publicaciones" (Events, news, announcements, and publications); and "lesbianas y gays latinos pa'qui y pa'lla" (latina lesbians and gays over here and over there).

But my favorite thing about *esto no tiene nombre* is "Cuéntame, una charla anónima" (Tell me, an anonymous interview). I love to do interviews; many of my earlier writings were features based on interviews. I like to dig in, to ask very personal questions about deep fears and desires, to expose humanity. The Cuéntame allowed this because it was anonymous—no one knew who I interviewed. I manipulated text to conceal the identity of the person interviewed. A few of these women were well known in their respective communities, and some were anonymous even to me. A few of the interviews were conducted via telephone and recorded with a tape recorder from Radio Shack, similar to the one Linda Tripp used to record Monica Lewinski (though *I* had permission).

I am amazed, to this day, that so many women trusted me with their intimacies. Each Cuéntame takes me back to each woman—the one who's married with children and always has a female lover on the side but won't call herself a lesbian; the one who allowed herself to come out with the help of booze and became an alcoholic; the one who hates herself for being fat; the burned-out suicidal activist; the twenty-two-year-old virgin who was turned on by feminine women; the one who used a white woman for sex and then dumped her for a Latina as fast as you can burn a tortilla; the one who thinks lesbians dress poorly; the one who drives fast cars and is afraid of women; the one who can barely restrain herself from coming when she climbs on top of a woman. Perhaps these interviews say as much about me as they do about the women I interviewed, since it was my questions that led to their responses.

In any case, I think *esto* was pretty damn cool, and I know that I am not alone in this sentiment. We had a small but faithful audience of lesbians who subscribed and gave subscriptions to their friends. We received letters of appreciation and pleas for lesbian connections from all over, including Latin America, Mexico, Cuba, and Europe. We had national distribution via Inland and Fine Print as of the fifth issue. We had grant moneys that continued to flow in and support our vision. We had contributors on every coast. We were filling a void with *esto;* we were fulfilling our mission.

Hurricane Andrew and the Eye of the Storm

But it wasn't all rosy behind the scenes between those of us at the core of *esto no tiene nombre*. It was difficult work, we all had full-time jobs, and, worst of all, we were lovers. Each of us was volatile and passionate about publishing, and we differed in opinion on process and strategy. Even so, those were some of the greatest times in my life, because in between the disagreements there was a lot of love, respect, and a collective twisted sense of humor. But when Hurricane Andrew ravaged South Florida on

August 23, 1992, we became part of the rubble. Vane and Patri were left homeless and moved to Miami Beach. Soon after, they separated, after eleven years of being together. My childhood house in Leisure City, where I still had a bedroom and many possessions, was destroyed, and my homeless family plus dog moved in with me. Margarita and I, already on shaky ground, broke up after she left me for a woman who had gotten her phone number from television, a result of my appearance on Telemundo. The four of us continued to publish *esto* even after our relationships fell all around us, but eventually, the beauty of publishing was not stronger than the hatred we came to have toward each other.

Hurricane Andrew hit right after Vane, Margarita, and I attended the Third Lesbian-Feminist Latin American and Caribbean Encuentro in Puerto Rico. One moment we were making international lesbian connections, selling subscriptions, and conducting interviews, and then we were in shock, our lives uprooted, the future uncertain. Although some of the contents could be found strewn throughout the fields of South Dade, Vanessa and Patricia's house literally disappeared, even the walls. Las Salamandras gave a hand to some lesbians affected by the disaster, including Vanessa and Patricia, but bypassed me and my family. Along with much of South Florida, we all went into a deep depression after Hurricane Andrew. I lost the house that had been my home for twenty-one years, and I lost my privacy and the home I had all to myself at the time of the disaster. We wrote an editorial about the devastation, which was published (in Spanish) in the issue of *esto* that followed the storm:

> The hurricane buried our books and memories, destroyed our refrigerator and sense of security, and drenched our mattresses and our souls. Andres left us unrecognizable pieces of our lives, destroyed our love and our nerves, stole our electricity, money, fine clothes, and the junk we had already forgotten about. He downed our telephone lines and our spirit, ripped out trees and roots. After Andrew we were ruined and miserable, with the heat of a summer without fans stifling our hopes. We looked at the rubble. We identified the photographs and porcelain figures that remained intact, the computer that still had its memory, the *estos* that remained dry, and the loves that remained in a state of transformation. We nourished ourselves with our own tears, hysteria, depression, bureaucracy, anger, and pain. Lesbian friends helped us. We bought beds, food, and underwear. Miraculously, *esto no tiene nombre*, revista de lesbianas latinas, takes shape again, inspires us. Life continues without being the same. We live knowing that walls crumble, that the illusion of security is history, and that we know nothing at all. (volume 2, number 1)

It wasn't just the hurricane that killed *esto no tiene nombre*. The end was gradual, like a cancer diagnosed in its early stages that kills you just the same. And we tried several times and in different ways to address the issues. In a nutshell, the problem was the combination of the workload required for producing *esto*, and the personalities of those of us at the core. I was doing too much of the work, and I was a bitch, all business. My focus was the end result, not the process. No one appreciated my badgering, and no one worked fast, or hard or long enough as was necessary to keep up with the production schedule. We tried bringing in people to work with us, to smooth things out, such as Lori Cardona, but by then our cancer had run amok. We were uncontrollable. Vanessa and Patricia finally pulled out, and Margarita and I invited Amy Concepción, who was Margarita's ex-lover, to join us. Amy was a wonderful co-editor, but then Margarita and I could not work together any longer.

Margarita wanted *esto* to end—she thought I was steering *esto* from our original mission because I was trying to make it too much like other national magazines. She didn't like my editing style. (True, Vanessa *was* a better editor.) She accused me of being too creative. Amy and I wanted to continue with *esto*; Margarita demanded that we cease publishing. She won.

conmoción, revista y red revolucionaria de lesbianas latinas

> **conmoción:** "commotion" (conmoción) and "with motion" (con moción), a powerful combination that alludes to social disturbances, earthly tremors, and all kinds of tumult. conmoción is a fury, a fervor, an endless fuck, a tempest you don't wanna tango with unless you're conmocionada, too!
>
> —de la tierra, "Las Sinvergüenzas"

That wasn't the end, though. Maybe I should have stopped, but I couldn't. By then, I was too obsessed, too invested. I had made too many connections, had gathered too much material, had raised too much money. Just as *esto* was in the process of reincarnating, we received the largest grant ever—$8,300 on May 3, 1994, from The Funding Exchange's Out, A Fund for Lesbian and Gay Liberation. We were also awarded another $2,500 from Astraea on April 14, 1994, and later, $2,000 from the Chicago Resource Center on June 30, 1995, and $1,000 from Mama Cash, from Amsterdam. If ever there was a time to think big, that was it. And think big I did.

The fine print in the editorial box reads in Spanglish, "*conmoción* is an international Latina lesbian vision that uses the published word to empower and terrorize, to destroy and create. we publish, support and develop any type of activity that leads to the betterment and greater visibility of Latina lesbians." And it lived up to its name. I was "la editora que echa humo" (the editor who emits smoke) and Amy Concepción, Cuban writer and good friend, was the associate editor. We formed a national editorial advisory board composed of Latina lesbian leaders and academics who helped us make connections within their community and solicit material, and who would be there should we run into glitches. We wrote grants and obtained the blessings, via letters of recommendation, from writers and academics who believed in our mission, including Cherríe Moraga, Luzmaría Umpierre, Lourdes Torres, Osa Hidalgo, Mariana Romo-Carmona, Marcia Ochoa, Terri de la Peña, Carmen Corrales, and Juana María Rodriguez. We circulated calls for submissions, signed contracts with eight distributors, doubled the print run, and took off. And we got Patri to do the graphics (this time, she got paid) and Margarita to contribute poetry and proofread in Spanish. Our base of support was possible because of *esto*. *Conmoción* was a continuation and expansion of *esto's* vision, pure and simple.

Besides being larger than *esto* and involving more people in the process, *conmoción* was constructed to have direct interaction with Latina lesbian groups and also with writers. La "cadena *conmoción*" focused on news about our groups and gatherings in América Latina and the United States. *La telaraña*, the Latina lesbian writers' web, was created as part of *conmoción*. Lesley Salas, from San Antonio, initially co-directed *La telaraña* with me. I edited a separate newsletter, *el telarañazo*, that supported emerging Latina lesbian writers. *El telarañazo* had information about where telarañeras were performing and publishing and gathering.

> **Telarañeras:** word weavers. Christened after fine and intricate spider webs as well as for "red," or "network." Those of us with a matrix of letters that squirm and squeal until they give birth to an urgent word. Those of us who envision text like sculpture, palabras like eagles, grammar like notas musicales, sentences like trains, paragraphs in the palm of our hands. Telarañeras, we prefer our words twisted and tongued and too too tough.
> —de la tierra, "Las Sinvergüenzas"

The first issue of *conmoción*, forty pages published in 1995, was devoted to activism. Carmelita Tropicana sings with a clenched fist on the cover (fig. 3); Rosita Libre de Marulanda reveals childhood experiences that

Figure 3. Cover of conmoción, *number 1 (1995). Image courtesy of the author.*

led her to founding La Liberación de la Teta (Titty Liberation) in New York City; Cherríe Moraga talks cultural activism; Achy Obejas is her writing-is-an-act-of-revenge self; Luzmaría Umpierre tells her story about homophobia in academia; Carmen Vazquez speaks of liberation; and I rant

211

with my "a Latina lesbian activist's survival guide: o, mejor dicho, activism de-mystified, de-glorified & de-graded" (which was later published in *Latino Heretics*, de la tierra 1999b). There are also poetry, tributes to activists who've passed on, lesbian journals, news about encuentros, reviews, essays, Cuéntame, a Spanish translation of "100 Simple Things You Can Do to End the Patriarchy" (which I had translated at the author's request, Nett Hart), and the beginnings of the *telaraña*. And then there's "La esquina de Erotiza Memaz," a perverted Dear Abby creation by Las Buenas Amigas from New York City that glorified lesbian sexuality.

The second issue of *conmoción* was forty-eight pages of erótica with Isabel Rosado's cuntal artwork on the front cover and Marcia Ochoa's bare-ass wonder photograph on the back. Inside you'll find Erika Lopez's strap-on cartoon, pics of breasts, vulvas, rear ends. There are writings and poetry on stripping for a living, dildos and feminism, sadomasochism, cybersex, and Doralisa Goitía's "The Colors of Transmission," which begins with a screaming statement, "PROMISCUITY IS A MOTHERFUCKER AND THE RESULT IS HIV." There's vaginal poetry, cunt stories, love letters, Loana DP Valencia's lunar cuento, "Bajando la luna" (Drawing down the moon, which subsequently won Best American Erotica of 1997), and omu's kinky "alfabeto incompleto" (incomplete alphabet). It was an openly sexual edition of *conmoción*, one that celebrated pleasure for the sake of pleasure.

The third issue of *conmoción*, which focused on identity, was published in 1996 (fig. 4). It would be the last, as production and distribution costs had skyrocketed; several of our large distributors had filed for bankruptcy and, thus, never paid for issues of *esto* or *conmoción* sold in bookstores. And I was in poor health, fighting for my life. A group of lesbians from San Francisco were guest editors for the final issue. They selected and edited most of the material but they didn't make a magazine out of it. After my health crisis was over, I published the last issue, fifty-two pages of writings and art that directly spoke of who we are.

Virginia Benavides's photograph of a witchy woman dancing in dark waters extends across the front and back cover of the identity edition. Intriguing artwork reigns, including Dina Bursztyn's ceramic *Totem Poles to Scare Lesbophobia*, Laura Aguilar's powerful self-portraits, and a funky androgynous collage by Elisa Galdo. There are thought-provoking essays, such as Juana María Rodriguez's "Pensando en identidad" (Thinking on identity), Theresa Becerril's autobiographical "Guns, Tetas & Me," Carmen Corrales's stunning "Amando a Cuba" (Loving Cuba), and Patricia Meoño Picado's analysis of Latin soap operas. Also included in this issue is a

conmoción
revista y red revolucionaria de lesbianas latinas

Guns, Tetas and Me ❖ Wanna be a puta? ❖ Misery ❖ English as My Second
Language ❖ Tres Boricuas Hablando ❖ The Language of Pain ❖ Altar
Propio ❖ 100% Latina Lesbian Checklist ❖ Películas ❖ Confessions of a

Chicana Ph.D. ❖ La esquina de Erotiza Memaz ❖ Combat ❖ Cadena
Conmoción ❖ Extraños en la Ciudad ❖ Telaraña ❖ Poesía ❖ Amando a
Cuba ❖ The Original Sin ❖ Perla ❖ Dina Ruled the Playground

identidad
conmoción #3 1996   **$5**

Figure 4. Cover of conmoción, *number 3 (1996). Image courtesy of the author.*

conversation between three boricuas, Susana Cook's trans-lesbian poem "I
Dress Therefore I Am," Maria de los Rios's story "The Language of Pain,"
and the "100% Latina Lesbian Checklist," which poked fun at the red
"100% Latina lesbian vision" logo on all the *conmoción* covers and made
it impossible to be 100 percent anything.

Conmoción was just a magazine. What made it so special is that it was us on each page. It took eighty-four contributors from thirty-eight cities to fill 140 pages. And gauging by subscriptions, sales in bookstores, and letters to the editor, lesbianas Latinas were grateful. Given that *conmoción* was distributed predominantly in the United States and Canada, we were surprised to receive correspondence from lesbians in Cuba, Guatemala, Chile, Mexico, Argentina, and Colombia. From the content of the letters it was clear that there was a need to connect with sisters across continents. And for Latinas living in the north, the impact was intense. As Brianna wrote in a letter to the editor published in the third edition, "The specific subject matter combined with such diverse writings evokes a feeling of sisterhood that gives me encouragement and hope in finding a community that I have been needing for a long time. You have shown me that my sisters are out there and that I am not alone in my experiences and feelings." In another letter published in the second edition, Ana Montero wrote that *conmoción* "shows that Latina lesbianas are coming out of the infamous closet to kick some ass with our own politics without waiting for the gringa dykes to give us space to speak our mind." *Conmoción* was a place where we could do the twist with our tongues and end up smiling regardless of the words exchanged.

It was impossible to continue publishing without money, though. In addition to the distributors that never paid for selling the magazines, grant proposals were rejected by foundations such as the Council of Literary Magazines, Ben and Jerry's, Digital Queers, The Sister Fund, National Association of Latina Lesbian and Gay Organizations, Womankind, and the Kimeta Society. We were also awarded funds by the Open Meadows Foundation, funds that we never received even after much badgering on my part. I tried to obtain funds for la telaraña in 1997, which had never received its own funding. But both Astraea and Chicago Resource Center rejected the proposals.

Besides running out of money for publication, I ran out of steam. I had been diagnosed with systemic lupus erythematosus in 1990. Mostly, I lived as I pleased. But I did have a life-threatening flare-up in 1995 that forced me to reconsider what I was doing with my life. Living on the edge had taken its toll. I loved publishing but it was a thankless job that I didn't get paid for. I was not surviving physically, economically, or even creatively. After much soul-searching, I decided to start anew—to break up with Gloria, my Colombian lover, get away from Margarita, get away from my family, and end *conmoción*. I did all of the above, and by 1999, I had my MFA in creative writing from the University of Texas at El Paso. Soon after, I was on my way to becoming a librarian at University at Buffalo (of the State University of New York).

And the Number Is? Shoddy Record Keeping

It's difficult to summarize the fruits *of esto no tiene nombre* and *conmoción* because, even after combing through the archives for weeks, the records are shoddy and incomplete.[4] Margarita kept track of the funds until January 21, 1994. The last subscriber she entered in the shorthand pad was #166. I know that there were more *esto* and *conmoción* subscribers. But with Lambda Community Center of Greater Miami, Inc. as our fiscal sponsor, our accounting was tricky. I gave Brian the receipts, and he gave us the money. I was not a consistent record keeper. The paper trail was all over the place—on pieces of paper jammed into folders, with *esto* records, with *conmoción* records, with Lambda Community Center records, in the computerized address list, (which "disappeared" several times due to electronic glitches), and who knows where else. I don't even know exactly how many subscribers we had. The mailing list had more than 2,000 names on it (not all paid subscribers). I recall mailing around 300 copies of *esto* (not all subscribers; there were many exchange subscriptions). From letters in the archives written by subscribers who didn't receive their issues, it's clear that our distribution was flawed.

Distribution was a nightmare, no matter how it was handled. I thought that if only we had Real Distribution, we would be sailing. We had been selling *esto* on consignment at a few bookstores and through a few individuals across the country. But in almost every single case, we were never paid, or we had to chase the bookstores down for a few bucks, and it wasn't even worth the phone calls. Inland Books became *esto's* first distributor in 1992, and Fine Print soon followed. *Conmoción* was distributed by a slew of companies, too many of them—Small Changes, Desert Moon, Fine Print, Golden Lee, Armadillo, Book People, RPM, and Doormouse (from Toronto). Most of them paid up; the largest ones didn't. I didn't even have the energy, in the end, to continue chasing after them all. Still, the distribution did result in *esto* and *conmoción* having national visibility. The magazines were in bookstores all over the country, and they sold well for "fringe" publications.

There was something worse than not getting paid, though. Our print run of *esto* was very small to begin with (200–500), so the issues were precious and I was guarded about sending them out. We had an agreement with Fine Print that unsold issues would be returned. At that point, Fine Print was the main distributor of *esto*, and they had what amounted to *esto*'s archives. They destroyed our archives. Today, there are very few original copies of *esto no tiene nombre* left; I do not even have an original set right now, although there are a few in storage in Miami that we plan to send to selected libraries and archives. Unfortunately, there are very few traces of *esto*. According to the WorldCat database, *esto* is only listed in the library catalogues of University of Arizona, University of Buffalo, and University of California at Berkeley.

Conmoción, though, is another story. By the time *conmoción* was published, the media and distribution machinery was already in place. And even though only three issues were published, *conmoción* had a print run of 1,000; most of the magazines were sent out to distributors. *Conmoción* just got around much more; there was more to go around. And *conmoción* had a bipad number—one of those computerized strings of numbers that you find in a bar code on products, issued on December 29, 1994, by the Council for Periodical Distributors Associations, bipad number 87175. Though it was not required, many distributors preferred titles with bar codes. It was part of playing the game Big. As a result, WorldCat lists nine lender libraries for *conmoción*. Cornell, New York Public Library, University of California at Riverside, California State University at San Bernadino, University of California at Santa Barbara, University of California at Berkeley, University of California at Santa Cruz, University of Buffalo, Michigan State University, University of Michigan Library, and University of Texas at Austin.

Traces of This, Which Has No Name

If one were to judge solely by the evidence from database and internet searches, *esto* and *conmoción* barely ever existed. On Google, "'esto no tiene nombre' +latina +lesbians" results in ten hits and "conmocion +latina +lesbians" yields twenty hits. The listings lead to bibliographies, resource listings, syllabi, contributors, articles, and reviews. The scant results place *esto* and *conmoción* in the almost forgotten past, in the poetic days of snail mail. The online revolution happened without us. I didn't have e-mail until 1995 and I learned how to use the internet, design web pages, and do research on academic databases just the other day in library school.[5]

I think Margarita was right—I was trying to do too much, thinking too big. I understand now the value of keeping a vision only as large as can be managed by those involved. *Conmoción* was too ambitious. It was practically a full-time job. It needed paid staff, a real office, high-tech equipment. The grant funds allowed *conmoción* to grow as it needed to, but they didn't go far enough.

Esto no tiene nombre and *conmoción* were tiny, unique publications, Latina lesbian megaphones. I feel fortunate to have been an integral part of their making. The early days of *esto no tiene nombre* were the happiest time in my life. I had a vision, I had hope, and I was not alone. There was a lot of love going around then—sexual love, spiritual love, friendship love, literature love, publishing love. Perfect love. I spoke with Patricia while writing this, to get her point of view, to help me fill in some blanks. While talking to her on the phone I thought of how much I still love her, how I wish we could still be doing it. *You can never go back.* My childhood home, intact in my mind's eye, was destroyed in the hurricane. *Esto* and *conmoción,* vivid and vibrant in my memory, are forever gone.

Of that era, Patri said, "It's a shame that moment didn't come at a time when we were more prepared, when we had more time to dedicate to it." And then she said, well, "everything is as it should be." Maybe. Today, Patricia is a science reference librarian at Florida International University and I am a reference and instruction librarian at University at Buffalo. I haven't spoken with Vanessa in years but I hear she is fine, working as a nutritionist in Miami. Margarita and I continue to love each other from a distance. Amy and I talk every once in a while. Gloria, the lover I broke up with, is a friend and a part of my family. Las Salamandras split up in 1994, before *conmoción* even began. I got an e-mail from one of them just the other day. I realize now, five years after cutting off family, friends, and magazines, that you can never truly free yourself from what you most love. Whenever I go to an event with Latina lesbian presence, *esto no tiene nombre* and *conmoción* are always riding on my shoulder.

Lovers and friends come and go, but magazines last forever.

27 de abril de 2000, Buffalo, Nueva York
revised 1 de noviembre de 2001, Buffalo, Nueva York

Notes

"Activist Latina Lesbian Publishing: *esto no tiene nombre* and *conmoción*," by tatiana de la tierra, is reprinted from *I Am Aztlán: The Personal Essay in Chicano Studies* (Los Angeles: UCLA Chicano Studies Research Center Press, 2004) and from *Aztlán: A Journal of Chicano Studies* 27, no. 1 (2002).

1. All translations from Spanish into English in this essay are my own.

2. Mari hit the clit right on. Turns out that I was a budding pornographer, but I didn't know that at the time. Much of my published writings to date are of the erotic variety. See de la tierra 2000.

3. Many of these phone interviews became quests for Latina lesbian herstory. Eventually, I researched Latina lesbian organizations in great detail and wrote about them. See de la tierra 1996.

4. After this writing, I found three more boxes of *esto* and *conmoción* materials in storage in Miami. The boxes contain an assortment of flyers, correspondence, fiscal papers, and copies of the magazines. Patri and I plan to send copies of *esto* and *conmoción* to selected libraries and archives with the intent of increasing public access to the magazines.

5. I became a librarian because I needed a survival mechanism and it seemed that I was already very "librarianish." I also wanted to find ways to use the tools and position of a librarian to continue with my brand of activism. I now work behind the scenes. Besides doing reference and bibliographic instruction, I examine subject headings for queer Latin texts, write book reviews, compile a comprehensive bibliography of Latin lesbian and gay materials, and scout out queer Latin titles in book fairs. I am also beginning to write and publish within the profession and hope to bring greater visibility to Latina lesbians and gays in this field. See de la tierra 2001.

Works Cited

Bathroom Sluts. 1991. Dykestyles series, Fatale Videos. Video cassette.

Conmoción: Revista y red revolucionaria de lesbianas latinas. 1995–1996. Miami Beach: Lambda Community Center of Greater Miami.

de la tierra, tatiana. 2001. "Latina Lesbian Literary Herstory: From Sor Juana to *Days of Awe*." In *The Power of Language/El poder de la palabra: Selected Papers from the Second REFORMA National Conference*, edited by Lillian Castillo-Speed, 199–212. Englewood, CO: Libraries Unlimited.

———. 2000. "Dancing with Daisy" and "Celestial Bodies." In *Gynomite: Fearless Feminist Porn*, edited by Liz Belile, 30–42. New Orleans: New Mouth from the Dirty South.

———. 1999a. "Jail Time for Beginners." *Tropic Miami Herald Sunday Magazine*, March 8, 18–21. Reprinted in *Latino Heretics*, edited by Tony Diaz, 67–74. Normal, IL: Fiction Collective Two.

————. 1999b. "A Latina Lesbian Activist's Survival Guide—o Mejor Dicho, Activism De-mystified, De-glorified and De-graded." In *Latino Heretics*, edited by Tony Diaz, 64–66. Normal, IL: Fiction Collective Two.

————. 1999c. "Las Sinvergüenzas." Unpublished essay.

————. 1996. "Latina Lesbians in Motion." In *The New Our Right to Love: A Lesbian Resource Book*, edited by Ginny Vida, 225–29. New York: Touchstone.

————. 1994. Interview. "El Noticiero de las Siete." *Caracol Televisión*. Colombia.

————. 1988. "Latin American Lesbian-Feminists Together in Mexico." *Visibilities* (September/October): 8–11.

de la tierra, tatiana, and Margarita Castilla. 1993. Interview. "La ola lesbiana." *El Show de Marcia Morgado*. WCMQ AM Radio. Miami.

de la tierra, tatiana, and Fabiola Restrepo. 1992. Interview. "Cuando su hijo es gay." *Contacto*, Telemundo Televisión. Miami.

Dress Up for Daddy. 1991. Dykestyle series. Fatale Videos. Videocassette.

Esto no tiene nombre, revista de lesbianas latinas. 1991–94. Miami Beach: Lambda Community Center of Greater Miami.

Moraga, Cherríe. 1983. *Loving in the War Years: Lo que nunca pasó por sus labios*. Boston: South End Press.

Moraga, Cherríe, and Gloria Anzaldúa, eds. 1981. *This Bridge Called My Back: Writings by Radical Women of Color*. New York: Kitchen Table.

Ramos, Juanita, ed. 1994. *Compañeras: Latina Lesbians, an Anthology*. New York: Latina Lesbian History Project, 1987. Reprinted 1994, New York: Routledge.

Restrepo, Fabiola. 2001. "El regalo." In *Conversaciones: Relatos por padres y madres de hijas lesbianas e hijos gay*, edited by Mariana Romo-Carmona, 21–14. San Francisco: Cleis.

Shanahan, Gloria L. 1994. "Tatiana no quiere que la amen a escondidas." *El Tiempo*, 18 May.

"Tatiana, la lesbiana." 1994. *Revista Semana* 11 October: 116. Unauthored article.

Trujillo, Carla, ed. 1991. *Chicana Lesbians: The Girls Our Mothers Warned Us About*. Berkeley: Third Woman.

Valencia, Loana DP. 1997. "Bajando la luna." In *Best American Erotica*, edited by Susie Bright. New York: Simon and Schuster.

Silencing Our Lady
La Respuesta de Alma

Alma López

In the beginning of a new millennium, *Our Lady* appeared in Santa Fe during Holy Week. Her appearance caused passionate discussions throughout the Americas. Hundreds met in a geographic space called Holy Faith to discuss and debate her contemporary apparition to a Chicana artist named Alma, a resident in the City of Angels. Thousands have also met, discussed, and debated *Our Lady*'s apparition in a space called Cyber in a world called the Wide Web.[1]

Before an Inquisition organized by the man, the priest, and the archbishop, Alma's Respuesta is as follows:[2]

I was born in Mexico and grew up in California. My family would visit our aunts, uncles, and cousins in Mexico at least once every two years. My parents felt it was important to nurture the relationship with our Mexican family, history, and culture. For these trips, my parents would save money for many months. On the morning of the trip we would pile up in the red Thunderbird and begin our long drive south at dawn.

In Mexico and in Los Angeles, the Vírgen de Guadalupe was always in a special place in our homes. Sometimes she was a migrant Vírgen. We always lived in overcrowded apartments and houses with two bedrooms at the most; one for my parents and the other one for all six kids. Often, when the house was too crowded and my mother needed to pray, she would take the Vírgen and a candle into the restroom or sometimes a closet.

On 21 April, I participated in the César Chávez Walkathon in East Los Angeles. We walked up Third Street past King Taco, around the Serbian Cemetery, and down Avenida César Chávez to East Los Angeles City College. After the march, we drove west on Avenida César Chávez past Soto Street to La Parrilla Restaurant for lunch. That day, I was in memory lane, walking and driving past murals portraying the Virgen de Guadalupe and heroes such as Zapata, Aztec warriors, and now César Chávez. I looked at some of these recently painted murals and saw that as Latinas we are still invisible. All of these murals neglected to portray female heroines such as UFW cofounder Dolores Huerta, poet Sor Juana Inés de la Cruz, Subcomandante Ramona, and Nobel Peace Prize winner Rigoberta Menchù.

The murals I grew up with rarely portrayed any strong Chicanas, except for the Judith Hernández *La Adelita* in Ramona Gardens.[3] I remembered my childhood and thought of my eleven nieces, most of them quickly approaching their teens. I remembered that as an artist one of the reasons I focus on female images is to add to the visual history a more complex identity from our lived realities as Latinas.

I remembered that one of the first digital murals I produced, as a California Arts Council Artist in Residence in collaboration with Judith Baca's UCLA César Chávez Center's digital mural course, was titled *Las Four* and installed in the new Estrada Courts Community Center in 1997. Soon after it was installed, the portable digital mural on vinyl portraying four young female residents of Estrada Courts Housing Project was slashed by young men.

At the time, I was most shocked by the violent attitude of the young men toward the young women. Referring to the young women as "hoodrats," they felt entitled to destroy the one image that featured their sisters. The excuse for the vandalism was that some of the young women portrayed had dated some of the young men in the neighborhood, and because the neighborhood was so small their dating possibilities were limited, so now one of the young women was dating someone outside of the neighborhood. The young women felt that the young men treated them as if they were neighborhood property. I also remembered how, at the request of one of the young women originally photographed on the front steps of their home, I replaced her, using Photoshop cut and paste techniques. She did not want to be part of the mural because she had a black eye her boyfriend had given her.

Currently, I feel like I am on trial. I am being forced to defend one of my digital prints in the *Cyber Arte: Tradition Meets Technology* exhibition at the Museum of International Folk Art in Santa Fe, New Mexico. The exhibition features four Chicana/Latina/Hispana artists who combine traditional cultural iconography with state-of-the-art technology. The artists include Elena Baca (photographer), Marion Martinez (sculptor), Teresa Archuleta Sagel (weaver), and me, Alma López. This exhibition was curated by Tey Marianna Nunn, a Latina scholar and art historian. Elena, Marion, Teresa, and Tey Marianna are Nuevo Mexicanas. The "offending"

Figure 1. Alma López, Our Lady, 2000. Digital print. Image courtesy of the artist.

work titled *Our Lady* is a small photo-based digital print on exhibition in a museum (fig. 1). It is not an object of devotion in a church.

Nowhere has there been such a strong response to my work as in Santa Fe. *Our Lady* has been exhibited in California, received a book cover award for a book published by the University of Arizona Press, and was shown on ABC/Channel 7 Vista L.A. The *Lupe and Sirena* image was exhibited throughout California, in Chihuahua, Mexico, and on the cover of the journal *Aztlán*.

223

From this experience I have learned that as an artist I may have an intended meaning in the work I produce, but that once on exhibit, how it is interpreted depends on the experiences of the viewer. My intention as an artist was not disrespectful in any way. However, some people in Santa Fe feel offended. Who are those offended? Why do they feel more entitled to this cultural icon than the Chicana/Latina/Hispana women in the exhibition? Why are they unable to make a distinction between an image in a museum and an image in their church? Why is the church in New Mexico targeting this image when they have so many of their own issues?

The protest against my digital print *Our Lady* is organized and led by community activist Jose Villegas and Deacon Anthony Trujillo. New Mexico Archbishop Michael J. Sheehan has joined them, calling the artwork "sacrilegious" and "a tart." Mr. Villegas, Deacon Trujillo, and the archbishop see the *Our Lady* digital print with exposed legs, belly, and a female angel's breasts as "offensive." Yet I know that many churches, in Mexico and Europe and the United States, house images of nude male angels and, most prominently, a crucifixion practically naked except for a loincloth. On the internet, the most vicious attacks have come from Santa Fe artist Pedro Romero Sedeño and Berkeley-based Tonatiuh–Quinto Sol publisher Octavio Romano. Their faith and masculinity are threatened by my portrayal of the Virgen as a contemporary Latina.

On March 17, I received an e-mail from Jose Villegas in which he described his upset feelings. He said that I have no right to express myself in regard to this particular cultural icon, and he threatened anyone who doesn't agree with his worldview. One week later, during a meeting with the museum and the Office of Cultural Affairs, he organized a rally that I saw on television.

On April 4, at 10:00 a.m. at the museum complex, a meeting of six to eight hundred people was rescheduled to a larger venue to allow anyone who was interested to participate. At this meeting, almost half inside were supporters, and I know that some outside were also supporters. Supporters seem to be primarily Latinas, artists, writers, professors, and women. The protestors seem to be primarily men, priests, and older women who were transported via buses from the local churches. Villegas, about three men, and a priest dominated the conversation. As curator Tey Marianna Nunn was about to speak, she was interrupted and the meeting was rescheduled.

On Monday, April 16, at 10:00 a.m. at Sweeney Center, anywhere from six to twelve hundred (reports vary, and some have told me that a smaller crowd gathered at this second meeting than were assembled at the first) met to discuss *Our Lady*. Unfortunately I was unable to attend this second meeting because of commitments to work, the cost of travel, anxiety about my physical safety, and because, at this point, I felt that if I had been present, I would be a target of discussion instead of participating in an open dialogue of concerns. When Elena and Marion, two artists featured in the exhibit, spoke in support of the exhibition, they were intimidated and harassed. Although this situation is very difficult and painful, I think that at some level there must be something positive about the dialogue it has prompted. This controversy must be about more than a small digital print. Among other issues, perhaps it's about local politics? Gentrification? Lack of opportunities for local artists? Fear of Latina women's liberation? Fear of change?

When I see *Our Lady* as well as the works portraying the Virgen by many Chicana artists, I see an alternative voice expressing the multiplicities of our lived realities. I see myself living a tradition of Chicanas who because of cultural and gender oppression have asserted our voice. I see Chicanas creating a deep and meaningful connection to this revolutionary cultural female image that appeared to an indigenous person at a time of genocide, and as an inspiration during liberation struggles such as the Mexican Revolution and the Chicano civil rights movement. I see Chicanas who understand faith.

Catholic or not, as Chicanas/Latinas/Hispanas, we all grew up with the ever-present image of the Virgen de Guadalupe. As an artist, I feel entitled to express my relationship to her in a way relevant to my own experiences. In doing so, I join many other visual, literary, and performance artists, such as Yolanda López, Ester Hernández, Santa Barraza, Delilah Montoya, Yreina Cervantez, Sandra Cisneros, and Raquel Salinas, all of whom have shared their own personal experiences in their works of the Virgen de Guadalupe.

More than twenty years ago, artists Yolanda López and Ester Hernández were threatened and attacked for portraying the Virgen in a feminist and liberating perspective. In 1978 Yolanda López received bomb threats for her portrayal of the Virgen wearing low-heeled shoes. In this image the Virgen walks with her head bowed, hands clasped, wearing a dress below the knee. I think that people were upset because the Virgen was able to walk away, especially if she didn't care to listen to someone's prayers.

Our Lady features two of my friends: performance artist Raquel Salinas as a contemporary Virgen dressed in roses and cultural activist Raquel Gutierrez as a nude butterfly angel. The two Raqueles and I grew up in Los Angeles with the image of the Virgen in our homes and community. The Virgen is everywhere. She's on tattoos, stickers, posters, air freshener cans, shirts, and corner store murals, as well as church walls. Many, including

225

myself, feel that because she is everywhere there is nothing anyone can do to change how the original image of the Virgen de Guadalupe is generally perceived.

Our Lady was inspired by our own experiences; by Raquel Salinas's one-person performance titled *Heat Your Own*; Raquel Gutierrez's experiences in Catholic school; and by a Sandra Cisneros essay, "Guadalupe the Sex Goddess." Sandra Cisneros writes: "She is a face for a god without a face, an indigena for a god without ethnicity, a female deity for a god who is genderless, but I also understand that for her to approach me, for me to finally open the door and accept her, she had to be a woman like me."[4]

When Cisneros wonders if the Virgen has a dark Latina vagina and nipples underneath her dress, I imagined roses. Roses were the proof of her apparition to Juan Diego. Abstracted plants and flowers are imprinted on her dress. Amid the other symbolism in her depiction and apparition, flowers and roses connect her to us as natives. Xochitl is flower. Xochitlalpan is the flower earth place that can be translated as paradise or heaven. When I imagined the image of *Our Lady*, I saw a contemporary representation of a Latina woman covered with flowers.

Even if I look really hard at *Our Lady* and the works of many Chicana artists, I don't see what is so offensive. I see beautiful bodies: gifts from our creator. Maybe because my mother breastfed me as a baby, I see breasts as nurturing. Maybe because I love women, I see beauty and strength. I also see the true representation of Mary. Mary was an awesome woman and mother with a difficult task. She had a child who was not her husband's, she kept her son safe from a murderous king, she suffered her son's struggles and death, and most of all she raised her son to have love and compassion for everyone, including female prostitutes. I think Mary was a lot like some of our mothers.

I am forced to wonder how men like Mr. Villegas, Deacon Trujillo, and Archbishop Sheehan are looking at my work that the horrible words they use to describe it are "blasphemy," "sacrilegious," "the devil," "a tart," "a stripper." I am forced to wonder: how do they perceive women and our bodies? I wonder: why do they think that our bodies are inherently ugly and perverted that they cannot be portrayed in an art piece in a museum especially when nude or practically nude male bodies live in churches? I wonder: where is their love and compassion for all men and women? I wonder: why are they attacking me for portraying my idea of a strong woman while protecting the sexual violence toward children and young women perpetrated by their own priests in their own churches in New Mexico? I wonder: will those priests ever be on public trial like I am today?[5]

This inquisition has been torturous. A few men self-righteously believe that they have the authority to dictate how a particular image should be interpreted. They believe they can tell me how to think. I am a woman who has grown up with the Virgen. Who are these men to tell me how to relate to her? Who are they to demand the censorship of an exhibition of four Latina artists curated by a Latina scholar? Who are they to believe that they hold the only and righteous worldview on this cultural icon? I wish they would realize that their perspective does not apply to everyone, not even all New Mexican Catholics. Not everyone is offended, and many more feel that the image should not be censored. E-mails, calls, and letters of support have included Catholics, Latinas/os, artists, educators, the governor and first lady of New Mexico, museum funders such as Neutrogena Corporation, free speech groups such as the New York–based National Coalition against Censorship, the ACLU, and various communities nationwide including Santa Fe. We all need to come to the conclusion that we can express our opinion, but no one has the right to silence anyone. I have the right to exhibit my work, and viewers have a right to voice their approval or disapproval.

I think that the museum and I are in a difficult situation and that the only fair solution to this issue would be to leave the work on exhibit. If the museum removes my work or makes it unavailable for the general audience in any way, they will be participating in censorship, acting against our first amendment rights, and losing credibility as a learning institution committed to present art that challenges and educates audiences. If I remove my work, I will be a Latina pushed to silence and invisibility. If my work is removed by the museum or by me, the message will be that I have no right to express myself as an artist and a woman. That, although all four artists and the curator are professionals in our fields, our work has no real merit and is unqualified unless it meets the approval of all. That the only voice that has value above everyone's including the museum, the artists in the exhibition, the curator, and people who expressed their support, is the voice of those who feel offended by my work.

I never thought that of necessity I would be siding with a museum since most of the time I feel extremely marginalized. In Los Angeles museums, Latino exhibitions are historical art phenomena. In the nearby city of Long Beach, the Museum of Latin American Art seems only to exhibit the art of non-US-born Latinos. In the case of the Museum of International Folk Art, I feel that the museum has made an admirable effort to listen to everyone's concerns by organizing public community meetings with budgets exceeding the *Cyber Arte* exhibition budget. However, I am beginning to feel that while attempts are being made to listen and mediate this conflict, the voices of the artists on exhibit and their supporters may be overlooked or even ignored; essentially, that the voices of the men organizing for the removal of the work will carry more weight than the voices of the women in the exhibition.

Many opinions and recommendations compete to be heard concerning this issue, I would ask that in considering such recommendations that they also consider the following questions. How rare are museum exhibitions by a Latina curator featuring Latina artists? What will be the effects of this controversy on future exhibitions of Latina/o artists? Will artists be censored to avoid any future possible controversies? Will work be removed for any reason if someone doesn't like it? What happens to the rights of artists and curators to create and exhibit without censorship? Will audiences be accorded intellectual respect to visit museums and make their own conclusions?

Author's Note

Since completing this essay, the New Mexico Museum Committee on Sensitive Materials recommended that *Our Lady* digital print remain on exhibit. The committee came to this conclusion after reviewing the museum's policies, curatorial process, and community response. The Museum of International Folk Art also decided not to extend the exhibition to February 2002, so it closed as originally scheduled on October 28, 2001.

However, Jose L. Villegas and Deacon Anthony Trujillo filed appeals and lawsuits against the museum. Tom Wilson, director of the New Mexico Museums, denied their appeals. "Nowhere in your appeal do you recognize the rights of all points of views to be heard, the hallmark of a free and democratic society," wrote Wilson to Villegas and Trujillo. "Nor do their requests address the importance of the museum as a place to present chang- ing ideas and concepts, a mission shared with other museums accredited by the American Association of Museums and one that is central to the educational responsibility of museums in today's world," said Wilson.[6] Mr. Villegas and Deacon Trujillo have filed their appeal to the Board of the New Mexico Museums, who will be having their regularly scheduled meeting in late September. Until the work is removed, Mr. Villegas and Deacon Trujillo are on a "holy fast" of breads and juices which they alternate weekly.

In May, New Mexican artists Pola Lopez and Delilah Montoya curated an exhibition of Nuevo Mexicana artists titled *Las Malcriadas* in Santa Fe in support of my work remaining on exhibit at the museum. They received very favorable press calling them "brave women." On Saturday, June 30, approximately three hundred protestors rallied, organized by America

Needs Fatima, a Catholic organization based in Pennsylvania with origins in Brazil. That same day, Las Malcriadas hosted a closing party where local artists spoke about their art, poets read their work, and local playwright Sylvia Vergara read passages of a recent play she wrote on the entire *Our Lady* controversy. Due to numerous requests to host *Cyber Arte: Tradition meets Technology Exhibition*, the museum and artists are considering packaging the entire exhibit for travel nationwide.

Appendices: Las cartas

26 March 2001

Dr. Thomas Wilson, Director
Museum of New Mexico
P.O. Box 2087
Santa Fe, NM 87501

Dear Dr. Wilson,

I am writing to thank you for your continued support of Los Angeles Chicana artist Alma Lopez, among others, in the current show at the Museum of International Folk Art. I understand you have received a certain amount of protest to the exhibition, and I thank you for maintaining your support for the innovative and provocative work of the artists.

I am quite familiar with Ms. Lopez' artwork and the richness of expression she brings to both traditional and contemporary Chicana/o images and issues. From her public artwork on billboards and murals all over the L.A. area to her "digital" collections online, I find her artwork a unique contribution to an evolving Chicana feminist sensibility, with an altogether consistent and visionary spirituality.

I should also say that I am not at all surprised by some negative reaction to her portrayal of the Virgen de Guadalupe. Dismay and even anger are to be expected—indeed, may be crucial—in inviting viewers to think about the many layers of meaning latent in the Virgen's image and her ramifications for Chicana/o gender ideology as well as spirituality.

And as a scholar of Chicana/o and Religious Studies, I must point out that this is not the first time that Chicana artists seeking to reclaim and transform traditional religious imagery have been threatened and silenced. I'm sure you are familiar with the work of San Francisco Chicana artists

Esther Hernandez and Yolanda Lopez, whose early work with the Virgen de Guadalupe received praise as well as various bomb threats, but is now widely recognized as a pivotal contribution to the Chicana and Chicano art "canon."

In closing, thank you again for your support of this amazing exhibition. Please do not hesitate to call if I can be of any assistance.

Sincerely,
Susana L. Gallardo, PhD (ABD), Department of Religious Studies, Stanford University

April 2, 2001

Dr. Joyce Ice, Director
Museum of International Folk Art

Dr. Tey Marianna Nunn, Curator
Museum of International Folk Art
(Curator of the *Cyber Arte* exhibition)

Dear Dr. Ice and Dr. Nunn,

Hello, as a Nuevo Mexicano and someone who has worked in the arts community for over twenty years I wanted to offer my own thoughts on the issues surrounding Alma Lopez's work. Although I have been away from my beloved homeland for eleven years now I still very much consider myself a New Mexican.

Primarily what I wanted to say is that this experience, as scary and painful as it is (I have been through my own controversies as a curator and formerly a New Mexico Arts Division employee), can be a real opportunity for a true and meaningful dialogue and the further deepening of the relationship between the communities of New Mexico and the cultural institutions that represent them. Of course, for this to occur there needs to be respect, reflection, commitment, and passion, all basic Catholic values.

I believe that this specific event is not only about the piece by Alma Lopez but also about the historic layered tensions between the community and the cultural institutions in New Mexico. There has been a long history of neglect, racism, and exploitation of the cultural resources of New Mexico and its people, and only relatively recently has it begun to change for the better. So this specific event is like touching a wound on the psychic body of our people.

If one is not aware of the work by many Chicana and other artists that has led to this piece it can appear as a shocking and disrespectful image of the virgin, but in art, context is everything. If we look at art history there are many images that created scandal in their times that seem totally banal to our contemporary eyes. I would encourage you to do whatever it takes to further contextualize the work, through exhibitions, readings, slide shows, etc. Having been through the culture wars of the 1980s and 1990s I know one of the most effective tools used against artists and cultural institutions was the de or re-contextualizing of artwork.

It is my strong belief that there must be solutions other than wholesale removal of the work. The solution is with the local community and the stewards of the institution. It would be a mistake to think that simply removing the piece would actually solve any of the deeper and long-term issues made manifest with this work.

I wish everyone there the strength, courage, and clarity of thought to struggle through this with dignity and respect. I will be in New Mexico the week before Easter and will come in to see the exhibit.

The very best regards,
Patricio Chávez
Artist, Community Activist

3 April 2001

Dr. Joyce Ice, Director
Museum of International Folk Art

Dr. Tey Marianna Nunn, Curator
Museum of International Folk Art
(Curator of the *CyberArte* exhibition)

Dear Dr. Ice and Dr. Nunn,

I am writing in support of Alma Lopez's image *Our Lady*, currently on exhibition in your CyberArte show at the Museum of International Folk Art in Santa Fe, and especially in support of her right as an artist to produce this image and your right as museum professionals to exhibit it to the public. It has been with utter dismay and indignation that I have been following the controversy ignited by Mr. Jose Villegas and his demeaning interpretation of Alma's vision of *Our Lady*, and I am deeply disturbed not only by the egregious lack of historical and political awareness demonstrated by Mr. Villegas in his diatribes against a well-respected (and respectful) Chicana artist, but even more so, by the fact that your museum board is actually going to meet this Wednesday to decide whether or not to censor Alma's image from the exhibit. As a Chicana writer and cultural critic who works on Chicana/o art, as a professor of Chicana/o Studies who often invites Ms. Lopez to lecture in her classes at UCLA, I can only shudder at the fascistic connotations of that action. The repercussions for all artists and museum professionals who fail to conform to the patriarchal status quo are painfully clear.

Although the attack on artistic freedom and the threat of censorship are more than enough cause for alarm, I think a deeper issue at the heart of Mr. Villegas's critique is that it is women who are in positions of power here: in the directorship of this museum, the organization of this exhibition, and the production of this image. If that were not so, he would not be demanding your resignation, and he would not be targeting the work of a lesbian artist. Mr. Villegas does not have a right to threaten your careers any more than he has a right to perpetrate a modern-day witch hunt on Alma Lopez; and yet, he is getting exactly the response he seeks. That the archbishop has gotten involved only underscores the fallacy of artistic freedom in a society in which, as the NEA debacle taught us over a decade ago, art is held accountable to church and state. Why is it that, instead of catering to Mr. Villegas, instead of meeting to discuss the removal of *Our Lady* from your exhibition, you are not taking him to task for his offensive remarks and the way in which he is slandering the reputations of your museum and the artist? I sincerely hope the Museum of International Folk Art, a museum I have always enjoyed and respected, does not fall prey to these McCarthyist tactics. I ask you to refuse to participate in an action meant to undermine your constitutional rights, and those of the artist, and I beg you not to capitulate to the arrogant demands and colonized interpretations of men who dwell in the backwater of cultural and sexual politics.

Again, I want to reiterate in the strongest possible terms my unconditional support of and admiration for the revisionist work of Alma Lopez. Your institution would be most remiss if it were to permit her contribution to be censored.

Respectfully yours,
Alicia Gaspar de Alba, PhD

Interim Director, LGBT Studies Program
Associate Professor of Chicana/Chicano Studies
UCLA

20 April 2001

Dear Alma,

I hope it is not too late to add my voice in support of your artwork. As you know, I have been an admirer of your work for many years, so please pass the following on to the museum.

I am a practicing, not just a cultural Catholic. My four children, including my three daughters, attend Catholic school and I have commissioned three santos from a New Mexico santero. I personally believe in the power of the Virgen to be a healer and a source of inspiration and comfort to me and my family. I took my children to the Basilica for the first time this past summer so that they too would know of her place in their Catholic, Mexican and Chicano history. (I am not unmindful of the controversies regarding her appearance, etc.)

But the issue today is not my personal beliefs, or those of any other viewer; the issue is our tolerance of your artistic vision, and the failure of the board to defend your right to that artistic vision against those who would for various reasons seek to deny you this right. I happen to love the image, but even if I didn't, I do, and Mr. Villegas should, respect that right, whether he agrees with it or not.

The museum's failing thus far seems to be that it has opened the door for a discussion of whether the piece should be removed. Enter the likes of Mr. Villegas. As others have already commented, where will the intolerance end? Will the Board allow Mr. Villegas, the archbishop, or anyone else, for that matter, to come to the museum and summarily order the removal of any other works, because they are sacrilegious, offensive, in bad taste, historically incorrect, badly composed, oddly dimensioned, or too big or too small? While the question may seem ludicrous, the answer seems to be yes, if enough people, especially the well connected, or of the threatening kind, say so.

Therefore, the museum should establish a standard. I recommend a ballot box at the entrance. Visitors may then vote on which, if any, pieces should be removed. If a piece receives enough votes, regardless of the reason, it will be removed. Of course that practice should be applied to all exhibitions at the museum, including those of folk, contemporary, conceptual, video, and other art forms. The board will be saving itself the trouble of calling special meetings whenever there are enough malcontents to warrant a review of the artistic vision of its invited artists or the curatorial prerogatives of its professional staff.

In short, this controversy is not your problem, Alma. And I hope it will not dissuade you from continuing to create works that question and inspire, not only aficionados like me, but especially young women like my daughters who need to interpret for themselves what their role in society is and need artists like you to help them do so.

Afectuosamente,
Armando Durón
Lawyer
Member, Chicano Art Collectors Anonymous

11 May 2001

Alma and Raquel,

I have been following up on the course of events of the "controversy" over Alma's art piece in which Raquel so beautifully represents *Our Lady*. The first time I saw it, I smiled and thought to myself, "Yeah, that's what our lady is all about." I mean really, that's what I have imagined her to be since I became an adult. She's chingona like that and proud, and causes controversy the way you are.

Since, I was a little girl, I have felt the oppression imposed on mujeres in society. Actually, when I was little, there was a period of time, where unaware of anatomy, I wondered what exactly made me different from little boys, and how did I know I was a girl. At four years old, I began my study of what made me different, what made me a girl. Not knowing that the difference is that boys have pee pees and girls don't, my first observation of difference was that girls had long hair and they couldn't go outside and play with pelotas or pretend to be in war. That's what made me a girl. My mom dressed me up in frilly little things and sat me down with a doll, and said sit there and stay clean. "Niñas like you, se sientan silensitas, you play quietly." That was my next observation, women were quiet, never yelled or spoke out; they sat silent with eyes on the ground (como la Virgen)

234

or looking out to nowhere. When they yelled they were irrational and emotional. Asi son las mujeres. . . . Disregarded either way.

Today, I am still suffering and my heart still bleeds from all the quiet that has been imposed on me and the quiet I see imposed on my sisters (mujeres in general). I was molested for several years by a family member, and I have been quiet. Don't share my anger, it's not ladylike. I've been feeling so angry at the quiet that we have to carry as mujeres. Worse than a cross, we carry an anvil on our back. For the sake of FAMILIA, we endure some of the worst tortures. I told my mom two years ago, she cried and felt bad, probably guilty, but she asked me not to tell. It would be too hard for the family. They wouldn't understand. My cousin would be hurt that it was her brother, maybe she wouldn't come over. No le digas a tu papa, she said. It would hurt him too much. Don't tell your boyfriend, he might think you come from a bad family. Don't tell. Don't tell. Don't tell. So when he comes over, I smile and I act cordial. Like a lady. But inside . . . inside . . . it's not quiet. It's all noise, earthquake and all the fire from hell. It's inside, so nobody gets hurt.

Pero yo, que? Me pudro?

The one thing that has made me strong is my mission to end the cycle of quiet, and the noise I hear from mujeres, artists like yourselves, que no se dejan. You give the voiceless and unimportant like me a voice. I'm an artist myself and fascinated by the archetype of Guadalupe/Tonanztin, who in my eyes is all woman with fire and pride in her eyes, just like you, Raquel. Not complacency. She's a warrior and carries a machete and she's beautiful and brown and strong the way you are. Funny coincidence, but I had been working on some sketches to do a portrait of a naked and pregnant Guadalupe. So when I read the stories and different points of view, I couldn't help but think, I love mi raza, but sometimes we are just as tapados as anyone else

I guess what I'm trying to say by writing this e-mail is, Thank You. Muchisimas gracias for creating empowering images of mujeres where we could see our reflection. It all begins there. We need to change the images that have controlled and kept us down for so long. Your work communicates the urgency in the need for us to love our bodies brown and round the way they are. It also communicates to me the need for us to keep our head up with our gaze always aflame, always watchful, and always aware, our souls ready to fight. The quiet has killed us for too long. I'm still a youngster and still learning how to yell. I'm trying not to let the anger eat me up. It's hard to live ashamed. But in the meantime thank you for speaking out for mujeres como yo. Your work saves us and our souls. The fact that you are willing to stand up for that is an inspiration to me. I hope I could one day follow your example of courage. So, no se dejen. Keep on talking, keep on painting, keep on yelling, just keep on.

Gracias con todisísimo el corazon,
Adriana
Santa Ana, Califas

Notes

"Silencing Our Lady: La Respuesta de Alma," by Alma López, is reprinted from *I Am Aztlán: The Personal Essay in Chicano Studies* (Los Angeles: UCLA Chicano Studies Research Center Press, 2004) and from *Aztlán: A Journal of Chicano Studies* 26, no. 2 (2001).

1. Please refer to www.almalopez.net for e-mails, news articles, and links specifically on *Our Lady*.

2. "La Respuesta," literally translated in English as "The Answer", was the title of Sor Juana Inés de la Cruz's letter to the Catholic Church in her defense of pursuing writing and reading in seventeenth-century Mexico. She was a poet, scholar, and nun. She felt she would not be honoring her creator if she did not use the mind she was given to seek knowledge. Sor Juana Ines died a few years after the church took away her library and stopped her from writing.

3. *La Adelita*, painted in Ramona Gardens Public Housing Project in 1976, is signed by Los Four, and usually Carlos Almaraz is given credit for design. However, anyone who studies the artwork of Judith Hernandez, Carlos Almaraz, and Los Four must agree that the primary Adelita figure is rendered much like the women in Ms. Hernandez's work.

4. Sandra Cisneros, "Guadalupe the Sex Goddess." In *Goddess of the Americas = La diosa de las Américas: Writings on the Virgin of Guadalupe*, 46–51 (New York: Riverhead Books, 1996).

5. In 1993, when former Archbishop Robert F. Sánchez resigned after his own sexual improprieties came to light, he was replaced by Archbishop Michael J. Sheehan who publicly promised to stop the rampant sexual abuses by parish priests. Archbishop Sánchez covered up hundreds of sexual offenses by parish priests because, over the span of eighteen years, he had sexual relationships with eleven women who were all in their twenties. Since Sheehan took over the job more than 150 claims have been settled. Over $3 million has been spent in an attempt to expiate this scandalous sin—not for victim counseling, but primarily on legal fees. The whereabouts of many of the perpetrators are currently unknown.

6. See Museum of New Mexico, "Museum Director Denies Appeal: Our Lady Stays," press release, 2001.

Breaking Down Glass Walls

Ruben Ochoa

¡Q-vo! In 1943, US bona fide sailors and servicemen roamed the barrios of East Los Angeles. They were not there for the culture and nightlife. They were there to dispose of an enemy. They were there for reprisal after a group of sailors declared they were attacked. The enemy could not be the Japanese; they were serving time in "relocation centers" throughout unknown deserts, unknown to themselves and their families. There was an additional enemy to fill the racial paranoid void lurking in the minds of Southern California's hysteria. This enemy did not tiptoe after hours and attempt to conceal their identities. They thumped and tapped their Stacy Adams as they Pachuco Hopped throughout the nightclubs of East Los, allowing them to be quite visible in their intentions to not conform to American standards. This put them in a space of contention with over two hundred sailors mobilized to confront them, which resulted in the Zoot Suit Riots.

By not succumbing to American assimilation those Mexican Americans ended up paying a heavy price for their defiance. Retribution, usually carried out by death, took the form of humiliation as well as dehumanization. One by one the pachucos were disconnected from reality and transported back in time to a sacrificial re-enactment for the Amerindian deity Xipe Totec. Absolutely not in the manner of being bludgeoned to death in the ritualistic fashion of drinking the blood of one's first kill. On the contrary, pachuco's skin became the prop for Xipe Totec's ceremonial use of skin, placing it over one's own body to signify renovation through death to insure the continuation of life. The pachucos were stripped and flayed of their visible markers, *sus trapos*, their zoot suits, their second skin, and left naked, jailed, and humiliated. All the while the press hailed the servicemen as heroes for stemming the spreading of corruption and contamination to others by pachucos.

Carrying this weight of historical fragility over my shoulders, my arms, my head, and my shoes, *Pachuco a la Vidrio* enters another space known for contention toward non-Anglicized artists, "The White Cube." The photos, formally taken to serve as documentation only, depict the glass encrusted zoot suit out of action. An aspect lost is the guerilla performance that disrupted the walls and minds of art patrons at the Escondido Center for the Arts, a museum filled mostly by Anglo patrons and Anglo artists. The only hint of Latino artists was the ploy of using an international Latino artist annually to fulfill a "diverse" quota—a strategy used by many Museum institutions. However, the work on display at the moment was a glass blown, art-for-art's sake exhibition, a calling card for an apolitical audience.

Just as the pachuco's clothes of the 1940s made meaning with their bodies, hateful and desirable, my suit acted in the same manner. The friction of glass resonated, this audible vibrancy of crashing glass, throughout the entire institution. The noise startled, disrupted, and yet enchanted the

Figure 1. *Ruben Ochoa and Joey Azul at the Escondido Center for the Arts. Photo by Pasha E. Turley.*

audience. Staff members, docents, and gallery attendees alike were shocked, alerting the security guards into action. But I had total agency. I strategically entered through the service entrance as an employee of the institution. I knew the space and they knew my face. I painted those white walls and installed those very works of glass on the pedestals with my own hands. But my appearance was no longer that of a laborer. I literally transformed and metaphorically jumped off a pedestal as a walking art piece subverting the institution. Thus forcing the museum to become my personal artist space.

Yet I did not act alone. I had an accomplice, Joey Azul. Azul appeared as one of them, but was recognized as the Other. Emphatically reading and pronouncing Azul's name and visually seeing Azul takes you beyond boundaries, genders, and ethnicities. Upon confrontation, one clearly sees that Azul is neither male nor a recipient of the Spanish surname by birth or marriage. This conscious and sadistic positioning is intentional. Causing

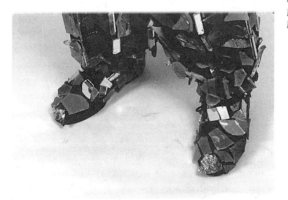

Figures 2, 3. Ruben Ochoa, details of Pachuco a la Vidrio, *1999. Glass and zoot suit; 5'8", US size 10, and 240 pounds minus 60 pounds for trapos. Photography by Patrick Miller.*

a conundrum with her verbal name and blond-haired, blue-eyed physical appearance. Especially effective when read on paper, her names signifies several other connotations.

As we continued to roam the halls of the museum, no one dared to strip us of our actions and glass suits. They physically could not without causing direct harm to themselves by handling raw shards of glass. This was the new improved *tacuche* zoot suit. I had the choice to shed my own skin and placed it onto others, not empowering them but myself. Audience members and patrons were allowed to wear my *trapo*, my coat, and *tando*, my brimmed hat. They animated themselves through fear and excitement by being encrusted in a glass zoot suit and becoming part of a pachuco aesthetic. The empowerment took place briefly right afterwards, when the audience member wanted to return to normalcy. Through fear of getting cut, they could not remove the *garras*, the suit, by themselves. I took on the position of Xipe Totec and flayed this added second skin. Orale!

Notes

"Breaking Down Glass Walls," by Ruben Ochoa, is reprinted from *I Am Aztlán: The Personal Essay in Chicano Studies* (Los Angeles: UCLA Chicano Studies Research Center Press, 2004) and from *Aztlán: A Journal of Chicano Studies* 28, no. 1 (2003).

I would like to give special thanks to Joey Azul, for her performance collaboration; Ray Estrella from El Pachuco Zoot Suits, located in Fullerton, CA, for donating the zoot suit; Harry Gamboa Jr., for his video collaboration; Cam La, for her immeasurable support; Patrick Miller, for his photography; Therman Statom, for donating the glass shards; and Pasha E. Turley, for her photography.

Jotería Identity and Consciousness

Anita Tijerina Revilla and José Manuel Santillana

As activist scholars, we feel that it is important to begin with our personal testimonies before sharing our research and vision of a collective Jotería identity and consciousness. We tell our queerstories as "counterstories" in the critical race theory tradition to position ourselves and illustrate that there is a direct connection between who we are as individuals and how we participate in an activist and academic community of queer Latina/os and Chicana/os.[1] These stories illustrate the diversity of Jotería identity, as the two of us have had very different experiences in our queer journeys.

Jota-historia, *Joto-historia*, and *Jotería-historia* are terms that we use intentionally to indicate the absence of queer history from traditional academic spaces. They refer to a process of reclaiming and documenting our personal testimonies and experiences.

Anita Tijerina Revilla's Jota-Historia

By the time I started graduate school at the University of California, Los Angeles (UCLA), I thought that it was quite possible that I was bisexual. I was certain that I was attracted to both women and men, but I had yet to have a romantic relationship with a woman. Through my mid-twenties, I was a self-presumed heterosexual. I had rarely questioned my sexuality, mostly because it was easy for me to maintain a "straight" identity. I was attracted to boys as a teen, and I dated men as a young adult. Heterosexual privilege, heteronormativity, and compulsive heterosexuality can easily lead some people to maintain a lifetime of heterosexual identity despite their diverse sexual desires.[2] Luckily, this was not my case.

I spent two years in Texas between receiving my master's degree and starting my doctoral program. In San Antonio, fabulous queers and their allies regularly surrounded me. I was one of the acknowledged "allies" in

241

my group of friends. We frequented the Bonham Exchange and several other gay clubs in town. We all went together—gays, lesbians, and allies. We had fun, and rarely did anyone question people's sexuality or their decision to be in a gay club if they were "straight," although the lines were at times blurry. One evening, a beautiful woman asked me to dance. As in the movies, the music faded away and a spotlight brightened the very spot where we stood. It was one of those moments that seem to last an eternity. To this day, I cannot remember what my answer was or whether I danced with her. What I do remember is that I was intensely attracted to her and had a deep desire for her, a desire I had never experienced for a woman before. The next day, I sat at the kitchen table with my mother and said, "Mom, I think that if I ever meet a woman that I'm attracted to, I will date her." My mom, a working-class Tejana who raised us on her own since the age of thirty, replied, "You know what *mija*? I think that I would do the same thing. I think I only married your dad because I was expected to." Ever since then, my mother and I have both openly proclaimed our desire for and attraction to both women and men.

Soon after, I entered a seven-year relationship with a man, my first adult long-term relationship. While I was in that relationship, I became a member of an organization called Raza Womyn de UCLA. The women in this organization were Chicanas/Latinas, feminists, labor organizers, and educators. Some were queer, others were allies, many were questioning their sexuality, and most were activists who also identified as muxeristas (Revilla 2010a, 2010b).[3] These women became participants in my research, which culminated in a dissertation and several published articles; they were my friends, fellow activists, and incredible teachers. As a member of this organization, I felt free to question my sexuality and to shift my sexual identity. I began to openly identify as bisexual, pansexual, and/or fluid, convinced that I had the right to love and desire any person, regardless of sex and gender identity. Since coming out as queer, I have predominantly dated women, while always honoring my ability and desire to love whomever I wish.

As a participant action researcher and member of this community, I learned and wrote about the fluidity of sexual identity and the importance of organizations that actively support people who are questioning their sexual identity and coming out as queer. This organization and its members epitomized a muxerista praxis, theory, and pedagogy that led to the early identification of a muxerista consciousness in my work. This in turn has served as a foundation for the Jotería identity and consciousness outlined below.

Jose Manuel Santillana's Joto-Historia

During my last year as an undergraduate at UCLA, in 2006, I enrolled in a Chicana/o studies course titled "The Chicano Movement and Its Political Legacies," with Professor Maylei Blackwell. It was in this class that I began my research on Gay and Lesbian Latinos Unidos (GLLU), formerly known both as Gay Latinos Unidos (GLU) and as Latinos Unidos (LU). The organization was founded in 1976 in Los Angeles to draw people together to support "Gay Latin/Heritage" issues. Co-founders included Rolando Palencia, José Ramírez, David Gonzales, Juan Villagómez, Ernesto Rojas, Ramón Márquez, and Davis Milhauser. In 1982 the group began publishing a monthly newsletter, *Unidad*, which lasted about fourteen years. GLLU called for educating all communities about the multiple and simultaneous oppressions that gay and lesbian Latina/os face in everyday life. Essentially, the organization successfully created a queer Latina/o network through its newsletter, community events, and active role in the larger Los Angeles area.[4] GLLU was one of a very few groups in Southern California organizing around gay and lesbian Latino issues in that era, and it opened the doors for future LGBT Latina/o groups like Bienestar.[5]

This was the first time I had conducted any research on queer Latina/o and Chicana/o activism, and I was excited when I began reading the material.[6] The paper became more than a research project: it was a way I could explore my own identity as a queer Chicano. I wanted to know about other people's experiences growing up in a society where white supremacy, patriarchy, and homophobia existed; I wanted to know how others had overcome these barriers and fought against oppression. As I interviewed past members of GLLU, I began making connections with their experiences. Many of them had felt, in the 1980s, that their sexuality was silenced in nonqueer activist organizations; two decades later, I felt the same. Their stories as queer Latina/o activists inspired me to continue doing both my academic work and my activism in the community. The research process gave voice to my experience as a young queer Chicano activist—to my Jotoness, or Jotería.[7]

Although I had begun educating myself about social justice issues during my first years of college, in no other class did I feel comfortable enough to express my experiences as a young Chicano queer growing up in central California. Class sessions provoked discussion of what it meant to be brown in the United States.[8] One session specifically focused on the United Farm Workers of America (UFW) and brought forth images of my *familia*, my grandmother Tomasa and my aunt Lupe, who took part in the farmworkers' movement in the late 1960s. This made me realize and affirm that my history as a brown person mattered. I began to see the women in my *familia* as part of a legacy that belonged to me and to many other young brown people. Just as the personal experiences of my *familia* mattered, so did my experiences as a queer person. Revisiting these experiences ignited the desire in me to pursue my work in documenting Latina/o and Chicana/o queerstories.[9]

The experience of growing up in Avenal, a small Mexican immigrant town in central California, informs my work. Who I was and where I came from is vital to understanding why my research is more than an academic project and is indeed a tool for survival and resistance—as is true for so many of us who engage in Jotería studies and activism. In doing this work, I had to go through a process of remembering. As hard as it was, I had to challenge myself by visiting the not-so-distant past. Bittersweet memories of the "Jem and the Holograms" doll recalled my struggle with gender. What did it mean to want a Barbie doll as a little queer boy? For me it meant humiliation and rejection by my *tías* and *tíos*. I remember my *tía* Angela storming into my cousin's room and shouting at me as I played Barbies with my *primas*, "What are you doing? Barbies are for girls, not little boys! Go play outside with the boys!" As a young "boy," I was prohibited from exploring my femininity. My gender was confined to other people's definition of maleness. Every touch, every brush to Jem's hair challenged this socially constructed maleness.

Other images come to mind: my grandmother and father working under the hot sun in the San Joaquin Valley fields while white ranchers watched over them. These experiences made me realize that racism had something to do with that fact that my *familia* was picking crops in the dirt and sweltering heat. I remember my father taking me to the fields on one of his workdays; I watched him as he picked onions for hours. At lunchtime, the ranch owner drove up to the workers in his truck and stood over them to make sure they were working quickly. The rancher would often blurt out racist slurs. I may not have realized what racism was then, but I knew there was a difference between the white ranchers and us brown people. I also understood that my family's encounters with racism (as well as my own) were important and their stories often untold; they represented our community's struggles. Although my experiences do not reflect those of the entire queer Chicana/o community, they provide an example of what many queer Chicana/os have endured growing up. Only by telling our stories can we open doors to our movements and new possibilities. As marginalized people, we must actively remember how we have survived and resisted.

Early in my research, I realized that there were few books and articles on queer Latina/o activism. Little had been written about the history of queer people within the Chicano movement, or about Latina/os in the gay rights movement.[10] Instead, I found that most Chicano movement literature revolved around heterosexually identified Chicano men, perspectives that contributed in one way or another to the homophobia and patriarchy of the Chicano movement. Figures such as Corky Gonzales, César Chávez, and José Angel Gutiérrez were easy to find in textbooks (Acuña 2004; Navarro 2000; Rosales 1997; Vigil 1999). Research on queer Latinos, meanwhile, typically dealt with HIV/AIDS prevention and treatment, while queer studies was dominated by white queer experiences and politics. The absence from textbooks of queer Latina/os and Chicana/os and their activism made me question the written histories of various movements. Why had the efforts of Jotería gone unnoticed? Did the absence of queer Latina/os and Chicana/os from history books mean that they did not take part in the important movements of the 1960s, 1970s, and 1980s? These questions were the starting point from which I worked.

I felt a great urgency to ensure that queer Latina/os and Chicana/os continued documenting Jotería activism. Members of queer Latina/o and Chicana/o activist organizations such as GLLU were growing older, and for the most part little had been done to document their experiences. At the same time, I felt it was necessary to uncover my own queerstory so that I could continue working toward the liberation envisioned by our queer Latina/o and Chicana/o community ancestors and predecessors, a world free from oppression and domination. I emphasize ancestors because as Jotería, our past is often erased and denied. Therefore, as Jota/os we must acknowledge and celebrate that we, too, have lineages. Thus far, I have documented the queer Latina/o and Chicana/o activism in which I participated. One of the goals of my research was to find multiple ways to bridge the gap between research and organizing, in particular the organizing that I do as a Joto activist.

Homophobia, patriarchy, and white supremacy are deeply embedded in our communities; consequently, there is a lack of literature that speaks to the collective experiences of Jotería. On one hand, homophobia and sexism have been problems in the Chicano community, preventing the Chicano movement from progressing. On the other hand, in the gay and lesbian rights movement there has been continued white supremacy, which has prevented this movement from fully including queer people of color. Too often, queer Latina/os and Chicana/os and other queer communities of color are pushed aside to the margins of society. Jotería's struggle must be acknowledged in and outside of the Chicano movement and the queer movement. One way to begin this process is to talk about the queer Latina/o and Chicana/o experience: we must write about it and document it.

By documenting Jotería organizing, we can begin to uncover queer-stories that have been systemically silenced and oppressed. Today, we still have very few books on queer Latina/o and Chicana/o activist organizations. Such organizations are often mentioned in passing in books and articles but are seldom documented in depth. While scholars like Horacio N. Roque Ramírez (2003), Juana María Rodríguez (2003), and Anita Tijerina Revilla (2010a, 2010b) have done great work, much more activist scholarship is needed. We should be able to research Jotería and queer Latina/o and Chicana/o organizing and find an array of books addressing the complex realities of our struggles. The queer Latina/o and Chicana/o experience must be told by and heard from all of our communities.

As a Joto scholar, I feel compelled to contribute to and help preserve our queerstories and experiences so that generations after us can reflect on our collective memory. Our community has always actively struggled against injustice; we must be able to understand, theorize, and analyze these struggles. This is why my research addresses race/white supremacy, gender/patriarchy, and sexuality/homophobia in the lives of queer Latina/o and Chicana/o student activists. My master's thesis examined the experiences of nine such students who participated in organizing the 2006 Jotería conference hosted at UCLA. I explored their involvement in social justice movements at the university and in their communities. This group of students eventually formed La Jotería de UCLA, a queer Latina/o Chicana/o student activist group that began in 2006.

I was delighted to find that much of what I was looking for and wanted to do in my own research had parallels in the work of Revilla, who defined a muxerista identity and consciousness in her own earlier research with Chicana/Latina student activists at UCLA. For her dissertation, Revilla conducted a five-year multimethod case study, including participatory action research, ethnography, interviews, and surveys, of Raza Womyn de UCLA, a Chicana/Latina activist organization founded in 1979. In her research, as in mine, race, class, gender, immigration, sexuality, and discrimination based on all of these were major issues within the lives of the participants and the driving force behind their activism. As members of the organizations we studied, we were fully invested in them, playing the roles of researchers and participants simultaneously.

After moving to Las Vegas in 2008, I began doing activist work with the immigrants' rights, feminist, and queer communities; Revilla was already documenting their work and was very engaged in local activism. Soon after, I asked her to serve on my thesis committee. Thus we have worked closely as activist scholars and as friends to formulate the findings shared below, which outline some emerging characteristics of Jotería identity and consciousness. The findings draw on our research projects and on what we have learned from our collective communities in Los Angeles and Las Vegas, as well as from the newly formed Association of Jotería Arts, Activism, and Scholarship (AJAAS).[11]

A Collective Jotería-Historia

Through our experiences as Jotería, we have come to understand living, loving, and surviving. The complexities and contradictions of being queer, Xicana/o, working-class, gender-fluid, and/or immigrant have guided our writing and activism. While some scholars have distanced themselves from including personal narrative in their writing, we find it necessary to interweave our own experiences into this work. This allows us to humanize our research and remain accountable to and connected to our community. This human connection, we believe, is essential to Jotería studies and the possibilities it offers within academia. Just as we cannot separate our various identities from one another, we cannot separate our writing from our activism. Our research speaks from the heart and is rooted in radical queer love. While academia has traditionally viewed the heart as negatively emotional and subjective, we believe it is empowering to work from a site that challenges the status quo. Similarly, our research participants and activist peers connect their activism with their academic journeys. Their will to survive and thrive in an academic setting is rooted in allowing themselves to show up authentically to school, home, and work—always being activists, queers, and seekers/producers of knowledge.

As activist scholars, we have highlighted the voices and queerstories of Latina/o and Chicana/o student activists at UCLA. Our research is driven by an urgency that could only exist for researchers who acknowledge and position themselves as part of the community they are researching. This is a political positionality that allows for the queer and brown to be at the center of knowledge production. Being able to view and theorize from our own perspectives has led us to important insights about Jotería activism, identity, and consciousness.

Below we share emerging characteristics of a Jotería identity and consciousness as expressed in both the academic and activist realms. This identity and consciousness builds on Revilla's (2004) muxerista framework. However, there are specific Jota/o tenets of this identity and consciousness, including but not limited to the characteristics listed below. Jotería identity/consciousness:

1. Is rooted in fun, laughter, and radical queer love,

2. Is embedded in a Mexican, Latin American, Indigenous, and African diasporic past and present,

3. Is derived from the terms *Jota* and *Joto* and has been reclaimed as an identity/consciousness of empowerment,

4. Is based on queer Latina/o and Chicana/o and gender-nonconforming realities or lived experiences,

5. Is committed to multidimensional social justice and activism,

6. Values gender and sexual fluidity and expressions,

7. Values the exploration of identities individually and collectively,

8. Rejects homophobia, heteronormativity, racism, patriarchy, xenophobia, gender discrimination, classism, colonization, citizenism, and any other forms of subordination,[12]

9. Claims and is aligned with feminist/muxerista pedagogy and praxis,

10. Claims an immigrant and working-class background/origin,

11. Claims a queer Latina/o and Chicana/o ancestry, and

12. Supports community members and family in their efforts to avoid and heal from multidimensional battle fatigue.[13]

Our research participants' vision for social justice came from a collective effort to transform their lives and their communities. It was by creating safe spaces that they were able to be active in making those changes happen. In doing so, they produced a specific language and culture that allowed them to empower themselves and to redefine what it means to be queer and brown. Jotería identity and consciousness spoke to them in ways that other identities did not, because it embraced various aspects of who they were.

Our research indicates that Jotería activists, students, and young scholars work to achieve social justice on two levels, externally and internally. Externally, they engage in a variety of collective actions that include protests, marches, rallies, cultural nights, meetings, conferences, and coalition building. In this way they maintain a much-needed visible presence both on and off campus. They challenge other organizations and community members, both Latina/os and others, on their heteronormative, racist, xenophobic, sexist, and homophobic attitudes. Internally, they go through a process of self-education, self-acceptance, self-empowerment, and healing. While some come to terms with their sexuality, others simultaneously explore their intersecting gender, working-class, and immigrant identities. They do so in a loving environment that helps guide them from feelings of marginalization and oppression to spaces of reclamation and transformation.

Various Latina/o and Chicana/o student organizations, queer organizations, and other civil rights movements keep making the same mistakes of the 1960s, 1970s, and 1980s. While some succeed in providing a healthy site for racial justice, they fail to fully include women and queers, or they fail to include issues of race in queer and women spaces. In an attempt to address these issues, the authors present some recommendations for organizations and movements that seek to create inclusive and transformational spaces.

1. Declare a "no one is free when others are oppressed" mindset: Many have made the mistake of failing to see how all our struggles intersect in one way or another. We must be able to make all connections as oppressed and marginalized people. This includes Jotería.

2. Denounce tokenism: The fact that an organization includes a queer-identified person does not in itself indicate that the organization is not homophobic. Many organizations and movements erect a false façade of inclusion. It is important to challenge this practice.

3. Recognize and challenge privilege: In order to create safe spaces, individuals need to recognize that they might be the beneficiaries of privilege, including but not limited to privileges based on whiteness, light skin, or socially constructed beauty; on passing or identifying as heterosexual, male, or gender-normative; or on citizenship. All of these must be explored, challenged, and dealt with in order to move toward social justice. Simply acknowledging that a privilege exists is not enough. We must explore ways to be authentic allies to others who do not share our privileges and avoid one-dimensional practices and understandings of who is oppressor and who is oppressed. We live layered and complex

existences, and therefore we must constantly build and expand upon a multidimensional critical consciousness and movement.

4. Create collective spaces: Hierarchically structured spaces tend to silence people and favor the voices of a few, while collectivity often places more value on democratizing processes. Importance should be given to creating a space that allows for different forms of participation, as well as finding ways to "step up and step back."

5. Create safe spaces: Organizations and movements should place value on loving environments that nourish self-growth and openness.

6. Ensure accurate representation: Organizations and movements must represent and reflect their membership. They must constantly revisit their goals, manifestos, mission statement, values, defining language, and name to make sure they are including everyone to whom they intend to open the space, even those who are not visibly at the table. As critical race theorist Mari Matsuda argues, we must ask: Who is *not* at the table, and how can we meet the needs of those members of our community who do not have the privilege to be at the table or even know that the table exists? (Matsuda et al. 1993)

7. Be an ally: Individuals, organizations, and movements must explore ways to value and outline effective practices for allies and must be allies to others as well.

8. Celebrate resistance and survival: Traditionally oppressed/silent organizations and movements need to actively celebrate their contributions to this world. They must be vocal and visible.

9. Work toward healing the wounds: Social justice advocates and activists tend to remain in the space of pain and struggle. We must work to heal the pain and to teach, organize, create, and write from a space of healing, love, and triumph.

We humbly offer these suggestions based on our experience and research, but we recognize the difficulties and challenges that exist in implementing them and acknowledge that many more recommendations could also be made. Homophobia, sexism, heteronormativity, classism, xenophobia, gender discrimination, and racism still exist in every part of our society. They are the systems of injustice used to marginalize our communities, and they work together to create borders and institutional discrimination. As Jotería activist scholars, we must continue to work against these structures of domination.

In doing so, we Jotas and Jotos place ourselves within a Jotería movement. We are part of a larger community where our identities, struggles, and collective healing can exist together. These conversations about movement building happen when groups seek to define their liberation. Many of the participants in our research have continued to pursue their vision of social justice long after graduating from UCLA. While some are doing so through established educational and nonprofit organizations, others are forming new organizations and spaces that embrace Jotería identity, consciousness, and growth. Some of the Jotería activists the authors studied have gone on to develop Xin Fronteras (an immigrant rights organization), a brand-new school, and a Latina/o bookstore. Others have received graduate degrees from the University of California, Berkeley, Columbia University, and San Francisco State University, among other institutions.

In Las Vegas, the authors have been working with the United Coalition for Im/migrant Rights (UCIR) and the local chapter of MEChA (Movimiento Estudiantil Chicano de Aztlán), both of which embrace a Jotería and muxerista multidimensional consciousness and practice. On a national level, we are active co-founders and leaders of the Association of Jotería Arts, Activism and Scholarship (AJAAS). There are so many fierce and amazing changes being made, and many more possibilities. Already, because of our Jotería and muxerista identity and vision, we have embarked on a path that is personally healing and transformative. We share this essay as an invitation for others to join us in this Jota y Joto muxerista journey.

Notes

"Jotería Identity and Consciousness," by Anita Tijerina Revilla and José Manuel Santillana, is reprinted from *Aztlán: A Journal of Chicano Studies* 39, no. 1 (2014).

This essay began as an excerpt from Santillana's thesis. His research built upon the work of Dr. Revilla on muxerista activism with Raza Womyn de UCLA, submitted as her dissertation to UCLA. The characteristics of a Jotería identity and consciousness and recommendations listed in the second half of the essay were created by both authors.

1. Counterstories are told from the perspective of marginalized people, as opposed to stories told by the dominant mainstream.

2. Heterosexism is a system of advantages that unfairly privileges heterosexuals. Heterosexual privilege is a set of unearned benefits and advantages that people who conform with or identify as heterosexual automatically inherit in

a heterosexist society. Heteronormativity is the belief in and enforcement of heterosexuality as "normal" and superior to any other sexual identity. Compulsory heterosexuality refers to the idea that heterosexuality is a mandatory, forced, or coercive sexual orientation/identity.

3. A muxerista is a person who identifies as a Chicana/Latina/o feminist and activist.

4. The term *queer* is an umbrella term used to refer to gay, lesbian, bisexual, and transgender people.

5. Bienestar is a nonprofit social service organization dedicated to positively affecting the health and well-being of the Latino community and other underserved communities in Southern California.

6. We use the term *Latina/o* to refer to people of Mexican, Caribbean, and South and Central American origin. We use the term *Chicana/o* to refer to people of Mexican descent living in the United States.

7. The term *Jotería* is also an umbrella term for gay, lesbian, bisexual, transgender, and other sexual expressions. It refers, however, to queer Latina/os and Chicana/os and gender-nonconforming individuals.

8. The term *brown* is a political, racial, and cultural classification that is based on human skin shade. We use the term to describe the racialized experience of Latina/os.

9. We use the term *queerstory* to make note of the fact that conventional historical accounts continue to be male-dominant, patriarch-centered, and heteronormative.

10. We write "Chicano movement" as opposed to Chicana/o movement to indicate that what most people acknowledge as the Chicano movement of the 1960s and 1970s was male-dominated and patriarchal.

11. AJAAS is an organization dedicated to advancing Jotería through practices that recognize the intimate connections between art, activism, and scholarship.

12. Citizenism is a system of advantages that unfairly privileges citizens of a nation-state.

13. Multidimensional battle fatigue refers to the depletion of energies that results from constantly struggling against discrimination and micro/macroaggressions. This idea expands on Will Smith's (2004) theory of racial battle fatigue.

Works Cited

Acuña, Rodolfo. 2004. *Occupied America: A History of Chicanos*. 5th ed. New York: Pearson Longman.

Matsuda, Mari J., Charles R. Lawrence III, Richard Delgado, and Kimberlé Williams Crenshaw. 1993. *Words That Wound: Critical Race Theory, Assaultive Speech, and the First Amendment*. Boulder, CO: Westview Press.

Navarro, Armando. 2000. *La Raza Unida Party: A Chicano Challenge to the U.S. Two-Party Dictatorship*. Philadelphia: Temple University Press.

Revilla, Anita Tijerina. 2004. "Raza Womyn Re-constructing Revolution: Exploring the Intersections of Race, Class, Gender, and Sexuality in the Lives of Chicana/Latina Student Activists." PhD diss., California State University, Los Angeles.

———. 2010a. "Are All Raza Womyn Queer? An Exploration of Sexual Identities in a Chicana/Latina Student Organization." *National Women's Studies Association Journal* 21, no. 3: 46–62.

———. 2010b. "Raza Womyn—Making It Safe to Be Queer: Student Organizations as Retention Tools in Higher Education." *Black Women, Gender, and Families Journal* 4, no. 1: 1–25.

Rodríguez, Juana María. 2003. *Queer Latinidad: Identity Practices, Discursive Spaces*. New York: NYU Press.

Roque Ramírez, Horacio N. 2003. "That's My Place!" Negotiating Racial, Sexual, and Gender Politics in San Francisco's Gay Latino Alliance, 1975–1983. *Journal of the History of Sexuality* 12, no. 2: 224–58.

Rosales, F. Arturo. 1997. *Chicano! The History of the Mexican American Civil Rights Movement*. Houston: Arte Público.

Smith, William A. 2004. "Black Faculty Coping with Racial Battle Fatigue: The Campus Racial Climate in a Post–Civil Rights Era." In *A Long Way to Go: Conversations about Race by African American Faculty and Graduate Students*, edited by Darrell Cleveland, 171–90. New York: Peter Lang.

Vigil, Ernesto. 1999. *The Crusade for Justice: Chicano Militancy and the Government's War on Dissent*. Madison: University of Wisconsin Press.

Memory of Struggle in Ciudad Juárez

Mothers' Resistance and Transborder Activism in the Case of the Campo Algodonero

Cynthia Bejarano

I remember as if it were yesterday. In January 2002, our unassuming group of border activists met with mothers whose daughters' bodies had been discovered, hidden in plain sight, near the intersection of Ejercito Nacional and Paseo de la Victoria in Ciudad Juárez, Chihuahua, Mexico. The bodies of the eight young women had been found several months earlier, on November 6 and 7, 2001, in two dried-up irrigation canals bordering a cotton field near the busy crossroads. Our organization, Amigos de las Mujeres de Juárez, based in New Mexico, announced through a Juárez radio station our alarm at what people were calling femicides or feminicides.[1] Samira Izaguirre, a well-known radio announcer, read our message to the families of victims, letting them know of our offer of assistance. We announced a meeting with families on the steps of the downtown cathedral, popular with local worshippers and tourists.

That frigid Saturday morning we crossed the Santa Fe Bridge from El Paso, Texas, into Juárez and walked six blocks to the main square, Plaza de Armas. There we waited on the cathedral's front steps. We stood out from the vendors, patrons, and passersby, and within minutes we were cautiously approached by three mothers who arrived independently of each other. We quickly realized they were mothers of the murdered girls found in November. These three women, Josefina González, Irma Monreal, and Benita Monárrez, would later become the lead petitioners in the case of *González et al. ("Campo Algodonero") v. México*, which was decided by the Inter-American Court of Human Rights on December 10, 2009.

This visit was the first of many our organization would make over the next several years as we crossed regularly into Juárez to meet with local organizations based in Ciudad Juárez and in the city of Chihuahua, 229 kilometers to the south. Mexican women's and human rights organizations, labor unions, students, academicians, attorneys, and the families of murdered and disappeared girls and women formed the core of a movement to demand investigations and accountability from authorities, to raise citizens' consciousness, and to obtain closure in these cases. To date, despite a favorable court ruling, justice is elusive.

This essay represents my secondary witnessing and testimonio based on observations as a transborder activist and on my academic work during the nearly decade-long struggle leading to the Campo Algodonero ruling. Through activist *encuentros*, public protests, marches, and other solidarity initiatives, we collectively built pressure for the case to be heard. The case was admitted to the Inter-American Court of Human Rights in 2007 and tried in Santiago, Chile, in November 2009. Benita Monárrez, Irma Monreal, and Josefina González offered damning testimony against the Mexican state's negligence and outright failure to properly investigate these crimes. The case offered families of the murdered women, or "witness-survivors," some vindication as they watched the Mexican state go on trial for negligence, corruption, and cover-ups in feminicide cases. "There are no survivors of feminicide," Fregoso and Bejarano write (2010, 11). "All we have are the voices of witness-survivors (families) who speak for them." For other witness-survivors, the ruling raised hopes that their own daughters' cases might one day be heard.

The court's ruling condemned the Mexican state for human rights violations and ordered various forms of reparation and redress. Not all of these have been fulfilled. Even so, the case was a landmark, providing "legal precedent for cases of gender violence in a non-war context and for enumerating feminicide in international law" (Fregoso and Bejarano 2010, 6). It also "establish[ed] a solid framework for legal interpretation with a gender perspective from which further development of the legal doctrine can take place" (Red Mesa and CLADEM 2010, 53).

In describing the Mexican and transborder mobilizations surrounding feminicidal violence in Ciudad Juárez, I will focus on the strategies witness-survivors and their allies used to confront hegemonic institutions and authorities leading up to the Campo Algodonero ruling.

Feminicides: A Legacy of Murder

The murders and disappearances of hundreds of women and girls from Juárez surely constitutes one of the worst epidemics of violence against women in recent history. Mexican sociologist Julia Monárrez Fragoso (2009) tracked the murders of 382 women and girls in Juárez between 1993 and 2004. She calls 144 of these deaths "serial sexual killings" based on where the bodies were discovered and the signs of torture and sexual violence they bore. Journalist Diana Washington Valdez (2006) estimates the total number of feminicides in 1993–2005 as closer to 470. Mexican government reports cite lower numbers. In addition to the serial sexual killings, hundreds of women and girls are killed for other reasons: they may be victims of intimate partner violence, random violence, or cartel or street violence, or involved in shadow economies. In total, according to Monárrez Fragoso, 1,436 women have been killed in Juárez from 1993 to early December 2012. This is based on her own research and data gathering since 1993.[2]

Women continue to disappear inexplicably from Juárez and the area around Chihuahua city. Estimates of the total number of women and girls still missing throughout Chihuahua state vary widely.[3] Official documentation of the missing is imprecise. The most accurate numbers appear to come from families who visit municipal police offices (*previas*) to file a missing person report; the families' investigations seem more meticulous than those of the authorities.

Although a number of victims shared physical features of beauty, dark skin, and long dark hair, many did not have these characteristics. Poverty is still the common denominator for most victims. Serial sexual victims were subjected to torture, rape, mutilation, and burning. Many were found in clandestine gravesites in desert areas like Lote Bravo or Lomas de Poleo, or in vacant city lots, while others were discarded in dumpsters or found dead on the side of the road. Most victims were young, typically fifteen to seventeen years of age. A number were maquiladora workers, while others were sales clerks or university or computer school students. Some had migrated from other Mexican states or elsewhere.

For years, the serial killings remained the subject of theorizing and speculation. Official investigations made little progress, though a handful of scapegoats were paraded in front of the media. But public pressure by families, activists, and organizations slowly gained momentum, leading to intense advocacy locally and globally.

The gruesome discovery of eight bodies at the Campo Algodonero in 2001 was a central catalyst. It took years to positively confirm the identities of Brenda Esmeralda Herrera Monreal, Laura Berenice Ramos Monárrez, Claudia Ivette González, María de los Ángeles Acosta Ramirez, Mayra Juliana Reyes Solis, Merlín Elizabeth Rodríguez Sáenz, and María Rocina Galicia; one woman remains unidentified.[4] When the bodies were discovered, people took to the streets, demanding that the government capture the assassins. Within days, two scapegoats were arrested. Bus drivers Gustavo "La Foca" González Meza and Victor Javier "El Cerillo" García Uribe confessed under torture to the cotton field killings. González Meza later died in prison. García Uribe was convicted in 2004 of the murder and sentenced to fifty years, but he appealed and was freed for lack of evidence on July 15, 2005 (Freeman 2005). Thus, the cotton field murders remain unsolved.

Mi Testimonio: El Rastreo del Campo Algodonero

Local activism around the femicides had remained consistent throughout the 1990s, although international attention waned somewhat toward the end of the decade. The Campo Algodonero case, however, shocked local and transnational activists and renewed solidarity initiatives. When our organization, Amigos de las Mujeres de Juárez, met Josefina, Irma, and Benita at the cathedral, we asked the mothers what we could do to assist them. Immediately, Benita mentioned that authorities would not allow them to enter the cotton field where their daughters' bodies had been found. The field had been cordoned off by police and searched in November and December 2001. Police had then assured witness-survivors there was nothing else to investigate, and they barred the public from the site. But the families, however, had lingering concerns that evidence was left behind.

We sought assistance from a Juárez-based volunteer rescue team, Grupo de Rescate Cobra, which had been conducting *rastreos*—searches—every weekend for the bodies of disappeared girls and women. Since the mid-1990s, various organizations and activists had participated in weekend *rastreos* in the desert outskirts of Juárez, looking for remains. Searchers would often unearth articles of clothing or personal belongings, and sometimes female bodies. *Rastreos* were often initiated by witness-survivors, who viewed the searches as a form of resistance when police were unwilling to search for the missing or did so carelessly.

On February 24, 2002, at least thirty volunteers gathered at the cotton field to search for evidence of the horrifying deaths. The group for the *rastreo* included witness-survivors, family friends, search and rescue volunteers, and students from Juárez, together with local and transborder activists from Las Cruces, New Mexico, and El Paso, Texas. Our "forensic" equipment consisted of fluorescent orange tape purchased at a US hardware store, as well as plastic grocery bags and tree sticks furnished by Grupo de Rescate Cobra.

The Grupo's blind organizer, who served as leader of our binational team, gave us our instructions, and we began searching the cotton field. We combed the area for any evidence visible to our untrained eyes. During the *rastreo*, Juárez municipal police stood guard along one edge of the cotton field, watching us as we cautiously watched them. Press photographers took snapshots of the volunteers as we formed human lines and walked along gingerly, scanning the cotton field and its bordering canals.[5]

Within a half hour, we heard loud shouts near a small group of trees above an irrigation canal. This *rastreo* had been seen as symbolic, as a sign of solidarity with witness-survivors, so I was stunned when the shouts indicated that something had been found. As a colleague and I approached a group crowding around the victims' mothers, we witnessed Josefina González, mother of Claudia Ivette González, clenching the cream-colored overalls that Claudia had worn the day she disappeared. Claudia Ivette worked at the LEAR 173 factory, a Juárez maquiladora owned by the US-based Lear Corporation. On October 11, 2001, Claudia Ivette arrived to work two minutes late and was not allowed to enter the factory.[6] Factory surveillance cameras caught the young woman's image as she left the factory and turned a corner; she was never seen alive again. Two fifteen-year-old boys volunteering with the Grupo de Rescate Cobra found Claudia Ivette's overalls in a plastic grocery bag, hidden inside a crevice of an irrigation canal wall.

Reporters' photographs showed Josefina clutching Claudia Ivette's overalls to her chest as tears ran down her face. Claudia Ivette fought for her life, her mother once told me. When her body was found, her murderer's skin was lodged underneath her fingernails. Josefina claimed that no DNA was ever taken from this evidence by authorities. The picture of Josefina grasping Claudia Ivette's overalls is emblazoned in my memory, just as it appeared in newspapers internationally. I watched helplessly as Josefina's eldest daughter tried to comfort her. The families who gathered that day had known one another only a few months, since convening with members of Amigos de las Mujeres de Juárez. They comforted one another awkwardly, brought together by a shared bond of trauma and death.

Our collective anger boiled over: we wanted a swift investigative response to such human tragedy. Municipal police were supervising the *rastreo*, but state police—*judiciales*—arrived within minutes after Claudia's overalls were found. The *judiciales* confiscated the overalls along with several piles of items that volunteers retrieved from a quarter-mile radius surrounding the area. Volunteers had discovered clothing and other personal artifacts near and inside the canals where the bodies were found. Women's undergarments, shirts, and a skirt, a few handbags and at least two bookbags, mismatched shoes, and a great deal of debris were found in the area. Items found were not typical of intentionally discarded items. Volunteers and witness-survivors were outraged that so much potential evidence had been left undiscovered three months after the women's bodies were found. They demanded that police explain why those articles were not found earlier. Police responded that this heavily trafficked intersection across from the Maquiladora Association headquarters was a popular place where people parked to have sex or came to dump debris. We were aghast at this comment.

State police cars encircled the area and everyone was asked to leave. The police placed all articles gathered in brown paper bags: underwear and handbags, socks and other clothing fell indiscriminately into the same "evidence" bags. No apparent effort was made to separate or label the articles that afternoon. What appeared to be forensics specialists wearing white gloves approached the irrigation canal as we were leaving; we watched police cordon off the area we had carefully inspected just minutes before. Authorities at the scene seemed as surprised as we were that anything had been discovered. We left skeptical of what would happen to the materials nonchalantly tossed into paper bags. We were disturbed by what we witnessed, yet triumphant that witness-survivors had entered the cotton field. As witness-observers, we served as a layer of protection for families, allowing them to mourn free from harassment at their daughters' final resting place.[7] In the following weeks and months, other *rastreos* in the city's outskirts ensued (as in previous years), with many families hoping to find traces of their own daughters in the desert.

These memories haunt me still. Ten years later, while watching *The Town*, a film about an armored car heist, I was reminded of the Campo Algodonero. One scene in the movie, in which bank robbers purchase discarded hair clippings from a barber to derail forensic DNA testing of hair follicles found at a crime scene, triggered a memory of the *rastreo*. I recalled that at the moment Josefina González discovered her daughter's overalls, an activist friend and I had inched away from the cotton field and walked inside a dry irrigation canal and through a tunnel underneath

Ejercito Nacional Street, several feet from where three of the bodies were found. As we emerged from the tunnel, we found clumps of long hair piled in a small mound. Five of the eight women allegedly had clumps of hair missing when their bodies were recovered; it was never confirmed, however, whether the different colored hair we saw belonged to any of the young women. One *judicial* claimed the clumps came from a nearby hair salon that would discard clients' cut hair in the tunnel leading to the cotton field. This was yet another quick-tongued policeman making another ludicrous comment about possible evidence.

Recovering Memory: The Significance of Witnessing a Decade Later

As years pass, some details of my activist work since 1998 begin to fade. But my memories of the *rastreo* at the Campo Algodonero remain vivid. There is a continuing need to remember in order to never forget, since feminicides are now archived from public memory even as new carnage unfolds. "The very act of remembering can serve as an impetus for action and empowerment. Being able to remember becomes a political act—an act of resistance and resilience—and can keep a community together" (Barbera 2009, 76). Witness-survivors, and by extension witness-observers, have a responsibility to always remember in order to maintain their struggle for resolution, justice, and a desire for secure communities.

Victims of trauma "badly need to regain their dignity and honour through a form of social recognition in which their private truth is openly recognised and becomes public truth, and their suffering is acknowledged and becomes part of social memory" (Agger et al. 2009, 207). The markings of trauma on individuals and their acts of remembering conducted on private and communal lands like the Campo Algodonero compel witness-survivors, community members, witness-observers, and public actors to take action. Now more than ever, it is critical to remember feminicides, since the news of recent women's disappearances is overshadowed by the reality of so many deaths of women, children, and men since 2007. Drug wars in Juárez caused by rival cartels vying for access to the US drug market caused tremendous human suffering and carnage, particularly from the years 2006 through 2012. The reality of feminicides has faded from public memory with this greater generalized violence. Feminicide is not recognized as an extreme form of community violence in the sense that activists and witness-survivors understand it. The act of remembering feminicides offers a history and cartography for highlighting negligence and corruption within government agencies, for conveying truths, and for sustaining advocacy for the countless people still missing throughout Chihuahua state. Critical action taken by witness-survivors and witness-observers can help avoid a repetition of past atrocities.

Publicly remembering through secondary observations as a witness-observer involves more than serving as an eyewitness to what is visible. Witness-observers participate in, articulate, and embody the anger, pain, resistance, and consciousness that unify them with witness-survivors and others. Serving as a witness-observer represents a synergy between seeing, hearing, feeling, and reacting to violence as a secondary witness to an atrocity. Secondary witnessing entails a communal pledge to tell the stories, in writing or orally, of our own observations and recollections. Just as important, we disseminate the testimonios of human rights activists and of victims, whose truths are often overlooked, dismissed, or silenced. Witness-observers commit to bearing witness and demanding justice to right the transgressions done to others.

Witness-Survivors and Their Resistance

When truth and reconciliation commissions, public hearings, or truth-telling mechanisms are not readily available for witness-survivors, there is a critical need to create ritual and ceremony to foreground the memories of trauma and death. Ceremony provides an occasion to recognize trauma publicly, to mourn together, and to denounce current and past atrocities in solidarity with others. Public ceremony and collective mourning also provide a measure of protection, albeit ephemeral, to witness-survivors, who are often targeted by state agents for scrutiny and threats.

Despite bearing the scars of trauma, witness-survivors have remained at the forefront of the effort to reconcile public and private memories of feminicides. They have sustained this through a commitment shared with other activists. The mothers of feminicide victims have always been at the heart of justice work, although siblings and fathers also form part of this anti-feminicide movement. Tragedy forced the mothers to come together and forge a shared identity. Despite their diverse personalities, migrant histories, and work backgrounds as housewives, cooks, maquiladora workers, and cleaning women, they are bound together as mothers, sharing their grief and their collective action against feminicide. They hunger for truth, knowledge, and justice.

Mothers from the anti-feminicide movement and mothers of the cotton field victims emerged as organic leaders within these groups of witness-survivors, coordinating activities with local activists—painting crosses on telephone and electric poles, making pink crosses and erecting them in public places. They set aside family and work obligations when necessary. Efforts to organize public protests, marches, and commemoration vigils began in their homes, at labor union halls, and in the modest offices of family-based or nongovernmental organizations.[8] Other mothers whose daughters had been reported murdered or missing joined the cotton field mothers in these efforts. Several of these mothers had initiated their own activities years before. Each year more witness-survivors joined the cadre of activist families that existed to collectively mourn, protest, and gain strength from one another.

Public protests at the Campo Algodonero began shortly after the news broke about the cotton field feminicides. Samira Izaguirre, the Juárez radio announcer, organized a candlelight vigil at the site on December 16, 2001, which drew an estimated 25,000 people (Washington Valdez 2006). Over the years, witness-survivors, anti-feminicide organizations, and women's and human rights organizations have held numerous public events at the Campo Algodonero. These memorial events have remembered ALL feminicide victims, and the cotton field has come to represent a space for public remembering and community mourning.

The space has become a site of resistance where remembering and witnessing are enacted through performances, street art, and active protest. One year after the discovery of the cotton field victims, a coffin was used to represent their deaths. Ballet Folklórico dancers performed, and for several years, artists and singers commemorated anniversaries of the murdered and disappeared women. Eight five-foot-tall pink crosses were erected at the cotton field where witness-survivors would stand together in prayer, protest, and song. Arturo Arias and Alicia del Campo affirm, "Memory is always centered in an act of recollection that evokes and appropriates the past as a way to signify our present—a reconstruction of a past according to our narrative of the present. These public acts of recollection, of memorialization, have the capacity to constitute communities, since the act of remembrance is and has to be a collective act" (2009, 11).

The protest site drew international supporters, ranging from a US Congressional Hispanic Caucus delegation to human rights rapporteurs, members of Amnesty International, and numerous others. The Campo Algodonero came to represent the resilience, resistance, and continued vigilance of the anti-feminicide movement, which encompasses witness-survivors, local and transborder activists as witness-observers, and international and local organizations. Our individual, collective, and social memories bound us together, creating community solidarity in confronting fear, rampant violence, and the erasure of memory.

Authorities made continuous attempts to remove the pink crosses, while witnesses insisted that they remain. After 2005, one could no longer enter this area without confronting law enforcement. Cement barricades permanently surrounded the entrance to the cotton field until 2007, when a private citizen purchased the property and the police presence disappeared. Years later, activists were forced to jump over street curbs to access the site; by 2009 the Campo looked like an abandoned lot, with construction taking place behind it to build a hotel. As the state sought to eliminate safe spaces for protest and businessmen worked to sanitize the city's image through urban development, activists worked to reaffirm their version of what happened at the Campo Algodonero.

In November 2009 a caravan called Exodo por la Vida de las Mujeres, made up of Mujeres de Negro de Chihuahua and fourteen other organizations, set out from Mexico City for Juárez, traveling by vehicle and on foot. As they went, they rang a large bell of justice, the Campana de Justicia, made from eighty-five kilograms of metal that had once been keys collected from women's organizations that participated in the Ni Una Muerta Más campaign in 2002. Leading the procession were witness-survivors from Juárez and Chihuahua City whose daughters had been killed or had gone missing since 1998. Arriving in Juárez, they ended the caravan at the Campo Algodonero. Alongside Mexican activists, families painstakingly clawed at the ground, digging out dirt with their hands and sticks to place small foot-long pink crosses at the spot where larger crosses had once been. Witness-survivors surrounded by witness-observers restored the iconic pink crosses and made proclamations while ringing the bell of justice. Among the mothers participating in the caravan was Irma Monreal, who was waiting for the Inter-American Court ruling in her daughter's case, *González et al.* (*"Campo Algodonero"*) *v. México*.

The Inter-American Court Ruling

The ruling in the case of *González et al.* was the culmination of a vigorous local, transborder, and transnational effort to bring this case first to the Inter-American Commission on Human Rights, and subsequently to the Inter-American Court of Human Rights. National and transnational solidarity builders served as interlocutors with witness-survivors and provided various types of support. These relationships resulted in testimony by experts on gender violence; access to women's and human rights networks; site visits to Juárez and reports by special rapporteurs on human rights; access to national and transnational legal assistance; and assistance establishing human rights observatories to ensure the Campo Algodonero case was heard.[9]

In March 2002, the three petitioners, Josefina González, Irma Monreal, and Benita Monárrez, together with the Red Ciudadana de No Violencia y Dignidad Humana (Network on Nonviolence and Human Dignity), submitted their petition to the Inter-American Commission on Human Rights. After hearing the complaint against the Mexican state in 2007, the commission presented evidence in the case before the Inter-American Court in 2008 (Red Mesa and CLADEM 2010). In 2009 the court held a public hearing on the Campo Algodonero case in Santiago, Chile, where these mothers gave their testimonies; additionally, twenty-three testimonies for both parties and expert reports were given in affidavit. Two witnesses for the state and two more experts—one for the state and the other for the commission—also testified (Red Mesa and CLADEM 2010, 47). The petitioners argued that "the inefficiency of the investigations shows lack of will from the Government to solve these crimes and to prevent them" (UN-INSTRAW 2010).

The court found Mexico guilty of failure to comply with its obligations to guarantee human rights, of gender stereotyping and discrimination, and of negligence to investigate these crimes including broad sweeping impunity, among other key rulings. It also recognized that petitioners and their next of kin had their human rights violated. The state generally was held responsible for not having protective measures for Brenda Esmeralda Herrera Monreal (age fourteen), Laura Berenice Ramos Monárrez (age seventeen), and Claudia Ivette González (age twenty). The court found a pattern of gender violence that led to the disappearances and murders of numerous girls and women (not solely the cotton field victims) and a failure of due diligence to investigate these crimes.

On December 10, 2009, the Inter-American Court issued a condemnation of the Mexican state for human rights violations in the Campo Algodonero case, with sixteen court-ordered resolutions that the Mexican state had to address. The court demanded that the government pay damages to the families of Claudia Ivette, Laura Berenice, and Brenda Esmeralda and also pay their legal expenses.[10] The Mexican government was required to make a public apology within six months and within a year to hold a memorial service and erect a public monument to the young women at the Campo Algodonero.

It took two years for this to occur. On November 7, 2011, the Mexican government inaugurated the monument to Laura Berenice, Claudia Ivette, and Brenda Esmeralda at the cotton field site. The area is enclosed by a pink metal fence, and a marbled tile half-circle wall serves as the monument, with a large pink cross at the center. The memorial ceremony was attended mainly by officials making empty promises, while the families that were present at the memorial heavily criticized the event. To protest the event and officials' failure to resolve these crimes, the mothers of the three girls did not attend.

At some point the property changed hands, going from private to federal ownership, and on January 26, 2012, the federal government gave the land to the city. As of early 2012, the monument was closed to the public, purportedly to allow the building of a statue dedicated to the victims (Gallegos 2012). In the fall of 2012 the monument was reopened to the public.

The Mexican government was also required to establish an electronic database of all missing women and to establish a DNA database, so families whose daughters might be missing can have their DNA included to check for positive matches. However, the website is often inactive and contains inconsistent data. Overall, the Mexican state must work toward reform of its legislative, executive, and judicial processes to reflect a gender perspective in crimes against women and girls, initiate crime prevention and victim assistance programs, and create public policies to bring about social and cultural change (Red Mesa and CLADEM 2010).

The ruling in *González et al. ("Campo Algodonero") v. México* serves as a living document representing the Inter-American Court's orders for reparations of damages by the Mexican state. "The sentence is in itself a form of reparation for all women and an exhortation to continue the process of cultural and social transformation toward the construction of egalitarian relations between men and women" (Red Mesa and CLADEM 2010, 68). We must work as global allies to ensure that the Mexican government abides by the court's sixteen resolutions so that justice is truly served.[11]

Sharing Testimony, Seeking Truth

I waited a decade to share my testimonio on the Campo Algodonero case and the events leading up to it. I hoped the court case would bring an end to a long legacy of violence. But despite the strides made by families and activists through the Inter-American Court ruling, Mexican authorities have yet to take full responsibility for their crimes of negligence, gender discrimination, and corruption. And the state has still failed to completely fulfill the court's mandates.

As a secondary witness, I cannot speak for the disappeared or the dead, but I can retell their story to help keep their memories alive. The families of the disappeared and murdered young women must be allowed public spaces to share their testimonios to remind society of lives lost and communities in mourning. Their testimonies illustrate a profound courage, resiliency, and determination to keep on living. Ultimately, each of us can only describe our own experiences in this anti-feminicide movement with any real clarity or conviction. Witness-observers must remain vigilant in monitoring the state's compliance with the court's ruling. It is everyone's responsibility to intervene when acts of violence occur in our communities.

As painful as it is to remember, these stories must be told. Our testimonios contribute to a framework of justice in which the public can seek truths surrounding crimes against humanity. In remembering and bearing witness as witness-observers, we assist witness-survivors and Mexican activists who are close to this struggle, so they need not carry the burden of traumatic memories alone. We join our voices with those of countless others involved in *observatorios comunitarios*, community observatories, monitoring the acts and negligence of the Mexican state so that we remember and never forget.

Postscript (2020)

Josefina González, mother of Claudia Ivette González, passed away in 2018. In 2019 a plaque remembering Josefina was placed at the Campo Algodonero permanent memorial. The memorial now pays tribute not only to Claudia Ivette but also to Josefina's motherist-activist efforts to seek justice for her daughter. Justice remained elusive for both mother and daughter.

Women and girls continue to disappear or are killed, like Isabel Cabanillas de la Torre, a mother, clothing designer, and Juárez activist and member of Las Hijas de Su Maquilera Madre (Daughters of Maquila Working Women), a young feminist activist collective working to end gender based violence in Juárez. Isabel was shot twice and killed on January 20, 2020, in downtown Juárez as she rode her bicycle home early that morning, after visiting with friends. On January 25, 2020, I joined thousands of protestors in downtown Juárez who initiated a binational march to protest Isabel's feminicide. We marched along Avenida Juárez yelling anti-feminicide chants: "Ni una mas, ni una mas, ni una asesinada mas!" (Not one more, not one more, not one more assassinated one!)

Notes

"Memory of Struggle in Ciudad Juárez: Mothers' Resistance and Transborder Activism in the Case of the Campo Algodonero," by Cynthia Bejarano, is reprinted from *Aztlán: A Journal of Chicano Studies* 38, no. 1 (2013).

1. Since the early 1990s, the terms *femicide* and *feminicide* have been used by scholars, activists, policy makers, attorneys, and families throughout Latin America, though they often prefer one term over the other. Both terms have been used to refer to the women and girls murdered throughout the state of Chihuahua. The term *feminicide* has been elaborated by Mexican scholars Julia Estela Monárrez Fragoso and Marcela Lagarde y de los Ríos. See Monárrez Fragoso's (2009) *Trama de una injusticia: Feminicidio sexual sistématico en Ciudad Juárez* for a comprehensive understanding of her body of work, and Lagarde y de los Ríos's (2010) preface to *Terrorizing Women: Feminicide in the Americas* for her development of the term *feminicide*. Fregoso and Bejarano (2010) also offer a detailed discussion of the femicide/feminicide discourse in the latter volume. I use the concept of feminicide that Rosa-Linda Fregoso and I conceptualized by building upon Diana Russell's work in *Femicide in Global Perspective* (2001) and the work of the above-mentioned Mexican scholars. We define feminicide as "the murders of women and girls founded on a gender power structure . . . as gender-based violence that is both public and private, implicating both the state (directly or indirectly) and individual perpetrators (private or state actors)." We note that it "encompasses systematic, widespread, and everyday interpersonal violence. . . . Feminicide is systemic violence rooted in social, political, economic, and cultural inequalities" (Fregoso and Bejarano 2010, 5).

2. Julia Estela Monárrez Fragoso, e-mail to author, December 5, 2012. For a detailed summary of Monárrez Fragoso's work in documenting the number of women murdered in Juárez, see Monárrez Fragoso (2009).

3. According to Monárrez Fragoso (2009), the number of disappeared women and girls varies greatly from one source to another, and exact numbers are impossible to obtain. A report from Mexico's National Commission on Human Rights indicates that 4,587 women disappeared from Ciudad Juárez between 1993 and 2003 (CNDH 2003). According to Monárrez Fragoso, this number reflects reports of disappearances and includes women who may have later been found alive. Another source states that over 1,000 women and girls have disappeared from the state of Chihuahua since the 1990s, based on tallies by local human rights activists and researchers (Fregoso and Bejarano 2010). Diana Washington Valdez suggests a range of 73 to 260 disappeared women, drawing on Amnesty International reports, interviews with victims' relatives in Juárez and El Paso, and Mexican law enforcement sources (e-mail to author, December 5, 2012).

4. Identification of the bodies was hindered by negligence and a lack of transparency on the part of Mexican authorities. The nongovernmental Argentine Forensic Anthropology Team (EAAF) was asked to begin their own forensic investigation in 2004. After DNA testing, the EAAF determined the identities of all but one of the cotton field victims. Prior to 2006, Guadalupe de la Rosa, Bárbara Aracely Martínez Ramos, and Verónica Martínez Hernández were also thought to be victims of the cotton field feminicides, but it was eventually confirmed that

they were not. Later, the EAAF made a positive identification of Verónica from remains recovered at the School of Medicine in Juárez (Red Mesa and CLADEM 2010; Mercedes Doretti, EAAF senior forensic anthropologist, e-mail to author, February 5, 2012).

5. For another description of this *rastreo*, see Diana Washington Valdez's *The Killing Fields: Harvest of Women* (2006). Washington Valdez was also present at this *rastreo*.

6. On October 12, 2001, Amigos members visited the Flores González family, founding members of Voces sin Eco, an organization formed by relatives of women and girls murdered in the 1990s. We asked Paula Bonilla Flores, one of the leaders of the group, whether Voces sin Eco was interested in our assistance. That day, her family had been looking for her daughter's friend, who had gone missing the day before; that girl was Claudia Ivette González, who worked with one of Paula's daughters.

7. Bearing witness as community observers means serving as active secondary witnesses.

8. Through Juárez colleagues, Amigos de las Mujeres de Juárez held meetings with families of cotton field victims at the hall of the Telefonistas, one of the largest labor unions in Mexico. These mothers later created their own organization, Integración de Madres por Juárez. Other women joined Nuestras Hijas de Regreso a Casa, formed in 2001.

9. Community observatories "serve as a mechanism for collective action that involves communities in witnessing, observing, and monitoring state agencies and ensuring that they exercise due process" (Fregoso and Bejarano 2010, 25).

10. The three victims' families were paid monetary reparations.

11. See www.campoalgodonero.org.mx for continuously updated discussions and monitoring of the case.

Works Cited

Agger, Inger, Lenin Raghuvanshi, Shirin Shabana Khan, Peter Polatin, and Laila K. Laursen. 2009. "Testimonial Therapy: A Pilot Project to Improve Psychological Wellbeing among Survivors of Torture in India." *Torture Volume* 19, no. 3: 204–17.

Arias, Arturo, and Alicia del Campo. 2009. "Introduction: Memory and Popular Culture." *Latin American Perspectives* 36, no. 5: 3–20.

Barbera, Rosemary. 2009. "Community Remembering: Fear and Memory in a Chilean Shantytown." *Latin American Perspectives* 36, no. 5: 72–88.

CNDH (Comisión Nacional de los Derechos Humanos). 2003. *Informe especial de la Comisión Nacional de los Derechos Humanos sobre los casos de homicidios y desapariciones de Mujeres en el municipio de Juárez, Chihuahua.* Mexico City: CNDH.

Freeman, Laurie. 2006. *Still Waiting for Justice: Shortcomings in Mexico's Efforts to End Impunity for Murders of Girls and Women in Ciudad Juárez and Chihuahua.* Washington, DC: Washington Office on Latin America.

Fregoso, Rosa-Linda, and Cynthia Bejarano, eds. 2010. *Terrorizing Women: Feminicide in the Américas.* Durham, NC: Duke University Press.

Gallegos, Rocio. 2012. "Ceden al Municipio terrenos del Memorial para mujeres asesinadas." *El Diario de Juárez,* January 27, B1.

Lagarde y de los Ríos, Marcela. 2010. "Feminist Keys for Understanding Feminicide: Theoretical, Political, and Legal Construction." Preface to Fregoso and Bejarano 2010.

Monárrez Fragoso, Julia E. 2009. *Trama de una injusticia: Feminicidio sexual sistémico en Ciudad Juárez.* Tijuana, Mexico: Colegio de la Frontera Norte.

———. 2010. "Las diversas representaciones del feminicidio y los asesinatos de mujeres en Ciudad Juárez, 1993–2005." In *Violencia contra las mujeres e inseguridad ciudadana en Ciudad Juárez, México,* edited by Julia Estela Monárrez Fragoso, Luis Ernesto Cervera Gómez, César M. Fuentes Flores, and Rodolfo Rubio Salas, 361–94. Mexico City: Colegio de la Frontera Norte and Miguel Ángel Porrúa.

Red Mesa and CLADEM (Red Mesa de Mujeres de Ciudad Juárez and Comité de América Latina y el Caribe para la Defensa de los Derechos de la Mujer). 2010. *Cotton Field: Proposals for Analysis and Monitoring of the "Cotton Field" Case Sentence, Regarding Human Rights Violations Committed by the Mexican State.* Mexico City: Heinrich Böll Stiftung and Ministerio de Asuntos Exteriores y de Cooperación. http://www.boell.eu/downloads/Campo_Algodonero_ENG.pdf

Russell, Diana E. H. 2001. "Defining Femicide and Related Concepts." In *Femicide in Global Perspective,* edited by Diana E. H. Russell and Roberta A. Harmes, 12–28. New York: Teachers College Press.

UN-INSTRAW (United Nations International Research and Training Institute for the Advancement of Women). 2010. "First Case of Feminicide before the Inter-American Court of Human Rights." http://www.un-instraw.org/index2.php?option=com_content&do_pdf=1&id=888.

Washington Valdez, Diana. 2006. *The Killing Fields: Harvest of Women.* Burbank, CA: Peace at the Border.

Brown and Down Theater in the Time of Pending Erasure

Ricardo Gamboa

Growing up, I listened as my Mexican American parents, aunts and uncles, and closest friends told the same stories over and over in the backyards and basements where our family parties happened on Chicago's South Side. This storytelling usually took place late at night, after guests had left and the music retrograded through time, stationing at Motown and old rancheras. The wails of racially oppressed US citizens and motherland denizens in despair, in English *y en español* respectively, made a perfect soundtrack for my family's stories about Mexican Americans' best-laid plans gone awry.

They would tell stories of frustrated immigrant parents, "American dream" aspirations, surviving gang violence and the Vietnam War, hours spent on assembly lines and picket lines, and doing whatever was necessary to attain a semblance of "a better life." I know there are people with families like mine across Chicago and the United States. I believe our families tell these same stories to one another because if they don't, who will? Their storytelling isn't just the drunken repetition of the ratchet of the earth. It is their attempt at oral history, their refusal to go quietly, and their swing in the fight against the obscurity that haunts their existence as Mexican Americans. It is theater, and to paraphrase the Black Panthers' maxim, theater that is a means of "survival pending erasure."

This recurring family scenario inspired my latest project, *Meet Juan(ito) Doe*, a collaboration with Chicago's Free Street Theater. The production is based on the stories of Chicago's omnipresent but underrepresented Mexican American and immigrant communities. *Meet Juan(ito) Doe* premiered to a sold-out audience on October 16, 2017, in a tiny storefront in the

Back of the Yards neighborhood on Chicago's South Side. It continued to sell out for its initial four-week run and two extensions before closing on December 15, 2017.

The play was developed over ten months by an ensemble of Chicago Mexican Americans, the majority of whom had never acted before. The development process included actor and ensemble training; collective study of social and political theory and the history of minoritarian performance art and social movements; and the organization of community events to create platforms for Chicago's Mexican American residents to share their personal narratives. My experience with *Meet Juan(ito) Doe* provides an optic on problems and realities confronting (Latino) theater and on the relationship between US theater and communities of color more broadly. Indeed, *Meet Juan(ito) Doe* represents the culmination of my fifteen years of theater making in Chicago, during which I have tried to navigate those realities and problems from a radical standpoint. I have never considered *Meet Juan(ito) Doe* "just a play." Like all my theater making, it is a radical political project that I believe illustrates theater's repressed potential for radical social change. So it is my hope that sharing my experience will help us reimagine what theater must do, especially as Mexican Americans, Latino/a/xe, and brown people under the shadow of pending erasure.

Background, or "The Personal Becomes Process"

The idea for *Meet Juan(ito) Doe* came to me in 2009 while I was working as artistic director of Teatro Americano, a theater program of Latinos Progresando, a nonprofit immigrant advocacy and legal services organization in Chicago. But the seeds had been planted several years before, in 2003, when I graduated from the University of Illinois at Urbana-Champaign and returned to Chicago to pursue an acting career in the city's revered theater scene. I discovered all too soon that "Chicago theater" wasn't *Chicago* theater at all. It did not reflect the Chicago in which I grew up: a Chicago that was black, brown, working-class, full of history, percolating with social conflict, authentic and ratchet, inspiring and heartbreaking, irreverent and real. Instead, "Chicago theater" was the product of white transplants by renowned institutions like the Steppenwolf Theatre, presenting theater as pasty as their flesh, delaminated from the communities and realities that make up Chicago. No plays about Chicago, by Chicagoans, performed by Chicagoans, much less any productions centering Chicago's working-class communities of color and their stories. This irrelevant mass of theater was validated by the canon and contemporary industry consensus. It occurred (almost exclusively) on Chicago's more affluent and white North Side, making it economically and geographically inaccessible to many Chicagoans of color, even if they wanted to masochistically sit through inconsequential, white-people-problems theater.

"Chicago Latino theater" offered no refuge, but rather replicated these dynamics. It was hardly Chicago Latino. Instead, as I discovered, it was an assemblage of transplanted Latino theater artists who had come to Chicago with BFAs or MFAs and careerist objectives to assimilate into mainstream "Chicago theater" and ascend to its venerable stages. The bodies, stories, and voices of actual Chicago Latinos were wholly absent from this "Chicago Latino" subset of theatrical production, which was seemingly committed to producing Latino theater as long as it was made by Latinos from anywhere but Chicago. Like its predominantly white counterpart, this work was not economically or geographically accessible to Chicago's working-class Latino communities. To me, "Chicago Latino theater" appeared as an amalgam of too many plays with too many monologues about the moon that were irrelevant to many local Chicago Latinos. It seemed to imitate mainstream, white theater aesthetics and conventions and to represent Latino identity and struggles for a white gaze and white audience consumption.

I returned home to make theater for my community in "Chicago's theater community," but found there was no place for me or my community in this theater system that called itself a "community." There was no space for the story of local activist Rudy Lozano, a Marxist labor and immigrant rights organizer who played a crucial role in the election of Chicago's first black mayor, Harold Washington. Lozano was shot three times in his kitchen while feeding his toddler son by a gangbanger who was paid only $1,500 for the hit by a still-undisclosed source. There was no space for the story of my parents, who bought hotdogs and drove to the suburbs of Chicago to stare at the big houses while learning to love each other and overcome the traumas of growing up in poverty with abusive and over-worked parents, against the backdrop of the hood and the Vietnam War. There was no space for the stories of all the boys and girls coming of age on stoops and in parks. There was no space for the stories of all the brown queers in drag or vaquero wear who came alive at night under the disco ball at La Cueva, one of the country's oldest Latino gay clubs, tucked away in the South Side Chicago immigrant mecca of Little Village. There was no space for the stories of so many people and places I loved, which were the worthy subjects and settings of epics that deserved to be represented and re-presented. This tragic reality drove me to Teatro Americano in 2008.

My arrival at Teatro Americano was also significantly motivated by my work with youth. At the outset of my acting career, finding myself unable to directly and meaningfully engage my communities through work in the "Chicago theater" scene, I assuaged my frustration by throwing myself into theater education and outreach. This at least engaged the children and schools of those communities. However, soon enough I realized that theater education and outreach replicated the same problematic power dynamics and relations I had identified within the larger theater community. Too often theater education and outreach meant white transplant theater artists entering communities of color and deeming what is appropriate and valuable for working-class children and youth of color to learn. Theater companies wrote curricula centering a predominantly white theatrical canon and contemporary offerings that did not reflect or relate to the lives of youth of color. Rather than providing a meaningful alternative or outlet, theater education and outreach was tethered to the ideologies and practices of standardized education that was designed not for the benefit of youth of color but for their systemic assimilation. The pedagogical approach I have seen used in school-based theater education and outreach programs is not creative or innovative enough and does not account for the cultural or geographic specificity or the social and political realities of youth of color.

It was the ability to articulate this critique of normative public education that landed me a job as a high school English teacher at a charter high school in Chicago. It was a dropout retrieval school for young adults seventeen through twenty-one years old that allowed them to graduate with high school diplomas. Almost the entire student body consisted of black and brown youth, living at or below the poverty line, who had intersected at one point or another with the foster or criminal justice system. I integrated arts into my English curricula, specifically theater and creative writing, and organized lessons to explore students' social context from a critical and social justice standpoint, with attention to cultural and geographic specificity. Within a month, my classroom became a real-life instance of all those movies that sensationalize unconventional, committed teachers who transform the education and lives of working-class youth of color by helping them find their voice and empowerment. Unlike the teachers in those films, I got fired before the end of the school year, although students would cut lunch period to sit in on my classes and participate. My employment was terminated for refusals to practice censorship in creative work and enforce punitive classroom management.

There is so much more to elaborate here, with more than enough conflict, drama, insights, and provocative themes to merit its own theatrical production. But what is noteworthy is how working at this school allowed me to bear witness to the transformative potential that theater can have, when braided with radical political and social analysis, in the lives of those of us struggling in the black holes of abjection. I accepted the opportunity to work with Teatro Americano because it allowed me to hire my former students with compensation and continue working with them so they did not feel abandoned and without recourse to pursue the creative abilities they had only begun to develop.

These experiences as a theater artist and educator converged to form the critical frame for my work at Teatro Americano during 2008–9. I always asserted that Teatro Americano understood theater as a serious means of resistance and social change. I described our rehearsal and training spaces as "wormholes" where we could embody and model alternative social relations and political principles to transform ourselves and temporarily create a new world, even if it only existed for the duration of rehearsal and training. Since oppression fundamentally targeted and managed our bodies while contouring our consciousness, much of the work in the rehearsal room included physically rigorous training along with intellectual discussions and research. I insisted that the world we were striving to create would not be confined to the content of our plays, but would also be woven into development and production processes. For example, if young actors identified hood materialism as a problem and discussed the pressures to wear "fresh" clothes or the recurring—sometimes even fatal—violence erupting over Nikes, we would agree that gym shoes would be left outside the door of the rehearsal room and that no one would wear clothing with brands or labels visible. We also removed social stratification by committing to create original work exclusively through nonhierarchical collaborative processes. To break the status quo relationship of theater production, in which a company creates work and then throws it out there for audience consumption without any community involvement, we decided our work would be affordable and geographically accessible to our audience or community and that development would incorporate community members through their stories, presentations, and feedback.

With regard to aesthetics and content, I decided our plays would focus on the realities and stories of Chicago's Latino immigrant community and diaspora. But I was adamant that the productions would not replicate docudrama or youth theater aesthetics that so often relied on direct testimony, making a spectacle of oppression for fetishized consumption of identity. Instead, our work would embrace artifice so that our productions would not just reflect our realities but also allow us to reimagine them. To counter the usual didacticism and inaccessibility associated with political theater, I reiterated that our plays must be entertaining, and indeed they often relied on genre mashups and subversion of popular media forms. I stressed to the ensemble that our works should never present definitive answers to the questions explored, instead leaving them open so that audiences could individually and collectively navigate the problematics themselves.

These principles guided the creation of the plays I directed at Teatro Americano from 2008 to 2009, when I left due to ongoing conflicts with management over compensation for me and my students. During my second year at Teatro Americano, I proposed the idea for *Meet Juan(ito) Doe* to a core of four young-adult actors as a play that would explore the realities of Latino immigrant youth and first- and second-generation youth in Chicago. We developed four monologues by sharing personal narratives, interviewing young Latinos, and conducting research, or "studies," through social media. We twice presented those monologues at community events before leaving Teatro Americano. I did not return to the idea of *Meet Juan(ito) Doe* until 2017, when the Joyce Foundation awarded resources to realize the production to me and Free Street Theater, where I had been developing work since 2011. The return to *Meet Juan(ito) Doe* was influenced by seven additional years of critical theater making, during which I refined my practice. I found the cultural politics of Chicago theater and local and national politics had not improved enough to make this play unnecessary, so I moved forward.

Context, or "Tell Me What You Walk Against and I'll Tell You Who You Are"

Meet Juan(ito) Doe began rehearsals in January 2017, in the wake of Trump's presidential election. While the country was bracing itself for executive leadership by an incompetent, despotic, corrupt, cis, straight, wealthy, white male racist, Chicago had been wrestling for years with its own racist neoliberal leader, our local Trump equivalent: Mayor Rahm Emanuel. Emanuel's policies had exacerbated the social problems facing the city's Latinos, defunding our communities while simultaneously enabling their gentrification; as a result, thousands of brown families had been displaced from Latino neighborhoods like Humboldt Park, Logan Square, and Pilsen in the space of less than a decade. This political context compounded the standing problematics of "Chicago" and "Chicago Latino theater" to renew the significance of *Meet Juan(ito) Doe*.

But 2017 was not 2009. In those eight years, driven by the rise of Black Lives Matter and intense activism around immigration led by undocumented youth, issues of racial justice had gained prominence on the national stage and in local theater. Theaters regularly held panels, talkbacks, and town halls, usually centered around casting scandals or controversial theater criticism, to address issues of theater and race. However, despite the proliferation of racial discourse there was little significant structural change in Chicago theater from a racial point of view. The overwhelming majority of theater was still white. For example, by this time Steppenwolf had grown to have over fifty ensemble members, but fewer than ten were people of color, and only one was Latina/o/x, actor and director Sandra Marquez. I believe Marquez's 2016 inclusion in the renowned ensemble spoke less to mainstream Chicago theater's embrace of Latinos and more to increased assimilation of "Chicago Latino theater" into that mainstream landscape. "Chicago Latino theater" had gained more legitimacy by this time, mainly through Teatro Vista, a company founded by mostly Latino transplants in 1990 that was hailed as respectable regional theater and as Chicago's premier Latino theater. (Teatro Vista frequently co-produced with the Goodman Theatre, where Henry Godinez, former artistic director of Teatro Vista, is artistic associate.) However, the problem of "Chicago Latino theater" displacing actual Chicago Latinos in theater was only extended. In 2015, as Teatro Vista celebrated its twenty-fifth anniversary, it had never produced a native Chicago Latino voice, and only one play in its entire production history even took place in Chicago. As was the case ten years earlier, "Chicago Latino theater" did not reflect local Latino communities and remained economically and geographically inaccessible to them.

Such discussions around the politics of place (and displacement) in culture work were not completely foreign to the theater scene, and in fact they infiltrated the theater establishment, especially after the social practice turn in the arts that invigorated socially engaged and community-based theater. Perhaps script changes in the Victory Gardens Theater production of Luis Alfaro's *Mojada*, an adaptation of Euripides's *Medea*, speak to the assimilation of socially engaged and community-based theater into mainstream theater output. Though it was originally set in his hometown of Los Angeles, Alfaro staged the play as taking place in Chicago, and he incorporated interviews with Mexican immigrant women from Pilsen as part of its development process. But Alfaro mediating the testimony of Mexican immigrants suggests that institutions like Victory Gardens still believed that these women were not capable of speaking for themselves. Rather, it used these imagined-as-inferior subjects and their experiences as fodder for content and to lend a sense of authenticity. This kind of inherently problematic work was exactly what Chicago's Museum of Contemporary Art (MCA) was planning with a project that was the antithetical doppelgänger to *Meet Juan(ito) Doe*.

In 2015, the same year I began writing grants with collaborators at Free Street Theater to support *Meet Juan(ito) Doe*, MCA announced plans for a multidisciplinary performance piece that would present "yet-to-be-recognized stories" of Chicago's "Chicano life." Designed by two of the museum's curators who were transplanted Latinos, this project planned to represent Chicano life in Chicago by importing two highly credentialled artists from Mexico! The Mexican dramaturges would work with a cohort of Chicago-based, transplanted Latino artists, who would serve as a resource so that the imported Mexican artists could be "introduced to artists and other civic, social, and community-invested individuals, and visit the communities of La Villita, Pilsen, and Albany Park." Through these visits, they would gain access to our communities and stories. According to the project outline, this binational team of artists would then participate in a "creative exchange" at the MCA to begin analyzing our stories. In 2017 these international Mexican artists would use their personal stories and the stories they had gathered with the help of native informants to create and perform a show at the MCA about Chicago's Mexican American community, for consumption by whoever goes to the MCA. The MCA's project encapsulated all the dynamics, logics, and power relations underpinning so many of my grievances with Chicago theater and Chicago Latino theater— sentiments that motivated me to create a theater alternative in my native Chicago in the first place and informed the design of *Meet Juan(ito) Doe*. While I did not have the language to analyze the problem in 2009, when the concept for *Meet Juan(ito) Doe* first emerged, I have since gained it and can elaborate clearly on the world of injustice all this creates.

Our theater system is a mashup of colonial logics and neoliberal capitalist and multiculturalist considerations. The fact that Chicago theater was operated by white transplants mirrored a colonial history in which white settlers deemed the indigenous people of color as "primitive" and "savages," beyond the frontiers of civilization and incapable of possessing culture. The newcomers styled themselves the cultural avant-garde of humanity, the only ones entitled to create legitimate culture. It should be no surprise that our theater system is still so white supremacist, hetero-patriarchal, and cultural chauvinist and elitist. Nor should it be surprising that the artists of color who are allowed to ascend within this theater system are those who are legible to power, who have the credentials and cultural capital that flatter and reify the system. Once these artists of color allow themselves to be drawn into this hegemonic theater, whether out of personal ambition or a warped sense of social mission, their inclusion in it is then touted as evidence of racial achievement and progress. Identity can be leveraged for careerist mobility or to litigate for inclusion in the dominant theater system. All this can be wedded with contemporary theater that is steeped in colonial logics, although its context is no longer just colonialism, but also capitalism.

In the context of a neoliberal capitalism that embraces difference and multiculturalism as long as it is profitable and unthreatening, theater needs people of color. The acquisition of the "best" of us allows theaters to appear invested in racial progress while affirming the classism and elitism of their structures (so still reinforcing racism). Moreover, in this moment of identity and racial conflict, our stories and struggles can be extracted for profit and to lend theaters authenticity and relevancy, providing their predominantly white audiences with comfortable consumption of narratives of racial oppression. Although this is often celebrated as better, more "diverse representation," it is not. Artists of color and the narratives they author for the white gaze, and for the profit margins of white institutions, become the stand-in for entire populations that are not present and that are often cut off from accessing these productions. This is not representational progress; it is using representation to expand the threshold of tolerance of the system. This yields big money for theaters that can say they are doing better on the representation front, seeming current and responsive to the times, as they petition for hundreds of thousands of dollars from donors and nonprofit foundations. By allowing theaters to tap big money to represent people of color struggles, this kind of inclusion does more to serve theater's interests in self-reproduction than it does for the communities and people of color whose struggles are depicted.

Our youth of color also become their targets. These youth are framed as culturally deprived (if not depraved) so as to justify theater education and outreach programs as a frontier for accumulation, given the industry that education and outreach has now become. But the paternalism underlying theater education and outreach is not exclusively directed toward youth. Instead, it advances a preeminent logic and notion that has roots in colonization and that pervades all arts and culture. People of color—working-class people of color specifically—can never be considered artistically or culturally credible. Our stories and struggles can make good culture, but we cannot. As a result, our stories and struggles must always be mediated by artists who are deemed credible and whose identity is meant to make them a suitable authority and proxy for those struggles. Vast amounts of money and resources are awarded for projects and programs that support the appropriation of struggles, that extract stories and testimonies from vulnerable people of color and their communities, and that compensate and confer value onto intervening white-run institutions and artists. Seldom compensated are the marginal people of color whom these white artists enlist in their work. When the project is over, the white mediators who parachuted into the communities depart just as rapidly, seldom leaving behind any resources for those communities to continue engaging in their own representation.

Dénouement, or "The Revolution Is in the Details"

Meet Juan(ito) Doe was designed to honor the lives and struggles of Chicago's Mexican American population, which makes up almost one-third of the city but is almost entirely absent from the Chicago's theater landscape. This would not be a play made for the white gaze—to satisfy the sensibility of a white literary manager, to exhibit our authentic and pathetic realities for a white audience, and so on. Instead, I designed *Meet Juan(ito) Doe* to be developed with, by, and for us, the South Side Chicago Mexican American and immigrant communities. I cast an ensemble of actual "brown, down, Chi-town" Mexican Americans from the city's South Side. Our community would be engaged by our community. We would take the promise of representation literally and radically rework it to do what becomes prohibitive in theater: self-representation. In an effort to destabilize the credentialization and professionalization that is used to marginalize people of color in the theater system, I cast an ensemble consisting almost exclusively of nonactors with little to no theatrical experience.

They embarked on a ten-month performance training and development process. Since the body is the site of oppression, performance training was physically rigorous in order to reclaim the body. Performance training exercises incarnated the principles upon which the show was founded. For example, because the show was about acknowledging and mobilizing a certain population and exalting our community's members and stories, an exercise during rehearsal might have the entire cast moving at top speed for long periods of time and agreeing without verbal communication to collectively lift a member of the ensemble, getting them as close to the ceiling as possible.

Development also included creative writing, reading anticolonial, decolonial, and radical writers, and, above all, collecting stories. However, stories were not collected in a way that would reinforce colonial anthropology's technology of ethnography. Rather, we created a series of events that provided our communities with opportunities for catharsis, communion, and commiseration. For example, we had a karaoke night in which song request slips were prompts, such as "my grandmother's favorite song," "the song that got us moving at basement parties," and the like, and there was space for participants to write a memory on the slip or share a personal story on stage before they sang. On another occasion, we held a drag *lotería* night at a Latino queer club on the South Side, playing rounds of *lotería* for donated prizes. In between rounds, cast members shared stories about coming out or queer relatives, and there were stations throughout the club for community members to do the same. Additionally, we held "drinking and writing" nights at local cafés in South Side Mexican immigrant communities, and we had a pop-up tent outfitted with typewriters and cases of Tecate that we deployed at community events, festivals, and parks, where passersby could sit and type up personal narratives.

The stories collected were not to be transcribed and composed into a script to be performed by actors representing those individual persons. We were not trying to celebrate individuals; rather, we were trying to speak to both a collective experience and a heterogeneous identity. On one hand, we wanted to generalize ownership of narratives and therefore looked for the commonalities between stories; on the other hand, we also identified anomalies and divergences that challenged conventional understandings of Mexicans in the United States. Indeed, we focused heavily on the geographic and cultural singularity of Chicago Mexican Americans and immigrants. This specific focus allowed us to zero in on who we were without being elided into dominant cultural identity narratives like the cliché "ni de aquí, ni de allá" narratives popularized by earlier Chicano cultural expression and exploration of Mexican diasporic identity. We were not the troubled bicultural figure of "Yo Soy Joaquín." Instead, we comfortably understood ourselves as Mexican-descended US racialized subjects, and as Chicago, South Side, and hood. But we also organized everything we encountered—not just stories, but also objects, emotions, and other material—in a matrix that helped us identify what was particular to Chicago and what would speak to Mexican Americans across the country. We wanted to create a play that would provide a much-needed honoring of place-based particularity, but that would also offer opportunities for mutual recognition among Mexican Americans and immigrants across the country. We decided that we would create longer original monologues from our "data." But I quickly referred to the monologues as "totems." We were to think of the characters and their speech as sacred objects or symbols that serve as an emblem of who we are.

This did not mean we created stereotypical portrayals of immigrants and gangbangers, but we did construct archetypical figures that were manifestations and encapsulations of an assembly of behaviors, psychologies, and performances. I was sure that these representations were filled with defiance and broken expectations, and I strongly underlined the need for us to avoid or oppose respectability politics. We were not looking to present stories of Mexicans "making it in the United States" according to capitalist, colonial, or nation-state standards of success and mattering. Our characters were those who were forgotten and left out of the frames of power. They were flawed because radical politics cannot happen without radical compassion. They were not antiheroes but heroes of the social antimatter, figures that are created in the abject spaces society makes as it creates spaces of privilege. But our play was not just a talking-heads play.

We realized there was so much about being Mexican American or an immigrant in Chicago that exceeded words. So we decided the play would oscillate between these totems and movement pieces that figuratively or literally depicted common affects, experiences, and places. These yielded moments that transported our audience to assembly lines, corner stores, Border Patrol offices, house parties, public transportation, or quinceañeras, among other locations. Actions such as pouring water from a Kool-Aid pitcher onto the backs of cast members to create literal "wetbacks" or parading a Chinese dragon–style puppet of a giant piñata, and scoring these moments with soundscapes composed of everything from popular songs to nostalgic television, marked this portion of the play with a quasi-surrealist aesthetic. I often define it as docu-surrealism, because I argue that surrealism is not an avant-garde endeavor but rather the only style that can accurately capture what it feels like to be Mexican American. Far from being the choreography of an inaccessible, intellectual, or masturbatory aesthetic, these movement pieces are democratic or populist cultural representation, I would argue, since they rely on understanding experience as the province of the commons. They frame Latino cultural experience and facilitate connection and identification around cultural experience in a way that is altogether beyond language, sidestepping language barriers and offering a para-linguistic means for audiences to connect and identify with one another. The kind of aesthetic experimentation that we found allowed me to understand that so often, the artists of color accepted by the mainstream theater system are embraced because their works flatter the aesthetics of that dominant apparatus. This results not only in the marginalization of bodies of color (apart from an exceptional few) but also in the marginalization of whatever aesthetic possibilities those bodies of color might have been able to bring to the stage. This is not just about artistic conceit, but about providing opportunities for actors and audiences to feel one another and ourselves differently. The stakes are greater than they might first appear, since it is my firm belief that in order to change social norms you must change the norms of sensation. Norms of sensation is a concept I use in my academic writing; it refers to the conditioned and naturalized desires and feelings that, I assert, are a principal basis for social reproduction—or its undoing.

From the beginning, I was determined to present the show on Chicago's South Side because that was where our audience was and because I wanted to protest the city's cultural geography. "Chicago theater" is exclusively located on the city's North Side, which is more white and affluent than other parts of the city and receives over 70 percent of all arts funding granted in Chicago. My close friend and collaborator Ruth Guerra rented to me her late father's storefront for a dollar a month. We renovated the storefront to make it a theater, one of only three operating on the entire South Side. The venue doubled as a center for the entire community, as every week hundreds of people came to the storefront to watch *Meet Juan(ito) Doe*. Almost completely absent from our audience was the city's mainstream theater press, the archivists of hetero-patriarchal and chauvinist cultural production. The mainstream press rarely reviewed work by artists of color if it did not occur in the sanctioned venues of the theater system. As a result, we asked our audience to write reviews after the show, which we collected, or to write reviews later and post them on social media. We amassed hundreds of reviews, the majority by fellow brown, down, Chi-towners who enthusiastically affirmed our work.

The establishment of our storefront theater and community center and the compilation of an archive of our work should also be read as political resistance through creative place making and place taking in a city and country that desires our erasure. We were modeling and seeding the possibility of an alternative cultural ecology by working mostly outside the existing theater system that expropriates and gentrifies our means of cultural production and by attending to our own self-representation. It is important to note that this cultural ecology operates on alternative values and protocols for production and advocates for a different metric by which to evaluate artistic excellence and legitimacy. It would be a mistake to reductively understand this as only articulating alternative models of theater making. It is about creating different aesthetic and political possibilities. You cannot change social norms without changing the norms of sensation. *Meet Juan(ito) Doe*, like all my work, is first and foremost a form of political resistance. Again: you cannot change social norms without changing the norms of sensation. *Meet Juan(ito) Doe* understands aesthetic experience as germane to politicization and change. As such, *Meet Juan(ito) Doe* was doubly invested in articulating a parallel universe of what constitutes Latino theater and what experience Latino theater could offer, as well as providing a radical intervention in this moment of "pending erasure."

I do not mean to sound grandiose in my assessment of theater and its potential. I write this as a brown, queer theater maker raised in the vulnerable communities of Chicago's South Side and as a person who has witnessed the transformative effects and political impact that theater can have on our lives and in our communities, which are in fact battlegrounds where our erasure is at stake. The notion of "pending erasure" is not activist paranoia or artist melodrama. Make no mistake: we Mexican Americans and immigrants, Latinos, Latinas, Latinxs, and racialized brown people are haunted by the possibility of erasure in the United States.

We are alive at a time when the president of the United States owes his election in part to his incessant deployment of anti-immigrant rhetoric, which is, more specifically, anti-Mexican hate speech. But Trump's promises to disappear Mexican immigrants with mass deportations only continue the practices of his predecessor, Barack Obama, who presided over 3 million immigrant deportations during his two terms. State violence inducing erasure of brown people is not limited to immigrant detention and deportations: it also includes police violence against Latinos (the second-largest group killed by police) and even the abandonment of Puerto Rico in the wake of Hurricane Maria, leaving those colonial subjects without the means of basic survival.

In recent years, our erasure has also taken the form of brutal, intersectional hate crimes against immigrants, like the shootings of Raul and Brisenia Flores, killed by vigilantes in Arizona, and the massacre of fifty queer Latinxs by shooter Omar Mateen at Orlando's Pulse nightclub. Erasure can even happen insidiously, latently, sanctioned by government and the market, when gentrification targets working-class Latino neighborhoods. Generations of brown people have struggled to survive gang violence or poverty and to secure their right to home ownership and quality schools, only to see their communities and histories displaced. Then there are those of us who do not die, who are not disappeared in the swoop of deportations or outbursts of violence, but who experience erasure on a continuum as a part of our ordinary existence in the modulated conditions of spaces we traverse every day, like the migrant farm, the block, the school, the office, the bar, and the bedroom.

So if theater has hitherto only reinforced this erasure in blatant and nuanced ways and has conscripted us in that erasure, the question becomes: What are you going to do about it? What are you going to make? For whom and for what?

Note

"Brown and Down Theater in the Time of Pending Erasure," by Ricardo Gamboa, is reprinted from *Aztlán: A Journal of Chicano Studies* 44, no. 1 (2019).

Field Reports

Turning Sunshine into Noir and Fantasy into Reality
Los Angeles in the Classroom

Alvina E. Quintana

David Reiff opens *L.A.: Capital of the Third World* with a series of LA jokes that his friends and acquaintances shared with him before he left New York to relocate to Los Angeles:

> "Their idea of reading is a long personalized license plate." "Don't forget to buy that beachfront property in Nevada while it's still affordable." "L.A.'s only contribution to civilization is being able to make a right turn on a red light." [An Annie Hall appropriation that Reiff describes as "life imitating kitsch."] "Just be sure to peek behind those facades every so often. Everything in L.A. is a stage set, up to and including the mountains. Those Santa Ana winds they all complain about are probably produced by a huge wind machine out at the Paramount sky lot." "Wasn't it Los Angeles that Gertrude Stein had in mind when she made that crack about there being 'no there there?'" . . . How are you going to know when you've gotten there, anyway? The whole place is just a hundred suburbs masquerading as a city." (1991, 17–18)

My first reaction to the jokes in Reiff's prologue was one of déjà vu. Struck by a series of powerful recollections, I was forced to reconsider some of the provincial attitudes I had encountered after leaving Santa Barbara, California, to relocate to the East Coast.

When I first heard comments about the laziness or stupidity of the average "laid back" Californian, whose primary concern in life was supposedly New-Age fanaticism or a narcissistic obsession with physical perfection (a preoccupation most commonly characterized as the "cult of the bod"), I was not only shocked but deeply offended. Over time, though, my defensive reaction began to shift from indignation to tolerance as I allowed myself to listen to the attitudes expressed by the inhabitants of my new and somewhat alien community. I began to understand how relocation had liberated me and fostered an awareness of the cultural baggage I carry with my native Californian status. Others' facile perceptions coerced me into reassessing my own assumptions and made me aware of individual's innocent but problematic tendency to turn a critical eye on unfamiliar terrain and self-righteously pass judgements that evoke the imaginary more then the real. Reiff's collection of LA jokes, which disregard the rampant social inequality and exploitation in Los Angeles, reduces the city to a vicinity overrun by the kind of carte blanche and frivolous sensibility that generally only flourishes with class privilege. Misleading as this portrait may be, a multi-million dollar movie industry produces and maintains this illusion of LA.

Although Reiff's brief survey reveals unquestionably problematic perspectives, his geographically based humor enables him to confront a series of provincial reactions; namely, for people living outside of Southern California, the name Los Angeles does not refer to a city any more than the name Hollywood refers to a neighborhood within that city. Rather, when speaking of LA, the public seems to unconsciously summon cinematic recollections. LA is a place that exists outside of reality, a place inhabited with superhumans or myths rather than real people. It is interesting, though not surprising, that New York wit represents Los Angeles as a haven of whites, "superficiality," and entitlement—the LA depicted in vintage cinema, the land of Hollywood and Vine, Lana Turner, tight sweaters, and dizzy, platinum blondes. But we must concede that regional ignorance is neither unusual nor limited to East Coast misconceptions about the American West. For the most part, Americans live as exiles within their own country; they are limited by provincial attitudes that encourage competitive views about geographic, racial, and ethnic difference. Ironically in this technologically advanced society, where many people have used the internet to explore the dry and desolate terrain of Mars, Americans remain marginally informed about American geography and racial, ethnic, or cultural difference(s).

I am a native of San Francisco and well aware of the way people in the Southwest conceive of the East Coast. The reaction of my best friend upon learning that I might accept a tenure-track appointment at the University of Delaware comes to mind: "You'll hate it, Alvina, the only tortillas they sell are in cans!" Aside from inspiring cultural anxiety about leaving the West, this comment tainted my arrival with a sense of panic that eventually dispatched at least twenty concerned members of the

English Department in pursuit of fresh tortillas and cilantro for their new Chicana "multiculturalist."

Yet, my relocation to Delaware has enabled me to modify my provincial attitudes about the East Coast and my California chauvinism. I remember my surprise when first exposed to Delawarean pride in their first-state status, a position to which I had never given much thought. The best I could do was muster a vague recollection of an early American portrait of George Washington crossing the Delaware River. And even that reference proved to be faulty, for as one of my colleagues pointed out, the painting depicts the Delaware river not the state! Today I recognize that my regional illiteracy was a consequence of my socialization to believe the many early explorers who described California as the "promised land," "beautiful," and "golden." I understand that, like other Americans, my concept of self and nation has been greatly influenced, or better yet, overdetermined by the prevailing attitudes of my homeland.[1]

Far from uncommon, geographical biases are indicative of the regional and cultural prejudices on which this country was founded. Even a cursory survey of American pioneering shows how Manifest Destiny was used to justify the distribution of territory away from indigenous peoples and excuse their dislocation or exile. The unsettling narratives of urban renewal and white flight from racially diverse suburban communities testify that, even as we approach the twenty-first century, many Anglo-Americans continue to inflect their cultural, racial, and regional biases by positioning themselves in opposition to racialized or ethnic groups they deem socially inferior. The "our forefathers" concept of the American Dream can be more realistically likened to the American horror film, as Ed Guerrero suggests, where "the social construction and representation of race, otherness, and nonwhiteness is an ongoing process, working itself out in many symbolic, cinematic forms of expression, but particularly in the abundant racialized metaphors and allegories of the fantasy, sci-fi, and horror" (1993, 56). Guerrero's analysis of film and Reiff's depiction of humor unveil a quintessential American ideology that naturalizes, through its social constructions, the marginalized, invisible, or inferior status of ethnic/racial difference (Hall 1996).[2]

The misconceptions revealed in Reiff's prologue are valuable because they underscore one of America's most haunting problems and thus provide a useful point of entry for addressing the fear that continues to augment social barriers and instill contempt. In fact, I was so impressed with David Reiff's book that in the spring semester of 1993 I decided to use it as a model for a course that would use the magic and allure of Hollywood to deepen student interest in and awareness of America. My course, "L.A.: City of the Angels," had broad campus appeal because of its promise for California dreaming while satisfying the university's "multicultural" requirement.[3]

In order to accomplish my goal of deepening student awareness about American diversity, I developed an interdisciplinary approach that emphasized history, political theory, film studies, and literature and enabled me to move my students from fantasy to actuality by introducing them to the Los Angeles recognized by the ordinary California resident. (One of my colleagues, without realizing it, provided the final push for this project when she suggested that in Delaware, diversity means "white" students from New Jersey, Pennsylvania, or New York.) My syllabus described the course in the following way:

> According to Ryzard Kapuscinski's report in *New Perspectives Quarterly,* "Los Angeles is the premonition of a new civilization. Linked more to the Third World and Asia than to the Europe of America's racial and cultural roots, Los Angeles will enter the 21st century as a multiracial and multicultural society." With this thesis in mind, the course will focus on Los Angeles as a center for multicultural production. We will study a variety of representations of L.A. reading, listening, and viewing. Our reading will feature contemporary writing produced by African Americans, Chicano/Latinos, Asian Americans, as well as Euro-Americans. In addition, we will examine a number of Hollywood films, considering how commercial film is shaped by cultural forces.

The reading list for the course included Mike Davis's *City of Quartz,* Ruben Martinez's *The Other Side/El Otro Lado,* Helen Hunt Jackson's *Ramona,* Chester Himes's *If He Hollers Let Him Go,* Ron Arias's *The Road to Tamuzunchale,* John Rechy's *The Miraculous Day of Amalia Gomez,* Michael Tolkin's *The Player,* Hisaye Yamamoto's *Seventeen Syllables and Other Stories,* and the edited volume *Invocation L.A.*

My hope was to challenge the East Coast students' stereotypic assessment of Southern California by considering the interconnections between regionalism and cultural/racial prejudice. The course experimented with notions of self-imposed exile in that I forced students to distance themselves from what they perceived to be their native understanding of Los Angeles, to deconstruct the way they, with the assistance of the Hollywood apparatus, had fabricated an "imagined community." I was working very deliberately to create a feeling of discomfort and unfamiliarity, a foreign sensibility that would challenge the student's preconceived ideas about the city. In many ways this teacherly structuring or planning compelled me to become theoretically cognizant of the way my own relocation to the East Coast disassociated me from many of the beliefs of my native land, challenging me to reassess my territorial attitudes about myself and my country.

The cinematic screenings enabled me to reproduce the apprehension that results from being thrust into a foreign environment. As a class, we viewed *L.A. Story, Chinatown, Colors, Blade Runner, El Norte, Zoot Suit, American Me,* and *The Player.* I was operating under the assumption that most of my students were aware of and probably had, for that matter, already seen *Boyz in the Hood.*[4] I selected the films screened in class with the intention of facilitating a sense of difference that would lead "mainstream" students into a process of self-discovery. Beginning with the familiarity of the comedic/ stereotypic as depicted in Steve Martin's *L.A. Story,* I asked students to write an essay that looked critically at the film, discussing whether it represented an LA of "Sunshine or Noir," in Mike Davis's terms (1992, 15-88).

In response to this assignment, one student opened his paper with the following quote from the film's leading character, a wacky TV weatherman (Steve Martin) who is trying to sort out his life:

> "Sitting there at that moment, I thought of something else Shakespeare said, 'Hey, life is pretty stupid with lots of hubbub to keep you busy, but really not amounting to much.'"

Without commenting on the insipid, trend-conscious sensibility of Martin's character, who exhibits no intellectual sophistication, my student launched into his analysis, stating that throughout *City of Quartz*:

> Davis exposes Los Angeles's myriad of woes, and offers little hope of remedy. Yet, this alone does not make Los Angeles noir. Steve Martin's romantic comedy *L.A. Story* demonstrates that, indeed, Los Angeles need not be considered in purely negative terms. Rather, Martin depicts a city that, though culturally vapid, possesses an underlying charm. Like *City of Quartz, L.A. Story* considers Los Angeles in a dualistic fashion. *L.A. Story* is both "sunshine," characterized by a light, playful atmosphere, and *noir,* characterized by an equally lighthearted rendering of a deeper, darker truth.

It was this "deeper, darker truth" that began to emerge as the course evolved. As we interrogated the "lighthearted" comfort of the comedic form, students began to enhance their awareness about multicultural concerns and the dystopic representations in *Bladerunner* and Ruben Martinez's *El Otro Lado.* Reflecting on three of the featured films, another student addressed the racial implications set forth by cinematic representation:

L.A. Story perpetuates the stereotypical, relegating minorities to service roles. The only "person of color" in the film, excluding Iman, is a waiter who relays the menu in rap. Even though the film is categorized as a comedy, full of slapstick humor, it is not immune from the kind of negative patterns of representation which are more blatant in such films as *Colors* and *Bladerunner*.

Overall, the students' responses to my writing assignments echoed the above examples, employing either a romantic sense of optimism (reflected in an acknowledgement of difference that self-consciously depicts both sides of the equation) or developing an oppositional perspective that challenged the narrative's representational practices.

The quotes from student papers are also useful because they serve as a template for understanding some common reactions that surface when students are faced with the task of interrogating a text in order to identify its "political unconscious." The first assignment provided the class with the opportunity to engage in a dialectical analysis that considered Los Angeles within the binary set of the Sunshine/Noir opposition. Students were thus motivated to understand the consequence of privilege, to discover that one person's sunshine is, more often that not, founded and sustained by another's darkness. Interestingly, some students responded by structuring arguments based on the ideology of romance and sentimentalism, while others offered critiques marked by their resistance and opposition to demeaning cultural representations.

The course readings and films during the early weeks of the term engaged students to the point where they began to follow Davis's example, reading literature, cinema, and current events critically, considering the relationship between dominant ideology and popular culture. During the final weeks, students were able to rigorously assess their course of study and reflect on cultural production as a means for articulating some of LA's social concerns. Contemplating the 1992 LA Rebellion, one student agreed with many political critics who suggest that "in reality" the "riots" should have been viewed as the first tremor of the social earthquake that is to come unless actions are taken to remedy ethnic/cultural unrest. Her final paper on the Community Arts Movement in Los Angeles argued that artistic communication leads to harmony and understanding. As supporting evidence, she cited Michael Newton, president of the Performing Arts Council of the Music Center of Los Angeles County:

"What the arts can do is release us from a state of being alone and remind us of our dependence on others and their dependence on us. The arts remind us that man can only fulfill his private passions, ideas, and dreams by sharing them with others."

It seems opportune to conclude this segment of my discussion concerning student reflections with a passage that summarizes the final sentiment of the class. In a paper entitled "Los Angeles's Burning Streets: Where Poetry and Rap Music Converge," the student suggested that:

> Along the brutal streets of Los Angeles, the poet and the rapper are one. Ice Cube, Kid Frost, Naomi Quinonez, and Wanda Coleman are the prophets of the modern urban nightmare. . . . Their words are as angry and violent as their world. It is a world that methodically stalks them, all the while threatening to destroy them. Somewhere, along a side street, another victim of Los Angeles dies, and close by these poets pronounce their frustration to a deaf world.

Although the course proved successful because the students developed a deeper appreciation for American diversity, it was for me an extremely difficult and challenging episode. Of my thirty students, only two were not white. For individuals unfamiliar with issues surrounding ethnic/racial diversity, multicultural studies courses run the risk of being reduced to consciousness raising groups wherein students want to discuss themselves; that is, their guilt, their anger, their frustrations, their prejudices, rather than the issues that the featured cultural producers raise.

I am reminded of the "classic example" Gloria Anzaldúa provides in the introduction to *Haciendo Caras*. Describing the dynamics in the US Women-of-Color class she taught at UC Santa Cruz, she reports:

> Two of the goals I had were for the 120 students to identify and interpret instances of Racism ("internalized dominance") and to both recognize their internalized Racism and oppression and to develop strategies against them. . . . I wanted to call attention to the dynamic of avoidance among us, of not acknowledging each other—an act of dehumanizing people like ourselves. Yet another goal was to encourage them to emerge from "blank-outness" and openly combat the dominant groups denial and erasure of ethnic subjectivity by allowing the students a relatively safe space to speak up and "expose" their feelings. At first, what erupted in class was anger—anger from mujeres of color, anger and guilt from whites, anger, frustration and mixed feelings by Jewish women who were caught in the middle (being white but often sympathizing with colored), and anger and frustration on my part from having to mediate between all these groups. Soon my body became a vessel for all the tensions and anger, and I dreaded going to class. Some of my students dreaded going to class. (1990, xix-xx)

As the "multiculturalist" in our department, I develop and teach courses like the one Anzaldúa describes above. Generally, I come away from the experience exhausted, extremely tempted to limit my future teaching endeavors to the "traditional" American literary canon. Teaching the canon would afford the opportunity to make a choice I do not have as a multiculturalist—the option of either emphasizing the aesthetic, rather than the political context that shaped it, or selectively explicating the text by limiting the analysis to formalistic concerns.

But I continue to avoid the easy path provided by apolitical approaches because my teaching experiences have made me realize that with the discomfort and tension, the anger, guilt, fear, and frustration, comes the opportunity for personal development and social change. In the end, my students, regardless of their East or West Coast status, have consistently come away from a demanding educational ordeal renewed and motivated to discover more about diversity, more about the so-called other. This was certainly the case with the "L.A.: City of the Angels" course. If I were to teach this class again, I would revise the reading requirements and course emphasis so that they could be used to illuminate today's cultural predicament.[5] In Mike Davis's terms, studying LA provides a method for "excavating the future." For instance, in a recent review of Quentin Tarantino's *Jackie Brown*, Joseph Giovannini alludes to the material and mythic importance of LA:

> Some people may believe there is no there there in Los Angeles, but ever since film noir of the 1940s and cinematic monuments like "Sunset Boulevard," the industry has known otherwise. Especially after "Shampoo," "Chinatown," and this year's "L.A. Confidential," the city has increasingly emerged as a character in movies.

On the last day of class, one of my students shared the following insight with me: "I can't wait to visit L.A., only now I know I've got to take lots of money." How's that for moving from fantasy to reality!

Notes

"Turning Sunshine into Noir and Fantasy into Reality: Los Angeles in the Classroom," by Alvina E. Quintana, is reprinted from *I Am Aztlán: The Personal Essay in Chicano Studies* (Los Angeles: UCLA Chicano Studies Research Center Press, 2004) and from *Aztlán: A Journal of Chicano Studies* 23, no. 2 (1998).

1. A recent double issue of *The New Yorker* (Feb. 23 & Mar. 2, 1998), subtitled the "California Issue," featured a number of articles that represented the state in general and LA in particular as the model for the future. With essays like "L.A. Glows: Why Southern California Doesn't Look Like Any Place Else," "Annals of Enterprise—The Comeback," and "Annals of Architecture—Desert Cool," the magic and allure of the place is packaged for East Coast/American consumption.

2. Speaking of difference and contestation, Stuart Hall explains that, "The play of identity and difference which constructs racism is powered not only by the positioning of blacks as the inferior species but also, and at the same time, by an inexpressible envy and desire; and this is something the recognition of which fundamentally *displaces* many of our hitherto stable political categories, since it implies a process of identification and otherness which is more complex than we had hitherto imagined" (1996, 167, emphasis in the original).

3. The University of Delaware requires all undergraduates to take three units stressing multicultural, ethnic, and/or gender related content. The requirement provides students with some awareness of and sensitivity to cultural pluralism, which the university views as necessary for educated persons in a diverse world.

4. *Poetic Justice* and *Menace II Society*, also relevant as examples of the gang genre and the overall course focus, had not yet been released.

5. Future courses might include films such as *To Sleep with Anger, Falling Down, South Central, Strange Days, Mi Vida Loca, L.A. Confidential, Devil in a Blue Dress, Jackie Brown, Bullworth,* and a variety of multicultural texts including but not limited to Karen Tei Yamashita's *The Tropic of Orange*, Cynthia Kadohata's *In the Heart of the Valley of Love*, Sanyika Shakur's *Monster: The Autobiography of an L.A. Gang Member*, and Luis J. Rodriguez's *Always Running*.

Works Cited

Anzaldúa, Gloria. 1990. *Haciendo Caras*. San Francisco: Aunt Lute Press.

Arias, Ron. 1987. *The Road to Tamazunchale*. Tempe, AZ: Bilingual Press.

Clinton, Michelle T., Sesshu Foster, and Naomi Quiñonez, eds. 1989. *Invocation L.A.: Urban Multicultural Poetry*. Albuquerque, NM: West End Press.

Davis, Mike. 1992. *City of Quartz*. New York: Vintage Press.

Giovannini, Joseph. 1997. "Tarantino's Los Angeles: Roadside Noir." *New York Times*, December 30.

Guerrero, Ed. 1993. *Framing Blackness: The African American Image in Film*. Philadelphia: Temple University Press.

Hall, Stuart. 1996. "New Ethnicities." In *Black British Cultural Studies*, edited by Houston Baker, Manthia Diawara, and Ruth Lindeborg, 163–72. Chicago: University of Chicago Press.

Himes, Chester. 1947. *If He Hollers Let Him Go*. New York: Thunder's Mouth Press.

Jackson, Helen Hunt. 1988. *Ramona*. New York: Penguin.

Kadohata, Cynthia. 1992. *In the Heart of the Valley of Love*. New York: Penguin Books.

Martinez, Ruben. 1992. *The Other Side/El Otro Lado*. New York: Vintage.

Rechy, John. 1993. *The Miraculous Day of Amalia Gomez*. Boston: Arcade Publishers.

Reiff, David. 1991. *L.A.: Capital of the Third World*. New York: Touchstone Press.

Rodriguez, Luis J. 1993. *Always Running*. New York: Touchstone Press.

Shakur, Sanyika. 1993. *Monster: The Autobiography of an L.A. Gang Member*. New York: Penguin.

Tolkin, Michael. 1995. *The Player*. Emerville, CA: Publishers Group West.

Yamamoto, Hisaye. 1988. *Seventeen Syllables and Other Stories*. Latham, NY: Kitchen Table Press.

Yamashita, Karen Tei. 1997. *The Tropic of Orange*. Minneapolis: Coffee House Press.

Ethnicity, Fieldwork, and the Cultural Capital That Gets Us There
Reflections from US Hispanic Marketing

Arlene Dávila

With global culture industries localizing their operations and targeting cultural differences, how are race, ethnicity, and cultural differences structured into their own workings and operations? Moreover, how do our own ethnicities, backgrounds, and identities as researchers mediate our access to and understanding of such processes? In what follows I explore these issues through an examination of my fieldwork experience, particularly my level of access to the corporate staff and the workings of the US Hispanic marketing industry during recently completed ethnographic research. Specifically, I want to call attention to the challenges posed to fieldwork and ethnography by the processes of globalization, in this case by the global integration and market segmentation of the advertising industry, in order to contend that our access or lack of access to such global industries is as revealing of their current operations as it is of the challenges and possibilities for contemporary fieldwork.

My argument addresses recent rethinking of anthropological fieldwork and, in particular, of the "field" as the place, space, and location where fieldwork is done. As Gupta and Ferguson note, anthropologists have long engaged in critical assessments of the concept of culture, the politics and practice of ethnography and ethnographic writing, and even the relationship between writers and their subjects, but less emphasis has been given to probing and deconstructing the field as the space of ethnographic work (1997). As a result, though increasingly self-critical, anthropological analyses have continued to privilege a space and location, fixity, and authority, recycling the same canonical assumptions that we have criticized so much about the concept of culture and about the anthropological endeavor. A face-to-face encounter with an informant and direct participant observation is still given more ethnographic validity and authority than any alternative method, just as fieldwork in the most exotic places abroad is still assumed to be the most valuable and authentic. Such hierarchies of scholarly validation have led to various exclusions, most notably the continued devaluation of work by women, who are more likely to encounter difficulties accessing "exotic" locations, and the familiar disregard of US-based anthropological work.[1] But what new problems and hierarchies of scholarly knowledge are created when our fieldwork sites disband, being no longer containable in one location or temporal moment, and when we are unable to access the multiple "sites" where the global phenomena that concern us take place?

Obviously, problems of access are not new to ethnographers studying institutions of power. Already in 1969, Laura Nader identified access as the most powerful obstacle to "studying up," while excessive bureaucracy and concerns over privacy have long been recognized as central variables affecting the study of formal organizations, such as private industries and corporations (Nader [1969] 1999; Schwartzman 1993). Today, however, the growing segmentation of culture industries across different transnational spaces and their growing embeddedness in the logics of private capital, which are generally antagonistic to the rules of full disclosure and critical inquiry, further complicate our access and understanding of such spaces and call us to rethink approaches to their study (Calabrese 1999; Miller 1999). Against this background, anthropologists have rightfully called for new methods with which to expand our research imaginary and pointed to the need to reformulate the ways research is conceived if we are to understand the multiple implications of cultural phenomena in the contemporary globalized and mass mediated world. Hence Gupta and Ferguson (1997) suggest that we are better off seeking to gain "situated knowledges" about processes and situations, without fetishising the field per se. In a similar vein, Marcus (1998) has advanced multiple recommendations for reshaping "fieldwork" spaces, such as by going beyond a particular space and instead following the thing, the person, or the event, while Hannerz (1998) and Foster (1999b) propose that we break from the possessive association of author and research and be more open to collective projects that allow us to supersede the challenges of time and space presented by the study of such global phenomena as contemporary advertising.

My discussion is located at the intersection of these debates; however, my aim is not to provide alternatives to the methodological challenges posed by globalization to the "ways" and "hows" of contemporary fieldwork, but rather to suggest that there is much to be learned from exploring the predicaments involved in accessing fieldwork sites and locations. What I call for is not so much a rethinking of fieldwork sites, or an end to the confining emphasis on fixity and location, as it is a critical engagement with the forces that mediate our entry into the very real spaces where globalization takes place, such as the closed quarters of a corporate boardroom or a New York City advertising agency. In particular, I am concerned with ethnicity, not because I am oblivious to the many other factors affecting the ethnographic study of formal organizations such as global advertising, but because I want to emphasize the structuring of ethnicity within contemporary global culture industries. Specifically, I seek to call attention to how such industries are increasingly tapping into cultural and ethnic differences and similarly incorporating such variables into their own operations. Finally, my analysis is also reflexive and speaks to the always present, though not always pursued, anthropological concern with how our subjectivities, backgrounds, and racial, ethnic, and social identities intersect with our ethnographic research.[2] My emphasis, however, will be in using this reflexive examination as a tool to analyze how ethnicity bears on the working of global culture industries such as advertising, and how, in turn, it may affect our ability to study their operations.

Before proceeding I should mention that I am a Latina born and raised in Puerto Rico, and now based in the United States, whose research has primarily revolved around analysis of Puerto Rican and US Latino cultural politics and commercial culture. This makes me a so-called native anthropologist insofar as the focus of my research is generally considered to be "my own group" and "my own culture," although I neither subscribe to the authenticating premises of this concept nor seek to comment here on the debate about the nature and authenticity of research by native anthropologists. It has already been amply noted that such works are oftentimes vested with greater authenticity as representative of the researcher's "own group," but are simultaneously considered a lesser type of anthropology given the discipline's continued emphasis on the putative distance between informant and researchers, who must deploy supposedly unique anthropological research skills.[3] Instead, in identifying myself as a Latina working in the marketing and commodification of US Latino culture, I seek to establish some of the factors that shaped my interest in probing how ethnicity and cultural backgrounds mediate our access and ability to conduct research on global cultural industries in a context where ethnicity and culture have become prominent marketing variables.

Contemporary US Hispanic marketing, a culturally specific and rapidly growing segment of US marketing, presents an interesting instance of these dynamics. As I discuss later, not only does this industry function as an intermediary between Anglo corporate America and US Latinos, it also maintains close transnational linkages with Latin America, and the nationalities and backgrounds of those employed in the industry are important in its workings and organization. In this context, my background was both a help and a hindrance in gaining access to the different levels and processes of this industry. It is what such issues of access reveal about this industry's organization around ethnic lines that is the main concern of this work.

My discussion draws from my previous ethnographic research on Puerto Rico's marketing industry (1993–95) and on US Hispanic marketing agencies primarily in New York City (1998–99).[4] I start by reviewing my research experiences in Puerto Rico in order to contrast the access I received there to my experience in New York City agencies and to suggest that my informants' reception of my work was indicative of the role and position of marketing in these different locations. I then devote the rest of the discussion to the US Hispanic marketing industry. In particular, I discuss how cultural differences among US Hispanic marketing staff—such as those of language use, nationality, and ethnic background—are incorporated into this industry in ways that maximize its ability to target its market constituency. I conclude by considering how these factors mediated my entrance to and understanding of this industry and how they suggest the place of cultural differences in the operations of contemporary culture industries.

The Marketing Context: Perspectives from Puerto Rico and the United States

Whether I would be granted access to US Hispanic marketing agencies in New York City was always an issue as I started to think about conducting ethnographic fieldwork on this industry and on its impact on the public definition and projection of US *latinidad*. Prior research and experience working with advertising agencies in Puerto Rico had introduced me to the secrecy that characterizes the marketing industry, to the bureaucracy involved in setting up meetings with informants, and to the difficulty involved in gaining access to strategic planning meetings with corporate clients. What I was surprised to learn, however, was the extent to which such issues would be directly tied to and revealing of the different contexts in which this industry operates in the States and on the island.

In Puerto Rico, though directly tied to transnational advertising networks, the industry operates as a national industry, an intrinsically Puerto Rican operation, whose production is geared to addressing the distinctiveness of the Puerto Rican consumer. This is not unique to Puerto Rico, but is a documented aspect of transnational advertising which, insofar as it operates in national terms—addressing a territorially and culturally distinct constituency and hiring local staff and personnel—sees and projects itself in a similar fashion irrespective of its direct connections with global advertising networks (Miller 1997). In fact, it is this self-presentation that feeds its profitability in local contexts, where advertisers can make connections with local elites and use the idiom of cultural distinctiveness to justify the development of new campaigns directed at the preferences of local consumers. It is also this stance that has prompted scholars to study marketing as a vector of cultural formation (Foster 1999a; O'Barr 1989; Wilk 1995). And indeed, in Puerto Rico, though most agencies are directly involved with global advertising networks, it is Puerto Ricans, construed as a nationally homogeneous constituency, who provide the sole consumer base, while the existence of any other type of consumer is never an issue.

At the time of my research, carried out in postindustrial and "post-work" Puerto Rican society (López 1994), the service industry was on a rapid rise, employing the brightest, most connected, and best-looking *blanquitos*, a popular appellate for the middle- and upper-class, highly educated, light-skinned Puerto Ricans on the island. They made up a privileged sector of the Puerto Rican economy, and one that was difficult to access. Specifically, in contrast to my informants working in US Hispanic marketing, whom I will consider later, those in Puerto Rico seemed to care little if they had already canceled or failed to appear for previous interviews at the arranged time and place. Talking with an anthropologist seemed to be the least of their priorities.

My research in Puerto Rico was not limited to this industry but revolved around larger issues of cultural politics and local cultural production, which arguably could have contributed to marketers' seeming disinterest in my work. After all, I was not exclusively focused on their work and operations, and never gained the level of familiarity and involvement as I later did with US Hispanic marketers. At the same time, the enthusiasm with which US Hispanic marketers greeted me from the inception of my research suggests that other factors, which I will consider later, were also at play. In any event, given that I was primarily concerned with how corporate marketing strategies impacted on local cultural politics, my research was not affected by my restricted access to the marketing industry. My interviews with the advertising staff and marketing representatives for some of the most heavily advertised US brands on the island provided enough information about how marketing strategies affected the island's status debate, their advertising both drawing from and fueling the island's cultural nationalism (Dávila 1997). Brands such as Clorox, Budweiser, and Winston had all become associated with Puerto Rican culture in one way or another, while advertising agencies like Lopito, Ileana, and Howie had become known for their pro–Puerto Rican stance in their product campaigns. And these were no small matters in Puerto Rico, a commonwealth of the United States where expressions of national pride have historically been viewed as suspect and subversive. Thus, poignantly, transnational marketing and advertising were not conceived as a threat to Puerto Rican culture, but rather had been popularly recognized even by island's elites and cultural nationalists as an important institution helping to fuel local cultural production. This stance was vividly reflected in the comment of one informant that "there are no gringos anywhere," emphasizing the marketing industry's autonomy from its corporate clients, as well as in the many nationalist intellectuals working at ad agencies where they saw themselves and their work as promoting and disseminating the value of Puerto Rican culture.

These were the types of issues that triggered my subsequent interest in the US Hispanic marketing industry and its role in the construction and public dissemination of a US Latina/o identity. I was particularly concerned with how the ethnic marketing industry was contributing to the current popularization of US latinidad, to the "salsa beats ketchup" phenomenon, and the seeming Latinization of US popular and mainstream culture. Because this industry's profitability is directly predicated on the existence of Latinos as an undifferentiated people and a market, it was my premise that marketing was greatly responsible for fueling the growing popularization of a common category of identification for the highly diverse peoples of Latin American background in the United States.

I was afraid that US marketers would likely be just as inaccessible as their Puerto Rican counterparts or even more so, in what I anticipated to be a more bureaucratic marketing environment. But to my surprise, my hunches were wrong. After placing random calls to Hispanic ad agencies in New York City to gauge the type of resistance my research was likely to encounter, I soon found someone who showed enthusiasm about my interest in the industry, who assured me that everyone would want to talk to me and that it would be an "important work." Most important, this person proceeded to give me names and numbers of people at other agencies I should contact to do my research—all of this over the phone! Obtained a year before I was ready to begin my research, the contacts he gave me meant little to me until later, when I learned that he had provided me with some of the actual founding figures of Hispanic marketing. They included people such as Castor Fernandes, Alicia Conill, and Daisy Exposito, founders of Castor Advertising NY, Conill Advertising NY, and The Bravo Group NY, respectively. These people did indeed require countless phone calls, letters, and pleas before they would talk to me, though this time I was pleased to have meetings canceled by agency founders and directors rather than by account executives at the bottom of an agency's hierarchy. These experiences confronted me early on with the difference that context could make both in the industry and in my ability to study its operations. Specifically, it was soon evident that for most US Hispanic marketers I encountered I was not a nuisance but a likely ally: someone who could potentially validate their work and their market, for whatever I wrote would be "publicity."

I was now an assistant professor, not a graduate student pursuing doctoral research, though this new status was not solely responsible for the more welcoming stance of US Hispanic marketers toward my work. Instead, I soon realized that it was the marginal position of the Hispanic marketing industry and of its prospective base of consumers—US Latinos—within corporate America that was behind it. That is, in contrast to the Puerto Rican marketers interviewed three years earlier, US Hispanic marketers were faced with the challenge not only of selling ideas and ad campaigns to their clients, but, more importantly, with the challenge of proving the existence and viability of "Hispanics" as a targetable market. As one noted: "We Hispanic marketers work twice as hard as do people in the general market. Not only are we in the business of selling marketing ideas but we are also selling our consumer, our market. We are constantly giving people lessons in Hispanic 101." Indeed, the US Hispanic market is not territorially contained as are Puerto Ricans on the island, but rather concerns an ethnic minority on US soil comprising over twenty-seven nationalities and a myriad of differences in variables such as language use, class, politics, ethnicity, and race. Latinos in the United States thus represented a diverse and phantom audience that many corporate clients found difficult to understand and address through advertisements.

Moreover, US Hispanic marketers were particularly frustrated to find that their consumer market was often considered an advertising-unworthy audience by corporate clients, most of whom were Anglos with little knowledge of the US Latino consumer and stereotypes of all Latinos as destitute and poor. The specter of Latinos' minority status loomed large in marketers' efforts; they needed to thoroughly prove the advertising worthiness of this population by emphasizing those qualities that rendered them a commercially viable population.

During my research, evidence of the second-class status of the Hispanic consumer included a 1998 memo by Katz Radio Group containing derogatory remarks about blacks and Latinos and implying that advertising for these audiences was appealing to "suspects, not prospects"; it became the subject of great controversy in the industry and public at large (*Hispanic Market Weekly* 1998). Further evidence came from the lagging advertising expenditures in this market. In 1999, in the midst of the so-called "Latin boom" in US popular culture, the Association of Hispanic Advertising Agencies estimated that Hispanic marketing received only 1 percent of all advertising spending in the United States. This was so even though Latinos made up 11.6 percent of the US population and were supposedly in vogue (Larmer 1999; Riley 2000).

Such disparities make US Hispanic marketers defensive and vulnerable and in greater need of validation of their industry and the viability of their market. Such conditions explain why, unlike their counterparts in Puerto Rico, many US marketers saw in my work a validation and recognition of their own efforts. This was so even when my work was ultimately critical of the essentialist definitions of Latinos so promoted by their commercial representations. In fact, in order to protect their market, the industry has oftentimes resorted to aggressive marketing appeals, and in particular, to images that homogenize Latinos' language use, media habits, values, and disposition in order to give the impression of a unified and sizeable market. The result is the pervasive picture of the Spanish-dominant, traditional, brand-loyal Latino, a faithful watcher of Spanish-language television—a stereotypical and patronizing portrayal of US Latinos.[5] In these constructions, the Spanish language is construed as the paramount basis of US latinidad, as evident in the industry's common designation of "Hispanic marketing" and "Hispanic-driven media." Indeed, this industry's premise and rationale for existence is not only that there are basic differences between Latinos and other consumers that need to be addressed through culture- and language-specific marketing, but also that there is a continuous influx into the United States of Spanish-speaking people who would not be reached by advertising were it not for this type of marketing.

Access to US Hispanic marketers was additionally assisted by the fact that I am an educated, Spanish-speaking, light-skinned Latina, who presented no threat to their normative ideal of latinidad. This image of the Spanish-speaking, light-complexioned, upward mobile Latino is one they themselves have cultivated and maintained as a means of proving to their clients the worthiness of what is generally considered a marginalized and destitute consumer. And in fact, just like the Puerto Rican marketers mentioned earlier, US Hispanic marketers are mostly from middle-class and upwardly mobile backgrounds and, most significantly, are Spanish-dominant. This, as I discuss later, is a pivotal trait in an industry predicated on the supposed language distinctiveness of Latinos, the greatest rationale for the development of customized campaigns for the US Latina/o consumer.

Yet as the staff at a Los Angeles marketing agency put it, US Hispanic marketing is ultimately "about corporate America, not corporate Hispanic America." Far from an isolated phenomenon, it is an ancillary segment of US marketing and corporate America, and the agencies' productions always depend on their clients' approval. Most of these are Anglo firms representing the local and transnational interests of corporations, adding to the interests screening and affecting the production of commercial representations of Latinos and, most significantly for the purposes of this work, requiring constant interaction between Anglo and Latino personnel in the creation of the ads. This structure in turn has contributed to an ethnic and linguistic division of labor within the industry that also mediated the level of my involvement and ability to study its operations. It is to these dynamics that I now turn.

US Hispanic Marketing and Its Ethnic Division of Cultural Labor

Hispanic marketing now spans a network of more than eighty advertising agencies operating in every US city with a sizable Latino population. Yet only thirty years ago, this industry consisted of little more than a couple of recently arrived Cuban expatriates who were intent on convincing a skeptical corporate America of the existence and profitability of a culturally specific market. Behind this growth were three interdependent and parallel developments: the federal designation in the 1970s of any person of Spanish descent in this country as "Hispanic"; the growing interest on the part of marketers in segmented and targeted campaigns; and the immigration of Cuban expatriates, who had been active in transnational advertising agencies in Cuba and had the expertise and contacts to establish their own agencies in New York, Miami, and later Los Angeles.[6] Today, however, it is not solely these early Cuban entrepreneurs who are marketing to Latino populations but hundreds of self-identified "Latinos" or "Hispanics" attracted to the business opportunity offered by what is now considered one of the fastest growing segments within US marketing.

As a result, US Hispanic marketing is not a homogenous industry but consists of staff who differ in, among other variables, their nationality, race, class, and language use (being Spanish or English dominant). Moreover, the industry's operations and profitability are predicated on this diversity to such an extent that it informs the location of different staff within different sectors of the industry. Specifically, the central place of the Spanish language in this linguistically distinct industry has led to a linguistic division of labor whereby Latin American professionals, who have kept their grammatically correct Spanish language skills, dominate in the creation and dissemination of "Hispanic" images. These are people who have relocated to the United States as adults, often to pursue advanced studies; many have had previous experience in the advertising and marketing industries of some of the major Latin American markets for US brands, such as Mexico and Puerto Rico. Recent imports are particularly common in creative departments, where demands for "perfect language skills" bar most US-born Latinos. For creative jobs, a "pure Latin American" coming from one of the major transnational advertising conglomerates in Latin America is the most favored due to his or her "fresh" and untainted language skills.

Indeed, more than one agency I encountered had just hired someone directly from South America to run their creative departments. Consider the three Mexican creatives who at one point worked at New York City's Castor Advertising. Rodolfo, who joined Castor after working at Ferrer Publicidad in Mexico, explained that he had been hired at Castor only because his CV landed in the hands of his friend Sergio, who already worked there. Sergio, in turn, had gotten his job in New York through yet another friend he met in the Dominican Republic, where he was sent on assignment by Mexico's Leo Burnett Advertising. When that friend migrated to the United States, Sergio came too, and through him, Rodolfo. In between, Sergio had worked in production in Venezuela, where he met Roberto Alcazar who, through his assistance, was eventually hired by Castor Advertising. Rodolfo, a former anthropology major at the University

Metropolitana in Mexico, even drew me a kinship chart to explain the multiple connections spanning transnationally to Latin America and, in particular, to countries with strong US advertising affiliates such as Mexico, Venezuela, and Puerto Rico.

Meanwhile, Latinos born and/or raised in the United States are more prevalent in production, client services, and research departments. These areas require what was described to me as "more Americanized" skills to handle corporate clients or negotiate with other segments of the industry. The industry craves highly educated bilingual Hispanics whose ethnicity does not present a problem to Anglo clients and who can accurately represent and translate Spanish creative concepts for Anglo clients. These are typically what writers, following Rubén Rumbaut, have called the "one-and one-half generation": individuals who were born in Latin America but were educated and came of age in the United States (Rodríguez 1999, 5). This provides them a simultaneous insider and outsider perspective into both US Hispanics and corporate America.

The inequalities embedded in this ethnic division are evident when we consider that within the advertising industry at large, creatives—that is, the staff who conceive an ad's creative strategy—generally gain more visibility and prestige than any personnel who deal with research, accounts, or clients. It is the creative who wins prizes and name recognition, what Dornfeld (1998) has called "career capital," distinctions stemming from Bourdieu's (1993) discussion of the anti-economic logic that predominates, to various degrees, in different fields of cultural production. It is this form of capital that over and above financial compensation provides an employee with prestige and connections in the industry, which will allow him to found his own agency at a later time. I say "him" purposefully because there is a gender disparity alongside this ethnic division of labor. While women have attained positions of power within the industry, the most renowned creatives I encountered during the course of my research (such as Tony Dieste, Roberto Alcazar, Luis Miguel Messiano, Sergio Alcocer, and Jorge Moya) were all Latin American–born men, as were most agency directors.

These are some of the distinctions that render the label of "Hispanic marketers" not a homogenous construct, just as "Latino" and "Hispanic" do not represent a unique identity. Therefore, contrary to the prevailing view of the relative advantages of native anthropologists, my background did not provide me an unqualified connection with my informants on the basis of a common identity. It did, however, contribute to my research by functioning as a conduit and trigger to conversations about the importance of culture, ethnicity, and national background in the workings and operations of this industry. For one, as documented in other contexts, evaluations of my insider status as a Latina served to reveal the "content" of a given identity—that is, the criteria participants associated with group membership (Lomba de Andrade 2000). Similarly, discussions about our respective accents, speech mannerisms, and fluency (or lack thereof) in Spanish pointed to their emphasis on Spanish as one of the primary defining variables of Latina/o identity. Most revealing, their own and my own background almost always surfaced during conversations, and it was clear that they saw me not as a Latina but as a Puerto Rican, just as they see themselves not as Hispanics or Latinos but rather as members of particular nationalities; these perceptions pointed to the distinctions along lines of nationality and language use that were commonly made by participants and their significance to members of this industry. As previously mentioned, these distinctions are not value neutral, but inform the hierarchical placement of Latino marketers within different sectors of the industry.

Nonetheless, in this industry Hispanic marketers function mostly as "cultural brokers" (Astroff 1997), people who provide the cultural know-how for addressing the Latino consumer but are not the ultimate decisive force in ad creation. Instead, such power is exerted by American investors of Anglo background, who have bought many of the Hispanic ad agencies, or else by the corporate clients who are always in charge of approving and validating the agencies' creations. And suggestively, for my research this became a coveted and inaccessible sector, not because clients were ever given the opportunity to reject me, but rather because my access to them was restricted by Latino marketers themselves who subserviently took to heart the industry's paramount concern with the protection of its clients.

Deference to clients is, of course, not unique to Hispanic marketers but is a common trait in the advertising industry; yet Hispanic marketers' dealings with their clients were additionally shaped by this industry's subordinate position. If I was given a contact on the client's side, it was usually a Latino or Latina working as a corporate representative or ethnic marketing director; these were contacts with whom agency staff had close relations and sometimes friendships, but who were peripheral to the companies' decision-making structures. Anglo personnel at client firms, in contrast, seemed to be omnipresent figures in the minds of the marketers, people they had to defer to and negotiate with but with whom they had few personal relations.

Once again, ethnicity played a role in the maintenance of such a distance, as suggestively expressed in Hispanic marketers' use of *gringos*, *Americanos*, and *Anglos* almost interchangeably to define their clients. This pointed to their general assumption and awareness that larger corporate America is white and that they saw themselves in opposition to a white Anglo-Protestant ideal, devoid of Blacks, Latinos, or other "ethnics." Within this discursive opposition between "Anglo client" and "Latino marketer," I was a temporary member of their Hispanic marketing community, someone who, like them, was peripheral and subordinate to the corporate client. The following statement from one marketer illustrates how they tended to assimilate me into the "Hispanic" category and how this category was, in turn, defined in opposition to "the Anglo":

> The Hispanic is a very particular race. It has 50 percent of similarities, in that we are all the same: *You and I are attached to our families, we love our families, we respect our ancestors and are proud of them, unlike the American.* We are proud of our roots and keep eating rice and beans. But we are 50 percent different in that the Cuban is different from the Argentinean and he in turn from the Colombian. . . . What we seek is to tap into that 50 percent that makes us all the same. (emphasis added)

I eventually made some contacts with corporate clients, but given that my ethnographic focus was the agencies and their staff, I was happy to limit my research into the corporate side of the business to attending marketing workshops and seminars and reading the trade literature. In exchange, I learned much about the business from the perspective of Hispanic marketers. The latter I found particularly open about their frustrations with corporate clients and other difficult topics, such as the extent to which race and racism permeated the industry and the relationships between the Latino agency staff and their Anglo clients. Perhaps they were even more open than they would have been if I had contacted or identified with their clients. Still, I was unable to access meetings with clients, the real spaces where the commodification of Latino culture takes place.

By calling attention to how ethnicity comes to bear in these culture industries and to its potential role in mediating our access to global industries, I am not proposing that we draw facile assumptions regarding who, on the basis of his/her racial, ethnic, or cultural background, is more likely to have comprehensive access to particular culture industries. Within the study of contemporary global industries—so segmentally organized around ethnicity, as evidenced in the case of Hispanic marketing and my two aforementioned studies—it is increasingly difficult and even irrelevant to distinguish who "belongs" more or less to the "people" one studies when our research concerns not groups or cultures but rather processes and institutional structures impacting the production of cultural representation within global industries. This is why I insisted on deconstructing my own and my informants' Latina/o identity and noted how this putative identity was helpful in some but not other contexts of my study. What I am proposing instead is that engaging these issues is not only essential but in fact may help us probe the operations of global culture industries such as advertising. For, insofar as global culture industries are structuring cultural differences into their own workings and operations—such as by localizing their staff and customizing their creations in ethnic and culturally specific ways—we are more than ever summoned to inquire into the place of ethnicity in the operations of these industries and in their reorganization to address such different constituencies.

Investigating how and in what ways our own identities and backgrounds affect our access to such processes points us to the structuring of race, ethnicity, gender, and nationality within these coveted spaces of globalization. In the case of Hispanic marketing, for instance, my informants' understanding of me as a Latina simultaneously suggested their views about the place of Latinos in the marketing industry and highlighted the pervasive distinctions between Latino marketers and Anglo clients informing their work and advertising creations. Their reception of my work also suggested the structural isolation of Hispanic marketing relative to other sectors of contemporary global marketing and the active role that ethnicity may play in this position and in our ability to study some marketing sectors in all of their complexity. In this way, our background, as perceived by our informants, can translate to more or less access to different sectors and stages of cultural production. Whether we are seen according to our professional identity—that is, as anthropologists, sociologists, or ethnographers—or in terms of our ethnicity, nationality, or gender conveys particular allowances or barriers that can reveal much about the manners in which ethnicity factors into the hierarchical organization of global marketing. Awareness of these issues does not guarantee access to all the different levels of cultural production within contemporary global culture industries, but it is certainly more likely to point us toward a closer understanding of the nuanced place of "culture" in their current operations.

Notes

"Ethnicity, Fieldwork, and the Cultural Capital That Gets Us There: Reflections from US Hispanic Marketing," by Arlene Dávila, is reprinted from *I Am Aztlán: The Personal Essay in Chicano Studies* (Los Angeles: UCLA Chicano Studies Research Center Press, 2004) and from *Aztlán: A Journal of Chicano Studies* 28, no. 1 (2003).

Arlene Dávila's recent book on this topic, *Latinos, Inc.: The Marketing and Making of a People,* was reviewed in *Aztlán: A Journal of Chicano Studies,* 27, no. 2 (fall 2002).

1. See Dell Hymes (1999) for a revealing assessment of changes and continuities in the discipline as a result of the changing contexts of and critical challenges to its premises and operations since the 1970s.

2. Indeed, while such issues have been amply discussed in the anthropological and ethnographic literature, they often take the form of methodological and theoretical considerations, and are less often reflected in the ethnographic record itself. See Abu-Lughod (2000) for a discussion of the need to further study what she calls the "politics of location" and how it affects research and writing. The ongoing gaps between theory and practice in the ethnographic record are discussed by, among others, Willis and Trondman (2000).

3. The location of "native anthropologists" in relation to the discipline is a long-standing issue that has been debated widely and is beyond the scope of this work. Readers may consult Limón (1991), Abu-Lughod (1991), and Jones (1970), among others.

4. My research in Puerto Rico included twenty-two interviews with members of the advertising and marketing industry, focusing primarily on those working on the campaigns of Bacardi, R. J. Reynolds, and Anheuser-Busch. The outcome of this research appears in Dávila (1997). My research in US Hispanic marketing was more extensive and included more than sixty interviews with different advertising staff at sixteen agencies, most of them in New York City, as well as participant observations of their meetings and conventions and other informal discussions in 1997–99. This information was supplemented by content analysis of their advertising disseminated in both the print and broadcast media, and monitoring of major developments in the Hispanic/Latino–oriented and general market industry in trade magazines and ethnic-specific media. See Dávila (2001).

5. In order to adhere to the primary concerns of this work, I will not delve here into the characteristics of the dominant commercial portrayal of Latinos. These issues are discussed in greater detail in Dávila (2001).

6. On this issue see Turow (1997).

Works Cited

Abu-Lughod, Lila. 2000. "Locating Ethnography." *Ethnography* 1, no. 2: 291–98.
———. 1991. "Writing Against Culture." In *Recapturing Anthropology: Working in the Present,* 137–62. Santa Fe: School of American Research.

Astroff, Roberta. 1997. "Capital's Cultural Study: Marketing Popular Ethnography of US Latino Culture." In *Buy this Book: Studies in Advertising and Consumption*, edited by Mica Nava, Andrew Blake, Iain MacRury, and Barry Richards, 120–38. London: Routledge.

Bourdieu, Pierre. 1993. *The Field of Cultural Production*. New York: Columbia University Press.

Calabrese, Andrew. 1999. "The Welfare State, the Information Society, and the Ambivalence of Social Movements." In *Communication, Citizenship, and Social Policy: Rethinking the Limits of the Welfare State*, edited by Andrew Calabrese and Jean-Claude Burgelman, 259–78. Lanham, MD: Rowman and Littlefield.

Dávila, Arlene. 2001. *Latinos, Inc.: The Marketing and Making of a People*. Berkeley and Los Angeles: University of California Press.

———. 1997. *Sponsored Identities: Cultural Politics in Puerto Rico*. Philadelphia: Temple University Press.

Dornfeld, Barry. 1998. *Producing Public Television*. Princeton, NJ: Princeton University Press.

Foster, Robert. 1999a. "The Commercial Construction of 'New Nations.'" *Journal of Material Culture* 4, no. 3: 263–82.

———. 1999b. "Globalization: A Soft Drink Perspective." Work in progress presented in the Anthropology Department, Syracuse University, October.

Gupta, Akhil, and James Ferguson, eds. 1997. *Anthropological Locations: Boundaries of a Field Science*. Berkeley and Los Angeles: University of California Press.

Hannerz, Ulf. 1998. "Transnational Research." In *Handbook of Methods in Cultural Anthropology*, edited by Russell Bernard, 235–58. Walnut Creek, CA: AltaMira.

Hispanic Market Weekly. 1998. "Oops." *Hispanic Market Weekly* 20 (18 May).

Hymes, Dell. 1999. *Reinventing Anthropology*. Ann Arbor: University of Michigan Press.

Jones, Delmos. 1970. "Towards a Native Anthropology." *Human Organization* 29, no. 4: 251–59.

Larmer, Brook. 1999. "Latino America." *Newsweek*, 12 July, 50–58.

Limón, Jose. 1991. "Representation, Ethnicity and the Precursory Ethnography: Notes of a Native Anthropologist." In *Recapturing Anthropology: Working in the Present*, 115–36. Santa Fe: School of American Research.

Lomba de Andrade, Lelia. 2000. "Negotiating from the Inside: Constructing Racial and Ethnic Identity in Qualitative Research." *Journal of Contemporary Ethnography* 29, no. 3: 268–90.

López, Milagros. 1994. "Post Work Selves and Entitlement 'Attitude' in Peripheral Postindustrial Puerto Rico." *Social Text* 38: 111–34.

Marcus, George. 1998. *Ethnography Through Thick and Thin*. Princeton, NJ: Princeton University Press.

Miller, Daniel. 1997. *Capitalism: An Ethnographic Approach*. Oxford: Berg.

Miller, Toby. 1999. "Television and Citizenship: A New International Division of Cultural Labor?" In *Communication, Citizenship, and Social Policy: Rethinking the Limits of the Welfare State*, edited by Andrew Calabrese and Jean-Claude Burgelman, 279–92. Lanham, MD: Rowman and Littlefield.

Nader, Laura. 1999 [1969]. "Up the Anthropologist—Perspectives Gained From Studying Up." In *Reinventing Anthropology*, 284–311. Ann Arbor: University of Michigan Press.

O'Barr, William. 1989. "The Airbrushing of Culture: An Insider Looks at Global Advertising." *Public Culture* 2, no. 1: 1–19.

Riley, Jennifer. 2000. "AHAA: Creating a Bridge Between Corporate America and the Hispanic Media." *Hispanic Magazine* (June): 40–46.

Rodríguez, America. 1999. *Making Latino News, Race, Language, Class.* Thousand Oaks, CA: Sage.

Schwartzman, Helen. 1993. *Ethnography in Organizations.* Newbury Park, CA: Sage.

Turow, Joseph. 1997. *Breaking Up America: Advertisers and the New Media World.* Chicago: University of Chicago Press.

Wilk, Richard. 1995. "Learning to Be Local in Belize: Global Systems of Common Difference." In *Worlds Apart: Modernity Through the Prism of the Local*, edited by Daniel Miller, 110–33. London: Routledge.

Willis, Paul, and Mats Trondman. 2000. "Manifesto for Ethnography." *Ethnography* 1, no. 1: 5–17.

We Morph War into Magic
The Story of the Border Fence Mural, a Community Art Project in Calexico-Mexicali

Ana Clarissa Rojas Durazo

> But the skin of the earth is seamless.
> —Gloria Anzaldúa, *Borderlands/La Frontera*
>
> I write to remember.
> —Cherríe Moraga, *The Hungry Woman*

I am looking at a picture of my great-great-grandfather. It was taken sometime in the 1880s. He sits on a horse at the US-Mexico border with the expanse of the Sonoran desert landscape all around. A palm tree to his right marks "the line," *la línea*. When I first came across the photograph, I was struck by the way it seemed to signal the shifting configuration of the landscape along the border. While leading scholars in border studies focus on the borderlands as a constant site of transition, there is a presumed static element in play, the US-Mexico border fence/wall (Lugo 2008). Although the borderline is perceived as static because it mostly has not moved since the end of the US-Mexican War defined it and the US Army Corps of Engineers mapped it, its making persists and its meaning remains in constant flux. The photograph offers insight into sociohistorical shifts in the configuration of the border landscape. It evokes the ways in which the US nation-project, through its b/ordering of "the line," marks lands and bodies with anchors of meaning. Border making along the US-Mexico border is a geopolitical project that chisels and sutures peoples, communities, and lands through interconnected forms of violence that inscribe the bordered sexual politics of gender racialities (Alba and Guzmán 2010; Fregoso and Bejarano 2010; Guidotti-Hernandez 2011; Lugo 2008; Monárrez Fragoso and Tabuenca Córdoba 2007).

317

This essay examines the ways communities inhabit the US-Mexico border, the ways we inscribe meaning onto border fences and concurrent processes of marking and fracturing bodies and lands. I wonder: what did this border, this palm tree, this "line," mean to my great-great-grandfather and great-great-grandmother, to my ancestors and the many generations since then, and to the countless others whose lives are shaped by the boundary? How do we live with and also contest, morph, and transform the geographies of violence on the US-Mexico border?

I approach these questions through a study of the binational community art project known as Border Metamorphosis, a five-year project in which 1,500 community members painted a 2.3-mile-long mural on the border fence between Calexico, California, and Mexicali, Mexico. I write, imagine, and reach toward the meanings refracted through my participation as a painter and as the daughter of lead organizer María del Carmen "Tiny" Durazo, drawing also on participant interviews and the print and media archive on the project. I ask how bordered subjects and border communities are made and remade through our efforts to metamorphose border walls, and how our practices transform the vestiges of colonial and neocolonial power that structure a sociality of division (Barron, Bernstein, and Fort 2000; Selz and Landauer 2006). How do border communities rearrange the geopolitical site of violent border-making processes, transforming meanings of belonging and community through creative practice and cultural production? What are the implications for how border walls that order socialities of racialized genders, sexualities, and nations might be reimagined and rearranged? Even the tallest, mightiest walls fall short of the flight of imagination.

Lacerating Life: Border Making

PREP: THE CLEARING

In the deepest summer suns of July and August 1997, 300 National Guard troops descended on the US-Mexico border in Calexico. First they went after the desert ecosystem: they vanquished 2,400 acres of vegetation, triggering soil erosion and killing thousands of eucalyptus, mesquite, and yucca trees, along with cottontails, jackrabbits, and other life forms.

THE CUTTING

After land and life were cleared, they cut incisions eight feet deep into the earth where once trees grew and wildlife roamed. They made a hole and another and another, perforating the skin of the seamless sands, penetrating deep into the desert's flesh with scything steel rods.

318

Erecting Walls

To mark the map, to delineate, to slice nations, bodies, life, sea, and air, they brought six miles of steel to build an edifice to structure the divide. Panel by panel, they assembled 1,800 slabs of rusted, recycled landing mats from the Vietnam War. They soldered the fourteen-foot-high corrugated iron panels imprinted with the memory of war and affixed them to the steel posts infiltrating the depths of the earth's desert (USACE 1997; Hill and Kelada 2010).

> The sea cannot be fenced . . .
> *Yemayá* blew that wire fence down.
> —Gloria Anzaldúa

It was the season of Operation Gatekeeper, the Clinton administration's project to continuously intensify the militarization of the US-Mexico border. The project deepened the material and symbolic divides between the US and Mexican sides of the border. One of the principal strategies written into law was the replacement of the porous chain link border fence with a solid wall (Cornelius 2001). The logic of US imperialism and war on the border legitimated the new border fence strategy: according to the Department of Defense, a wall would "secure" the nation from the threat of a criminality constituted as the confounded movements of people and drugs (Nevins 2001; Payan 2006; USACE 1997). The discursive formations of national security, as enunciated through the "war on drugs" and the criminalization of migration, for example, obscure an imperial desire for migration (of peoples and plants) from the south. It elides US trafficking of racial, sexual, and gendered political economies invested in "securing" difference and dichotomy.[1] The heightened militarization of the border in the era after Operation Gatekeeper is marked by the expansion of border walls that mark particular geographies and bodies as criminal and expendable, making it increasingly difficult and indeed deadly to cross (Cornelius 2001; O'Leary 2009).[2]

Border walls signal the material, cultural, and social geographies of exclusion; they define territories, they animate the power to exclude. Their purpose is to produce compliant subaltern subjectivities, eliciting incessant participation in the constant remaking of the subject's subalternity. The practice of power over life, domain over life, is implicit in the work of constructing the sovereign (Agamben 1998). Border walls are assembled to disunite, to dissuade, and to disappear resistant subaltern subjectivities. The nation-building project becomes a modality of sanctioned forgetting that makes it possible for borderland communities, many of which live with military occupation, to forego resistance, because when the state kills people on the border, it is doing so under law, making such killing (inhumanely) tolerable. Nation-building projects and the metonymic border walls become a vital tool that produces ways of seeing, or not seeing, categories of criminality that conjure perceptions of territories, languages, and belonging.

Yet, in Calexico, a group of community members gathered in fall 1997 to discuss the new wall and its impact on transnational community relations in Calexico-Mexicali, a sprawling border metropolis in California's Imperial Valley. They were angered by the fourteen-foot-tall barrier that was erected without consultation or even any attempt at communication with local communities. Three hundred National Guard troops, deployed by the Department of Defense to install the fence, arrived in the hottest days of the summer, when the thermometer climbs past 120 degrees and most people try to stay indoors. The community felt that they installed the fence covertly, working through the night over a couple of weeks. People were angered by what they experienced as a deceitful maneuver that explicitly disregarded them. The community dialogue was hosted by the Calexico Beautification Committee, which ironically found out about the construction only when Imperial County supervisor Wayne Van De Graaff showed up at a meeting to complain about graffiti on the "new border wall."

My mother, María del Carmen "Tiny" Durazo, was a member of the committee. She said that people expressed the most concern over what they interpreted as a breach in the "sister communities" relationship between Mexicali and Calexico. Before, people could see and even touch each other through the porous chain link fence. With the new solid barrier, they could no longer "see each other." It was through the act of seeing that they remained connected, they felt.

Transnational social and kin formations and interdependent political economies shape quotidian life on the border and borderland intersubjectivities. These connections continuously undo the imperialist project of maintaining the US-Mexico divide that didn't quite end in 1848 with the so-called end of the US-Mexican War. The act of seeing each other contests the unrelenting effort to scribe criminality and exclusion onto bordered bodies. People used the chain link fence in ways that contested the material limitations on the free movement of people across the border. Every time I went home, I could see and almost touch Mexicali. In ways that have grown familiar through such visual virtual practices as Skyping, seeing can evoke the sense of touch. What is perceived visually is experienced as within reach, increasing the realm of the possible while shrinking the sense of material distance and division. Maurice Merleau-Ponty considers the possibility of being and becoming as emergent through the act of seeing and being seen: "my body simultaneously sees and is seen . . . through [vision] we come in contact with the sun and the stars, . . . we are everywhere all at once" (1964, 162, 187). His phenomenological understanding of inter-subjectivity considers it as emergent through multisensory and complex embodied and situated experiences that hinge on sight: we come into being by seeing and being seen. This helps explain how seeing each other across the border can carry the possibility of a more collective definition of cross-border self/selves that may counter attempts at individuation and division.

The ability to see each other across the border was not only displaced or blocked by the new border wall; it was replaced by the hypervisibility of the state and its 24/7 gaze on the border subject, who can forever see the central tower from which he or she is watched. In his work on panopticism, Michel Foucault (1995) considers the ways in which hypersurveillance imposes particular knowledges/disciplines onto bodies. New stadium lights, infrared technologies, and ground sensors installed through Operation Gatekeeper intensified the border subjects' understanding of themselves as subject to surveillance. As Nicole Guidotti-Hernández and Evelyn Nakano Glenn document, the state's unceasing gaze fosters gendered, sexualized, and racialized subjects who internalize exclusionary notions of citizenship and belonging (Glenn 2004; Guidotti-Hernández 2011; Spivak 1988). Althusserian interpellation also emerges through the specular practices of advanced military technologies that produce subjectification (Althusser 1971). The citizen is made through nation-state recognition; when the state sees us, the state constitutes us. The dismay expressed by residents on both sides of the border, when they realized that the new fence and surveillance technologies meant that they could no longer see each other, was a response to the epistemological and ontological attacks that threatened border inter-subjectivities and collective transborder being, belonging, and knowledges.

In the community dialogue, the room was filled with grief, disappoint-ment, disillusionment, anger. The community had experienced a loss and was unsure of the possibilities for redress, or even what redress might look like. They grew angrier when they found out that the new fence was made of materials that had been used in warfare. This added insult to injury, deepening the divide between (transnational) friends as it symbolically and materially represented the violence and destruction of war (fig. 1). The border itself was created through war and has been remade continuously through formal institutionalization, expansion, and militarization of the

Figure 1. The new border fence made of corrugated iron landing mats recycled from an earlier war. Photograph by Armando Rascón.

border zone over the last 150 years (Dunn 1996; Hernández 2010). Even the old border fence was a symbol of war, consisting of recycled chain link fence from the World War II–era Japanese internment camp in Crystal City, Texas. The new barrier "was a slap in the face to our community," said Durazo. But the fence was up. What could be done?

Border Fence-ing: Morphing Already Under Way

> This is my home, this thin edge of barbwire.
> —Gloria Anzaldúa

I grew up on both sides of the border, living in Mexicali and crossing, sometimes daily, to visit family, go to school, or work in Calexico. So many of us did the same. When crossing wasn't an option, families and friends in all kinds of formations gathered on both sides of the chain link fence. Newborns met kin for the first time; loved ones sat in lawn chairs telling stories, sharing food through the wire; friends hung out after school, playing volleyball across the fence, listening to music that seemed to fade the fence; lovers gazed at each other, touching hands and skin in the spaces between the metal mesh. On the border, we learned to love through walls.

The fence, both old and new, is a part of our lives, of the geography of families and of love. Those of us who cross on a regular basis get to know its texture, temperament, and tonality. We come to know the landscape, how to read the map for crossing: today is a good day for crossing, or maybe not so much. Border communities develop a relationship with the ever-present fence. We learn to live with it but we also dream it into something else: we morph it into volleyball nets and bedroom sheets; displays for vendors selling blankets, ceramic suns and *ollas*, Aztec calendars, piñatas; showcases for *nacimientos, luminarias y lucecitas* at Christmastime. The chain link fence was first installed in 1951, and for nearly fifty years border communities pushed the porosity of the fence in search of malleability, turning it into something far from its intended purpose of division and separation. A brief walk or drive along the border fence reveals the many cutouts, dug-ups, decorations, and transformations. Crossers constantly turn the fence into a pathway, cutting through the separation. We live amid the markers of geopolitical separation, and when we symbolically and materially turn them into something else, we undo their capacity to divide. A life lived on the borderlands yields profound insight into the feebleness of a power that strives to separate. In the words of Norma Alarcón, "deterritorialized populations often reconstruct an imaginary . . . to mediate a critique of geopolitical nationalisms, as well as a 'third space' through which to situate the critique that alleviates the 'us vs. them' syndrome produced by geopolitical nationalisms" (Alarcón 1994).

As borderlands people and border crossers, we practice a kind of transborder *rasquachismo* in our everyday lives, defiantly and creatively bridging divides, inventing paths where there were walls, transforming the monster objects of war into magic.[3] As Gloria Anzaldúa puts it, "The border is the locus of resistance, of rupture, implosion and explosion, and of putting together the fragments and creating a new assemblage" (2009, 177). Border artist Armando Rascón from Calexico collected bits and pieces of discarded or cut-out fence in a box below his bed when he was a child and later used them for art projects and installations (Bonetti 2002). Rosa María Villanueva from Mexicali collects *piedras*, stones near the border, and paints life on them, scenes of women laughing, dancing, sleeping, working; her paintings breathe life and movement into rock. But we are all artists when fences are our everyday reality. We stitch together the wounds of separation through imagination, piecing life together through objects and memories of deaths and wars. We make homes of barbwire.

"Let's Paint a Mural!"

Pies para qué los quiero si tengo alas para volar.
—Frida Kahlo

Nothing happens in the "real" world unless it first
happens in the images in our heads.
—Gloria Anzaldúa

It was unexpected, but not entirely a surprise, when Durazo, who had defied the divide all her life with constant movement across the border, asked, "Why don't we paint a mural?" She thought of bringing the community on both sides together to paint a mural along the wall. An English teacher at Calexico High School, Durazo had designed the Calexico Unified School District Service Learning Program and was active in statewide and national conversations on emerging service-learning pedagogies in the 1990s. She envisioned the mural as a project that could involve the entire community and especially young people in schools. Durazo was concerned about budget cuts to school art and music programs and community youth groups. The cuts had increased in tandem with the militarization of the US-Mexico border and the intensification of the drug war. Calexico was quickly becoming a drug corridor where young people faced heightened risk of getting caught up in addiction and violence related to the war on drugs.

As a cultural arts activist, Durazo believed that when young people express themselves creatively, they develop the imagination and agency they need to better negotiate and survive and even transform the risk of living on the border in the drug war era. Shortly before the mural art project, she began serving on the Imperial County Council for the Arts "in order to learn how to build a home for artists in Calexico." She envisioned Calexico as a place where young people and artists could build community through art, where they could learn, grow, and thrive as artists. She was struck by the potentially transformative ways that art could make a difference. In *Chicana Art*, Laura Pérez contends that art practice leads to a kind of healing: "The arts optimally embody and facilitate the critical, truth-seeking, and daring consciousness that is necessary to both social and spiritual well-being" (2007, 306).

The mural idea caught on, and Durazo began organizing. Members of the Calexico Beautification Committee tracked down Rascón, the artist who had grown up in Calexico and was known for his border art. The committee discussed their ideas about the mural design with Rascón. Durazo noted that an image invoking friendship would assert the transnational community's sense of connectedness. Rascón pointed to the friendship bracelet on his wrist, and Durazo said, "Even if they put up a fence, we can take away the barrier by affirming our friendship." As energy for the project grew, Durazo formed the first Calexico Arts Commission to bring the mural to life. Hildy Carrillo secured support from the city council and served as adviser to the commission, and community members Sheila Dolente, Brenda Hinojosa, Steve Wong, and Reynaldo Ayala joined the commission as members. Durazo served as chairperson and mural project director.

In the early stages of the project development, the community began a letter-writing campaign to express their rage and concern about the wall. "The federal government got heat from the community about the fence," said Durazo. Since the border fence is federal property, "we used this [strategy] as leverage to get the fence art in with DC." Eventually the federal government approved the mural project, something the community felt they would have previously shut down with no consideration. The combination of the mounting community pressure and an unusually community-oriented border patrol chief in neighboring El Centro, Tom Walker (who did not last long in his post), led to a memorandum of understanding that turned the fence into federally recognized public art and also established joint local and federal control of the fence going forward. US Border Patrol representatives apologized to the community and agreed to consult local residents about all future changes to the fence. A couple of years later, when it came time to replace the chain link fence on the south side of the city, the community organized a committee that demanded, and received, "a fence you could see through."

After Rascón was hired as lead artist for the mural, my mother and I met him at his gallery, Terrain, in San Francisco. He proposed a geometric pattern of interlinking circles and diamonds inspired by a 3,400-year-old Olmec jade axe handle said to be a symbol of communication. He felt that connecting to one of the earliest cultures of the Americas would question the legitimacy of the US-Mexico border divide and the border fence. Rascón wanted to connect the border community to Olmec cosmovisions to show that indigenous knowledges in the Americas might offer different ways to interpret, assign meaning to, and rearrange the structures and knowledges of coloniality, in particular the border fence (Mignolo 2005). Durazo felt that expressing a connection to Olmec culture and affirming friendship and communication would honor the lives and histories of indigenous and migrant peoples in the Americas in light of escalating attacks on migrants in the borderlands. The intention to honor migrants and indigenous knowledge predating national borders eventually led to the temporary cessation of migrant arrests at the border fence mural site.

After nearly a year of planning, the painting began in October 1998 with a celebration marking the Olmec harvest festival. Mexicali and Calexico community members came together to inhabit the public space previously inaccessible and guarded by the Border Patrol. Over the next three years, 1,500 multi-generational border community members, from one to ninety years of age, took part in painting a 2.3-mile-long mural along the US side of the border fence.[4] Through a broad grassroots community outreach campaign, anyone and everyone was invited to paint. Folks arrived from Mexicali with passports or without. They jumped over fences or came in through the *garitas* (border crossing points). They came in school buses and vans filled with members of the Conservation Corps or with elders from the De Anza assisted living center.

Stitching Wounds: We Morph Border Walls into Art

> We can transform our world by imagining it differently . . .
> willing it into creation.
> —Gloria Anzaldúa

> Quality, light, color, depth . . . awaken an echo in
> our bodies and . . . the body welcomes them.
> —Maurice Merleau-Ponty

Candis takes the colored *velas* and arranges them in four directions on a napkin on the floor. To mark the beginning. She didn't learn this in the highlands of her Mixé pueblo, Paso de Águila, on the Oaxaca-Veracruz border; the coloniality of Mexican nationalisms penetrated even where few cars reached and tried to take traditions away. But she returned to them and relearned the Maya tradition of burning color candles. Each color a direction. An element. An energy. A welcoming.

The colors brought life to the decaying border fence. Vivid blue melded the fence into sky, bringing a healing water from the direction of the sea to cleanse the fence of all it has seen, to renew and regenerate. Jade green served as conduit for *energía espiritual* to heal the land's wounds, to sing trees into it. Yellow looked to the east to honor the rising sun and usher new life. Bright red in the center formed an omniscient orb, the eye that sees the pulsing of life, the memory of bloodshed and of life birthed, seeing on its way to becoming. Color was everywhere; it flew through the air, filling buckets, streaking clothes, dotting flesh, animating steel. And we came

Figure 2. We morph border walls into art. Photograph by Armando Rascón.

alive with possibility. The border fence became the palm tree in my great-great-grandfather's picture. "The painter's way of seeing is reconstituted by the marks he makes on the canvas" (Berger 1990, 10). The brilliant interwoven stitch danced across the fence, healing wounds. The stitch forged an unbreakable pattern, a bond invoking what Anzaldúa calls the "refusal-to-be-split themes of the border artist," a chain of unending color (Anzaldúa 2009, 181).

As the painting neared completion, the size, color, and content of the mural seemed to diminish the prominence of the border fence, in effect visually shrinking the fence. The temporality and fiction of the fraction became visible, undoing the divide. As the mural transformed the border fence, a place mired in meanings and histories of violence became a space filled with color, joy, and love (fig. 2).

> The painter "takes his body with him."
> —Maurice Merleau-Ponty, quoting Paul Valéry

> Free the body, and the mind will have a chance to follow.
> —Cherríe Moraga

There was a movement in the making, deep below the border fence, where the earth's heart beats strong. I knew this moment, like many others, carried with it the possibility of rearranging the architecture of violence—not just in my own body, but on the land's map, in the community, on the border. I took paintbrush to blue paint and turned the fence into a sea.

The new border fence marked one of the many ways the US nation-project aims to subjugate borderlands inhabitants by arranging the spatial configurations of power through the landscape, which is then activated as a weapon against its inhabitants (Guidotti-Hernández 2011). The border mural project, like many Chicana/o mural projects, recognized the symbolic and material implications of reclaiming and recodifying the public art site as part of the sociopolitical and cultural intervention (Latorre 2008; Pérez 2007). In "Border Arte," Anzaldúa speaks to this recurring practice as it manifests in border art: "the border is a historical and metaphorical site, *un sitio ocupado*, an occupied borderland where individual artists and collaborating groups transform space, and the two home territories, Mexico and the United States, become one" (2009, 184). The border mural art project stitched not only the fence but also a community fractured by coloniality.[5]

The mural project had a significant impact on the painters, as revealed in the archive, interviews, and conversations, and as I myself witnessed and experienced through my own participation. It also transformed community relations. The confounding deployments of militarism and border organization conjure a community that is divided between migrants who cross the border and nonmigrants who live on the border. As the nation-project sets out to elicit participation in producing a community that surveils itself with regard to notions of belonging and citizenship, a culture of policing bodies, gestures, clothing, and language is created to measure belonging (Bejarano 2005). The border mural project narrowed the distance between "migrants" and "citizens," between nations, between men and women, and between migrants and the border patrol. It made visible the way we are made to depend on border-making notions of gender, nation, citizenship, and race.

> Through arts . . . we can become more in touch with our full humanity.
> —Incite! Women of Color Against Violence, SisterFire tour

Because the border fence extended into the desert landscape, nonmigrant painters shared aspects of the migration experience. On several occasions the painters heard gunshots and thought they were being shot at by border patrol; they collapsed to the ground in fear. More than once, painters were caught in desert sandstorms. My mother recalls a few occasions when painters "huddled together, holding hands through the storms deep in the desert, unable to see anything." My mother recalls that the painters started coming down with eye and respiratory infections as the mural approached the New River, the most polluted waterway in the United States. The border fence ends at the New River; crossing the river is one of the limited options available to migrants because it is the one place the border patrol won't go. The river is a death trap. Many would-be crossers drown, while others are exposed to pesticides, bacteria, and viruses, including the pathogens that cause cholera, hepatitis, typhoid, tuberculosis, encephalitis, and polio. Operation Gatekeeper's slogan, "prevention [of migration] through deterrence," comes to mean that only deadly pathways will be left for migrants (Chacón and Davis 2006; Cornelius 2001; Nevins 2001). Both of these experiences involved the sense of sight: temporary blindness due to weather and to illness offered people the possibility of new ways of seeing themselves—as human beings, as painters, as migrants—and new ways of seeing their relationality.

The border mural project worked as a heuristic device that countered the state's framing of the border wall and as an epistemic intervention in militarization by countering the state's attempts to objectify and fix border communities through hypersurveillance. The community reclaimed "seeing." As Guidotti-Hernández (2011) puts it, "seeing" challenges the fundamental strategy of the nation-state along the border: the elimination of historical memory and of a sense of knowing the other. The mural project's grassroots fundraising strategies fostered collective intersubjectivities (Incite! 2007) and deepened a sense of community excitement about the mural. Two-thirds of the project budget, $50,000 of the $75,000 total, was raised through community activities like special events and raffles. When a community funds a project, there is the possibility for greater accountability to that community, so grassroots fundraising can function as a community-building strategy. In this case it nurtured a collective sense of agency and responsibility for the mural project.

Beyond B/ordering Bodies: Morphing Borders that Racialize Genders and Sexualities

Border making is a gendering process that maps, surveils, conditions, and attacks bodies by marking racialized genders and sexualities in particular ways (Alba and Guzmán 2010; Fregoso 2003; Fregoso and Bejarano 2010; Segura and Zavella 2007). Colonial maps and border walls are drawn not just on the topography of lands but on our bodies, on our relationalities and kinship formations. As the border fence morphed, were narratives and structures of racialized sexualities and genders morphed too? In what ways did the border mural art project contest, decolonize, and rewrite the structural and imagined landscapes of racialized gender subjectivities on the border (Lugones 2007)?

Delving into the historical record of the border mural project as documented in books and print media, I found that the work of Chicanas and Mexicanas—their leadership, labor, and *energía* that made the mural project a possibility—was obscured if not entirely omitted (Barron, Bernstein, and Fort 2000; Bonetti 2002; Selz and Landauer 2006). Beyond assessing their contributions to the mural, I also want to elucidate the contours of the community mural project and the associated community transformations that were made possible by the work and vision that border Chicanas/ Mexicanas brought to it.

The etymological and historical roots of the term *sex* signal a cutting, a separation of bodies. According to Ramón Gutiérrez (2010), bodies are marked through racial and colonial mythologies and narratives that highlight the space where science and religion conjoin to calibrate the complex colonial ordering of racialized genders and sexualities. This b/ordering of bodies, communities, and peoples is historically and continually activated in ways that entrench colonial heteropatriarchal social orders through the practice of effacing and abnegating Chicana/Mexicana power (Blackwell 2011). While the colonial racial coding of gendered/sexed hierarchies instigates, depends on, and promotes violence against gender/sexual queering and subjugated sexualities/genders, it has historically activated a denial of and attack on Chicana/Mexicana and indigenous women's leadership. An instructive historical account is the case of Toypurina, an indigenous Tongva/Gabrieliña medicine woman who led an insurrection at the San Gabriel Mission in what is now Southern California. As documented by Antonia Castañeda (2005), when indigenous men were punished for revolting, they were specifically and menacingly castigated for following the leadership of an indigenous woman. Is the repeated erasure of Chicana leadership on the border mural project a reenactment of colonial gender, racial, and sexual disciplining?

Chicana/Mexicana leadership in the border mural art project, muted out of the historical records, included various official roles. Durazo formed and then chaired the Calexico Arts Commission, and she served as director of the mural project and as its service learning coordinator. Brenda Hinojosa and Carmen Durazo successfully secured the first California Arts Council Challenge Grant ever received by a community in the Imperial Valley. In addition, Chicanas and Mexicanas played a wide range of unofficial roles in initiating, conceptualizing, and leading the project. It is vital to recognize their labor and leadership so as to counter the complicity with colonial racial gendering processes that continuously enact the various violences of heteropatriachy on the border and in Mexican/Chicana/o communities. The recognition of their leadership also opens space for historicizing, analyzing, and learning from border Chicana feminisms that engender politically transformative projects. These projects unquestionably remap gender relations, whether or not they enunciate gender focality and declare themselves as feminist (Blackwell 2011).

Stories abound of the many ways in which Mexicana artists, including Frida Kahlo and María Izquierdo, were discouraged and prevented from painting murals (Luke 2011). The patriarchal Mexican nationalism of the early twentieth century regulated the size and placement (in public space) of mural projects through a masculinist frame, treating muralism as strictly a male art form "unbecoming" of Mexican women.[6] The modernist era in Mexico emerged conversant with European patriarchal enunciations of artistic expression of the time (McCaughan 2012).

Both the Mexican muralist movement and the Mexico City student art movement in the late 1960s were highly influential in inspiring a Chicana/o art movement whose key murals, according to Guisela Latorre, "possess a gendered history that historically and discursively relegated women to the margins and subsequently rendered them completely invisible" (2008, 176). By contrast, the border mural art project put paintbrushes in the hands of Mexicanas and Chicanas of all ages. When they set out to paint the site of a border wall and a borderland policed and coded by militarized hypermasculinities and masculinist nationalisms (American, Mexican, and Chicano), the painters and the project contested the racially coded gender borders that prevent women from claiming public space and from reimagining and remaking our worlds through murals (fig. 3). "I don't see myself as different from men," said Durazo. "Start thinking of yourself as an artist who's about to make her mark," read an announcement recruiting painters for the mural in the *Valley Women Magazine* (Clarke 1999).

Gender morphing also emerged with regard to the mural's content. Mexican and Chicana/o modernist mural techniques often enshrine hyper-hetero-masculinist figures. On so many of my beloved *panadería* calendars, a limp and dying Ixtacihuatl is draped across the arms of a virile Popocatepetl, his rippling biceps growing bigger each year (Rueda Esquibel 2006). Such images are consistent with Mexican nationalist and Chicana/o nationalist

Figure 3. Mi tía Alba García, born and raised in Calexico, who returned from San Diego to paint the mural. Photograph by Ana Clarissa Rojas Durazo.

Indigenism projects. But they invigorate a colonial, heteropatriarchal sociality that promotes violence against women by representing indigenous women as passive victims while agrandizing men's physical strength and its capacity to dominate a gendered passive subject (Contreras 2008; Latorre 2008; Rodríguez 2009). By contrast, the border mural featured a repeating geometric pattern, designed by Rascón in conversation with Durazo's ideas about the accessibility, content, and meaning of the mural (fig. 4). In a context where the measure, mark, and surveillance of feminized bodies by the state and culture is key to nation building, it was refreshing to see a mural design that did not feature bodies marked by inclusion/exclusion and violence (Cantú 2009; Luibheid 2007; Peña 2010).

Durazo wanted youth, elders, and people of all ages and abilities to paint, consistent with Chicana feminist mural practices that have often led to collective community mural painting. The project thus expanded the concept of a mural artist by inviting nonartists to paint, and it stimulated cross-racial solidarity by including non-Chicana/o painters (Latorre 2008). The border mural art project outreach materials advised, "If you think you definitely are not the artsy type, then by all means, there's a project that's going to prove you wrong" (Clarke 1999). The mural project considered anyone who showed up at the site to be an artist, fostering cross-racial,

Figure 4. María del Carmen "Tiny" Durazo and Armando Rascón. Photograph by Ana Clarissa Rojas Durazo.

transnational community building through dialogue, consciousness raising, and mural art practice.

Chicana leadership shaped the unique contours of the mural project from its transnational character and organization to its content. When I worked with the feminist organization Alaíde Foppa in Mexicali on an anti-violence project, I learned that they considered gender-making processes and violence on the border to be shaped by transnational racializing and nation-building discursive formations. According to this approach, the strategies for undoing border violence should therefore be transnationally informed. By fostering transnational relations, the mural project countered the violence of separating communities and Chicanas/Mexicanas north and south of the borderline. It provided a practical and analytic building block to counter the many ways in which this division hinders activism, knowledge production, collective intersubjectivities, and the possibility of reducing border violence.

Chicana/Mexicana leadership opened a space for deeper transformative consideration of the myriad forms of violence deployed on the border. Based on my observation, women's feminist leadership in the project was key in countering and humanizing the militarized hypermasculinities of the border patrol and building community accountability. Statistics show that women and children are at greater risk than men of experiencing sexual violence or being injured or killed while navigating treacherous border crossings. It is possible that the safety of migrant women was enhanced by the mural project's creation of a temporary buffer and friendly no-arrest migrant zone at the mural site (Marrujo 2009; O'Leary 2009).

As the border fence morphed, so too did the militarized hypermasculinities of the border patrol. Sylvanna Falcón (2006) has studied rape and sexual violence as an effect of militarization along the US-Mexico border. The militarization of the border patrol, she contends, leads to the internalization and institutionalization of hypermasculine militarized subjectivities. According to Cynthia Enloe (2000), where there is a military presence, the gendering/sexual ordering of that space is shaped by ideologies that intertwine militarism and sexuality in such a way as to produce masculinities that advance the military's goals. The heteropatriarchal order of the border patrol and the military continually deploys racial-gender constructs that promote violence against Latinas. In her analysis of the heightened violence suffered by the children, partners, and spouses of "a relative in uniform," Enloe posits that militarized training produces a masculinity capable of killing an enemy. She highlights "the potential incompatibility between a social role intended to nurture and sustain another human being and a profession designed to wield violence in the name of the state" (Enloe 2000, 51).

When the leaders of the mural project invited border patrol agents to participate, they created the potential for an intervention in an otherwise highly controlled military training. Structurally, the entrenched masculinized hierarchies of the Border Patrol command were interrupted during their participation in the mural project because in that effort they responded to Chicana civilian and community leadership. When agents took brush in hand and participated, they became painters, and something happened to their bodies. Their faces were rearranged. I saw it with my own eyes. They smiled more. It was as if the weapons they still carried no longer fit. Institutionally, border patrol duties were subverted by the painting; instead of arresting, detaining, and deporting, they painted, carried paint, brought food, and helped with setup, takedown, and cleanup. Their work with the project allowed them to participate in both mural making and community making. This in turn fostered a nurturing humanity that countered the institutional training and mandates of the Border Patrol.

Agents desisted from their duties; they saw migrants cross and did not arrest them. Plenty of people jumped the fence to join the painters on the US side. The painters from Mexicali sometimes lingered all day, sitting on top of the border fence, hanging out, talking with painters and even with agents. In this artistic and social exchange, the migrants and Mexicali folks who had been constructed as enemy subjects and threats to national security by border patrol training were humanized. Migrants became part of the mural project or were able to cross through it; it became a safe buffer zone. They were free, like the birds I love to watch as they fly freely across the fence.[7]

Folks from the Mexicali side brought food and drinks; they broke bread with Border Patrol agents. The mural project suspended and subverted the agents' otherwise potentially violent war subjectivities. Durazo recalled that agents expressed a feeling of shame at the idea of arresting anyone in the vicinity of the mural and within view of the painters. The mural project fostered a strong community sensibility as people spoke with pride and a renewed sense of collective agency that inspired a kind of community accountability to the mural. It reconnected a transnational community that had been divided by the fence. Not a single arrest was made at the border mural site for the three years the painters were there. The mural project was a striking, if temporary, intervention in the border war and the war against migrants.

Speaking of the transformative power of art, Merleau-Ponty (1964) wrote that a painter is born through the act of painting, gaining a new visibility, "seeing anew." The border mural project offered a new way of seeing that served to undo the ways that violence and war splinter bodies, kinship structures, and communities. The project countered the hypersurveillance of border militarization so that subjects emerged through practices and imaginings that interrupted the epistemologies of the state. When we became painters, we saw the world anew. We saw what was made unseen in ourselves and one another and on the natural landscape deep into the earth that grieves, heals, and renews; we became healers stitching across divisions. As the site(s) and sight(s) of division were transformed by a work of art, we too were transformed. It was a reminder of the ways in which our practices create meanings and magic that we routinely invoke, as generations of communities along the border have done since before the creation of a US-Mexico border.

The border art project recently celebrated the tenth anniversary of the mural's completion. I want to recognize and thank my mother, María del Carmen "Tiny" Durazo, along with Armando Rascón, Brenda Hinojosa, Hildy Carrillo, Steve Wong, Manina, the *tías* and *primas* and all the members of the community who made this mural a possibility. They labored with hearts on their paintbrushes to build the dream that a little art project could, if for an instant, call up the power to stop a war.

Notes

"We Morph War into Magic: The Story of the Border Fence Mural, a Community Art Project in Calexico-Mexicali," by Ana Clarissa Rojas Durazo, is reprinted from *Aztlán: A Journal of Chicano Studies* 38, no. 1 (2013).

I write with deepest love and gratitude to honor my mother's labor, her vision, and her spirit that teaches me every day how to do the work of brewing justice. I write in awe of the spirit and dedication, the smiles and the tremendous effort it took for an entire community to imagine and paint itself, and the border fence, anew. A note of gratitude to Gloria Anzaldúa for her mentorship and guidance.

1. M. Jacqui Alexander reminds us that "the state has an abiding investment in war, in owning and deploying the means of violence and coercion in the society" (2005, 114). She comments on the importance of thinking about both discursive and material processes because of the ways in which public symbols are used to engender US preeminence in the creation of new social orders and to legitimate war.

2. The synchronicity of Operation Gatekeeper and Proposition 187, both mobilized in California in 1994, worked to expand the borderlands and the logics, practices, captivities, and casualties of the border war. In explaining his concept of "governmentality," Foucault argues that "criminality was constituted as an object of knowledge [through which] a certain 'consciousness' of criminality could be formed (including the image which criminals might have of themselves, and the representation of criminals which the rest of us might entertain)" (1984, 338).

3. On *rasquachismo*, a concept elaborated by Tomás Ybarra-Frausto and Amalia Mesa-Bains, see Barnet-Sánchez (2005).

4. While the initial idea was to paint the mural on both sides of the fence, discussions with the community in Mexicali led to the discovery that much of the border fence stood on the private property of Mexicali residents, which made it difficult to get approval. Still, many community members in Mexicali were deeply invested in the vision of the mural, and they participated in mural activities, including painting.

5. Although my tendency is to recognize the multiplicity of border communities participating in the project, the people involved in the project I spoke with, as well as the project documents I analyzed, all spoke of community in the singular, emphasizing their consternation at the attempt to divide with the border fence. Respecting the spirit of the project, I have adhered to their usage of "community" as a singular noun.

6. Rosa-Linda Fregoso's "Toward a Planetary Civil Society" (2003) is an excellent account of the contemporary ordering of Mexican women's gender/sexuality through new (transnational) nationalist public discourses on morality

and the continued bifurcation (and gendering) of public/private domains along the US-Mexico border. She cautions, in her analysis of the violence and responses to violence in Juárez, that among the dangerous consequences of this recent iteration of patriarchal transnational nationalism is a kind of violence emerging from social and political institutions that blames women for the violence they experience.

7. Armando Rascón took a beautiful series of photographs of Mexicali painters sitting on the ledge, "as if like birds," he said.

Works Cited

Agamben, Giorgio. 1998. *Homo Sacer: Sovereign Power and Bare Life*. Palo Alto, CA: Stanford University Press.

Alarcón, Norma. 1994. "The Work of Armando Rascón: T(r)opographies for a Critical Imaginary." In *Occupied Aztlán: Armando Rascón: Adaline Kent Award Exhibition*, 11–15. Exhibition catalog. San Francisco: San Francisco Art Institute.

Alexander, M. Jacqui. 2005. *Pedagogies of Crossing: Meditations on Feminism, Sexual Politics, and the Sacred*. Durham, NC: Duke University Press.

Althusser, Louis. 1971. "Ideology and Ideological State Apparatuses." In *Lenin and Philosophy and Other Essays*, 85–126. New York: Monthly Review Press.

Anzaldúa, Gloria. 1987. *Borderlands/La Frontera: The New Mestiza*. San Francisco: Aunt Lute.

———. 2009. "Border Arte: Nepantla, el Lugar de la Frontera." In *The Gloria Anzaldúa Reader*, edited by AnaLouise Keating, 176–86. Durham, NC: Duke University Press.

Barnet-Sánchez, Holly. 2005. "Tomás Ybarra-Frausto and Amalia Mesa-Bains: A Critical Discourse from Within." *Art Journal* 64, no. 4: 91–93.

Barron, Stephanie, Sheri Bernstein, and Ilene Susan Fort. 2000. *Made in California: Art, Image, and Identity, 1900–2000*. Berkeley: University of California Press.

Bejarano, Cynthia L. 2005. *¿Qué Onda? Urban Youth Culture and Border Identity*. Tucson: University of Arizona Press.

Berger, John. 1990. *Ways of Seeing*. New York: Penguin.

Blackwell, Maylei. 2011. *¡Chicana Power! Contested Histories of Feminism in the Chicano Movement*. Austin: University of Texas Press.

Bonetti, D. 2002. "Ugly Fence Becomes Work of Art: Artist Makes Mural of Mexican Border." *San Francisco Chronicle*, January 8.

Cantú, Lionel Jr. 2009. *The Sexuality of Migration: Border Crossings and Mexican Immigrant Men*. New York: New York University Press.

Castañeda, Antonia I. 2005. "Malinche, Calafia y Toypurina: Of Myths, Monsters and Embodied History." In *Feminism, Nation and Myth: La Malinche*, edited by Rolando Romero and Amanda Nolacea Harris, 82–97. Houston: Arte Público.

Chacón, Justin Akers, and Mike Davis. 2006. *No One Is Illegal: Fighting Racism and State Violence on the U.S.-Mexico Border*. Chicago: Haymarket Books.

Clarke, T. 1999. "That Border Art Project We Can All Do." *Valley Women Magazine* (Imperial Valley Press, El Centro, CA), Summer, 1.

Contreras, Sheila Marie. 2008. *Bloodlines: Myth, Indigenism, and Chicana/o Literature*. Austin: University of Texas Press.

Cornelius, Wayne A. 2001. *Death at the Border: Efficacy and "Unintended" Consequences of US Immigration Control Policy, 1993–2000*. Working Paper. San Diego: Center for Comparative Immigration Studies, University of California.

Dunn, Timothy J. 1996. *The Militarization of the U.S.-Mexico Border, 1978–1992: Low-Intensity Conflict Doctrine Comes Home*. Austin: University of Texas, Center for Mexican American Studies.

Enloe, Cynthia. 2000. *Maneuvers: The International Politics of Militarizing Women's Lives*. Berkeley: University of California Press.

Falcón, Sylvanna. 2006. "Securing the Nation through the Violation of Women's Bodies: Militarized Border Rape at the US-Mexico Border." In *Color of Violence: The Incite! Anthology*, edited by Incite! Women of Color Against Violence, 119–29. Boston: South End Press.

Foucault, Michel. 1995. *Discipline and Punish: The Birth of the Prison*. New York: Vintage.

Fregoso, Rosa-Linda. 2003. *meXicana Encounters: The Making of Social Identities on the Borderlands*. Berkeley: University of California Press.

Fregoso, Rosa-Linda, and Cynthia Bejarano, eds. 2010. *Terrorizing Women: Feminicide in the Américas*. Durham, NC: Duke University Press.

Gaspar de Alba, Alicia, and Georgina Guzmán, eds. 2010. *Making a Killing: Femicide, Free Trade, and La Frontera*. Austin: University of Texas Press.

Glenn, Evelyn Nakano. 2004. *Unequal Freedom: How Race and Gender Shaped American Citizenship and Labor*. Cambridge, MA: Harvard University Press.

Guidotti-Hernández, Nicole M. 2011. *Unspeakable Violence: Remapping US and Mexican National Imaginaries*. Durham, NC: Duke University Press.

Gutiérrez, Ramón A. 2010. "A History of Latina/o Sexualities." In *Latina/o Sexualities: Probing Powers, Passions, Practices, and Policies*, edited by Marysol Asencio, 13–37. New Brunswick, NJ: Rutgers University Press.

Hernández, Kelly Lytle. 2010. *Migra! A History of the U.S. Border Patrol*. Berkeley: University of California Press.

Hill, Linda, and AlexandraMary Kelada. 2010. "The US-Mexico Border, San Diego and Imperial Counties: Changes to Policy and Structure, with Concomitant Trends in Injury and Death Rates." *SciTopics*, October 6.

Incite! Women of Color Against Violence. 2007. *The Revolution Will Not Be Funded: Beyond the Non-Profit Industrial Complex*. Boston: South End Press.

Latorre, Guisela. 2008. *Walls of Empowerment: Chicana/o Indigenist Murals of California*. Austin: University of Texas Press.

Lugo, Alejandro. 2008. *Fragmented Lives, Assembled Parts: Culture, Capitalism, and Conquest at the U.S.-Mexico Border*. Austin: University of Texas Press.

Lugones, Maria. 2007. "Heterosexualism and the Colonial/Modern Gender System." *Hypatia* 22, no. 1: 186–209.

Luibheid, Eithne. 2007. "'Looking Like a Lesbian': The Organization of Sexual Monitoring at the United States–Mexican Border." In Segura and Zavella 2007, 106–33.

Luke, Gregorio. 2011. "Murals Under the Stars: David Alfaro Siqueiros." Lecture at Museum of Latin American Art, Long Beach, CA, July 31.

Marrujo, Olivia T. Ruiz. 2009. "Women, Migration, and Sexual Violence: Lessons from Mexico's Borders." In *Human Rights along the U.S.-Mexico Border: Gendered Violence and Insecurity*, edited by Kathleen Staudt, Tony Payan, and Z. Anthony Kruszewski, 31–47. Tucson: University of Arizona Press.

McCaughan, Edward J. 2012. *Art and Social Movements: Cultural Politics in Mexico and Aztlán.* Durham, NC: Duke University Press.

Merleau-Ponty, Maurice. 1964. *The Primacy of Perception.* Evanston, IL: Northwestern University Press.

Mignolo, Walter D. 2005. *The Idea of Latin America.* Malden, MA: Blackwell.

Monárrez Fragoso, Julia Estela, and María Socorro Tabuenca Córdoba, eds. 2007. *Bordeando la violencia contra las mujeres en la frontera norte de México.* Tijuana, Mexico: Colegio de la Frontera Norte.

Nevins, Joseph. 2001. *Operation Gatekeeper: The Rise of the "Illegal Alien" and the Making of the U.S.-Mexico Boundary.* New York: Routledge.

O'Leary, Anna Ochoa. 2009. "In the Footsteps of Spirits: Migrant Women's Testimonios in a Time of Heightened Border Enforcement." In *Human Rights along the U.S.-Mexico Border: Gendered Violence and Insecurity*, edited by Kathleen Staudt, Tony Payan, and Z. Anthony Kruszewski, 85–105. Tucson: University of Arizona Press.

Payan, Tony. 2006. *The Three U.S.-Mexico Border Wars: Drugs, Immigration, and Homeland Security.* Westport, CT: Praeger Security International.

Peña, S. 2010. "Latina/o Sexualities in Motion: Latina/o Sexualities Research Agenda Project." In *Latina/o Sexualities: Probing Powers, Passions, Practices, and Policies*, edited by Marysol Asencio, 188–206. New Brunswick, NJ: Rutgers University Press.

Pérez, Laura E. 2007. *Chicana Art: The Politics of Spiritual and Aesthetic Altarities.* Durham, NC: Duke University Press.

Rodríguez, Richard T. 2009. *Next of Kin: The Family in Chicano/a Cultural Politics.* Durham, NC: Duke University Press.

Rueda Esquibel, Catrióna. 2006. *With Her Machete in Her Hand: Reading Chicana Lesbians.* Austin: University of Texas Press.

Segura, Denise A., and Patricia Zavella, eds. 2007. *Women and Migration in the U.S.-Mexico Borderlands: A Reader.* Durham, NC: Duke University Press.

Selz, Peter, and Susan Landauer. 2006. *Art of Engagement: Visual Politics in California and Beyond.* Berkeley: University of California Press.

Spivak, Gayatri Chakravorty. 1988. "Can the Subaltern Speak?" In *Marxism and the Interpretation of Culture*, edited by Cary Nelson and Lawrence Grossberg, 271–315. Basingstoke, UK: Macmillan.

USACE (US Army Corps of Engineers). 1997. "Fence Construction and Maintenance Calexico, California. Final Environmental Assessment, JTF-6 Border." Department of Homeland Security Library, Fort Worth District, Texas. http://www.dhs.gov/xlibrary/assets/nepa/Mgmt_NEPA_FEA-FONSIJTF6brdrfence-constr-maintcalexicoCAmar1.pdf.

The Chicanx Poster Workshop
A Space Where Subjectivity Is Produced

Carlos Francisco Jackson

I frame my printmaking and writing practice as that of a cultural worker. After starting in 2003 as a lecturer at the University of California (UC), Davis, in 2007 I became an assistant professor in the Chicana and Chicano Studies Department, where I assumed leadership of the art curriculum after the retirement of Malaquias Montoya in 2008. Assigned the task of establishing a community-based art center, I served from 2005 to 2015 as founding director of the Taller Arte del Nuevo Amanecer (TANA). In 2009 TANA moved to its current location in Woodland, a largely Chicana/o and Latina/o community ten miles north of UC Davis. I have been deeply committed to teaching and expanding access to the Poster Workshop, a curricular space within the Chicana/o Studies Department that is now held at TANA's Woodland facility.

Paper is the primary material I utilize in my practice. It is the substrate for poster production and the material that facilitates dialogue within the Poster Workshop. In the workshop, subject formation occurs through a praxis that combines dialogue about critical issues facing the community with strategies to achieve transformation. The Poster Workshop at UC Davis is in its twenty-seventh year, and during its existence several thousand individual poster projects have been produced by students and community members. These posters are now held within the department's Chicana/o Studies Poster Archive. My review of the archive demonstrates students and community members engaging in a rigorous process of interrogating and creating new identities and subjectivities. In this respect, Chicanx posters demonstrate that Chicanx identity is fluid, in development, and open for creation, a finding that contests the widespread notion that Chicanx identity is a fixed category that is manifested in predictable ways. According to cultural critic and feminist theorist Rosa-Linda Fregoso, "Chicano" is a self-identified category and identity produced through efforts to achieve social justice. She resolves the question of what "Chicano" represents "by de-emphasizing the biological claims to authenticity, yet accentuating its productive quality. In this respect, Chicano refers to a space where subjectivity is produced" (Fregoso 1993, xix). Her analysis is useful in thinking through Chicanx posters and the Poster Workshop as spaces for subjectivity creation.

I write this essay at a time when postrace and post-Chicano discourse is being adopted and manifested within new scholarship and cultural critique. It is also a time when social media and digital design have become the dominant forms of communication, especially among younger generations of cultural workers. In light of these forces, the Chicanx poster might seem to be a cultural form that is irrelevant to the contemporary moment. I argue that it is not, and I will share some brief reflections on how the poster (and by extension the Poster Workshop) remains a relevant tool for creating community while facilitating the formation of Chicanx subjectivity. In this context, I honor paper as a meaningful and necessary substrate that facilitates this process.

This essay discusses the methods that I use to teach the Poster Workshop courses at UC Davis and relates those methods to the way Chicana/o art was integrated as a central element of the Chicana/o studies curriculum during formation of the discipline. Utilizing archives in the Ethnic Studies Library at the University of California, Berkeley, I review the establishment of the Chicano Art Center at UC Berkeley, precursor to the UC Davis community-based arts curriculum, and show how arts curriculum was a core element in the formation of Chicana/o studies. I ask: if artistic studio/workshop courses had been valued and expanded within Chicana/o studies in its early days, would there be more spaces today for community-based and decolonial artistic methodologies within the discipline? Would there be more opportunities for Chicanx artists to serve as faculty within Chicana/o studies, leading the discussion, not as objects of study but as intellectual guides? Lastly, I discuss the development of community-based arts curriculum within Chicana/o studies at UC Davis and the methodologies of the Poster Workshop as it is taught today. I argue that the artistic and cultural methods that were effective during the Chicana/o movement remain relevant and should be expanded so that artists are centered within the discipline, not simply as objects of study but as educators and producers of knowledge. Throughout this discussion, I recognize paper as the material that facilitates the historical and contemporary practice of Chicanx poster making, which is one artistic method of many that remain relevant to social justice community-based efforts.

Throughout my time at UC Davis, I have continuously questioned my practice as an educator and administrator for both university and community arts curricula. I teach a range of courses in my department, but my primary courses are the introductory and advanced Poster Workshops. In interrogating my practice, I question whether the Poster Workshop remains a relevant curricular emphasis within Chicana/o studies. Today, social media is the primary platform and digital media a primary tool used to disseminate content for social justice movements. The majority of students who are currently establishing creative careers, because they were inspired to become social protest image makers, are seeking instruction in the technical aspects of digital graphics programs such as Illustrator, InDesign, and Photoshop, as well as coding/programming applications. The screen-printed poster is no longer the most effective means for disseminating information and supporting social movements, which were the two primary purposes of poster making when the Chicana/o studies curriculum was in its most formative stage.

Chicana/o art scholarship has characterized the poster as a relic of the earliest phases of the movement. The seminal exhibition *Just Another Poster?* (2000–3), and its accompanying catalog, framed Chicana/o print production into periods. Terezita Romo outlines three broad phases of Chicana/o poster making: the first is "Seize the Moment: The Chicano Poster, Politics, and Protest, 1965–1972"; next is "Synthesis: The Chicano Poster and Cultural Reclamation, 1972–1982"; and last is "Selling the Vision: The Chicano Poster as Art, 1983–Present." She further states,

> The evolution of the poster began in 1965 with the production of graphic work for the United Farm Workers' organizing and boycotting efforts, both within and outside the union. During the 1970s, the artistic process and iconography developed further with the advent of artist-led collectives throughout California . . . In the early 1980s, the Chicano poster entered an era of commodification . . . within each of these phases, Chicano poster production was marked by distinct changes in intent and iconography. (2001, 93)

Romo thus sees Chicana/o poster making as primarily relevant to the community during the first period, 1965–72. The second period marked a departure from the direct militancy of earlier prints in favor of artistic production that "had as a central goal the formation and affirmation of Chicano cultural identity" (100). In an article on the print archive of Self Help Graphics & Art, Colin Gunckel affirms this analysis. Referring to Romo's second period, he states, "In fact, the first decade of [Self Help's] existence (1972–82) coincides precisely with Tere Romo's astute periodization of Chicano silkscreen production and its tendency toward 'cultural reclamation'" (2011, 159). Within this chronological framework, the third and current phase is that of "fine-art" printmaking, which is aimed at producing a market for Chicana/o art. In this way, the Chicana/o "poster" morphed into the Chicana/o "print." Whereas the poster engages social movements and community and is not handled as a precious item, the print is fragile/precious, numbered and signed, so that it can be exhibited and sold within artistic environments. Today I continue to teach the Poster Workshop, and I believe its processes and outcomes remain relevant, ultimately challenging this periodization.

While scholars in Chicana/o studies historicize the poster, it is also at the farthest reaches of the periphery within contemporary art discourse. The orientation of mainstream art discourse and practice is to seek validation through the exhibition of artwork in commercial galleries and mainstream art museums. These hegemonic structures frame the poster as didactic propaganda and/or as a product of "design." I've often asked myself, are Chicanx posters "art"? Am I teaching "art making"? If hegemonic art structures see the poster as propaganda, and Chicana/o scholars see the poster as a relic of a movement that currently has no form (in a postmovement era), then what relevance does the poster have to my practice as an artist and faculty member within Chicana/o studies?

The spring 2015 issue of Aztlán produced an important dossier titled "Teaching Chicana/o and Latina/o Art History in the Twenty-First Century." Alma López's article, "Artists as Migrant Workers: From Community to University Teaching," provides a powerful statement about the role of the Chicanx artists within both Chicana/o studies departments and art departments. López states, "We are rarely employed as tenure-track faculty in art departments. In fact, I can't think of a single tenure-track Chicana artist in a University of California art department." Furthermore, "It has become commonplace for academic departments, including Chicana/o studies departments, to require those applying for a full-time tenure track position—even if the position is to teach studio art—to have a PhD. In fact, in the last few years all the arts-related teaching jobs in academic departments such as Chicano studies in which I was interested required a PhD" (López 2015, 183). López's article makes clear that institutional support for established and emerging Chicanx artists is in a state of crisis.

In my view, this lack of institutional support is not due to any lack of quality or quantity with respect to artists; rather, the main issue is how artistic methodologies from the Chicanx community have been supported and taught inside the academy. López highlights an important question: how has Chicana/o studies taken ownership of the cultural/artistic methods that emerged out of the movement? How have those practices become part of the curriculum and scholarship that advances the creation of culture? Chicana/o studies departments that teach Chicana/o art, not simply as an object of study but as a method of creation, are extremely rare. I ask: how do we work within neoliberal institutions to effect a shift so that artists can have a place within the discipline, in the classroom/workshop, leading and participating in the dialogue?

The introduction of an arts curriculum into the Chicano Studies Program at UC Berkeley is an important example that is also foundational to the history of the Poster Workshop. The Chicano Studies Program (as it was then called) came into being as a result of the Third World Liberation Front (TWLF) strike at UC Berkeley in 1969. TWLF was a coalition of students seeking to decolonize the university. Toward this end, they sought to establish a set of academic programs and departments to facilitate the broader self-determination efforts that were at the heart of the civil rights struggles of historically marginalized communities in the United States. The TWLF strike began in January 1969 and concluded with a negotiated settlement in April. By the fall of that year the Chicano Studies Program was created and began offering courses within the Department of Ethnic Studies, established under the agreement in response to the TWLF demand for a Third World College.[1]

As stated in an early working paper titled "The Conception of a Third World College," the "goal of the Third World College will be to provide an education of the highest quality while allowing students to retain *their cultural identity*, thus enabling them to return to their communities to live and to create an atmosphere conducive to political, social, and economic changes."[2] This ideology underpinned the formation of a Chicano studies that was, in the words of Chela Sandoval, "outlaw studies." Sandoval states that "Chicano studies can be conceived as outlaw studies. It defies disciplinary categorization. Its aim is to advance the knowledge required to comprehend colonizer and colonized psyches, bodies, and cultures throughout the Americas" (Davalos et al. 2002, 149). Chicano studies was "outlaw" because it created methodologies that produced decolonial and oppositional forms of knowledge, beginning the process of undisciplining the academy to support Chicana/o community self-determination.

By the 1970–71 academic year, Chicano studies at UC Berkeley was offering the courses Chicano Art History (118) and Art Workshop (119). In 1972, Advanced Art Workshop (140) was added, along with courses in creative writing and contemporary Chicano theater.[3] As stated in a 1972 letter, "In the area of Art, Chicano Studies has developed the Chicano [Art] Center, under the direction of Malaquias Montoya. Students learn skills in poster making and mural painting, skills which they in turn make available to the community. Hundreds of posters have been produced which are veritable history of La Causa. Our library is in the process of collecting these. In addition, we have over 1,000 color transparencies of important Chicano Art Work."[4] The Chicano Art Center was an off-campus insurgent art center located at a site that had previously been the Anna Head School for Girls, at 2538 Channing Way in Berkeley. It was here that Montoya and his students had made posters for the TWLF strike through an occupation of the space in 1969. In 1970 Montoya worked to establish the space as an off-campus studio to facilitate the development of an arts curriculum for the Chicano Studies Program. Both Montoya and Luis Valdez taught courses during the 1970–71 academic year at this location, with Valdez leading the Chicano Theater Workshop course. Montoya taught the Art Workshop curriculum until 1974.[5]

The formation of the Chicano Studies Program at UC Berkeley was marked by a deep commitment to valuing art practice as an activity central to the discipline. Chicano art practice was a curricular and intellectual engagement aligned with the critique, analysis, and investigation of culture, history, and society. The Art Workshop, as stated in the 1972 syllabus, was "mainly designed to give Chicano students an awareness of art as a medium of culture and of communication."[6] The Advanced Art Workshop syllabus from the same year was "designed for advanced students interested in developing their art as a means of social and political communication." The course offered "mural painting and advanced poster art" as the two media that students would use to engage the community through the development of new "cultural symbols and forms."[7] From the very formation of art practice within Chicano studies in 1969, professors named the curriculum a "workshop," not a "studio."[8] The term "workshop" signaled a praxis based on community engagement and dialogue that were not valued within traditional studio art courses.

The program identified the mural and poster as unique visual forms ideally situated to work toward three goals: to develop new symbols/signs to represent the new ideology and identity of the movement, to communicate those signs/symbols to a broader Chicano/Latino community, and to develop the visual arts as a tangible tool to support social movements. As stated explicitly in its syllabus, the Art Workshop was "designed to show the relationship between artistic creation and community action, as both an educational tool and as a catalyst for social change."[9] As the mural and poster were accessible visual forms utilized during the emergence of the student movement and labor movement across the United States, these methods became central visual tools to encourage transformation backed by rigorous community engagement and research.

The Chicano Art Center was both a community resource and a classroom for UC Berkeley students. Romo states that while "the class [Art Workshop] was listed as meeting for three hours twice a week, Montoya conducted it as an open studio from eight in the morning until six in the evening, Monday through Thursday" (2011, 34). At the beginning of the quarter, the Art Workshop and Advanced Art Workshop were structured around demonstrations and instruction, and then "for the rest of the semester the class became a 'continuous, ongoing print shop'" (55). The insurgent nature of the Chicano Art Center and its community-based oppositional praxis is clearly evident in archival materials that document the space, which I located in an unorganized storage cabinet at the UC Berkeley Ethnic Studies Library. These materials include slides showing the Chicano Art Center's environment and some of the posters produced during the early phase of the Art Workshop (figs. 1, 2). The center, as represented in these slides, is a space where a collective of students, or perhaps community members, are actively working on developing screenprint posters. The walls are covered with political graffiti and posters from floor to ceiling, giving a sense of the intensity of the work under way. These archival materials demonstrate what must have been a powerful dialogue facilitated through the activity of poster making. I imagine discussion, debate, problem solving, and celebration occurring within this space, all facilitated through the collective making of prints.

In 1989, fifteen years after resigning from UC Berkeley, Montoya accepted a teaching position in the Chicana/o Studies Department at UC Davis. Tasked with leading the community-based art curriculum, Montoya taught courses called Mural Workshop (CHI 171), Poster Workshop (CHI 172), Survey of Chicana/o Art (CHI 70), and Cultural Expression through

Figure 1. Chicano Art Center, 1969. Image courtesy of the Chicano Studies Collection, Ethnic Studies Library, University of California, Berkeley.

Figure 2. Chicano Art Center, 1969. Image courtesy of the Chicano Studies Collection, Ethnic Studies Library, University of California, Berkeley.

348

Silkscreen (CHI 73). In its structure, the curriculum resembled the one instituted in the early days of Chicano studies at UC Berkeley. Montoya's hiring demonstrated the UC Davis faculty's commitment to and valuing of studio/community–based art creation as a key component of the inter-disciplinary Chicana/o Studies Department. This complemented the art focus of the Native American Studies Department, where faculty member George Longfish was already teaching art courses while also directing the department's Gorman Museum.

Since 2003 I have taught the Poster Workshop (CHI 172) twenty-one times. I teach the workshop with limited material requirements, so that students who are on financial aid or come from low-income backgrounds can afford to take a studio course. Students typically create three poster projects in editions of twenty to twenty-five, although the edition size can be significantly larger if there is a need to support a large community campaign. Within the upper-division Poster Workshop, dissemination of the posters to local community organizations or for community events is required. The Poster Workshop is divided into two parts: the first three weeks are dedicated to instruction, and the following seven weeks consist of poster production. Before production begins, workshop participants are expected to develop a poster topic that is relevant to the community and to their lives.

Throughout the period that I have directed the Poster Workshop at UC Davis, I have changed the course structure minimally, although I have significantly revised how assignments are framed within the syllabus. Montoya's 1999 Poster Workshop syllabus calls on students to "be responsible for selecting a particular theme, researching it and making an informal presentation to the class before beginning their prints." This direction is followed by a series of possible themes, including "Middle East, Health Rights, Drugs, Unemployment (workers), Capitalism, Racism, Imperialism, Central American, Props. 187, 209, 227, Women's Issues, Aids, Chiapas."[10] I was an enrolled student in this 1999 workshop and recall how important the syllabus and its direction were to my understanding of what I should do in the course. As the faculty member now responsible for leading the Poster Workshop, I outline the process for developing poster topics in the following manner:

> The issues addressed in the posters created by workshop participants should engage this idea: that there is a role for all types of work in the collective effort to create self-determination for a community that has been historically denied the structural and individual resources to

achieve it. Visual artists, designers, and cultural workers of all types can and should contribute to visualizing the imaginary that is a new, better, and more equitable future. Equity and representation should be at the center of the themes and images put forward by workshop participants. Posters can be broadly defined but also should have a tangible application within community.[11]

I encourage students to engage the broader community through their poster making, but also to see themselves as creating community within the workshop. The community I ask students to create is one where there is no center or periphery; rather, it is a community that is infinitely generous in its boundaries. In this way students are urged to create the workshop as a world where many worlds are possible. I recognize that this is an aspiration and that it requires constant interrogation of privilege. What students share in the workshop is a common commitment to engage in social justice efforts through their contributions to community. The workshop could very easily be taught in a hierarchical manner, with the artists acting as the voice for the community and expecting special privilege in their process of creation. Having experienced spaces that are directed in this manner, I actively work to facilitate a different form of engagement.

Critics often frame Chicana/o poster making as an essentialist practice that manifests predictably around stereotypical representations of identity. A critical article written by Josh Kun (2005) in the *Los Angeles Times Magazine*, profiling an emerging generation of Mexican American and Latina/o artists, reinforced the notion that posters are relics of the movement and stereotypical forms of Chicana/o art. Kun quotes Los Angeles artist Camille Rose Garcia: "The Chicano tradition of activism and social commentary is so important to me . . . but if your work is only about identity, a lot of people can't relate to it." For some time now I have been confused by suggestions that Chicana/o art is "only about identity." I would argue instead that Chicanx art is an expansive method that seeks to manifest social justice. That said, I understand the perspective of critics who believe that art practice centered on identity reinforces hierarchies through forms of art-ethnography and ultimately creates exclusive boundaries around the possibilities of subject formation. Derek Conrad Murray follows that line of inquiry when he states, "The artist-ethnographers are said to achieve their success at the expense of the communities that they represent, and in the process reinscribe the hierarchical abjector-abjected relationship between mainstream and subaltern" (Murray and Murray 2006, 34). In this case, Murray discusses visual art that engages identity as a "voice for the voiceless," whereby the artist represents the voice of the community and reinforces its position of authority over expression, language, and representation.

I have tried to keep this critique in mind when leading the Poster Workshop. I have organized the workshop around the expectation that students will speak from their individual subjectivity, requiring a rigorous process of dialogue within the workshop and among organizations within the community. Both the individual experience and the broader community dialogue creates powerful engagement, which ultimately results in praxis. In its current manifestation, the workshop demands that students speak not "for" the community but rather "from" their experiences "within" the community. According to Fregoso, there is a form of "paternalism in claiming to speak for the community as though its members cannot speak on their own behalf. This is why the video artist Frances Salomé España insists . . . that she speaks not *for* the Chicano community, but *from* the specificity of her experience as a Chicana in L.A." (Fregoso 1993, xix, italics in original). At its best, the workshop is a cacophony of voices as students work together to relate their experiences, education, and passions to the lived realities of their real and imagined communities.

The workshop becomes a powerful educational space, at times a potentially liberatory space, as the course progresses. During the first three weeks I am at the center of the course, outlining the structure for engagement within the workshop and providing technical instruction on screen printing, but during the remaining seven weeks my role recedes. Students are expected to engage with rigor and focused presence while operating within the space. A principle of the workshop, which is constantly reinforced, is that if a student is not working on developing their poster while in the studio, but has some free time, that student should make every effort to assist another student with poster production. Peer assistance can involve racking prints, helping to clean someone's screen, coating screens, or engaging in dialogue around the technical questions of developing the imagery. In my experience, the work that students do to support each other's poster production is a key way to manifest praxis. While the instructor ensures that the foundational approach of the workshop is maintained and that students have the technical instruction necessary for successful screen printing, it is through student-to-student engagement that transformation occurs.

The posters they produce are one outcome that can be used to assess student performance within the traditional grading model of the university.

Yet the engagement within the workshop is the more significant result of the course and ultimately provides the tool that can be replicated in other spaces. This engagement is an "outlaw" method that emerged out of the movement and established itself during Chicana/o studies' formative stage, yet remains relevant and contemporary.

Two posters in the UC Davis Chicana/o Studies Poster Archive, created during the 2015–16 academic year, illustrate the dialogic process of the workshop. One was made by a student who is a straight cisgender male and identifies as Mexican/Chicano. The other is by a student who identifies as a queer, nonbinary Chicanx/Mexicanx. The two students worked independently but eventually developed projects that were heavily informed by each other.[12] Both posters used eyeglasses to metaphorically represent the perspective or lens through which to view the world. The first poster narrates the story of a woman who is wrongfully convicted for the murder of her abusive partner. Inside the lens the student wrote "white patriarchy" and "'Justice' system" to signal how victims of injustice are framed by colonial logic (fig. 3). On the other hand, the lenses in the second poster represent how oppositional forms of knowledge inform current social justice movements. This poster shows a pair of eyeglasses viewing the US flag; one lens contains the famous *Daily News* cover that addressed the acquittal of George Zimmerman in the death of Trayvon Martin (fig. 4). Looking through the lenses in this poster represents the consciousness developed through education, what Gloria Anzaldúa called "taking inventory" and "winnowing out the lies" (1987, 82). Neither of these posters would have been possible without a dialogic process among the students and a foundational expectation that they would address issues that are pressing within their community context. I was deeply inspired by the dialogue and engagement these two students developed during their time in the Poster Workshop, and I know this to be one of many similar engagements that have produced powerful outcomes.

In my experience, the poster workshop remains a relevant method. I recognize and appreciate the scholarly efforts that have proposed periodization of the Chicana/o poster, rendering it an artifact of the movement. Yet I have witnessed countless students address contemporary issues that are quite literally matters of life and death. I recognize that this is in some ways a subjective judgment, yet I believe my engagement and the poster archives provide evidence to support it. I also recognize that digital media are the most effective tools we have today to disseminate information. Community organizations doing social justice work often

Figure 3. Student artist, White Patriarchy, 2015. Screen print, 24 × 18 inches. Created at the UC Davis Chicana/o Studies Poster Workshop. Image courtesy of the UC Davis Chicana/o Studies Poster Archive.

Figure 4. Student artist, American Dream/American Nightmare, 2015. Screen print, 18 x 24 inches. Created at the UC Davis Chicana/o Studies Poster Workshop. Image courtesy of the UC Davis Chicana/o Studies Poster Archive.

need designers who can manipulate and generate imagery and content via digital media and platforms, perhaps more than they need a screen-printed poster. Despite this, there continues to be a high demand from community organizations and campaigns for handmade screen prints that engage and support their efforts. The material of the workshop—paper—and the process of poster making facilitate a dialogue that is highly speculative and at the same time relevant to contemporary issues. It is speculative in that the process and the imagery produced allow for the creation of community and for representation of a world in which social justice is possible. Quite simply, what feels endlessly relevant to me is the space that is created through the facilitated process of collectively creating posters. The space encourages dialogue and engagement that results in praxis and, ultimately, transformation.

Notes

"The Chicanx Poster Worship: A Space Where Subjectivity Is Produced," by Carlos Francisco Jackson, is reprinted from *Aztlán: A Journal of Chicano Studies* 42, no. 1 (2017).

1. The Chicano Studies Program was one of four programs established as part of the new Department of Ethnic Studies. Documented in the Third World Liberation Front strike newspaper, 1969, carton 120, Third World Strike at University of California, Berkeley collection, Ethnic Studies Library, University of California, Berkeley.

2. Third World Liberation Front, "The Conception of a Third World College," working paper, February 7, 1969, Chicano Studies Collection, Ethnic Studies Library, University of California, Berkeley.

3. "Chicano Studies Bulletin, Spring 1971," carton 7:16, Chicano Studies Collection, Ethnic Studies Library, University of California, Berkeley.

4. "Response to Ad Hoc Committee to Review Ethnic Studies Questionnaire," 1972, carton 2:1, Chicano Studies Collection, Ethnic Studies Library, University of California, Berkeley. The center is misnamed in the letter as the Chicano Center; its actual name was the Chicano Art Center.

5. Myrtha Chabran and Malaquias Montoya, "Reassessment of Chicano Studies," March 27, 1974, Chicano Studies Collection, Ethnic Studies Library, University of California, Berkeley.

6. Malaquias Montoya, syllabus for "Ch.S. 119: Art Workshop," 1972–73, carton 7:37, Chicano Studies Collection, Ethnic Studies Library, University of California, Berkeley

7. Malaquias Montoya, syllabus for "Ch.S. 140: Advanced Art Workshop," 1972–73, carton 7:37, Chicano Studies Collection, Ethnic Studies Library, University of California, Berkeley.

8. "Chicano Courses Offered 1969–1972," from "Schedule of Classes 1969–1974," carton 7:14, Chicano Studies Collection, Ethnic Studies Library, University of California, Berkeley.

9. Montoya, syllabus for "Ch.S. 119."

10. Malaquias Montoya, syllabus for "Chicano Studies 172: The Poster—A Silkscreen Workshop," Winter 1999, University of California, Davis (in author's personal collection).

11. Carlos Francisco Jackson, syllabus for "Chicana/o Studies 172: The Poster Workshop," Summer Session 1, 2015, University of California, Davis (in author's personal collection).

12. I interviewed the two students (whose names are withheld for privacy) in the Chicana/o Studies 172 Poster Workshop, June 1, 2016.

Works Cited

Anzaldúa, Gloria. 1987. *Borderlands/La Frontera: The New Mestiza*. San Francisco: Aunt Lute.

Davalos, Karen Mary, Eric R. Avila, Rafael Pérez-Torres, and Chela Sandoval. 2002. "Roundtable on the State of Chicana/o Studies." *Aztlán: A Journal of Chicano Studies* 27, no. 2: 139–52.

Fregoso, Rosa Linda. 1993. *The Bronze Screen: Chicana and Chicano Film Culture*. Minneapolis: University of Minnesota Press.

Gunckel, Colin. 2011. "Art and Community in East LA: Self Help Graphics & Art from the Archive Room." *Aztlán: A Journal of Chicano Studies* 36, no. 2: 157–70.

Kun, Josh. 2005. "The New Chicano Movement." *Los Angeles Times Magazine*, January 9.

López, Alma. 2015. "Artists as Migrant Workers: From Community to University Teaching." *Aztlán: A Journal of Chicano Studies* 40, no. 1: 177–88.

Murray, Derek Conrad, and Soraya Murray. 2006. "Uneasy Bedfellows: Canonical Art Theory and the Politics of Identity." *Art Journal* 65, no. 1: 22–39.

Romo, Tere. 2001. "Points of Convergence: The Iconography of the Chicano Poster." In *Just Another Poster? Chicano Graphic Arts in California*, exhibition catalog, edited by Chon A. Noriega, 93–108. Santa Barbara: University Art Museum, University of California.

———. 2011. *Malaquias Montoya*. A Ver: Revisioning Art History, vol. 6. Los Angeles: UCLA Chicano Studies Research Center Press.

Place and Perspective in the Shadow of the Wall
Recovering Ndé Knowledge and Self-Determination in Texas

Margo Tamez

In 2013, five years after the United States constructed an eighteen-foot-high, steel and concrete, gulag-style wall along the Texas-Mexico border, colonialist laws and practices work to conceal the violent effects of the wall, militarization, and necropolitics on local Indigenous peoples. Along the border, the wall slices through Indigenous peoples' lands, separating them from subsistence lands, sacred sites, and customary places collectively shared. Land loss and ongoing destruction of Indigenous lifeways has increased displacement, further fragmenting Indigenous families and disrupting their connection to ancestral communities.[1]

On the Texas border, Ndé (known to anthropologists as "Lipan Apache") experienced extensive land loss and atrocities over generations as settlers enacted colonial violence to target Indigenous peoples and lands. Current experiences of violent dispossession are known through collective memory of Ndé elders and community experts. Land loss seriously denies Indigenous peoples' existence. Continuing dispossession undermines Indigenous continuity. Ndé women are key actors in the movement to revitalize Indigenous languages, food systems, and governance.

As physical and psychosocial architecture, the border wall embodies the US government's use of carceral, or prisonlike, structures and systems to enforce its sovereignty. The government's heavy-fisted procedures for exerting domination over Indigenous peoples reassert Americanization as an authoritarian project along the Lower Rio Grande. Americanization operates to police Indigenous land and water protectors deemed nonassimilating, poor, leftist, nonconforming, and dissident for refusing violent dispossession and settler democracy. Settler democracy in Texas, at the border, functions to uphold powerful interest groups' de jure and de facto immunity to exercise impunity against Indigenous peoples resisting systemic racism and discrimination and exercising Indigenous rights. Some of the effects are to intensify race- and gender-based violence, atrocities, massacres, trafficking, land dispossession, militarization, paramilitary activities, and official repression. Indigenous survival depends on land protection, on human rights protection, and rights to transmit knowledge to the community. Indigenous peoples must be able to produce, reproduce, and disseminate memory and knowledge to future generations and must be free to exercise and access justice. The rights to knowledge and to truth, and to name—actively repressed in this region both before and after construction of the wall—are being redefined by Indigenous peoples such as the Ndé.

This essay critiques the repression of Indigenous land-based knowledge in southern Texas. Through the lenses of place and perspective, I draw upon Indigenous peoples' historical knowledge to counter a carceral order of subjugation exemplified by the border wall. Indigenous peoples' resistance is built upon anti-colonial consciousness, collective memory, and clan-kinship forms of social organization and self-determination in the Texas-Mexico borderlands. I am interested in recovering histories of Indigenous communities where armed resistance to occupation and dispossession in the region occurred across generations. One example is El Calaboz Ranchería and its related sister communities in Cameron County, an area that has received little attention by scholars. Place and perspective constitute Indigenous lenses on the necropolitical, a core characteristic of the subjugation imposed upon Indigenous peoples. Dispossession and subordination—social, economic, and legal—is a theme running through intergenerational narratives about being dominated and traumatized through violence in Ndé peoples' homeland. For instance, Texas roadside history markers portray a violent process of Spanish, Anglo, and Texan race-based blood wars—aimed at removing, subjugating and controlling Indigenous peoples. Such structures celebrate Indigenous destruction as necessary and sanctioned. These hagiographic records chronicle and constitute an official settler memory of Texas. My work here aims to unsettle that project.

Indigenous traumatic memory is a broad band of brightly hued threaded contexts in the Ndé view of occupation. Yet Indigenous knowledge and knowing from an Ndé perspective is hemmed in and driven under, out of sight of official inspection, in the larger colonial weavings of official history, which normalize dominion as desirable colorizations. I entered the Indigenous knowledge stream in 1962, when I was born into it, and I have lived it into the present. Throughout this essay I provide fragments of Indigenous orality and memory to embody the repression.

In order to reflect on the wall as a weaving of many competing and shared histories, it is necessary to take account of Indigenous adaptations and continuity in spite of the settler society. Through the spaces between the thick steel bars of the wall, Ndé grandmothers stare down the Texas-Mexico border, a key structure of authority and power embedded in local memory and deeply naturalized and familiar to our sense of place. The naturalizing of dispossession and borders and the constraints imposed upon Indigenous peoples' ability to adapt have played a role in their present-day struggles to defend their rights to know, to collective memory, to self-determination, and to decision making regarding their lives, customary lands, territories, and resources beyond borders.

Personal memories of my own life experiences, conversations with Ndé people, and the insights I gleaned through research in 2010–12 inform my process of knowledge recovery with, for, and alongside Ndé elders, women, and hereditary chiefs. While working on collaborative history projects related to collective land rights on the Texas-Mexico border, I sought to develop and clarify the Indigenous, international law, and human rights legal principles that confront the pillars of racism, ideology, and discrimination that uphold the Texas-Mexico border wall.[2] Personal memory contradicts and unsettles the many erasures and denials that underlie popular distortions of Ndé peoples' history under colonization—distortions that have been mainstreamed in Texas. Through fragments brought into the order of English and the Western dominant mode of scholarly interchange, I posit that Indigenous place and perspective are both dynamic and severely threatened by the framework of domination that usurps indigeneity, Indigenous presence, and Ndé memory.

I. History on Trial

Ndé lineal and inherent relationships with homelands near, along, and across the Rio Grande have too long been denied, relegated to the frozen anthropological artifacts and lethal footnotes left behind by militarized ethnographies. These are the foundations of the American canon of social Darwinism and embedded militarized anthropology camouflaged as empirical science and objectivity. For example, American anthropologists Morris

Opler (1907–96) and Harry Hoijer (1904–76) designed and disseminated a discourse, made official through their state-supported projects, which I have described as "Apache studies." The effort to undermine Ndé knowledge systems, mother tongues, and motherlands was always kept hidden through methods and approaches that enabled Opler and Hoijer to access "data" to construct "Apaches" in ways that directly upheld US imperialism. Rarely do "Apache studies" texts offer an Indigenous perspective on the structurally unequal and unbalanced power relationship between the white American male anthropologist and Indigenous "subjects" from the US-Mexico borderlands. Opler's and Hoijer's careers were founded on the extraction of knowledge from Indigenous peoples. Many of their initial contacts occurred within US carceral systems designed to permanently incarcerate Indigenous peoples in various types of open-air containment pens.

Opler's and Hoijer's "subjects," often the adult and elderly survivors of late nineteenth-century extermination wars against "Apaches," were undergoing processes of violent Americanization. Many had been abducted, captured, and taken prisoner during the nineteenth-century wars to occupy the Ndé homelands in the territory that is now the US Southwest and northeastern Mexico. Opler and Hoijer constructed a simple discourse with far-reaching impacts on Indigenous social actors, whose descendants today are targeted by the US war on terror as it unfolds discursively, rhetorically, and physically in the Texas border region. All too often, states such as Texas officially deny that Indigenous peoples still exist within their political borders. Yet few scholars have connected the purported absence of Ndé in Texas to the Opler-Hoijer effect—that is, the administrative extinction of Ndé in connection with anthropological authenticity after the extermination period. This bias profoundly affects settler narratives that constitute "Lipan Apaches" as relics of the American Indian wars in Texas, not contemporary social actors beyond linear time and beyond domestic borders.

There is an inherent, underlying reality of Ndé claims to Indigenous proprietary title, to a homeland in Texas and northeastern Mexico, and this claim applies continuing pressure on the legitimacy of Texas and the United States. Along the wall, the persistence of Ndé memory and evidence of community treaties, land grants, and other legal mechanisms establishing Indigenous collective ownership of lands cast doubt on the state's and nation's fictive claims to sovereignty and dominion.[3] Subverting the reality of Ndé survival and extreme marginalization in Texas and northeastern Mexico works to obscure the fact that Ndé peoples have continuously defended a homeland

and challenged colonizers' claims to Indigenous customary lands. Violence has imposed and continues to impose constraints that have subjected a large population of diverse Indigenous peoples to the hegemony of a much smaller Anglo and elite Hispanic ruling class. Nonetheless, Indigenous and related peoples have maintained social, cultural, and legal practices across clan and kinship organization for centuries. Ndé have maintained a dynamic relationship to a homeland and have never relinquished or surrendered these lands voluntarily or through legal mechanisms. Today, Ndé claims to self-determination are supported by the total absence of proof that they ever ceded the traditional homeland. On the contrary, elders and chiefs argue that there exists ample evidence of a violent, forced severance of Ndé peoples from their lands since the inception of "Texas."

One of the myriad ways in which the settler-colonizer has maintained dominance over numerous Indigenous groups in southern Texas is through political control over naming. Texas and Texans officially deterritorialized Indigenous peoples by aggregating them under names that highlight the colonizers' cultural and ideological roots in the discourses of conquest. Naming bodies, places, and concepts demarcates settler ecologies as it deterritorializes Indigenous collective identity and ownership. Naming cartographically erases the embedded Indigenous knowledge system in the region and makes Indigenous people "foreigners" in our homelands. This is accomplished legally, socially, culturally, economically, and commercially through mining, agricultural, and ranch-based economic systems in a globally interconnected capitalist world system.

Indigenous peoples in southern Texas have also struggled with colonial land relations dominated by powerful legal and international entities such as the Catholic Church, which has maintained its economic control over Indigenous peoples and lands for centuries. The Catholic Church has been a persistent institution in Ndé peoples' lives in the histories of Spain, Mexico, Texas, the Confederate states, and the US Southwest. Hence, the colonial taxonomy of Indigenous peoples in Texas demands to be understood as a matrix, prism, and mirror reflecting dominant classification systems rooted in a colonizer's multicontextual, violent dynamic. The present-day taxonomy of "Mexican," "Mexican American," "Native American," "Hispanic," "Latino," and "Indian" is continuously imposed by the state, citizens, and the mainstream media. Racist views relegating Indigenous peoples to the status of minorities in our own homelands are uncritically adopted by civil society within the framework of domination, which is experienced as the norm of social relations in the border region.

Ndé have reorganized to contest this domination over resources, naming, and governance. Ndé seek to recover, protect, and reclaim our land, bodies, memory, and natural resources required for self-determination in southern Texas. The colonial project failed to quench the human spirit and will, and Ndé people refused to be removed from Kónitsąąíí gokíyaa, the Ndé homeland in North America. Recovering Kónitsąąíí gokíyaa is a path of resistance against US and Mexican militarization of the Texas-Mexico border today.

Ndé traditional knowledge is rooted in intergenerational orality—creation stories, emergence stories, stories transmitted from grandmothers to granddaughters. It is embedded in Ndé pictographs across the Texas-Mexico landscape, and in the fragments of the photographic past within communities. Both reveal glimpses into the lives of Indigenous communities in a region that underwent extensive ethno-genesis as a strategy and into lives of survival and adaptation to violence (figs. 1, 2). Moreover, traditional knowledge has been continuously practiced and kept vibrant, shared between and across communities, into the present day. But in a climate of low-intensity warfare, which we have experienced in our familiar places throughout the twentieth century and into the period of wall construction, traditional knowledge is under repeated attack. Formalized militarization against Indigenous peoples in the Texas-Mexico border region was always and continues to be a process of integrating repression, armed conflict, and extraction. In Indigenous eyes, armed occupation preceded the wall construction. This is an old story, one that requires analytical tools developed by local knowledge keepers.

The oral tradition that recounts extermination, persecution, racism, and gender violence became central to my analysis of Ndé family-based and land-based governance principles and ontologies, which have never been fully relinquished (M. Tamez 2010a). Women's activism and analysis were central to the process of rebuilding clan relationships and revitalizing the connection between clan genealogies and Ndé governing principles on a traditional land base. This movement, spearheaded by Ndé women, galvanized Ndé hereditary chiefs to reinstate decision making through lineal relationships, sacred councils, chiefly societies, elder councils, and women's justice spaces. In principle, Ndé leaders' legal cases—in and out of court—challenged the US government's use of sovereign immunity, impunity for human rights violators, and inaccurate historical narratives that erased the unresolved issues of Ndé land claims and self-determination. Ndé rejected the Western and state-driven definitions of the "law" and

Figure 1. Ndé-Nahua girls from El Calaboz, ca. 1941. Photograph courtesy of Margo Tamez.

Figure 2. Ndé-Tlaxcalteca-Nahua extended family on a feast day by the levee near the Rio Grande River, ca. 1942. Photograph courtesy of Margo Tamez.

sought to decolonize the Western patriarchal definition of the "family" as powerless before the state. Ndé human rights defenders worked to revitalize Ndé kinship decision-making structures and societies in the traditional homeland. This was central to self-determination in the heavily militarized, "constitution-free" zone of impunity.[4]

From 2007 to 2010, as I worked to revitalize Ndé knowledge in partnership with Ndé elders, chiefs, and women leaders, I witnessed a collective and shared history emerging. While conducting interviews I began to gain a proper understanding of the human rights implications when entire communities of Indigenous peoples are dispossessed of their customary lands. Community historians owned, managed, and curated documents that provided me with Indigenous peoples' legal perspectives on land defense over nineteen generations. As I studied the community members' genealogies, *testamentos*, maps, letters, and photographic collections, it became clear that Ndé dispossession had occurred in the course of numerous waves of occupation and armed resistance going back to the late fifteenth century. *Terra nullius* declarations, papal bulls, the Doctrine of Discovery, and the legal constructions of the framework of domination were among the devices used by Spain, Mexico, Texas, and the United States.

Learning about how the colonial system used this framework over generations to maintain "law" became a process of examining intimate and collective disorder in the lives of my own kin and clans. Internal colonialism among and between Indigenous peoples, settlers, capitalists, and militarized society was built on pillars of cultural, racial, and political exclusion. "Lipan Apaches" were always constructed in European and Euro-American doctrine as official state enemies who could be dispossessed and exterminated at will. In essence, Ndé lands, Ndé peoples, Ndé rights, and Ndé power were villainized again and again, by one colonial regime after another. The colonial invention of "Lipan Apaches" was designed to legally privilege and enfranchise settlers while ostracizing and marginalizing the internal Native "enemy." Ndé were continually denied real access to justice on issues of recognition, rights, and redress. This underlying truth gave shape to a system of erasure that precluded Indigenous peoples along the border wall from legibility in the contemporary period.

I had the opportunity to interrogate these issues and to reflect on the processes of Ndé colonization and deterritorialization alongside human rights legal experts and Indigenous advocates (Dulitzky and Tamez 2012). I interviewed leaders involved in the revitalization of Ndé memory and decision-making processes in relationship to sacred bonds to ancestors, kinship networks, and homelands. They conveyed a knowledge tradition anchored in a conception of an Ndé homeland defined by intimate aware-ness of and relationship to land, water, medicinal plants, food systems, and burial grounds (fig. 3). Elders and chiefs also made reference to Ndé knowledge found inside Texas museums and national parks and on roadside state "history" plaques. Their stories counternarrated history lessons that formed a crucial body of Indigenous consciousness and knowledge.

Reflection—turning inward to see beneath skin, to understand the heart of human experience, to harmonize and make order from the disorder imposed by external systems—made me recognize the entangled layers of violence embedded in Indigenous memory in southern Texas. Indigenous

Figure 3. Ndé-Tlaxcalteca male relatives share harvest responsibilities in traditional fields (milpas) near the river, ca. 1946. Photograph courtesy of Margo Tamez.

leaders, through their analysis of Indigenous rights and responsibilities, established a critical terrain that I navigated. The impunity operating on the Texas-Mexico border suppressed Indigenous experience. The framework of responsibility and remembering foregrounded the Indigenous history of defense, death, and resilience (M. Tamez et al. 2012, 50–65).

In my field notes, I trace where and when community members' analysis nudged me to interrogate the oral histories of hunted, massacred, lynched, abused, exploited, starved, and disappeared family members from the 1872–1935 period. Comparing the documented testimonials to Indigenous community records, I read the weavings of violence alongside Ndé peoples who taught me the relationships between the mission, ranch, baptismal, and economic ledgers tied to dispossession. Decolonizing the methodology motivated me to examine community documents through an Indigenous lens in partnership with elders. We discerned patterns whereby nineteen generations of Ndé and related Indigenous peoples were subjugated, coerced, and forced into carceral and contained spaces tied to economic projects involving priests, politicians, merchants, soldiers, elites, and sometimes other Indigenous peoples. These containment systems worked to fragment bands, clans, and families and to fragment knowledge and memory.

Over centuries, Ndé gradually lost vital, intimate relationships with each other and with the land as the Ndé worldviews and knowledge system were violently and systematically targeted for destruction. Texas and the United States instituted laws that enfranchised settlers, not Indigenous peoples. Ndé forged intercultural relationships with similarly oppressed Indigenous peoples and were violently assimilated into a large, colonized labor pool in Texas. The lie used to justify land theft was always coded in racial and imperialist terms: exterminable Indians were reconstructed as "Mexicans." As a result, Indigenous peoples lost juridical personality, the right to recognition of indigeneity, and the right to know their own languages, religions, kinship systems, lands, and worldviews. Through colonization across many carceral spaces—mines, missions, jails, prisons, households (domestic slavery), assimilative schools—Ndé were subject to disciplining and socializing "instruction." Colonizing agents forced the people to behave, think, work, and exist under the gaze of the aggressor— that is, the settler nation and its police.

Ndé ancestors and currently living elders, women, and hereditary chiefs have testified in international law arenas about these interlocking race- and gender-based capitalist systems that have consumed the Ndé aboriginal lands, bodies, minds, and resources. In 2009, hereditary Cúelcahén chief

Daniel Castro Romero Jr. submitted a formal intervention at the United Nations Permanent Forum on Indigenous Issues in which he denounced the border wall construction by the United States and its ongoing denial of formal recognition of the peoples of the Ndé nation. The same year, Eloisa García Tamez testified in US federal court, in the 5th District of Brownsville, Texas, to convey her ongoing refusal to relinquish her lands without "free, prior, and informed consent" and without recognition of her inherent Indigenous rights, which are protected under the United Nations Declaration on the Rights of Indigenous Peoples. In 2009, I joined several law and science professors from the University of Texas at Austin in presenting arguments on the United States' violation of Indigenous peoples' human rights through the construction of the Texas-Mexico border wall. In the shadow of the wall, the growing national and international realization that Ndé never surrendered or ceded the traditional homeland confronts the nation-state and the state of Texas.

II. Being Ndé in South Texas

Growing up in South Texas and in the unseen spaces between Matamoros, Progreso, Reynosa, Premont, Kingsville, Raymondville, and San Patricio, and especially in the low-lying rancherías in between, I learned to discipline myself to avoid physical violence, punitive verbal abuse, malnourishment, slaps, beatings, molestation, and other forms of indignity directed toward me—a brown body and physical reminder of indigeneity. Powerful individuals and groups exercised enormous racial authority in southern Texas, visiting their rage on the poor brown Indigenous children, workers, and families navigating the hostile spaces of South Texas from the mid-twentieth century to the present.

My mind, spirit, and body learned to curl under the normalization of active containment of Indigenous will. My recent research on the border wall convinces me that the substructure of settler history must be deeply interrogated in order to truly comprehend the magnitude of the hate against survivor Ndé peoples who defy internal displacement, that is, deterritorialization, and who are actively recovering indigeneity in the arena of international human rights law.

My mother's womb was my first home. My father's songs of hope and my mother's voiced resistance to the settler policing in South Texas flowed through the placental juices to shape my early consciousness. As my mother and father crisscrossed our traditional Ndé territory in 1961–62, I was logging miles as an unborn subject in an extensively policed colony known as "deep" South Texas. Decades later, I would recognize the systemic and technological links between the South Texas cattle, textile, and oil empires and Argentina and South Africa. As a child, I knew only the contained, open-air, policed lands of my people. I eventually moved outside those lands, to southern Arizona, Washington state, and finally British Columbia, Canada. Now, though I have been disciplined by Texas state schooling and indoctrinated to view the world through the mythical lenses constructed by the settler society, I defiantly see the larger patterns. I recognize the many ways in which Indigenous peoples have been forced to be the fire beneath the burning "melting pot" of Euro-America. The erasure of the mega-transfer of Indigenous resource wealth is part of the masking of ongoing colonialism that is at the core of Indigenous peoples' acute marginalization.

My mother voiced loud counternarratives to the ongoing occupation of the Indigenous mind. Growing up in San Antonio in HUD housing, I remember her resisting assimilation to the white-streaming as she prepared tortillas, beans, corn, squash, and roasted meat in her small kitchen. My parents and elders "teethed" me on their hard-as-bone back talk. Talking back to white and elite rule was part of a long family history of defiance. Oral history instructed us about the ancestors' defenses and their resistance to surrendering.

To survive the process of assimilation imposed by the Catholic and state schools, the poisoning by pesticide used in our living areas, and the policing overseen by Fort Sam Houston, we had to adapt to being fractured selves. This contradiction, of course, was not tenable, and the punitive measures we all experienced at work, in school, and in society revealed that we were constantly navigating states of "being in trouble" and being watched. Systems indoctrinated us to verbally "give up" our lands. Forced to say the Pledge of Allegiance and to sing the Texas state anthem, we were forced to kill, exterminate, and abolish the "Indian" inside ourselves. We internalized white and Hispanic myths of "Texas" and "South Texas" and ingested the repeated history and government lessons that "pioneers" were our heroes and the legitimate founders of our consciousness. While our families lived a marginal existence in barrios, ranchitos, campos, and rancherías in every county of Ndé country, we were disciplined into pledging multiple allegiances to the Texas creation myth and genocide denial, despite the fact that Texas had vigilantly erased the legal fact of Ndé proprietary title to lands, territories, and resources. In a web of interrelated kinship systems, our relatives were eking out humble existences, rooting into and clutching onto place. Wave after imperialist wave, the people were learning to drive their knowledge and mother tongues underground. The people adapted to systems in deep conflict with the culture and worldviews of land, place, and collective power.

In these travels between ancestral birthplaces along the Rio Grande River, behind barbed wire fences erected by settlers, we traversed the terrain lying between Kįgołgah (Many Houses, i.e., San Antonio) and Kónitsąąíí (Big Water, i.e., the Rio Grande). These were lands where *we* were the majority, though ordered as a menial "ethnic minority," a peon Indigenous labor class. On the roads between our customary places, from one labor site to another, our parents and grandparents, cousins, uncles and aunts passed by the roadside history markers. Incised into metal, our ancestors' revolutionary struggles were recast as skirmishes and uprisings of "renegades," "horse thieves," and "raiders," the iconic terms describing official Indigenous "enemies" of the cattle kings, oil barons, agribusiness interests, and railroad industrialists that dominated settler society.

III. 1962–1972

My family made frequent journeys between San Antonio, Austin, Corpus Christi, and the many rancherías where our people lived in the rural countryside. We traveled long distances, as many of our ancestors did before us, to participate in traditional family feasts within our territory and to fulfill community obligations.

I remember the importance of shutting my mouth and holding my body very still when we approached the first, then the second, and then the third checkpoint. The armed white Rangers and Texas highway patrol positioned their roadblocks strategically between San Antonio and Cameron County, the southernmost county in Texas. When I grew into young adulthood, I learned that it was *we*, the dark people, Ndé, who provided justification for the construction of an elaborate, militarized, open-air checkpoint system far inland from the border—*inside the colony*.

IV. 2012–1978

As an adult, looking back, I feel my body automatically clench when I enter the internal checkpoint zone between the Lower Rio Grande Valley and San Antonio. When I cross the US border overland, between British Columbia and Washington state, or between Mexico and the United States, my body continues to feel the numbing sensation learned in southern Texas during childhood. My body remembers the many times when they herded my family members' bodies, managed and policed our movement within the barbed-wired, railroaded, roadside industrial landscapes of southern Texas settler society. To resist the body's memory of fear, we tried to make jokes, to hum, sing, or perform our own counter-storytelling. As we came into the checkpoint, the armed Texas guards halted these adaptive tendencies.

I remember the incongruity. As we approached the checkpoints, the armed men in uniforms were only small dots on the horizon of the dashboard. Their existence, down the road and in the imminent future, fractured our thoughts. My parents grew tense, exchanged worried glances, changed their natural behaviors, became stone statues. We were bad. We were the ones needing to visit family members in nearly every county between San Antonio and the Rio Grande. There must be something wrong with our families. The existence of Ndé families in the majority of counties in southern Texas and across all border counties is proof of our much longer presence in occupied lands.

V. AD 1435 to present

Shizhazhii Ndé á'gó nant'ánhíh. Shi Cúelcahén á'gó Gochishndé Kónitsąąíí gokíyaa. I am the daughter of hereditary chiefly families of the Tall Grass and Lightning Peoples of the Big Water. I am related to Nakaiyéndé á'gó Sumandé (Nahua and Jumano) peoples.[5] I am a direct lineal descendent of Kónitsąąíí Ndé. These chiefly peoples intermarried with other chiefly peoples descended from Mariana de Moctezuma, daughter of Moctezuma Xocoyotzin II, whose daughters walked with Indigenous and European legal devices called Crown land grants into our Ndé homeland. In the Lower Rio Grande Valley, along the Texas-Mexico border, Ndé, Nahua, Tlaxcalteca, and European peoples converged through Indigenous intercultural exchanges predating colonization and through the introduction of missions, presidios, mines, land grants, agriculture, and trade systems. These created new relationships based on capitalism, greed, subjugation, and exploitation.

VI. 2006–2011

Violence undergirds the power relations between Indigenous communities, Anglo Texans, Hispanic Texans, and the two nation-states. The Texas-Mexico border is targeted for an intensified Americanization drive, as evidenced in a 2011 study commissioned by the Texas Department of

Agriculture, *Texas Border Security: A Strategic Military Assessment* (McCaffrey and Scales 2011). The traditional logics and discourses of the colonial condition work to obscure how the oligarchy of private, powerful elites along the border sculpted this war "within." This report makes clear that the nation-state is engineering new "enemies" who purportedly threaten national sovereignty, and the new war against terror has once again shifted to the Texas-Mexico border. Indigenous peoples readapt and reposition themselves. Indigenous knowing forms a bond between ancestral and contemporary ways of indigeneity. Dismantling the border wall, one legal fiction at a time, Ndé reclaim a right to remember, a right to truth, and a right to recovery and document collective memory.

VII. 2011

In June 2011, Ndé elders, hereditary chiefs, women, children, activists, academics, and invited human rights experts assembled in El Calaboz Ranchería, located in Cameron County, Texas, on the border with Mexico. The ranchería is what is left of my maternal clan's ancestral land in Kónitsąąíí gokíyaa. As a clan among chiefly families, we decided to address key issues of border violence. Indigenous knowledge, lands, and human rights reclaimed the center (Lipan Apache Women Defense 2011). The assembly located the gathering in Kónitsąąíí gokíyaa, the traditional Ndé motherland, and in El Calaboz, "earthen dugout dungeon." An Ndé community with violent, colonial memories and histories, invaded in 1749 through co-organized Spanish and Tlaxcalteca colonization of "la Gran Apachería," lit up possibilities and hope.

In the process of "getting underneath"[6] and "getting to the point"[7] about the forces that led to the border wall construction, the leaders and activists remapped violence through community testimony. Some people used colonial records, photo collections, state archives, and memory of bloodstained lands and forced disappearances stemming from the nineteenth- and twentieth-century sites of massacres, long repressed and now being uncovered by the chiefs. The Cúelcahén (Tall Grass People) chiefs at the El Calaboz assembly moved to challenge the hegemonies of Mexican, Anglo, and Hispanic stories as offical experience imposed on Ndé and all related Indigenous peoples in the region. The assembly undertook crucial first steps to recover and reclaim relationships, oral traditions, community documents, and, most important, Ndé continued existence. The assembly decided that the wall is built upon an archaeology of carceral systems birthed by settler society and premised on the death and bare existence of Ndé. The ethnographic "Lipan Apache" savage, based on a racist, nineteenth-century ideology, was repudiated as a false version of Ndé identity. Texas roadside historical plaques, the Institute of Texan Cultures in San Antonio, and the Witte Museum, among others, were named as perpetrators of the continuing loss and theft of Ndé culture. Ndé repudiate the settler history, which scripts "Lipan Apaches" as static, primitive savages and the Mexican Indigenous peoples as an exotic and folkloric backdrop to a violent order of racist systems.

VIII. 1546–1749

El Calaboz, El Ranchito, La Encantada, Los Ebanos, El Granjeno, Las Milpas, Los Indios, and Las Rusias are key places where Ndé, Nahua, Tlaxcalteca, and Europeans converged and clashed before and after 1749. The construction of the "Lipan Apache" as an ethnicity and an "enemy" accompanied the violent suppression of indigeneity across many cultures in the Texas-Mexico region. *Un calabozo* in Spanish is a dungeon or jail. As the name El Calaboz suggests, Indigenous experience has too often been beaten, incarcerated, and buried underground.

IX. 2009

On a hot August afternoon in 2009, while we were driving together alongside the border wall, my mother, elder Eloisa García Tamez, declared,

> One thing we learned after [Michael] Chertoff ordered the taking of our lands was that the journalists writing the news stories always took the government's perspective, and they always censored out the fact of indigeneity. Now . . . we gave detailed interviews, and educated them about our perspectives. Yet, on nearly all the stories, they "omitted" [she gestures quotation marks with her fingers] that we are the original landowners, the Lipan Apaches. Why is that? People who now call themselves "Hispanics" and vote with the Anglos, whose Indigenous ancestors actually lived here for hundreds of years, have negated the fact of Indigenous peoples *all around them*. What does that say? (E. Tamez 2009)

Chief Romero put it to me this way: "It is interesting to me that when a land dispute arises, the majority of Anglos and Hispanics are 'surprised' [he gestures quotation marks with his fingers] to read that Lipans are not in war paint, that we are their next-door neighbors, we don't wear buffalo robes in public, we are veterans of war, pay taxes, get college degrees, and take on major law cases for our rights as the landowners" (Romero 2012).

X. 50,000 BC to present

Traditional knowledge locates Ndé physically, spiritually, linguistically, economically, and politically as coming from the lands now known as the Yukon, British Columbia, and Alaska borderlands. More than seven hundred years ago, around AD 1300, ancestors *dáhi'ash* (traveled together) to the Lower Rio Grande area and northeastern Mexico. Through the dissemination of creation stories, maintained and handed down through knowledge keepers and transmitted orally at reunions and feasts, the Ndé oral tradition on *kótsoi łeesh goołgaiyé háá'áhí* (river-earth-plains-landmark) inherently binds Ndé to place. This is the Ndé legal perspective in federal and international courts.

XI. 2012

It is certain that Ndé never ceded lands, territories, or revenue-sharing rights, or "gave" or "surrendered" the homeland to the Catholic Church, Spain, Anglo-Saxon settlers, Texas, the United States, or any other *mangááni* (foreign) settlers or corporations. There was a reassertion of plural Indigenous kinship relations between Indigenous peoples. This knowledge system is deeply connected to women's resource and economic circuits among the peoples, predating the nation. Ndé remapping of indigeneity *re-indigenizes the* extended family and confronts the anthropological "tribe" and "ethnic group." Indigenous women's oral traditions fundamentally challenge the false categorizations and aggregations of Indigenous peoples into state-focused identities of "Indians," "Mexicans," and "border people."

The function of carceral systems is to impose domination and assimilation and to destroy Indigenous collective consciousness and resistance. Missions, haciendas, ranchos, mines, forts, schools, checkpoints, and borders function to aggregate indigenous peoples into monolithic pools of minority laborers without self-determination. The effects of violent Othering and criminalization fractures Indigenous peoples' potential for accessing justice and building empowerment from a plural indigenous base into a hegemonic counterforce.

XII. 1910–1938

In Indigenous women's memory and oral history, dispossession and violence are interwoven. The burning of fields, lynchings, and mass killings that occurred in Cameron County are interconnected. Stories from the close of the nineteenth century and the first three decades of the twentieth century reveal that Ndé in El Calaboz maintained intimate relationships with kinship households in Tamaulipas and Coahuila, on the south side of the Rio Grande River. The tendency in domination histories to erase Indigenous women's inherent land ownership and deeply rooted governance systems obstructs their access to justice and participation at the household, ranchería, community, and national level.

XIII. Activist Research in the Shadow of the Wall

Ndé peoples' efforts to protect and revitalize Indigenous knowledge systems confront and challenge Euro-American colonial claims to Ndé lands and natural resources (fig. 4). As Ndé continue to take their arguments to the international legal arena, they are reaching beyond US borders to strategize effective challenges to US impunity. This outreach is of great consequence. Ndé decolonizing practices expose the ongoing dangers and threats against Indigenous peoples by the assimilative projects and systems of violent repression in contexts of environmental and cultural expropriation.

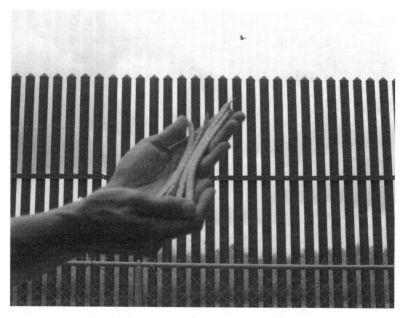

Figure 4. Mesquite pods, Ndé First Foods recovery project, July 2011. Photograph courtesy of Margo Tamez.

My intervention here, as an Ndé scholar, activist, poet, legal defender, and community member, is to reclaim place and self-determination in the decolonization of Texas. The border wall controversy provides a context in which to reexamine Indigenous peoples' truths and experiences. This is necessary to advance Indigenous peoples' and Indigenous researchers' fundamental human rights in a zone of escalating armed conflict.

Indigenous memory and experiences expose persistent forms of impunity, racism, gender violence, and genocidal systems currently operating to marginalize the nonassimilative Ndé elders, women, and hereditary chiefs. As Indigenous human rights defenders work to recover Indigenous lands, territories, rights, and futures, they enact critical disruptions of state violence. As an Indigenous researcher and Indigenous human rights defender, the state and private interests conduct surveillance upon me. Their technologies are embedded in nearly invisible laser strips implanted along the wall's perimeter. My body's thermal heat activates the radar as I investigate dispossession and the archaeologies of discontent beneath the wall (fig. 5).

Figure 5. Margo Tamez examining soil erosion and desertification of wetlands near the wall, July 2009. Photograph courtesy of Margo Tamez.

The state's aggressive policy abuses against Indigenous peoples in the homelands target Indigenous revolutionary consciousness and Ndé human rights defenders in particular. Myriad actors are involved in the state's patriarchal, racist, sexist, supremacist, and xenophobic practices against Ndé peoples. Indigenous inherent relationships with the land predate the state's questionable claims to sovereignty, which are based on settler legal fictions stemming from the Doctrine of Discovery and the Western legal concept of *terra nullius*—empty lands.

My research journey with and alongside Ndé social actors exposes the cracks in a Texas discourse about a state that is officially without Indigenous peoples, yet has a plethora of official roadside history markers that enshrine violent narratives of genocide. Denial of the disturbing realities puts further pressures upon Indigenous peoples to exhume persistent and traumatic memories. Indigenous human rights defenders have taken steps to demand the opening of an international transitional justice space in which to redress the issues of the descendants of Indigenous genocide survivors, who are also directly affected by the border wall today.

Ndé knowledge, memory, and perspectives deserve critical attention, both on their own terms and as counternarratives that fracture the "bulletproof" veneer of Texas and the United States. These counternarratives link elders', women's, and hereditary chiefs' memories of childhood, adolescence, and adulthood and interweave their knowledge of the lands, bodies, and spirits under domination. The effect is to unsettle the dominant discourses, customs, and legal practices that have structured the permanent political marginalization of Ndé peoples. Ndé can demand the right to know and the right to truth. They can seek redress, restitution, and reparation for the cultural, spiritual, social, economic, and political harms that threaten and deprive Ndé of the human right to know their Indigenous language, spiritual practices, histories, traditions, kinship structures, economic systems, lands, and food systems, and to preserve and protect natural resources.

Carrying out Indigenous research with, for, and alongside Ndé peoples challenges an Indigenous activist-scholar to immerse herself in all aspects of protecting Indigenous peoples and knowledge. This model is conducive to supporting human rights–based approaches, even though that system has its own set of challenges and colonial histories. Indigenizing human rights in this region of armed conflict makes it possible to build collaboration across and along international borders.

We commit to extensive hours documenting, relearning principles and protocols of Indigenous thought, and enacting Indigenous advocacy for the right to know and to remember. We are becoming bridges in the resurgence movement in which Indigenous voices, issues, and principles forge terrains where the settler and sovereignty are exposed by the subjugated. In this subjugation, Indigenous peoples' bodies, lands, and memories are exposed as sites of suffering and recovery, even reconciliation. Without truth, however, there can be no reconciliation.

Women's participation in decision making on legal, economic, and political matters directly challenging state and patriarchal violence is altering the current-day perception of Indigenous peoples and Indigenous self-determination movements. Civil society's perception of the critical and positive transformational aspects of Indigenous women's leadership is creating openings for us to demand collectively the creation of transitional justice spaces to disrupt authoritarian violence.

Ndé women's work—to expose carceral spaces that impinge on Indigenous knowledge, to reclaim forms of self-determination through the extended family, and to strategize on collective stewardship of natural resources and decision making in all areas that affect collective rights— has bolstered the legitimacy of elders and hereditary chiefs. This is an important area that poses a threat to the violent authoritarian state in a constitution-free zone.

"I know what this wall is: it's a prison," said elder Eloisa García Tamez in one of many long walks we took together along the wall. According to the Working Group on Human Rights and the Border Wall at the University of Texas School of Law, the construction of the Texas-Mexico border wall "involves massive violations of human rights" (Gilman 2008, 2).[8] "That line is a political line, not a cultural line," said José Emilio García, my grandfather, whose grandfather was a traditional Comanche healer and whose grandmother was "Lipan Apache."

For Indigenous peoples, decolonizing, remembering, and reinstituting indigeneity in a conflict zone that numbs residents into mere existence in open-air carceral systems has become a new site for human rights scholarship and advocacy (fig. 6). There is scant attention to this area. For Ndé, this is a critical site of memory, and if Ndé and related Indigenous peoples have their way, the result will be the establishment of a Truth and Memory Commission (Tamez et al. 2012). Developing a base for implementing the rights of Indigenous peoples in the United States, in Texas, and in the Inter-American law system is a crucial next step in that direction.

Figure 6. Action research: Margo Tamez documenting Indigenous perspectives on the wall's impacts on local families, July 2011. Photograph courtesy of Margo Tamez.

Postscript (2020)

In this essay, I bring into relief the effect and affect of a gulag wall in the Ndé Dene peoples' still-existing and still inhabited ancestral villages and places along the lower Rio Grande River and northern bank of the Texas-Mexico border. I have crucial kinship ties in these communities, and I use diverse methods and strategies to bring awareness of the wall and its antecedents: preceding causes and events, the processes of colonization, dispossession, and refusal.

I seek and enact a critical kinship form of solidarity building, inviting readers to go on a journey with me through different temporal and spatial trajectories of Ndé Dene memory and place. Drawing on the concept of Indigenous storywork (Archibald 2008), I interrogate the role of intimate witnessing, as a daughter, grand-daughter, and descendent of Ndé foremothers since time immemorial, and my responsibilities to engage and to witness indigenous storying from a contemporary Aboriginal perspective. This braiding is necessary to decolonize the layers of Euro-American settler and Indigenous inter-group violence, which negatively overwrite and suppress Ndé Dene place, identity, and perspectives in Texas.[9]

This essay gives readers permission to be uncomfortable in unsettling hegemonic ways of thinking and knowing; it invites them to feel, to recognize, to acknowledge, and to challenge the gendered, racial, sexual, and cognitive violence underpinning the settler colonial identities established to normalize colonization and resource theft of Indigenous peoples. These identities naturalize and inscribe a gendered hegemony onto Indigenous peoples' places which are inscribed as "Texas"/"Texan"/"Tejano", or "Mexico"/"Mexican", or "Aztek"/"Aztlán", or "American." By witnessing and historicizing Ndé place, through Ndé women's history, oral traditions, and anticolonial land protection, I call for critical consciousness to interrogate colonizing hegemonic claims to place as a Ndé Dene ontological and epistemological resistance to violent erasures.

The essay asks readers to think critically about not only the epistemologies, ontologies, axiologies, and methodologies of diverse Aboriginal peoples in ongoing struggles with settler colonial erasure, and with deep-time belonging in place, but also the serious risks and violence of mapping erasure onto Ndé Dene places in Texas, a process that is ongoing. It is a call to decolonize Texas—conceptually, cognitively, ethically, morally, and physically.

I have this unique and very special honor to re-share and, thus, to re-imagine this essay and make a prominent space in this powerful collection for Indigenous autobiography and nonapology as critical, interlocking decolonial, feminist methodologies of resistance against violence and genocide.

I engage these as I re-energize Ndé Dene women's experience, intimate memory, collective memory, and oral history in order to bring meaning to the suppression of the Ndé Dene peoples' genocide-based trauma. On many levels, the wall construction process, and the community's resistance to it, have excavated and unburied the Ndé Dene people's intergenerational post-genocide memory, which is deeply embedded in the cellular kinship structure of key families and in the lands and waters where these events and processes transpired. Thus, trauma-informed epistemologies in the walled region of Texas give rise and resurgence to the pedagogy of hidden Indigenous genocide in critical ways. The significant role of the storyteller—that is, of being seen and heard—and the role of those who witness and who make space for Ndé Dene memory, struggles, and ways of resisting erasure are in themselves key agentic acts in the decolonization of the deep and bloody history of group-on-group violence and dispossession in Texas.

The US wall and the dispossession processes, from 2006 through 2013, are the focus of the essay, which relates the Ndé Dene peoples' perspectives of, and in, the shadows of the genocide and brings into relief their/our collective trauma. Of significant concern is the gathering of Ndé Dene peoples to protect and defend the Ndé women who take up active refusal to the US government's occupation of Ndé lands. Indigenous women's communication of kinship and traditional knowledge using current-day technologies also works to reshape knowledge and relationships with the digital and cyber domains. This innovation enables Ndé women to widely convey the fact that the Ndé struggle for land protection—between recognition and self-determination for Indigenous women's belonging and place on the land—is an anti-capitalist, anti-misogynous, and anti-patriarchal struggle for Ndé women and girls.

The essay doesn't attempt to resolve the tensions and contradictions that are long-term effects of the Dene peoples' continuing struggles not only in Texas but also beyond its borders. Glen Coulthard (2014) argues that the Dene Nation's "articulations of recognition were informed by a land/place-based ethics of reciprocity that fundamentally challenged the assumed legitimacy of colonial sovereignty over Dene lands as well as the capitalist social relations surrounding them" (150). It was Ndé Dene women who organized critical resistance to the wall, enacted and launched lawsuits against powerful US officials and agencies, took the case to two international legal systems outside the United States, and articulated a different social, spiritual, economic, cultural, and political paradigm for the Ndé Dene peoples' struggle for recognition along the lower Rio Grande River. Between 2007 and 2013, Ndé Dene women filed a national lawsuit and launched a two-year land-protection standoff against three US militarized units and an extensive team of US and private attorneys. The conditions imposed upon Ndé Dene women in the decades preceding and during construction of the wall critically resonate with Dene Nation struggles in Denendeh (in the Northwest Territories of Canada) across similar periods.

From the perspectives of Indigenous peoples whose lands, communities, sacred sites, cemeteries, communal gathering areas, and customary territory are currently captured, and contrary to current popular belief, the wall is not a stand-alone fixture. Further, the wall and the militarized surveillance systems that interface with it are not history- or memory-neutral. The wall is an extension of embedded settler, colonial, imperialist, and capitalist impulses on the part of the United States to gain control over resources and pathways to effect the normalization of capitalist, corporate structures. In the walled zone, nothing is neutral, not even silence.

Another important point this essay introduces and establishes is my ongoing engagement with Achille Mbembe's theory of necropower and the necropolitical. Key to necropower are four objectives: to gain operational control over the Indigenous space and place; to marginalize *spatially, to the extreme, remote fringes*, surviving Indigenous groups; to diminish existence to the harshest and most deprived conditions, structurally and economically; and to harvest and exploit Indigenous peoples, to debase them to a crouching form of humanity.

Necropolitical strategies work through an interlocking construction, which gives settlers control over production and distribution, the police and military, and the processes of disposability. Maintaining control over the consciousness of a large population requires disciplinary control over thought that is not relegated to just one place and institution. The goal of necropower was never about any one space of ultimate disciplinary control per se. Rather, it seeks to establish a constellation of spatial exclusion, alienation, and social death that is normalized on Indigenous bodies, especially those who *survive* genocide and *remain*. They are an *abhorrence* and a constant reminder of bloody violence and mass death. Mbembe (2003) argues that "the colonial state derives its fundamental claim of sovereignty and legitimacy from the authority of its own particular narrative of history and identity. This narrative is itself underpinned by the idea that the state has a divine right to exist; the narrative competes with another for the same sacred space. Because the two narratives are incompatible and the two populations are inextricably intertwined, any demarcation of the territory on the basis of pure identity is quasi-impossible" (27).

Mbembe's ongoing articulations of necropower and the necropolitical, social and civil death, and enslavement, as well as different forms of political violence in the twentieth and twenty-first centuries, offered tools at a time when I could find little that reflected my Ndé experiences in a walled gulag space. Since 2009 his work has deeply informed my own exploration and interrogation of Texas settler colonialism, the carceral, militarism, walls, and the crucial epistemological systems of Apache-Comanche survivor communities. Oral histories from Indigenous villages throughout southern and southwestern Texas provide evidence for an organized theory of Indigenous genocide in and around El Calaboz and similar villages on the Rio Grande River.

Mbembe was the first scholar to theorize in depth the uses of social and political power through the lens of necropower and necropolitics. In "Necropolitics," he states (or guides, or warns) that we must give serious consideration to "those figures of sovereignty whose central project is not the struggle for autonomy but *the generalized instrumentalization of human existence and the material destruction of human bodies and populations*" (2003, 14; italics in original). He argues, further, "Such figures of sovereignty are far from a piece of prodigious insanity or an expression of a rupture between the impulses and interests of the body and those of the mind. Indeed, they, like the death camps, are what constitute the *nomos* of the political space in which we still live" (14). When the sovereign entity enables, allows, constitutes, and structures death (whether political, social, or material) of certain Indigenous people, this is where and when the death of one group and the life of another secures a deeply embedded knowing, both subconscious and felt, of being constituted into political, social, and material existence.

I offer readers crucial reflexivity through my experiences as a walled-in community member and as a witness to my mother, elders, and relatives who are walled in; the relatives who died during and after the walling in; and the subsistence traditions that died during and after the walling in. As a human rights advocate and researcher for three Ndé legal resistance and refusal cases (which are currently in a diasporic limbo in Syilx territory), I have come to grips with the mental and emotional processing necessary to endure—to feel, know, and work through—the personal trauma connected to the deliberate and persistent en masse, state-sanctioned human rights violations against Indigenous peoples, between 2009 and the present, in and near El Caeboz and within the walled region of the lower Rio Grande River.

Notes

"Place and Perspective in the Shadow of the Wall: Recovering Ndé Knowledge and Self-Determination in Texas," by Margo Tamez, is reprinted from *Aztlán: A Journal of Chicano Studies* 38, no. 1 (2013).

1. It is important to recognize that the wall on the Texas-Mexico border predominantly affected poor, marginalized peoples who make up Native American communities and multiheritage Indigenous communities. Both have ties to the affected region of Texas-Mexico going back hundreds of years prior to the construction of the border, and even predating the nation. Indigeneity in Texas border communities is masked, at times, by the officially prescribed aggregations of "Latina/o," "Hispanic," "Mexican," and "Mexican American." See Wilson et al. (2008, 2010).

2. I have written in other places about critical dimensions of Indigenous peoples' and Indigenous women's resistance to the border wall, the state, and oligarchic violence. See Tamez (2008a, 2008b, 2009, 2010b, 2011, 2012a, 2012b) and Gilman and Tamez (2011).

3. See Guzman and Hurwitz (2008, 9) for a summary of the Lipan Apache Aboriginal Title claims against the United States before the Indian Claims Commission (ICC), Docket no. 22-0, and the ICC decision on February 19, 1976.

4. The American Civil Liberties Union defines the US border as a "constitution-free zone," where normal constitutional protections, such as the one against arbitrary search and seizure, do not apply (ACLU 2008).

5. Ndé peoples in the transboundary region are a plural indigenous society with roots in reciprocal, familial, economic, and political governance and trade systems. These interweave Ndé experiences with and alongside Purépecha, Tlaxcalteca, Nahua, Coahuilteco, Mescalero, Comanche, Kikapu, Jumano Apache, and related peoples. All are indigenous to the broader region and North America, which is currently trifurcated by the US-Mexico and the US-Canada borders.

6. Richard Gonzalez, Ndé council member, statement to assembly at El Calaboz Ranchería, June 24, 2011.

7. Eloisa García Tamez, Ndé elder, statement to assembly at El Calaboz Ranchería, June 24, 2011.

8. Gilman continues: "The construction of the wall along the Texas/Mexico border will destroy important environmental resources, will involve the unfair and discriminatory taking of private property without a clear and fair process and will affect the means of subsistence and way of life of persons living in border communities, including the members of several indigenous groups. In response to this looming threat, a multi-disciplinary collective of faculty and students at the University of Texas at Austin formed to analyze the human rights impact of the construction of a border wall on the Texas/Mexico border. This project is facilitated through the Rapoport Center for Human Rights and Justice at the University of Texas Law School and is supported by the University of Texas office of Thematic Initiatives and Community Engagement. The Working Group includes faculty and students from the Geography Department, the Anthropology Department, the LBJ School of Public Affairs, the Teresa Lozano Long Institute of Latin American Studies and the Immigration Clinic, Environmental Clinic and Rapoport Center at the Law School. The Working Group is collaborating with affected individual property owners, indigenous communities, environmental groups, Environmental Sciences faculty at the University of Texas at Brownsville and other academics and advocates to carry out work on this project" (2008, 2).

9. Meaning, original (native; Indigenous) peoples having existed in a place, region and period of time before European colonists' arrival.

Works Cited

ACLU (American Civil Liberties Union). 2008. "Fact Sheet on U.S. 'Constitution Free Zone.'" http://www.aclu.org/technology-and-liberty/fact-sheet-us-constitution-free-zone.

Archibald, Jo-Ann. 2008. *Indigenous Storywork: Educating the Heart, Mind, Body and Spirit*. Vancouver: UBC Press.

Dulitzky, Ariel, and Margo Tamez. 2012. "The Situation of the Texas-Mexico Border Wall: A Request for Consideration under the Early Warning and Urgent Action Procedures of the United Nations Committee on the Elimination of Racial Discrimination." Report submitted by the Human Rights Clinic of the University of Texas School of Law and Lipan Apache Women Defense to the UN Committee on the Elimination of Racial Discrimination.

Gilman, Denise. 2008. *Obstructing Human Rights: The Texas-Mexico Border Wall: Background and Context*. Austin: University of Texas, Working Group on Human Rights and the Border Wall. http://www.utexas.edu/law/centers/humanrights/borderwall/analysis/briefing-INTRODUCTION.pdf.

Gilman, Denise, and Margo Tamez. 2011. "Brick by Brick: Using Human Rights and Critical Perspectives of Indigenous Peoples' Social Movements to Build Momentum against the Texas/Mexico Border Wall." Under review.

Guzman, Michelle, and Zachary Hurwitz. 2008. *Violations on the Part of the United States Government of Indigenous Rights Held by Members of the Lipan Apache, Kickapoo, and Ysleta del Sur Tigua Tribes of the Texas-Mexico Border*. Austin: University of Texas, Working Group on Human Rights and the Border Wall. http://www.utexas.edu/law/centers/humanrights/borderwall/analysis/briefing-violations-of-indigenous-rights.pdf.

Lipan Apache Women Defense. 2011. "Indigenous Peoples' Knowledge, Lands & Human Rights, Texas-Mexico Border." Poster for El Caloboz Gathering, June 24–26. http://lipanapachecommunitydefense.blogspot.com/2011/05/el-calaboz-2011-gathering.html.

McCaffrey, Barry R., and Robert H. Scales. 2011. *Texas Border Security: A Strategic Military Assessment*. Mico, TX: Colgen LP. http://mccaul.house.gov/uploads/Final%20Report-Texas%20Border%20Security.pdf.

Mmembe, Achille. 2003. "Necropolitics." Translated by Libby Meintjes. *Political Culture* 15, no. 1: 11–40.

Romero, Daniel Castro, Jr. 2012. Interview by Margo Tamez, El Calaboz Ranchería, Texas, June 26.

Tamez, Eloisa García. 2009. Interview by Margo Tamez, El Calaboz Ranchería, Texas, August 19.

Tamez, Margo. 2008a. "El Calaboz Ranchería and the Border Wall." ePortfolio. https://mysite.wsu.edu/personal/mtamez/calaboz/default.aspx.

———. 2008b. "Space, Position, and Imperialism in South Texas: Dr. Eloisa García Tamez v. US Secretary Michael Chertoff, US Department of Homeland Security, US Border Patrol, US Army Corps of Engineers." *Chicana/Latina Studies* 7, no. 2: 112–21.

———. 2009. "Open Letter to Cameron County Commission." *The Crit: A Critical Legal Studies Journal* 2, no. 1: 110–29.

———. 2010a. "Nádasi"né" nde' isdzáné begoz'aahi' shimaa shini' gokal Gową goshjaa haánáidiłí texas-nakaiyé godesdzog" (Returning Lipan Apache Women's Laws, Lands, and Power in El Calaboz Ranchería, Texas-Mexico Border, 1546–2009). PhD diss., Washington State University.

———. 2010b. "Restoring Lipan Apache Women's Laws, Lands, and Strength in El Calaboz Ranchería at the Texas-Mexico Border." *Signs* 35, no. 3: 558–69.

———. 2011. "'Our Way of Life Is Our Resistance': Indigenous Women and Anti-Imperialist Challenges to Militarization along the U.S.-Mexico Border." In "Invisible Battlegrounds: Feminist Resistance in the Global Age of War and Imperialism," special issue, *Works and Days* 57/58, vol. 29, nos. 1–2: 281–318.

———. 2012a. "On Being 'Indian,' Unsilent, and Contaminated along the US-Mexico Border." In *Companions in Wonder: Children and Adults Exploring Nature Together*, edited by Julie Dunlap and Steven R. Kellert, 251–57. Cambridge, MA: MIT Press.

———. 2012b. "The Texas-Mexico Border Wall and Ndé Memory: Confronting Genocide and State Criminality, Beyond the Guise of 'Impunity.'" In *Beyond Walls and Cages: Prisons, Borders, and Global Crisis*, edited by Jenna M. Lloyd, Matt Mitchelson, and Andrew Burridge, 57–73. Athens: University of Georgia Press.

Wilson, J. Gaines, Jude Benavides, Karen Engle, Denise Gilman, Anthony Reisinger, Jessica Spangler, and Joe Lemen. 2010. "Due Diligence and Demographic Disparities: Effects of the Planning of U.S.-Mexico Border Fence on Marginalized Populations." *Southwestern Geographer* 14: 42–56.

Wilson, J. Gaines, Jude Benavides, Anthony Reisinger, Joseph Lemen, Zachary Hurwitz, Jessica Spangler, and Karen Engle. 2008. *An Analysis of Demographic Disparities Associated with the Proposed U.S.-Mexico Border Fence in Cameron County, Texas.* Austin: University of Texas, Working Group on Human Rights and the Border Wall. http://www.utexas.edu/law/centers/humanrights/borderwall/analysis/briefing-papers.html.

Bibliography of Chicana/o Autobiography and Personal Essays in Spanish and English

Primary Literature

Books

Acosta, Oscar Zeta. 1972. *The Autobiography of a Brown Buffalo*. San Francisco: Straight Arrow Books.

———. 1973. *The Revolt of the Cockroach People*. San Francisco: Straight Arrow Books.

Anaya, Rudolpho A. 1986. *A Chicano in China*. Albuquerque: University of New Mexico Press.

Arteaga, A. 1997. *House with the Blue Bed*. San Francisco: Mercury House.

Baca, Jimmy Santiago. 1992. *Working in the Dark: Reflections of a Poet of the Barrio*. Santa Fe: Red Crane Books.

Barrera, Aída. 2001. *Looking for Carrascolendas: from a Child's World to Award-Winning Television*. Austin: University of Texas Press.

Campobello, Nellie. 1988. *Cartucho; and, My Mother's Hands*. Austin: University of Texas Press.

Chacón, R., and J. Meketa. 1986. *Legacy of Honor: The Life of Rafael Chacón, a Nineteenth-Century New Mexican*. Albuquerque: University of New Mexico Press.

Cisneros, Sandra. 2015. *A House of My Own: Stories from My Life*. New York: Alfred A. Knopf.

Corona, Bert. 1994. *Memories of Chicano History: The Life and Narrative of Bert Corona*, edited by Mario T. García. Berkeley: University of California Press.

Corral, Jesús C. 1984. *Caro Amigo: The Autobiography of Jesús C. Corral*. Tucson: Westernlore Press.

Demarco, T. 2000. *Vinny Castilla*. Childs, MD: Mitchell Lane Publishers.

Elizondo, Virgilio P. 1988. *The Future Is Mestizo: Life Where Cultures Meet*. Oak Park, IL: Meyer-Stone Books.

Frías, G. 1982. *Barrio Warriors: Homeboys of Peace*. Los Angeles: Díaz.

———. 1989. *Barrio Patriots: Killing and Dying for America*. Los Angeles [?], n.p.

Fuente, Mario de la, and Baye de Mente. 1972. *I Like You, Gringo—But!* Phoenix: Phoenix Books.

Galarza, Ernesto. 1971. *Barrio Boy*. Notre Dame: University of Notre Dame Press.

Galindo, R., and E. Marcus. 1997. *Icebreaker: The Autobiography of Rudy Galindo*. New York: Pocket Books.

Galvan, Jesse. 1992. *The Way Back: The Autobiography of Jesse Galvan, Jr.: Businessman, Comedian, Federal Employee*. San Antonio: Watercress Press.

García, Lionel G. 1994. *I Can Hear the Cowbells Ring*. Houston: Arte Público Press.

García, Mario T. 2000. *Luis Leal: An Auto/Biography*. Austin: University of Texas Press.

García, Ricardo L. 2001. *Coal Camp Days: A Boy's Remembrance*. Albuquerque: University of New Mexico Press.

Gilbert, Fabiola Cabeza de Baca. 1989, 1954. *We Fed Them Cactus*. Albuquerque: University of New Mexico Press.

Gonzales, George L. 1987. *The Other Side of the Coin*. Ogden, UT: n.p.

Gonzales, Ray. 1993. *Memory Fever: A Journey Beyond El Paso del Norte*. Seattle: Broken Moon Press.

González, Rigoberto. 2013. *Autobiography of My Hungers*. Madison: University of Wisconsin Press.

Guerrero, Salvador. *Memorias, a West Texas Life*. Lubbock: Texas Tech University Press, 1991.

Guevara, Rubén Funkahuatl. 2018. *Confessions of a Radical Chicano Doo-Wop Singer*. Oakland: University of California Press.

Hart, E. T. 1999. *Barefoot Heart: Stories of a Migrant Child*. Tempe: Bilingual Press/ Editorial Bilingüe.

Herrera, Jess Robert. 1992. *Memories of My Life*. San Francisco: J. R. Herrera.

Herrera, Juan Felipe. 1997. *Mayan Drifter: Chicano Poet in the Lowlands of America*. Philadelphia: Temple University Press.

Jaramillo, Cleofas M. 1941. *Shadows of the Past (Sombras del pasado)*. Santa Fe: Seton Village Press. Reprint, Albuquerque: University of New Mexico Press, 2000.

———. 1955. *Romance of a Little Village Girl*. San Antonio, Texas: Naylor Co. Reprint, Albuquerque: University of New Mexico Press, 2000.

Jiménez, Francisco. 1997. *The Circuit: Stories from the Life of a Migrant Child*. Boston: Houghton Mifflin.

Johnson, Kevin, R. 1999. *How Did You Get to Be Mexican?: A White/Brown Man's Search for Identity*. Philadelphia: Temple University Press.

López, Arcadia H. 1992. *Barrio Teacher*. Houston: Arte Público Press.

López Tijerina, Reies. 2000. *They Called Me 'King Tiger': My Struggle for the Land and Our Rights*, translated and edited by José Angel Gutierrez. Houston: Arte Público Press.

Lucas, María Elena. 1993. *Forged Under the Sun: The Life of Maria Elena Lucas*. Ann Arbor: University of Michigan Press.

Marichal, Juan, with Charles Einstein. 1967. *A Pitcher's Story*. Garden City, NY: Doubleday.

Maril, Robert Lee. 1992. *Living on the Edge of America: At Home on the Texas-Mexico Border*. College Station: Texas A & M University Press.

Martin, Patricia Preciado. 1983. *Images and Conversations: Mexican Americans Recall a Southwestern Past*. Tucson: University of Arizona Press.

Martínez, Adrian. 1986. *Adrian: An Autobiography*. Written with Felix Garcia. Austin: Morgan Printing and Publishing.

Martinez, Domingo. 2012. *The Boy Kings of Texas: A Memoir*. Guilford, CT: Lyons Press.

Martínez, José. 1970. *A Foot in Two Worlds*. Chicago: Children's Press.

Martínez, Rubén. 2001. *Crossing Over: A Mexican Family on the Migrant Trail*. New York: Metropolitan Books.

Martínez, Víctor. 1996. *Parrot in the Oven: Mi Vida: A Novel*. New York: HarperCollins.

Mendoza, Lydia. 1993. *Lydia Mendoza: A Family Autobiography*. Houston: Arte Público Press.

Mora, Pat. 1993. *Napantla: Essays from the Land in the Middle*. Albuquerque: University of New Mexico Press.

Moraga, Cherríe. 1983. *Loving in the War Years: Lo Que Nunca Paso Por Sus Labios*. Cambridge, MA: South End Press.

Morales, Dionicio. 1997. *Dionicio Morales: A Life in Two Cultures*. Houston: Piñata Books.

Nava, Julián. 2002. *Julian Nava: My Mexican-American Journey*. Houston: Arte Público Press.

Navarrette, Rubén. 1993. *A Darker Shade of Crimson: Odyssey of a Harvard Chicano*. New York: Bantam Books.

Núñez Cabeza de Vaca, Alvar. 1993. *The Account: Alvar Núñez Cabeza de Vaca's Relación*. Houston: Arte Público Press.

Osío, Antonio María. 1996. *The History of Alta California: A Memoir of Mexican California*. Madison: University of Wisconsin Press.

Pérez, Ramón Tianguis. 1991. *Diary of an Undocumented Immigrant*. Houston: Arte Público Press.

Pineda, Albino R. 2008. *Among the Repatriated: Autobiography of a Mexican American*. Philadelphia: Xlibris.

Ponce, Mary Helen. 1993. *Hoyt Street: An Autobiography*. Albuquerque: University of New Mexico Press.

Prieto, Jorge. 1989. *Harvest of Hope: The Pilgrimage of a Mexican-American Physician*. Notre Dame: University of Notre Dame Press.

Ramos, J. 2002. *Atravesando Fronteras: La autobiografía de un periodista en busca de su lugar en el mundo*. New York: Rayo.

———. 2003. *No Borders: A Journalist's Search for Home*. New York: Rayo.

Recinos, Harold J. 1989. *Hear the Cry!: A Latino Pastor Challenges the Church*. Louisville: Westminster/John Knox Press.

Ríos, Alberto. 1999. *Capirotada: A Nogales Memoir*. Albuquerque: University of New Mexico Press.

Rivas, R. A. 1977. *Survival: My Life in Love and War*. Hicksville, NY: Exposition Press.

Rodríguez, Luis J. 1994. *Always Running: La Vida Loca, Gang Days in L.A.* New York: Simon and Schuster.

Rodríguez, Richard. 1983. *Hunger of Memory: The Education of Richard Rodríguez: An Autobiography*. New York: Bantam Books.

———. 1992. *Days of Obligation: An Argument with My Mexican Father*. New York: Viking.

———. 2002. *Brown: The Last Discovery of America*. New York: Viking.

Romano-V., Octavio Ignacio. 1990. *Geriatric Fu: My First Sixty Five Years in the United States*. Berkeley: TQS Publications.

Roque Hernández, Lamberto. 2002. *Cartas a Crispina*. Oaxaca, Mexico: Carteles Editores.

Ruiz, D. V. 1981. *A Soul in Exile: A Chicano Lost in Occupied Land*. New York: Vantage Press.

Ruiz, R. E. 2003. *Memories of a Hyphenated Man*. Tucson: University of Arizona Press.

Salas, Floyd. 1992. *Buffalo Nickel*. Houston: Arte Público Press.

Sanabria, R. 2001. *Stewing in the Melting Pot: The Memoir of a Real American*. Sterling, VA: Capital Books.

Santos, John Phillip. 1999. *Places Left Unfinished at the Time of Creation*. New York: Viking.

Soto, Gary. 1985. *Living Up the Street: Narrative Recollections*. San Francisco: Strawberry Hill Press. Reprint, New York: Dell, 1992.

———. 1986. *Small Faces*. Houston: Arte Público Press.

———. 1988. *Lesser Evils: Ten Quartets*. Houston: Arte Público Press.

———. 1990. *A Summer Life*. Hanover, NH: University of New England Press.

Stavans, Ilan. 2001. *On Borrowed Words: A Memoir of Language*. New York: Penguin.

Taylor, Sheila Ortiz, 1996. *Imaginary Parents: A Memoir*. Albuquerque: University of New Mexico Press.

Torres, Olga Beatriz. 1994. *Memorias de Mi Viaje: Recollections of My Trip*. Albuquerque: University of New Mexico Press.

Treviño, J. S. 2001. *Eyewitness: A Filmmaker's Memoir of the Chicano Movement*. Houston: Arte Público Press.

Trujillo, Charley, ed. 1990. *Soldados: Chicanos in Viet Nam*. San Jose, CA: Chusma House.

Tywoniak, Frances Esquibel, and Mario T. García. 2000. *Migrant Daughter:: Coming of Age as a Mexican American Woman*. Berkeley: University of California Press.

Urrea, Luis Alberto. 1998. *Nobody's Son: Notes from an American Life*. Tucson: University of Arizona Press.

———. 1999. *Wandering Times: Western Notebooks*. Tucson: University of Arizona Press.

Villegas de Magnon, Leonor. 1993. *The Rebel*. Houston: Arte Público Press.

Villaseñor, Victor Edmund. 1991. *Rain of Gold*. Houston: Arte Público Press.

———. 1994. *Walking Stars: Stories of Magic and Power*. Houston: Piñata Books.

———. 2001. *Thirteen Senses: A Memoir*. New York: Rayo.

Zúñiga, José. 1994. *Soldier of the Year*. New York: Pocket Books.

Anthologies with Chicano Autobiographies

Anzaldúa, Gloria A. 1990. *Making Face, Making Soul: Haciendo Caras: Creative and Critical Perspectives by Women of Color.* San Francisco: Aunt Lute Foundation Books.

Augenbraum, Harold, ed. 1993. *Growing Up Latino.* Boston: Houghton Mifflin.

Augenbraum, Harold, and Margarite Fernandez Olmos, eds. 1997. *The Latino Reader: An American Literary Tradition from 1542 to the Present.* Boston: Houghton Mifflin.

Binder, Wolfgang, ed. 1985. *Partial Autobiographies: Interviews with Twenty Chicano Poets.* Erlangen, W. Germany: Verlag Palm and Enke.

Cortez, Jaime, ed. 1999. *Virgins, Guerrillas and Locas: Gay Latinos Writing on Love.* San Francisco: Cleis Press.

Delgado, Richard, and J. Stefancic, eds. 1998. *The Latino/a Condition: A Critical Reader.* New York: New York University Press.

Fernández, Roberta, ed. 1994. *In Other Words.* Houston: Arte Público Press.

González, Ray, ed. 1994. *Currents from the Dancing River.* New York: Harcourt Brace.

Heide, Rich, ed. 2002. *Under the Fifth Sun: Latino Literature from California.* Santa Clara, CA: Santa Clara University.

Hernández-Gutiérrez, Manuel de Jesús, and David William Foster, eds. 1997. *Literatura Chicana, 1965–1995: An Anthology in Spanish, English, and Calo.* New York: Garland.

Horno-Delgado, Asunción., eds. 1989. *Breaking Boundaries: Latina Writing and Critical Readings.* Amherst: University of Massachusetts Press.

Howe, Elizabeth Teresa. 2015. *Autobiographical Writing by Early Modern Hispanic Women.* Farnham, UK: Ashgate.

Kabalen de Bichara, Donna M. 2013. *Telling Border Life Stories: Four Mexican American Women Writers.* College Station: Texas A&M University Press.

Kanellos, Nicolás, ed. 1995. *Hispanic American Literature: A Brief Introduction and Anthology.* New York: Longman.

Ludwig, Ed, and James Santibanez, eds. 1971. *The Chicanos: Mexican American Voices.* Baltimore: Penguin Books.

Noriega, Chon A. and Wendy Belcher, eds. 2004. *I Am Aztlán: The Personal Essay in Chicano Studies.* Los Angeles: UCLA Chicano Studies Research Center Press.

Payne, James Robert, ed. 1992. *Multicultural Autobiography: American Lives.* Knoxville: University of Tennessee Press.

Ramos, Juanita, ed. 1994. *Compañeras: Latina Lesbians: An Anthology.* New York: Routledge.

Siems, Larry, ed. 1992. *Between the Lines: Letters between Undocumented Mexican and Central American Immigrants and Their Families and Friends.* Hopewell, NJ: Ecco Press.

Tatum, Charles M., ed. 1992. *New Chicana/Chicano Writing.* Tucson: University of Arizona Press.

Vázquez, Francisco H., and Rodolfo Torres, eds. 2003. *Latino/a Thought: Culture, Politics, and Society.* Lanham: Rowman and Littlefield.

Personal Essays

Acosta, Oscar Zeta. 1996. "Autobiographical Essay." In *Oscar "Zeta" Acosta: The Uncollected Works*, edited by Oscar Zeta Acosta and Ilan Stavans, 3–15. Houston: Arte Público Press.

———. 1998. "Life in the Trenches." In *The Latino/a Condition: A Critical Reader*, edited by Richard Delgado and J. Stefancic, 332–38. New York: New York University Press.

Alvarez, Jorge. 1970. "Autobiography in Maize." *El Grito* 3, no. 2: 44. Reprinted in *El Espejo–The Mirror. Berkeley: Quinto Sol Publications, 1972. Reprinted in From the Belly of the Shark*, edited by Octavio Ignacio Romano-V. and Herminio Ríos C., 248. Berkeley: Quinto Sol Publications, 1973.

Alvarez, Julia. 1997. "An Unlikely Beginning for a Writer." In *Mascaras*, edited by Lucha Corpi, 188–99. Berkeley: Third Woman Press.

Anaya, Rudolfo A. 1990. Interview with John F. Crawford. In *This Is About Vision: Interviews with Southwestern Writers*, edited by William Balassi, John F. Crawford, and Annie O. Eysturoy, 82–93. Albuquerque: University of New Mexico Press.

———. "Rudolfo A. Anaya: An Autobiography." In *Rudolfo A. Anaya: Focus on Criticism*, edited by César A. González-T., 359–89. La Jolla, CA: Lalo Press.

Anonymous. 1994. "Hombre de Palabra." Oral history. In *Compañeras: Latina Lesbians: An Anthology*, edited by Juanita Ramos. New York: Routledge.

Anonymous. 1994. "Homofobia: El miedo de una sociedad." Oral history. In *Compañeras: Latina Lesbians: An Anthology*, edited by Juanita Ramos, 44–53. New York. Routledge.

Anonymous. 1994. "It Took Everything I Had." Oral history. In *Compañeras: Latina Lesbians: An Anthology*, edited by Juanita Ramos, 44–53. New York: Routledge.

Anzaldúa, Gloria A. 1981. "La Prieta." In *This Bridge Called My Back*, edited by Cherríe Moraga, Gloria A. Anzaldúa, and Toni Cade Bambara, 198–204. Watertown, MA: Persephone Press.

———. 1997. "Movimientos de rebeldía y las culturas que traicionan." In *Latinos and Education: A Critical Reader*, edited by Antonia Darder , 259–65. New York: Routledge.

Archambeau, Ernest R. 1946. "Spanish Sheepmen on the Canadian at Old Tascosa." *Panhandle-Plains Historical Review* 19: 45–73.

Baca, Jimmy Santiago. 1990. Interview with John F. Crawford. In *This Is About Vision: Interviews with Southwestern Writers*, edited by William Balassi, John F. Crawford, and Annie O. Eysturoy, 180–93. Albuquerque: University of New Mexico Press.

———. 1994. "Imagine My Life." In *Currents from the Dancing River*, edited by Ray Gonzalez, 514–21. New York: Harcourt Brace.

Baez, Joan. 1971. "Thoughts on a Sunday Afternoon." In *The Chicanos: Mexican American Voices*, edited by Ed Ludwig and James Santibanez, 255–60. Baltimore: Penguin Books.

Balanta, Beatriz E. 2019. "The Hidden Costs of a Life of the Mind." *Latin American and Latinx Visual Culture* 1, no. 3: 78–82.

Barraza, Santa C. 2001. "The Maguey: Coming Home." *Aztlán: A Journal of Chicano Studies* 26, no. 1: 199–202.

Barrera, Nancy. 1984. "Mi Sueño." *Revista Mujeres* 1, no. 2: 13–14.

Benavídez, Max. 1997. "Subterranean Homesick Blues." *Aztlán: A Journal of Chicano Studies* 22, no. 2: 139–49.

Black, Charlene Villaseñor. 2017. "Chicana Art Historian at the Crossroads." In *On Second Thought: Learned Women Reflect on Profession, Community, and Purpose*, edited by Luisa Del Giudice, 171–84. Salt Lake City: University of Utah Press.

Brinson-Piñeda, Barbara. 1985. Interview. In *Partial Autobiographies: Interviews with Twenty Chicano Poets*, edited by Wolfgang Binder, 16–27. Erlangen, W. Germany: Verlag Palm and Enke.

Brito, Mónica. 1990. "An Autobiography." *Llueve Tlaloc*, no. 17: 35.

Bruce-Novoa, Juan. 1990. "Mexico in Chicano Literature." In *Retrospace: Collected Essays on Chicano Literature Theory and History*, Juan Bruce-Novoa, 52–62. Houston: Arte Público Press.

Calvillo, Daniel. 1991. "Mi Diario (Segmentos)." *Llueve Tlaloc*, no. 18: 1–6.

Canon, James. 1999. "My Lessons with Felipe." In *Virgins, Guerrillas and Locas: Gay Latinos Writing on Love*, edited by Jaime Cortez, 65–80. San Francisco: Cleis Press.

Castillo, Ana. 1985. Interview. In *Partial Autobiographies: Interviews with Twenty Chicano Poets*, edited by Wolfgang Binder, 28–38. Erlangen, W. Germany: Verlag Palm and Enke.

Cervantes, Lorna Dee. 1985. Interview. In *Partial Autobiographies: Interviews with Twenty Chicano Poets*, edited by Wolfgang Binder, 39–53. Erlangen, W. Germany: Verlag Palm and Enke.

Chávez, César E. 1966. "The Organizer's Tale." *Ramparts* 5, no. 2: 43–50.

———. 1969. "Nonviolence Still Works." *Look Magazine*, April 1), 3.

———. 1973. "The Organizer's Tale." In *Chicano: The Evolution of a People*. Compiled by Renato Rosaldo, Robert A. Calvert, Gustav L. Seligmann, 297–302. Minneapolis: Winston Press.

———. 2002. "From 'The Organizer's Tale.'" In *Under the Fifth Sun: Latino Literature from California*, edited by Rich Heide, 291–96. Santa Clara, CA: Santa Clara University; Berkeley: Heyday Books.

Chávez, Denise. 1989. "Heat and Rain (Testimonio)." In *Breaking Boundaries: Latina Writing and Critical Readings*, edited by Asuncion Horno-Delgado, 27–32. Amherst: University of Massachusetts Press.

Cisneros, Sandra. 1985. Interview. In *Partial Autobiographies: Interviews with Twenty Chicano Poets*, edited by Wolfgang Binder, 54–74. Erlangen, W. Germany: Verlag Palm and Enke.

Cisneros, Sandra. 1986. "Living as a Writer: Choice and Circumstance." *Revista Mujeres* 3, no. 2: 68–72.

———. 1987a. "Do You Know Me? I Wrote *The House On Mango Street*." *The Americas Review* 15, no. 1: 77–79.

———. 1987b. "Ghosts and Voices: Writing from Obsession." *The Americas Review* 15, no. 1: 69–73. Reprinted in *Hispanic American Literature: A Brief Introduction and Anthology*, edited by Nicolas Kanellos, 45–49. New York: Longman, 1995.

———. 1987c. "Notes to a Young(er) Writer." *The Americas Review* 15, no. 1: 74–76. Reprinted in *Hispanic American Literature: A Brief Introduction and Anthology*, edited by Nicolas Kanellos, 50–52. New York: Longman, 1995.

———. 1990. "Only Daughter." *Glamour*, November, 256, 285. Reprinted in *Mascaras*, edited by Lucha Corpi, 118–23. Berkeley, CA: Third Woman Press, 1997.

Cornejo, Kency. 2019. "Writing Art Histories from Below: A Decolonial *Guanaca*-Hood Perspective." *Latin American and Latinx Visual Culture* 1, no. 3: 72–77.

Coronado, Raúl, Jr. 1999. "Dallas, Summer 1986." In *Virgins, Guerrillas and Locas: Gay Latinos Writing on Love*, edited by Jaime Cortez, 47–51. San Francisco: Cleis Press.

Coronel, Antonio Franco. 1994. "De cosas de Californio de Antonio Franco Coronel." In *Nineteenth-Century Californio Testimonios*, edited by Rosaura Sánchez, Beatrice Pita, and Bárbara Reyes, special edition of *Crítica: A Journal of Critical Essays* (Spring): 123–36.

Corpi, Lucha. 1985. Interview. In *Partial Autobiographies: Interviews with Twenty Chicano Poets*, edited by Wolfgang Binder, 75–85. Erlangen, W. Germany: Verlag Palm and Enke.

Cruz, George Xavier. 1988. "Being Hispanic in Houston, TX: From the "Barrio" and Back Again." *The Americas Review* 16, no. 1: 53–64.

Cuadros, Gil. 2002. "Indulgences." In *Under the Fifth Sun: Latino Literature from California*, edited by Rich Heide, 488–94. Santa Clara, CA: Santa Clara University; Berkeley, CA: Heyday Books.

Cunningham, Veronica. 1985. Interview. In *Partial Autobiographies: Interviews with Twenty Chicano Poets*, edited by Wolfgang Binder, 86–92. Erlangen, W. Germany: Verlag Palm and Enke.

Dávila, Arlene. 2003. "Ethnicity, Fieldwork, and the Cultural Capital That Gets Us There: Reflections from US. Hispanic Marketing." *Aztlán: A Journal of Chicano Studies* 28, no. 1: 145–161.

de Hoyos, Angela. 1985. Interview. In *Partial Autobiographies: Interviews with Twenty Chicano Poets*, edited by Wolfgang Binder, 109–16. Erlangen, W. Germany: Verlag Palm and Enke.

de la tierra, tatiana. 2002. "Activist Latina Lesbian Publishing: Esto no tiene nombre and conmoción." *Aztlán: A Journal of Chicano Studies* 27, no. 1: 139–78.

de Leon, Eduardo S. 1996. El Chicano y el Joto. *Latino Studies Journal* 7, no. 3 (Fall): 26–42.

Chavez, Denise. 1990. Interview with Annie O. Eysturoy. In *This Is About Vision: Interviews with Southwestern Writers*, edited by William Balassi, John F. Crawford, and Annie O. Eysturoy, 156–69. Albuquerque: University of New Mexico Press.

Franco, Jean. 1990. "Joseph Sommers: A Personal Memoir." *Crítica* 2, no. 2: 16–18.

Franco, Juan Roberto. 1978. "Name Frames II: The Nomenclature of an Autobiography." *Nuestro* 2, no. 8: 36–37.

Gallegos, Magdalena. 1985. "The Swallowtail Butterfly." *Colorado Heritage*, no. 2: 21–26.

Gamboa, Harry, Jr. 1997. "Phantoms in Urban Exile." *Aztlán: A Journal of Chicano Studies* 22, no. 2: 197–203.

Garcia, Jerry. 2004. "The Measure of a Cock: Mexican Cockfighting, Culture, and Masculinity." In *I Am Aztlán: The Personal Essay in Chicano Studies*, edited by Chon A. Noriega and Wendy Belcher. Los Angeles: UCLA Chicano Studies Research Center Press.

Gil, Carlos B. 1989. "Washington's Hispano American Communities." In *Peoples of Washington: Perspectives On Cultural Diversity*, edited by Sid White and S.E. Solberg, 159–93. Pullman: Washington State University Press.

Valdez, Luis. 1994. Interview with Elliot Gilbert. *Low Rider Magazine* 16, no. 11: 22, 27.

Gómez-Peña, Guillermo. 1991. "El performance como peregrinación binacional." In *Visual Arts on the U.S./Mexican Border*, edited by Harry Polkinhorn, 73–95. Calexico, CA: Binational Press.

González, Michelle. 1986. "Reflexiones de una estudiante chicana." *Fem* 10, no. 48: 40–41.

Gonzales, Rebecca. 1985. Interview. In *Partial Autobiographies: Interviews with Twenty Chicano Poets*, edited by Wolfgang Binder, 93–94. Erlangen, W. Germany: Verlag Palm and Enke.

Groth, Gary. 1989. "The Hernandez Bros. Interview." *The Comics Journal, no. 126*: 60–111.

Guerra, Erasmo. 1999. "Sexmoneylove." In *Virgins, Guerrillas and Locas: Gay Latinos Writing on Love*, edited by Jaime Cortez, 93–98. San Francisco: Cleis Press.

Guerra de Ord, Angustias de la. 1994. "Del testimonio de Doña Angustias de la Guerra de Ord: Ocurrencias en California, relatadas a Thomas Savage en Santa Barbara, 1878." *Crítica* (Spring): 68–74.

Hernández-Cancio, Sinsi Mercedes. 1990. "To Tell One's Story: Women's Self-Definition in Latino Male/Female Relationships." *Latino Studies Journal* 1, no. 2: 74–93.

Herrera, Juan Felipe. 1989. "Memoir: Checker-Piece." In *Best New Chicano Literature*, edited by Julian Palley, 83–87. Tempe: Bilingual Press.

———. 1991. "Mission Street Manifesto: Circa 1959–1982." *Guadalupe Review*, no. 1: 175–216.

———. 1992. "Blowfish: An Autobiography." In *New Chicana/Chicano Writing 1*, edited by Charles M. Tatum, 119–41. Tucson: University of Arizona Press.

Huerta, Dolores. 1972. "Dolores Huerta Talks." *La Voz del Pueblo* 3, no. 8: 8–10, 22.

Lichty-Uribe, Pat. 1994. "I Had a Choice." In *Compañeras: Latina Lesbians: An Anthology*, edited by Juanita Ramos, 28–34. New York: Routledge.

López, Alma. 2001. "Silencing Our Lady: La respuesta de Alma." *Aztlán: A Journal of Chicano Studies* 26, no. 2 : 249–67.

López, Enrique Hank. 1971. "Back to Bachimba." In *The Chicanos: Mexican American Voices*, edited by Ed Ludwig and James Santibanez, 261–70. Baltimore: Penguin Books.

Lorenzana, Apolinaria. 1994. "Memorias de Doña Apolinaria Lorenzana 'La Beata' dictadas por ella en Santa Barbara en Marzo de 1878 a Thomas Savage, Bancroft Library 1878." *Crítica: A Journal of Critical Essays* (Spring): 1–14.

Lorenzo, Orestes. 1993. "Power of Love." *Hispanic* (May): 50, 52, 54.

Luna, Jesús. 1973. "Luna's Abe Lincoln Story." In *Chicano: The Evolution of a People*, edited by Renato Rosaldo, Robert A. Calvert, and Gustav L. Seligmann, 347–55. Minneapolis: Winston Press.

Machado de Ridington (Wrightington), Juana. 1994. "Los tiempos pasados de la alta California: Recuerdos de la Sra. Doña Juana Machado de Ridington, Bancroft Library 1878." *Crítica: A Journal of Critical Essays* (Spring): 15–29.

Martínez, Elisa A. 1983. "Sharing Her Tiny Pieces of the Past." *Nuestro* 7, no. 7: 51–52.

Martínez, Jesús. 1993. "National Identity and Binational Migration: An Autobiography." *San Jose Studies* 19, no. 1: 89–103.

Martínez, Oscar. 1993. "Gregorio Hernandez Moreno: Diary of an Undocumented Worker." *Journal of Borderlands Studies* 8, no. 2: 59–72.

Mendoza, Lupe. 1984. "¿Porque lo podemos hacer—a poco no?" *Revista Mujeres* 1, no. 2: 33–37.

Mohr, Nicholasa. 1986. "On Being Authentic." *The Americas Review* 14, nos. 3–4: 106–9.

Molleur, Suzanne. 1974. "A Chicano Bishop Looks at His Church: An Interview with Bishop Flores." *Saint Anthony Messenger* 82, no. 5: 37.

Montoya, Margaret E. 1998. "Masks and Acculturation." In *The Latino/a Condition: A Critical Reader*, edited by Richard Delgado and J. Stefancic, 435–41. New York: New York University Press. Reprint, 1998.

———. 1998. "Masks and Identity." In *The Latino/a Condition: A Critical Reader*, edited by Richard Delgado and J. Stefancic, 37–43. New York: New York University Press.

Mora, Pat. 1990. Interview with Tey Diana Rebolledo. In *This Is About Vision: Interviews with Southwestern Writers*, edited by William Balassi, John F. Crawford, and Annie O. Eysturoy, 128–39. Albuquerque: University of New Mexico Press.

Moraga, Cherríe. 1981. "La Güera." In *This Bridge Called My Back*, edited by Cherríe Moraga, Gloria A. Anzaldúa, and Toni Cade Bambara, 27–34. Watertown, MA: Persephone Press.

———. 2003. "Queer Aztlán: The Re-Formation of Chicano Tribe." In *Latino/a Thought: Culture, Politics, and Society*, edited by Francisco H. Vázquez and Rodolfo Torres, 258–74. Lanham, MD: Rowman and Littlefield.

Morales, Tomás. 1985. "Entering the 'New World' of College." *Nuestro* 9, no. 9: 48.

Negrón-Muntaner, Frances. 1999. "Beyond the Cinema of the Other, or Toward Another Cinema." *Aztlán: A Journal of Chicano Studies* 24, no. 2: 149–54.

Nericcio, William Anthony. 1988. "Autobiographies at La Frontera: The Quest for Mexican-American Narrative." *The Americas Review* 16, nos. 3–4: 165–87.

Noriega, Chon A. 2002. Research Note. *Aztlán: A Journal of Chicano Studies* 27, no. 2 (Fall): 1–8.

Ochoa, Rubén. 2003. "Breaking Down Glass Walls." *Aztlán: A Journal of Chicano Studies* 28, no. 1: 175–78.

Olivas, Michael A. 1990. "The Chronicles, My Grandfather's Stories, and Immigration Law: The Slave Trader's Chronicle as Racial History." *Saint Louis University Law Journal* 34, no. 3: 425–41.

―――. 1998. "'Breaking the Law' on Principle." In *The Latino/a Condition: A Critical Reader*, edited by Richard Delgado and J. Stefancic, 320–31. New York: New York University Press.

Ortega, Emmanuel. 2019. "Spanish Colonial Art History and the Work of Empire." *Latin American and Latinx Visual Culture* 1, no. 3: 83–86.

Osuna de Marrón, Felipa. 1994. "Recuerdos de Doña Felipa Osuna de Marrón natural de San Diego donde vive actualmente con varios papeles originales pertenecientes al archivo particular de la misma señora, que los obsequio a la Bancroft Library 1878." *Crítica A Journal of Critical Essays* (Spring): 45–53.

Peffia, Terry de la. 1991. "Beyond el Camino Real." In *Chicana Lesbians: The Girls Our Mothers Warned Us About*, edited by Carla Trujillo, 85–94. Berkeley: Third Woman Press.

Paredes, Américo. 1993. "The Hammon and the Beans." In *Growing Up Latino*, edited by Harold Augenbraum, 159–64. Boston: Houghton Mifflin.

Pérez, Emma. 1991. "Gulf Dreams." In *Chicana Lesbians: The Girls Our Mothers Warned Us About*, edited by Carla Trujillo. Berkeley: Third Woman Press.

Pérez, Eulalia. 1994. "Eulalia Perez, una vieja y sus recuerdos dictados a la edad avanzada de 139 anos, San Gabriel, California, 1877." *Crítica: A Journal of Critical Essays* (Spring): 31–44.

―――. 1997. "An Old Woman Remembers." In *The Latino Reader: An American Literary Tradition from 1542 to the Present*, edited by Harold Augenbraum and Margarite Fernandez Olmos, 72–80. Boston: Houghton Mifflin.

Pérez, Vincent. 1999. "Heroes and Orphans of the Hacienda: Narratives of a Mexican American Family." *Aztlán: A Journal of Chicano Studies* 24, no. 1: 33–106.

Pesqueira, Randy. 1999. "Daddycakes." In *Virgins, Guerrillas and Locas: Gay Latinos Writing on Love*, edited by Jaime Cortez, 53–57. San Francisco: Cleis Press.

Pico, María Inocenta. 1994. "Cosas de California contadas a Thomas Savage en Avila y San Luis Obispo por Doña Maria Inocenta Pico, viuda de Don Miguel Avila, 1878 Bancroft Library." *Crítica: A Journal of Critical Essays* (Spring): 57–66.

Pineda, Cecile. 1997. "Deracinated: The Writer Re-Invents Her Sources." In *Mascaras*, edited by Lucha Corpi, 56–70. Berkeley: Third Woman Press.

Ponce, Mary Helen. 1983. "El jabon de Doña Chonita." *Nuestro* 7, no. 10: 44–45.

―――. 1994. "The Day Rito Died." In *Currents from the Dancing River*, edited by Ray Gonzalez, 197–203. New York: Harcourt Brace.

―――. 1997. "On Language." In *Mascaras*, edited by Lucha Corpi, 110–17. Berkeley: Third Woman Press.

Prado, José M. 1994. "From Farm Work to a Washington Fellowship." *The Hispanic Outlook in Higher Education* 4, no. 12: 6–7.

Prida, Dolores. 1989. "The Show Goes On (Testimonio)." In *Breaking Boundaries: Latina Writing and Critical Readings*, edited by Asuncion Horno-Delgado, 181–88. Amherst: University of Massachusetts Press.

Quinn, Manuela (Nellie). 2002. "From the Original Sin." In *Under the Fifth Sun: Latino Literature from California*, edited by Rich Heide, 229–36. Santa Clara, CA: Santa Clara University; Berkeley: Heyday Books.

Quintana, Alvina E. 1998. "Turning Sunshine into Noir and Fantasy into Reality: Los Angeles in the Classroom." *Aztlán: A Journal of Chicano Studies* 23, no. 2: 179–189.

Ramírez, Walter C. 1993. "Diary of a Madman." In *New Chicana/Chicano Writing 3*, edited by Charles M. Tatum, 115–40. Tucson: University of Arizona Press.

Reynoso, Cruz. 2002. "Brief Remembrances: My Appointment and Service on the California Court of Appeal and Supreme Court, 1976–1987." *Berkeley La Raza Law Journal* 13, no. 1: 15–27.

Rips, Geoffrey. 1983. "Living History: Emma Tenayuca Tells Her Story." *Texas Observer*, October 28, 7–15.

Rivera, Edward. 1993. "First Communion." In *Growing Up Latino*, edited by Harold Augenbraum, 211–49. Boston: Houghton Mifflin.

Rodríguez, Richard. 1974. "Going Home Again: The New American Scholarship Boy." *American Scholar* 44, no. 1: 15–28.

———. 1989. "An American Writer." In *The Invention of Ethnicity*, edited by Werner Sollors, 3–13. New York: Oxford University Press.

———. 1993. "Aria." In *Growing Up Latino*, edited by Harold Augenbraum, 305–28. Boston: Houghton Mifflin.

———. 1997. "Prologue: Middle-Class Pastoral." In *Literatura Chicana, 1965–1995: An Anthology in Spanish, English, and Calo*, edited by Manuel de Jesús Hernández-Gutiérrez, and David William Foster, 62–65. New York: Garland.

———. 1998. "A Scholarship Boy." In *The Latino/a Condition: A Critical Reader*, edited by Richard Delgado and J. Stefancic, 419–20. New York: New York University Press.

Romo, Ricardo. 1986. "A Westside Story." *Texas Observer* 78, no. 25: 10–12.

Roque Ramírez, Horacio N. 1999. "El Sereno." In *Virgins, Guerrillas and Locas: Gay Latinos Writing on Love*, edited by Jaime Cortez, 5–12. San Francisco: Cleis Press.

Ruelas, J. Oshi. 1987. "Moments of Change." *Revista* Mujeres 4, no. 1: 23–33.

Salseda, Rose. 2019. "Creating Equity in Academia for Latinx Art History." *Latin American and Latinx Visual Culture* 1, no. 3: 87–91.

Sandoval, Anna. 1999–2000. "Building Up Our Resistance: Chicanas in Academia." *Frontiers: A Journal of Women Studies* 20, no. 1: 86–92.

Sandoval, Lito. 1999. "I Love You Also." In *Virgins, Guerrillas and Locas: Gay Latinos Writing on Love*, edited by Jaime Cortez, 27–30. San Francisco: Cleis Press.

Schirra, Roger. 1999. "News of Your Country." In *Virgins, Guerrillas and Locas: Gay Latinos Writing on Love*, edited by Jaime Cortez, 83–92. San Francisco: Cleis Press.

Seguín, John N. 2003. "The Making of a Tejano: The Personal Memoirs of John N. Seguín." In *Latino/a Thought: Culture, Politics, and Society*, edited by Francisco H. Vazquez and Rodolfo Torres, 102–21. Lanham, MD: Rowman and Littlefield.

Sierra, Rubén. 1979. Untitled autobiography. *Metamorfosis* 2, nos. 1–2: 5.

Small, Mario. 1996. "West Indian Latino." *Latino Studies Journal* 7, no. 3: 43–47.

Smith, Norman. 1986. "Buffalos and Cockroaches: Acosta's Siege at Aztlán." In *Contemporary Chicano Fiction: A Critical Survey*, edited by Vernon E. Lattin, 82–93. Binghamton, NY: Bilingual Press/Editorial Bilingüe.

Solís, Manuel. 1996. "Growing Up Tejano." *Latino Studies Journal* 7, no. 3: 17–25.

Soriano, Diane H. 1984. "'Ni he tenido tiempo para mi': Entrevista con Gabriella S. Mejia." *Revista Mujeres* 1, no. 2: 38–41.

Sosa, Maribel. 1999. "Sense and Responsibility." *Frontiers: A Journal of Women Studies* 20, no. 1: 97–104.

Soto, Gary. 1993. "Being Mean." In *Growing Up Latino*, edited by Harold Augenbraum, 274–79. Boston: Houghton Mifflin.

Thomas, Raul. 1999. "They Say I'm One of Those: Excerpts from Dicen Que Soy." In *Virgins, Guerrillas and Locas: Gay Latinos Writing on Love*, edited by Jaime Cortez, 33–45. San Francisco: Cleis Press.

Thwaites, Jeanne. 1992. "The Use of Irony in Oscar Zeta Acosta's *The Autobiography of a Brown Buffalo*." *The Americas Review* 20, no. 1 (Spring): 73–82.

Tijerina, Aleticia. 1994. "I Am the Lost Daughter of My Mama's House (Oral History)." In *Compañeras: Latina Lesbians: An Anthology*, edited by Juanita Ramos. New York: Routledge.

Trujillo, Carla. 1992. "Confessions of a Chicana PhD: On Lesbians, Class, and Interracial Relationships." *Out/Look* 4, no. 3: 22–27.

Urrea, Luis Alberto. 1994. "Father's Day." In *Currents from the Dancing River*, edited by Ray Gonzalez, 198–11. New York: Harcourt Brace.

Vallejo, Manuel Salvador. 1994. "De notas históricas sobre California de Jose Manuel Salvador Vallejo, Sonoma, California, 1874." *Crítica: A Journal of Critical Essays* (Spring): 91–104.

Vallejo, Platón Mariano Guadalupe. 1994. "From Memoirs of the Vallejos." *Crítica: A Journal of Critical Essays* (Spring): 106–22.

Vela, Richard R. 1978. "Autobiography with Horses." *De Colores* 4, nos. 1–2: 52.

———. 1978. "Poetry." *De Colores* 4, no. 1–2: 50–52.

Vicioso, Sherezada (Chiqui). 1989. "An Oral History (Testimonio)." In *Breaking Boundaries: Latina Writing and Critical Readings*, edited by Asuncion Horno-Delgado, 229–34. Amherst: University of Massachusetts Press.

Villalón, Joel Antonio. "Boots." 1999. In *Virgins, Guerrillas and Locas: Gay Latinos Writing on Love*, edited by Jaime Cortez, 13–25. San Francisco: Cleis Press.

Villanueva, Alma Luz. 1985. Interview. In *Partial Autobiographies: Interviews with Twenty Chicano Poets*, edited by Wolfgang Binder, 201–2. Erlangen, W. Germany: Verlag Palm and Enke.

———. 1997. "Abundance." In *Mascaras*, edited by Lucha Corpi, 36–55. Berkeley, CA: Third Woman Press.

Villegas, Ygnacio. 2002. "From Boyhood Days." In *Under the Fifth Sun: Latino Literature from California*, edited by Rich Heide, 8–10. Santa Clara, CA: Santa Clara University; Berkeley: Heyday Books.

Viramontes, Helena María. 1989. "'Nopalitos': The Making of Fiction." In *Breaking Boundaries: Latina Writing and Critical Readings*, edited by Asuncion Horno-Delgado, 33–38. Amherst: University of Massachusetts Press. Reprinted in *Making Face, Making Soul: Haciendo Caras: Creative and Critical Perspectives* by *Women of Color*, edited by Gloria Anzaldúa, 291–294. San Francisco: Aunt Lute Foundation Books, 1990.

Waldron, Lawrence. 2019. "Color in the Curriculum or in Ourselves? Why I Thought I Had to Choose." *Latin American and Latinx Visual Culture* 1, no. 3: 92–95.

Williams, Norma. 1988. "A Mexican American Woman Encounters Sociology: An Autobiographical Perspective." *American Sociologist* 19, no. 4: 340–46.

Zamora, Bernice. 1985. Interview. In *Partial Autobiographies: Interviews with Twenty Chicano Poets*, edited by Wolfgang Binder, 221–29. Erlangen, W. Germany: Verlag Palm and Enke.

———. 1997. "Silence at Bay." In *Mascaras*, edited by Lucha Corpi, 20–34. Berkeley: Third Woman Press.

Zamora, Rodolfo. 1999. "The Lost City." In *Virgins, Guerrillas and Locas: Gay Latinos Writing on Love*, edited by Jaime Cortez, 59–63. San Francisco: Cleis Press.

Secondary Literature

Abrahão, Maria Helena Menna Barreto. 2012. "Autobiographical Research: Memory, Time and Narratives in the First Person." *European Journal for Research on the Education and Learning of Adults* 3, no. 1: 29–41.

Adams, Timothy Dow. 2001. "Heightened by Life" vs. "Paralyzed by Fact": Photography and Autobiography in Norma Cantu's Canicula. *Biography* 24, no. 1: 57.

Alvarez, Francisco R. 1993. "*The Autobiography of a Brown Buffalo* de Oscar Zeta Acosta: Escritura, ser e idcología en la autobiografía chicana de los 70." *Monographic Review*: 162–75.

Alvarez-Borland, Isabel. 1994. "Displacements and Autobiography in Cuban-American Fiction." *World Literature Today* 68, no. 1: 43–48.

Bell, Michael Davitt. 1982. "Fitting into a Tradition of Autobiography." *Change* 14, no. 7: 36–39.

Bello, Ruth T. 1988. "Being Hispanic in Houston, TX: A Matter of Identity." *The Americas Review* 16, no. 1: 31–43.

Bellver, Pilar. 1999. "La historia oral como autobiografía cultural: Dos ejemplos chicanos." *Aztlán: A Journal of Chicano Studies* 24, no. 2: 49–72.

Blackwell, Maylei. 2011. *¡Chicana Power! Contested Histories of Feminism in the Chicano Movement*. Austin: University of Texas Press.

Bost, Suzanne. 2019. *Shared Selves: Latinx Memoir and Ethical Alternatives to Humanism*. Urbana: University of Illinois Press.

Bruce-Novoa, Juan. 1985. "Mexico en la literatura chicana (II)." *La Comunidad*, no. 268, September 8, 14–15.

———. 1986. "Homosexuality and the Chicano Novel." *Confluencia* 2, no. 1: 69–77.

———. 1990. "Mexico in Chicano Literature." In *Retrospace: Collected Essays On Chicano Literature Theory and History*, edited by Juan Bruce-Novoa, 52–62. Houston: Arte Público Press.

———. 1996. "The U.S.-Mexican Border in Chicano Testimonial Writing: A Topological Approach to Four Hundred and Fifty Years of Writing the Border." *Discourse* 18, nos. 1–2: 32–53.

Brumble, H. David. 2018. *Street-Gang and Tribal-Warrior Autobiographies*. London and New York: Anthem Press.

Calderón, Héctor. 2004. *Narratives of Greater Mexico: Essays on Chicano Literary History, Genre, and Borders*. Austin: University of Texas Press.

Castillo-Garsow, Melissa, and Jason Nichols, eds. 2016. *La Verdad: An International Dialogue on Hip Hop Latinidades*. Columbus: Ohio State University Press.

Christopher, Renny. 2002. "Rags to Riches to Suicide: Unhappy Narratives of Upward Mobility: *Martin Eden*, *Bread Givers*, *Delia's Song*, and *Hunger of Memory*." *College Literature* 29, no. 4: 79–109.

Dalleo, Raphael, and Elena Machado Sáez. 2007. *The Latino/a Canon and the Emergence of Post-Sixties Literature*. New York: Palgrave Macmillan.

Davis, Rocío G. 2002. "Metanarrative in Ethnic Autobiography for Children: Laurence Yep's *The Lost Garden* and Judith Ortiz Cofer's *Silent Dancing*." *MELUS: Multi-Ethnic Literature of the United States* 27, no. 2: 139–56.

Delgadillo, Theresa. 2015. *Latina Lives in Milwaukee*. Urbana, Chicago, and Springfield: University of Illinois Press.

Espinoza, Dionne, María Eugenia Cotera, and Maylei Blackwell, eds. 2018. *Chicana Movidas: New Narratives of Activism and Feminism in the Movement Era*. Austin: University of Texas Press.

Fachinger, Petra. 2001. "Lost in Nostalgia: The Autobiographies of Eva Hoffman and Richard Rodriguez." *MELUS: Multi-Ethnic Literature of the United States* 26, no. 2: 111–27.

Fernández, Roberta. 1997. "Depicting Women's Culture in Intaglio: A Novel in Six Stories." In *Mascaras*, edited by Lucha Corpi, 72–96. Berkeley: Third Woman Press.

Fernández-García, Andrea. 2020. *Geographies of Girlhood in US Latina Writing: Decolonizing Spaces and Identities*. Cham, Switzerland: Palgrave Macmillan.

Fischer, Michael M. J. 1986. Ethnicity and the Post-Modern Arts of Memory. In *Writing Culture: The Poetics and Politics of Ethnography*, edited by James Clifford and George E. Marcus, 194–233. Berkeley: University of California Press.

Flores, Juan. 2000. *From Bomba to Hip-Hop: Puerto Rican Culture and Latino Identity*. New York: Columbia University Press.

Flores, Lauro. 1990. "Chicano Autobiography: Culture, Ideology and the Self." *The Americas Review* 18, no. 2: 80–91.

Gamio, Manuel. 1980. "Señora Flores de Andrade." In *Mexican Women in the United States: Struggles Past and Present*, by Magdalena Mora and Adelaida del Castillo, 189–92. Los Angeles: UCLA Chicano Studies Research Center.

García, Mario T. 2016. *Literature as History: Autobiography, Testimonio, and the Novel in the Chicano and Latino Experience*. Tucson: University of Arizona Press.

Garcia, Michael Nieto. 2014. *Autobiography in Black and Brown: Ethnic Identity in Richard Wright and Richard Rodriguez*. Albuquerque: University of New Mexico Press.

Gatto, Katherine M. 1998. "Mambo, Merengue, Salsa: The Dynamics of Self-Construction in Latina Autobiographical Narrative." *Philological Papers* 48: 84–90.

Griffiths, Morwenna. 1994. "Autobiography, Feminism, and the Practice of Action Research." *Educational Action Research* 2, no. 1: 71–82.

Guzmán, Romeo, Carribean Fragoza, Alex Sayf Cummings, and Ryan Reft, eds. 2020. *East of East: The Making of Greater El Monte*. New Brunswick and Newark: Rutgers.

Hannabuss, Stuart. 2000. "Being There: Ethnographic Research and Autobiography." *Library Management* 21, no. 2: 99–107. https://www.emerald.com/insight/content/doi/10.1108/01435120010309425/full/html.

Hernandez, Ellie D. 2009. *Postnationalism in Chicana/o Literature and Culture*. Austin: University of Texas Press.

Hernández-Cancio, Sinsi Mercedes. 1990. "To Tell One's Story: Women's Self-Definition in Latino Male/Female Relationships." *Latino Studies Journal* 1, no. 2: 74–93.

Herrera-Sobek, María. 1997. "Geography of Despair: The Mean Streets of L.A. of Luis Rodriguez's *Always Running*." *Latino Studies Journal* 8, no. 2: 56–67.

Hunsaker, Alan C. 1990. Book review of *The Autobiography of a Brown Buffalo* and *the Revolt of the Cockroach People*. *Hispanic Journal of Behavioral Sciences* 12, no. 3: 328–34.

Iwabuchi, D. S., and R. Stuhr-Rommereim. 2003. *Autobiographies by Americans of Color, 1995–2000: An Annotated Bibliography*. Albany, NY: Whitston Publishing Co.

Jiménez, Luis A. 1995. "Nineteenth Century Autobiography in the Afro-Americas: Frederick Douglass and Juan Francisco Manzano." *Afro-Hispanic Review* 14, no. 2: 47–52.

Keating, AnaLouise, and Gloria González-López, eds. 2011. *Bridging: How Gloria Anzaldúa's Life and Work Transformed Our Own*. Austin: University of Texas Press.

Kowalczyk, Kimberly A. 1988. "Oscar Zeta Acosta: The Brown Buffalo and His Search for Identity." *The Americas Review* 16, nos. 3–4: 198–209.

Kridel, Craig. n.d. "An Introduction to Biographical Research." American Educational Research Association website. http://www.aera.net/SIG013/Research-Connections/Introduction-to-Biographical-Research.

López, Marissa K. 2011. *Chicano Nations: The Hemispheric Origins of Mexican American Literature*. New York: New York University Press.

Marinic, S. 1996. *Contemporary Autobiography in the Mexican American Borderland: Richard Rodriguez in Perspective*. Salzburg, Austria: University of Salzburg.

Márquez, Antonio C. 1984. "Richard Rodriguez's *Hunger of Memory* and the Poetics of Experience." *Arizona Quarterly* 40, no. 2: 130–41.

———. 1988. "Self and Culture: Autobiography as Cultural Narrative." *Bilingual Review* 14, no. 3: 57–64. Reprinted in *Discurso literario: Revista de temas hispanicos* 7, no. 1 (1990): 51–66

McKenna, Teresa. 1997. *Migrant Song: Politics and Process in Contemporary Chicano Literature*. Austin: University of Texas Press.

Méndez-Negrete, Josie. 2020. *Activist Leaders of San José: En sus propias voces*. Tucson: University of Arizona Press.

Molloy, Sylvia. 1991. *At Face Value: Autobiographical Writing in Spanish America.* Cambridge: Cambridge University Press.

Murray, David. 1988. "Authenticity and Text in American Indian, Hispanic and Asian Autobiography." In *First Person Singular: Studies in American Autobiography,* edited by A. Robert Lee, 177–97. New York: St. Martin's Press.

Nericcio, William Anthony. 1988. "Autobiographies at La Frontera: The Quest for Mexican-American Narrative." *The Americas Review* 16, nos. 3–4: 165–87.

Neumaier, Diane. 1990. "Judy Baca: Our People Are the Internal Exiles." In *Making Face, Making Soul: Haciendo Caras: Creative and Critical Perspectives by Women of Color,* edited by Gloria Anzaldúa, 256–70. San Francisco: Aunt Lute Foundation Books.

Nuiry, Octavio Emilio. 1993. Book review of *Growing Up Latino. Hispanic* (August): 62.

Oboler, Suzanne, ed. 2009. *Behind Bars: Latino/as and Prison in the United States.* New York: Palgrave Macmillan.

Ocasio, Rafael. 2000. "Autobiographical Writing and 'Out of the Closet' Literature by Gay Latino Writers." *Antípodas: Journal of Hispanic and Galician Studies,* nos. 11–12: 273–82.

Olazagasti-Segovia, Elena. 2000. "The Mother Figure." *Latino(a) Research Review* 4, no. 3: 40–42.

Padilla, Amado M. 2003. "The Origins of the Hispanic Journal of Behavioral Sciences: A Personal Memoir." *Hispanic Journal of Behavioral Sciences* 25, no. 1: 3–12.

Padilla, Genaro M. 1984. "The Self as Cultural Metaphor in Acosta's *The Autobiography of a Brown Buffalo.*" *The Journal of General Education* 35, no. 4: 242–58.

———. 1988. "The Recovery of Chicano Nineteenth-Century Autobiography." *American Quarterly* 40, no. 3: 286–307.

———. 1988. "'Yo Sola Aprendi': Contra-Patriarchal Containment in Women's Nineteenth-Century California Personal Narratives." *The Americas Review* 16, nos. 3–4: 91–109.

———. 1991. "Imprisoned Narrative? or Lies, Secrets, and Silence in New Mexico Women's Autobiography." In *Criticism in the Borderlands: Studies in Chicano Literature, Culture, and Ideology,* edited by Héctor Calderón and José David Saldívar, 43–60. Durham, NC: Duke University Press.

———. 1993. "Discontinuous Continuities: Remapping the Terrain of Spanish Colonial Narrative." In *Reconstructing a Chicano/a Literary Heritage,* edited by Maria Herrera-Sobek, 24–36. Tucson: University of Arizona Press.

———. 1993. *My History, Not Yours: The Formation of Mexican American Autobiography.* Madison: University of Wisconsin Press.

Paredes, Raymund A. 1992. "Autobiography and Ethnic Politics: Richard Rodriguez's *Hunger of Memory.*" In *Multicultural Autobiography: American Lives,* edited by James Robert Payne, 280–96. Knoxville: University of Tennessee Press.

Pines, Paul. 1992. Book review of *Working in the Dark. Multicultural Review* 1, no. 3: 48.

Portales, Marco A. 1998. Book review of *From Labor to Letters: A Novel Autobiography. MELUS: Multi-Ethnic Literature of the United States* 23, no. 1: 177–81.

Portillo, Annette Angela. 2005. "Outlaw Genres: Reconceptualizing Life Stories by Chicanas and Native American Women." PhD diss., Cornell University.

Postlewate, Marissa Herrera. 2003. *How and Why I Write: Redefining Hispanic Women's Writing and Experience.* New York: P. Lang.

Ramírez, Arthur. 1975. Book review of *The Autobiography of a Brown Buffalo* and *The Revolt of the Cockroach People. Revista Chicano-Riquena* 3, no. 3: 46–53.

Randolph, Donald A. 1988. "Autobiography as Pain: Anthony Quinn's *The Original Sin." The Americas Review* 16, nos. 3–4: 144–64.

Rebolledo, Tey Diana. 2005. *The Chronicles of Panchita Villa and Other Guerrilleras: Essays on Chicana/Latina Literature and Criticism.* Austin: University of Texas Press.

Rivera, Tomás. 1984. "Richard Rodriguez's *Hunger of Memory* as a Humanistic Antithesis." *MELUS: Multi-Ethnic Literature of the United States* 11, no. 4: 5–13.

Rockwell, Susan L. 1994. Book review of *My History, Not Yours: The Formation of Mexican American Autobiography. Explorations in Sights and Sounds,* no. 14: 62–64.

Rodríguez, Luis J. 1991. "Literacy and the Writer's Spirit." *Guadalupe Review* no. 1: 277–80.

Rodríguez, Randy A. 1998. "Richard Rodríguez Reconsidered: Queering the Sissy (Ethnic) Subject." *Texas Studies in Literature and Language* 40, no. 4: 396–424.

Romero, Lora. 1993. "'When Something Goes Queer': Familiarity, Formalism, and Minority Intellectuals in the 1980s." *Yale Journal of Criticism* 6, no. 1: 121–42.

Romero, Osvaldo. 1974. Book review of *The Autobiography of a Brown Buffalo. Oester* 4, no. 2: 141.

Rose, Shirley K. 1987. "Metaphors and Myths of Cross-Cultural Literacy: Autobiographical Narratives by Maxine Hong Kingston, Richard Rodriguez and Malcolm X." *MELUS: Multi-Ethnic Literature of the United States* 14, no. 1: 3–15.

Roybal, Karen R. 2017. *Archives of Dispossession: Recovering the Testimonios of Mexican American Herederas, 1848–1960.* Chapel Hill: University of North Carolina Press.

Sabat-Rivers, Georgina. 1983. Book Review of *A Woman of Genius: The Intellectual Autobiography of Sor Juana Inés de la Cruz. Nuestro* 7, no. 6 (August): 62–64.

Saldívar, José David. 1992. "The School of Caliban: Pan-American Autobiography." In *Multicultural Autobiography: American Lives,* edited by James Robert Payne, 297–325. Knoxville: University of Tennessee Press.

Saldívar, Ramón. 1985. "Ideologies of the Self: Chicano Autobiography." *Diacritics* 15, no. 3: 25–34.

———. 1990. *Narrative: The Dialectics of Difference.* Madison: University of Wisconsin Press.

Sánchez, Rosaura. 1995. *Telling Identities: The Californio Testimonios.* Madison: University of Wisconsin Press.

Sánchez González, Lisa. 2001. *Boricua Literature: A Literary History of the Puerto Rican Diaspora.* New York: New York University Press.

Schilt, Paige. 1998. "Anti-Pastoral and Guilty Vision in Richard Rodriguez's *Days of Obligation." Texas Studies in Literature and Language* 40, no. 4: 424–32.

Scotto, Barbara. 1990. Book review of A Summer Life. *Wilson Library Bulletin* 65, no. 3: 142–43.

Shirley, Carl R. 1988. *Understanding Chicano Literature*. Columbia: University of South Carolina Press.

Simerka, Barbara. 1997. "The Construction of the Liminal Subject: Monica Palacios's *Latin Lezbo Comic* as Dramatic Autobiography." *MELUS: Multi-Ethnic Literature of the United States* 22, no. 1: 89–104.

Smith, Norman. 1986. "Buffalos and Cockroaches: Acosta's Siege at Aztlán." In *Contemporary Chicano Fiction: A Critical Survey*, edited by Vernon E. Lattin, 82–93. Binghamton, NY: Bilingual Press/Editorial Bilingüe.

Smith, Sidonie, and Julia Watson. 2010. *Reading Autobiography: A Guide for Interpreting Life Narratives*. 2nd ed. Minneapolis: University of Minnesota Press.

Staten, Henry. 1998. "Ethnic Authenticity, Class, and Autobiography: The Case of Hunger of Memory." *PMLA* 113, no. 1: 103–17.

Stuhr-Rommereim, Rebecca. 1997. *Autobiographies by Americans of Color 1980–1994: An Annotated Bibliography*. Troy, NY: Whiston Publishing Co.

Torres, Héctor A. 1992. "Chicano Narrative: The Dialectics of Difference." *College Literature* 19, no. 3: 265–70.

Torres, Lourdes. 1991. "The Construction of the Self in U.S. Latina Autobiographies." In *Third World Women and the Politics of Feminism*, edited by Chandra Talpade Mohanty, 272–87. Bloomington: Indiana University Press.

Trouve, Maria del Carmen. 1997. "La mujer en la negociación de la identidad chicana: *The Autobiography of a Brown Buffalo*, de Oscar Zeta Acosta." In *Jornadas de la asociación argentina de estudios americanos: Ponencias*, edited by Rolando Costa Picazo, 377–86. Rio Cuarto, Argentina: Editorial de La Fundación, Universidad Nacional de Rio Cuarto.

Turner, Elizabeth Hayes, Stephanie Cole, and Rebecca Sharpless, eds. 2015. *Texas Women: Their Histories, Their Lives*. Athens: University of Georgia Press.

Velasco, Juan. 2004. "*Automitografías*: The Border Paradigm and Chicana/o Autobiography." *Biography* 27, no. 2: 313–38.

———. 2016. *Collective Identity and Cultural Resistance in Contemporary Chicana/o Autobiography*. New York: Palgrave Macmillan.

Vizcaíno-Alemán, Melina V. 2017. *Gender and Place in Chicana/o Literature: Critical Regionalism and the Mexican American Southwest*. Cham, Switzerland: Palgrave Macmillan.

Vilaseca, David. 2010. *Queer Events: Post-Deconstructive Subjectivities in Spanish Writing and Film, 1960s to 1990s*. Liverpool, UK: Liverpool University Press.

Walker, Anthony. 2017. "Critical Autobiography as Research." *The Qualitative Report* 22, no. 7: 1896–1908.

Walker, Madeline Ruth. 2011. *The Trouble with Sauling Around: Conversion in Ethnic American Autobiography, 1965–2002*. Iowa City: University of Iowa Press.

———. 1995. "*Los laberintos de la mexicanidad: La construcción de la identidad en la autobiografía chicana contemporánea*." PhD diss., University of California, Los Angeles.

Woods, Richard D. 1988. *Mexican Autobiography: An Annotated Bibliography / La autobiografía Mexicana: Una bibliografía razonada*. New York: Greenwood Press.

Zamora, Emilio. 2015. "José de la Luz Sáenz: Experiences and Autobiographical Consciousness." In *Leaders of the Mexican American Generation: Biographical Essays*. Edited by Anthony Quiroz, 25–55. Boulder: University Press of Colorado.

Zavala, Iris M. 1982. "Ideologías y autobiografías: Perspectivas femeninas." *Third Woman* 1, no. 2: 35–39.

Websites

Research Connections: Resources for Biographical and Documentary Research. American Educational Research Association website. http://www.aera.net/SIG013/Research-Connections.

Research Methodologies for the Creative Arts and Humanities: Life Histories /Autobiographies. Edith Cowan University website. https://ecu.au.libguides.com/c.php?g=410634&p=2798897.

Contributors

ALEJANDRO ANREUS is professor of art history and Latin American studies at William Paterson University in Wayne, New Jersey. He is the author of *Orozco in Gringoland* (2001), *Luis Cruz Azaceta* (2014), co-editor and contributor of *The Social and The Real, Political Art of the 1930s in the Western Hemisphere* (2006); *Mexican Muralism, A Critical History* (2012); and the *Blackwell Companion to Modern and Contemporary Latin American and Latina/o Art* (forthcoming). His articles and essays have appeared in *Art Journal*, *Encuentro de la Cultura Cubana*, *Commonweal* and *Diario de Cuba*. He is currently completing a monograph on Cuban American painter Arturo Rodríguez.

JUDITH F. BACA is one of America's leading visual artists. She has been creating public art for four decades. Powerful in size and subject matter, Baca's murals bring art to where people live and work. In 1974 Baca founded Los Angeles's first mural program, which produced over four hundred murals and employed thousands of local participants. It evolved into an arts organization known as the Social and Public Art Resource Center (SPARC). Her best-known work is *The Great Wall of Los Angeles*, a half-mile-long mural located in the San Fernando Valley. The creation of *The Great Wall* employed more than four hundred youth and their families from diverse social and economic backgrounds, artists, oral historians, and scholars. Baca is an emeritus professor of the University of California, Los Angeles, where she taught in the Department of Chicana/o Studies and the Department of World Arts and Cultures from 1980 until 2018.

SANTA C. BARRAZA, a native of Kingsville, Texas, is a contemporary Chicana/Tejana artist and educator. She is professor of art at Texas A&M University–Kingsville. She has exhibited widely in the United States and in Mexico, Argentina, Spain, Germany, Italy, Austria, and France. Her work has been shown in exhibitions at National Gallery of American Art in Washington, DC, Los Angeles County Museum of Art, INTAR Latin American Gallery in New York, Mexican Fine Arts Center Museum in Chicago, Centro Cultural de la Villa in Madrid, Museum of Modern Art in Mexico City, and Santo Domingo Museum of Art in Oaxaca, among others. She is the recipient of many awards, including most recently the 2014 Lifetime Achievement Award from the Mexic-Arte Museum of Austin. Her artwork appears in *Santa Barraza: Artist of the Borderlands*, edited by Maria Herrera-Sobek (2001), which was awarded the 2002 Southwest Book Award from the Border Regional Library Association. In 2012 Barraza was featured and recognized for her contributions to Texas history in the exhibition *Women Shaping Texas in the 20th Century* at the Bullock Texas State History Museum in Austin.

CYNTHIA BEJARANO is Regents Professor and the College of Arts and Sciences Fulton Endowed Chair in the Department of Interdisciplinary Studies and Gender and Sexuality Studies at New Mexico State University. Her publication and research interests include immigrant and migrant advocacy and social justice, immigrant youth and education at the border, and border violence (broadly speaking) and gender-based violence at the US-Mexico border. She is author of the book *"Qué Onda?" Urban Youth Cultures and Border Identity* (2005) and co-editor (with Rosa-Linda Fregoso) of the anthology *Terrorizing Women: Feminicide in the Américas* (2010), which was published in Spanish in 2012. She was co-founder of Amigos de las Mujeres de Juarez, an organization that worked to end violence against women in Chihuahua, Mexico, and the borderlands. Bejarano is also an advocate for farmworker students, serving as the principal investigator of the US Department of Education's College Assistance Migrant Program since 2002 at her institution.

WENDY LAURA BELCHER is professor of African literature in Princeton University's Department of Comparative Literature and Department of African American Studies. She is working to bring attention to early African literature and how African thought has shaped global history. She was for eleven years, from 1996 to 2007, the managing editor of *Aztlán*. She is the author of *Abyssinia's Samuel Johnson: Ethiopian Thought in the Making of an English Author* (2012) and co-editor and co-translator (with Michael Kleiner) of *The Life and Struggles of Our Mother Walatta Petros: A Seventeenth-Century African Biography of an Ethiopian Woman* (2015), perhaps the first African biography of an African woman. Her books in progress are *Ladder of Heaven: The Miracles of the Virgin Mary in Ethiopian Literature and Art* and *The Black Queen of Sheba: A Global History of an African Idea.*

Max Benavidez headed the communications offices for UCLA, Caltech, and Claremont McKenna College; consulted for the Ford Foundation, Corporation for Public Broadcasting, and Harvard Medical School; served as a professor at USC's Annenberg School, Sotheby's Institute of Art, and UCLA; published scores of articles on arts and culture, digital media, marketing, film, education, and literature; lectured widely in the United States and abroad; and authored several books, including *Dracula In Beverly Hills* (2020), *Gronk* (2007), and *Graciela's Dream* (2005). Benavidez received his BA in philosophy from UCLA and his PhD in new media from Claremont Graduate University. He has been an Ahmanson Foundation Fellow and a Getty Trust Scholar. In 2016-17 he was named a Fulbright US Scholar and conducted research on communications and diversity at the Grand Écoles in Paris, Marseille, and Aix-en-Provence.

Charlene Villaseñor Black is professor of art history and Chicana/o studies at the University of California, Los Angeles, associate director of the Chicano Studies Research Center, editor of *Aztlán: A Journal of Chicano Studies*, and founding editor-in-chief of *Latin American and Latinx Visual Culture*. She publishes on a range of topics related to Chicanx studies, contemporary Latinx art, and the early modern Iberian world. In 2016 she was awarded UCLA's Gold Shield Faculty Prize for Academic Excellence.

Arlene Dávila is professor of anthropology and American studies and founding director of The Latinx Project at New York University. She studies the political economy of culture and media, consumption, immigration and geographies of inequality and race. These research interests grew out of her early work in Latinx art and culturally specific museums and spaces in New York City and have developed through her continued involvement in Latinx advocacy and interest in creative industries across the Americas. She has authored six books, including her most recent work, *Latinx Art: Artists, Markets and Politics* (2020).

Tatiana de la Tierra (1961–2012) was a Latina lesbian poet, editor, and activist. Among her publications are *For the Hard Ones: A Lesbian Phenomenology/Para las Duras: Una Fenomenología Lesbiana* (2002) and the chapbooks *Porcupine Love and Other Tales from My Papaya* and *Píntame Una Mujer Peligrosa*. Her writing has appeared in anthologies, including *Bend, Don't Shatter: Poets on the Beginning of Desire* (2004) and *Ultimate Lesbian Erotica 2005* (2004) and journals, including *Cimarron Review, El Andar, Flyway,* and *La Revista Calaca*. She was the founder and editor of the magazines *Esto No Tiene Nombre, Conmoción,* and *La Telaraña*.

HARRY GAMBOA JR. is an artist, author, and educator. He is the founder and director of the international performance troupe Virtual Vérité (2005–17). He is also a co-founder of Asco (1972–85), the Los Angeles–based performance group. He is co-director of the Photo/Media Program at California Institute of the Arts. His work has been exhibited internationally at Smithsonian National Portrait Gallery; Marlborough Contemporary, New York; Whitney Museum of American Art, New York; Museum Ludwig, Cologne, Germany; Centre d'Arts Plastiques Contemporain Bordeaux, France; De Appel, Amsterdam; Lentos Kunstmuseum Linz, Linz, Austria; Nottingham Contemporary, Nottingham, England; Smithsonian American Art Museum; Le Musée d'Art Contemporain, Marseille, France; Museo Universitario Arte Contemporáneo (UNAM), Mexico City; Tate Liverpool; Museo del Palacio de Bellas Artes, Mexico City; Musée de l'Élysée, Lausanne; Los Angeles County Museum of Art; Centre Pompidou; Statens Museum for Kunst, Copenhagen; and Museum of Modern Art, New York. He is author of *Xoloitzcuintli Doppelgänger and Other Stories*. His recent essays have appeared in *Pfeil No. 10* (Hamburg), and *Exploring Commonism A New Aesthetics of the Real* (2018). He is the author of *Urban Exile: Collected Writings of Harry Gamboa Jr.* (1998).

RICARDO GAMBOA is a brown, non-binary, and queer activist, artist, and scholar creating radically politicized art, media, interventions, and knowledge in their native Chicago and New York City. A doctoral candidate of American studies at New York University, Gamboa pursues research interests that include aesthetics, politics, arts activism, history of capitalism, social movements, and artificial intelligence.

JERRY GARCIA was born and raised in Quincy, Washington. After graduating high school, he served three years in the US Army. Garcia went on to receive his BA and MA at Eastern Washington University and his PhD from Washington State University. He is currently the vice president of Educational Services at the Sea Mar Museum for Sea Mar Community Health Centers in Seattle, Washington. Garcia had academic appointments with Iowa State University and Michigan State University, and he is the former director of the Chicano Education Program and the College Assistance Migrant Program at Eastern Washington University. Garcia's research focus is on Chicano history, Latin American history, and the history of Mexico; Asians in the Americas, immigration, empire, masculinity, and race in the Americas. He has published five books and over fifteen peer-reviewed articles. His forthcoming publications include

"Mexicans, Race, and Immigration: Historicizing the Postville, Iowa Raid of 2008" and a manuscript that examines the Chicano movement in the state of Washington.

CARLOS JACKSON, a visual artist and writer, was born and raised in Los Angeles, California. He attended the University of California, Davis where he received an MFA. In 2002 he was awarded a full fellowship to attend the Skowhegan School of Painting and Sculpture in central Maine. For the 2003-4 year he held the David Shainberg Endowed Fellowship at the Fine Arts Work Center in Provincetown, Massachusetts. Since 2004 he has served as founding director of Taller Arte del Nuevo Amanecer, a community-based art center managed by the Chicana/o/x Studies Department at UC Davis, where he also serves as professor and chair.

ALMA LÓPEZ is a visual artist. Her work has been exhibited in over one hundred solo and group exhibitions internationally. She is the co-editor, with Alicia Gaspar de Alba, of *Our Lady of Controversy: Alma Lopez's "Irreverent Apparition"* (2011). Currently Lopez is an assistant professor in residence in the César E. Chávez Department of Chicana/o Studies and the LGBTQ Studies Program at UCLA. She teaches courses on art censorship, queer art, Chicanx/Latinx art, public art, and digital art. She may be reached at http://almalopez.com.

RENEE M. MORENO is professor in Chicana/o Studies at California State University, Northridge. She directs the Chicana/o Studies Writing and Tutoring Center and is active in the National Council of Teachers of English. Her research interests are on rhetoric and composition, storytelling, and counter-stories about communities.

FRANCES NEGRÓN-MUNTANER is an artist, writer, scholar and professor at Columbia University, where she is also the founding curator of the Latino Arts and Activism Archive. Among her books and publications are *Boricua Pop: Puerto Ricans and the Latinization of American Culture* (CHOICE Award, 2004), *The Latino Media Gap* (2014), and *Sovereign Acts: Contesting Colonialism in Native Nations and Latinx America* (2017). Her most recent films include *Small City, Big Change* (2013), *War for Guam* (2015), and *Life Outside* (2016). For her work as a scholar and filmmaker, Negrón-Muntaner has received Ford, Truman, Rockefeller, and Pew fellowships. In 2008 the United Nations' Rapid Response Media Mechanism recognized her as a global expert in the areas of mass media and Latin/o American studies. Negrón-Muntaner is also a recipient of the Lenfest Award, one of Columbia University's most prestigious recognitions for excellence in teaching and scholarship (2012), an OZY Educator Award (2017), and the Latin American Studies Association's Frank Bonilla Public Intellectual Award (2019). Negrón-Muntaner served as the director of Unpayable Debt, a working group at Columbia University that studied debt regimes in the world and was a lead collaborator in two of its main projects, *NoMoreDebt: Caribbean Syllabus* (first and second editions), and Valor y Cambio (Value and Change), a storytelling and community currency project in Puerto Rico and the United States (valorycambio.org).

CHON A. NORIEGA is professor in the UCLA Department of Film, Television, and Digital Media, director of the UCLA Chicano Studies Research Center at UCLA, and consulting curator at the Los Angeles County Museum of Art. He is the author of *Shot in America: Television, the State, and the Rise of Chicano Cinema* (2000) and editor of numerous books dealing with Latino media, performance, and visual art. He was the editor of *Aztlán: A Journal of Chicano Studies* from 1996 to 2016. Noriega has developed many art projects, including *Home—So Different, So Appealing*, an exhibition for the Getty Foundation's Pacific Standard Time initiative "L.A./L.A.: Latin American and Latino Art in L.A."; *L.A. Xicano*, which comprised five exhibitions for the Getty Foundation's first Pacific Standard Time initiative, "Art in L.A., 1945–1980"; and *Phantom Sightings: Art after the Chicano Movement*. He has helped preserve independent films and video art, including the first three Chicano-directed feature films, as a part of the Chicano Cinema Recovery Project, which he organized. He was awarded the Getty Postdoctoral Fellowship in the History of Art.

RUBEN OCHOA is a Los Angeles–based artist whose practice engages space as both a concept and a form. Sourcing from construction materials associated with inherent histories, Ochoa's works expose the ideological and broader sociopolitical and economic relationships that facilitate the way in which the spaces we inhabit and move through are assembled. His work has been shown in solo exhibitions at Museum of Contemporary Art in San Diego, Wadsworth Atheneum Museum of Art in Hartford, and SITE Santa Fe in Santa Fe, and in numerous group exhibitions, including the 54th Venice Biennale Collateral Event (The Future Generation Art Prize Exhibition), Nasher Sculpture Center in Dallas, and 2008 Whitney Biennial in New York. His work is in many public collections, including the Smithsonian American Art Museum, Los Angeles County Museum of Art, Museum of Contemporary Art San Diego, and Hammer Museum in Los Angeles. In

2019, Ochoa completed *Mis Marcadores*, his first public art commission, located at the San Ysidro Land Port of Entry for GSA Art in Architecture program. He has received two California Community Foundation Fellowships and a Guggenheim Fellowship. He received his BFA from Otis College of Art and Design and his MFA from University of California, Irvine.

Vincent Pérez, associate professor of English at the University of Nevada at Las Vegas, does research in Chicanx and Latinx literature and popular culture and Hemispheric American literary studies. He is an affiliate faculty member of the Department of Interdisciplinary, Gender, and Ethnic Studies and the Latinx and Latin American Studies Program. He is a member of the Quechan (Kwatsáan) Indian Tribe of the Fort Yuma–Quechan Indian Reservation. His scholarship investigates how literary texts operate as repositories of cultural memory and counter-history. He has published in American (US), Mexican American, and African American literary studies in a range of scholarly journals. His book *Remembering the Hacienda: History and Memory in the Mexican American Southwest* (2006) examines early Mexican American novels and autobiographies in relation to the nineteenth-century hacienda and ranch social economy of the Mexican Southwest. His next book project is an interdisciplinary study of early immigration narratives. Anthologies in which his articles appear include *Look Away: The U.S. South in New World Studies* (2004), *María Amparo Ruiz de Burton: Critical and Pedagogical Perspectives* (2004), and *Recovering the US Hispanic Literary Heritage* (2003) and *A History of California Literature* (2015).

Alvina E. Quintana is associate professor emerita in women and gender studies at the University of Delaware. Aside from teaching ethnic studies and writing at San Francisco State, University of California, Santa Cruz, and University of California, Santa Barbara, she taught courses in literature and gender studies and Latinx cultural studies at the University of Delaware from 1990 to 2016. Her book publications include *Feminist Cyberspaces: Pedagogies in Transition* (2012), for which she was co-editor, and for two books that she edited: *Reading U.S. Latina Writers: Remapping American Literature* (2005) and *Home Girls: Chicana Literary Voices* (1996). She has published various articles on multicultural literature and cinema studies. Her research focuses on feminist theories, sexuality and difference, new technologies, and Latinx cultural practices. She is currently working on a documentary film that explores notions of transculturation and the Black Pacific.

CATHERINE S. RAMÍREZ, associate professor of Latin American and Latino studies at the University of California, Santa Cruz, is a scholar of migration, citizenship, race, and gender. Her book, *Assimilation: An Alternative History*, is forthcoming from the University of California Press. She is also the author of *The Woman in the Zoot Suit: Gender, Nationalism, and the Cultural Politics of Memory* (2009) and several essays on science fiction, race, gender, and futurity. She is the recipient of a fellowship from the Center for Advanced Study in the Behavioral Sciences at Stanford University, an Andrew W. Mellon Foundation Sawyer Seminar grant, a Ford Foundation Postdoctoral Fellowship, and the Excellence in Teaching Award, UC Santa Cruz's highest teaching honor. She holds a PhD in ethnic studies, with a designated emphasis in gender and women's studies, from the University of California, Berkeley.

ANITA TIJERINA REVILLA is an activist scholar and professor in the Department of Chicana(o) and Latina(o) Studies at California State University, Los Angeles. Her research focuses on student movements and social justice education, specifically in the areas of Chicana/Latina, immigrant, feminist and queer rights activism. Her expertise is in the areas of Jotería (queer and Latinx) studies, Chicanx education, Chicana/Latina feminism, and critical race/ethnic studies. After receiving her bachelor's degree from Princeton University and a master's degree from Teachers College, Columbia University, she earned her doctorate from the UCLA Graduate School of Education in Social Sciences and Comparative Education, with an emphasis in race and ethnic studies. She is working on a book about feminist, queer, and immigrant rights activism in Las Vegas and Los Angeles titled "Muxeristas y Jotería: From Los Angeles to Las Vegas and Beyond."

ANA CLARISSA ROJAS DURAZO grew up in the bordered tierras de Mexicali y Calexico, Baja California/California. Her roots trace to Nogales and Douglas, Arizona/Sonora, and Guadalajara, Jalisco. She is a recognized scholar-activist whose transdisciplinary research explores the architecture of violence: the interrelatedness of myriad modalities of violence inclusive of state violence, institutional entanglements, and intimate expressions of violence. Her work foregrounds the possibilities for the transformation of violence anchored in the praxis of shifting away from settler colonial logics and structures toward indigenous and decolonial knowledges otherwise. Rojas Durazo is an internationally published poet who believes in caracoles and trusts the creative spirit. She is co-editor of *The Color of Violence: The INCITE! Anthology* (2016); *Community Accountability: Emerging Movements to Transform Violence,* a special issue of *Social Justice* (2012); and *Ending Heteropatriarchal Violence in Chicano Studies,* a special issue of *Chicana/Latina Studies* (2014). Her recent publication, "For Breath to Return to Love: B/ordering Violence and the War on Drugs" was awarded the Antonia I. Castañeda Prize from the National Association of Chicana and Chicano Studies. Rojas Durazo is assistant professor of Chicana/o studies at the University of California, Davis.

JOSÉ MANUEL SANTILLANA is a doctoral candidate in the Department of Gender, Women and Sexuality Studies at the University of Minnesota. His activism and organizing efforts focus on interrogating and disrupting white supremacist–settler colonial(ism)–heteropatriarchy. His research explores Mexican social life in rural Central California, where there is ongoing environmental degradation. His areas of expertise are Jotería studies, Chicanx studies, critical race and ethnic studies, women of color feminism, and environmental studies. He received his BA in Chicanx studies from the University of California, Los Angeles and his and MA from California State University, Northridge. His master's thesis is titled "La Jotería de UCLA: Queer Latina/o Chicana/o Student Activism."

MARGO TAMEZ (she/her/hers) is a Ndéé Dene (Lipan Apache, Dene nation) poet, historian, and Indigenous feminist from El Calaboz, Texas. Born in Kónítsajįgokĺyąą (Big Water Peoples' Country in South and Southwest Texas), she and her ancestors came from and were raised in remote, rural and urban Lipan-Jumano Apache kinship communities along the Pecos, Colorado, San Antonio, Trinity, Nueces, Frio, Guadalupe, and Rio Grande rivers. Her work blurs boundaries between law and Indigenous matriarchy; history and poetics; Indigenous feminist methodologies and philosophy; memory, visuality, digital expression and language; and auto-ethnography and genocide studies. For her, decolonizing the archives involves spiritual relationality with and on earth and recognizing the difficult human conditions. She is concerned with power, violence, masking ideologies, knowing, and mobilizing Indigenous epistemology, and she recovers, organizes, and builds on community-based archives, collective and individual story, and dissidence to create meaningful multi-media works reflecting the experiences of othered, non-recognized, Indigenous peoples in Texas. Tamez is interested in the spaces of abjection—where settler-colonizers violated Indigenous laws, imposed conditions of bare life, and enacted conditions for monstrosities (the killing field, walls, the camp, death march, exile, erasure, censure, impunity zones)—as instrumental spaces of epistemology and pedagogy. Her work sustains focus on articulating Indigenous post-genocide memory, which enmeshes and juxtaposes national histories and violence, while erasing or distorting Ndéé traumatized communities. She engages resistance and refusal within coloniality, echoing her foremothers' refusals to dispossession and carceral enclosure as a form to know and understand intergroup, organized violence enacted on Apache, Comanche, and Nahua peoples by Basque, Irish, Scottish, German, Mexican, and Tejano settlers. Tamez is an associate professor in the Indigenous studies program, UBC, Unceded Syilx territory, British Columbia.

Index